LINKING SCIENCE & LITERACY
IN THE K-8 CLASSROOM

LINKING
SCIENCE
& LITERACY
IN THE K–8 CLASSROOM

Edited by Rowena Douglas, Michael P. Klentschy,
and Karen Worth, with Wendy Binder

NSTApress
NATIONAL SCIENCE TEACHERS ASSOCIATION
Arlington, VA

NATIONAL SCIENCE TEACHERS ASSOCIATION

Claire Reinburg, Director
Judy Cusick, Senior Editor
Andrew Cocke, Associate Editor
Betty Smith, Associate Editor
Robin Allan, Book Acquisitions Coordinator

Will Thomas, Jr., Art Director
Tracey Shipley, Assistant Art Director, Cover and Inside Design

PRINTING AND PRODUCTION Catherine Lorrain, Director
Nguyet Tran, Assistant Production Manager
Jack Parker, Electronic Prepress Technician

NATIONAL SCIENCE TEACHERS ASSOCIATION
Gerald F. Wheeler, Executive Director
David Beacom, Publisher

LIBRARY OF CONGRESS CATALOGING-IN-PUBLICATION DATA

Linking science & literacy in the K-8 classroom / edited by Rowena Douglas ... [et al.].
     p. cm.
 Includes bibliographical references and index.
 ISBN-13: 978-1-933531-01-4
 ISBN-10: 1-933531-01-0
 1. Science--Study and teaching (Elementary)--United States. 2. Science--Study and teaching (Middle school)--United States. 3. Language arts (Elementary)--United States. 4. Language arts (Middle school)--United States. I. Title: Linking science and literacy in the K-8 classroom. II. Douglas, Rowena.
 LB1585.3.L556 2006
 372.3'5--dc22
                              2006004318

Contents

Section 4:
Science and Reading

Contents

Section 1:
Linking Science and Literacy in the Classroom

Section 2:
Science and Oral Discourse

Section 3:
Science and Writing

Section 4:
Science and Reading

Section 5:
Science, Literacy, and Culture

Section 6:
Implementation and Policy Issues

*Chapter 13, "Professional Development and Strategic Leadership to Support Effective Integration of Science and Literacy," is copyright © 2005 Horizon Research, Inc., and is reprinted with permission from the Horizon Research, Inc., website (*www.horizon-research.com*).

About the Editors

Rowena Douglas, who has taught science at all educational levels, is assistant executive director for professional development at the National Science Teachers Association. She was formerly a program director with the Division of Elementary, Secondary, and Informal Education at the National Science Foundation and state science supervisor for the Ohio Department of Education.

Michael P. Klentschy is superintendent of the El Centro School District in El Centro, California. He has also served in teaching and administrative positions in the Los Angeles Unified School District and the Pasadena Unified School District since the mid-1960s. Among other honors, he was named the 2005 Administrator of the Year by the National Science Education Leadership Association.

Karen Worth, a senior scientist with the Education Development Center in Cambridge, Massachusetts, has taught at the elementary and college levels, and worked for more than two decades on curricula and teaching related to science and literacy. She teaches early childhood and elementary education at Wheelock College.

Wendy Binder, author of the book's case stories, is a project director in the Professional Development Division of the National Science Teachers Association. She has taught science at the elementary and middle school levels and has been a curriculum developer at the National Science Resources Center and senior program associate at the Leadership and Assistance for Science Education Reform (LASER) Center.

Introduction

Karen Worth
Center for Science Education
Education Development Center, Inc.

The connection between science and literacy is the subject of much attention in the science education community. This attention comes in large part from three sources. One is the growing body of research and practice in science teaching and learning that suggests that language is essential for effective science learning—for clarity of thought, description, discussion, and argument, as well as for recording and presentation of results. In addition to engaging in direct investigation of scientific phenomena, students make meaning by writing science, talking science, and reading science. At the root of deep understanding of science concepts and scientific processes is the ability to use language to form ideas, theorize, reflect, share and debate with others, and ultimately, communicate clearly to different audiences.

The second source is a related body of research and practice from the literacy community that suggests that students improve their skills in many areas of literacy when those skills are practiced in engaging contexts. One such context is inquiry-based science, where instruction includes direct experience, is explicit, focuses on substance rather than on form, and offers sufficient opportunity to engage in meaningful use of language. This context can be particularly important for second-language learners and students from diverse languages and cultures.

And, finally, the attention to the science and literacy connection is also a result of the current emphasis on literacy and mathematics in the No Child Left Behind (NCLB) legislation, with the resulting lack of focus on science instruction. While this may change somewhat when science becomes a tested subject area, the primacy of literacy and mathematics at the K–8 level is likely to remain, and thus this introduction requires a cautionary note. If we are not careful and clear, the current privileging of literacy instruction over all other areas of learning can lead to connections being forged between literacy and science in which reading and writing instruction substitute for, rather than add to, direct experience and scientific reasoning.

In response to the growing interest in science and literacy integration, the National Science Teachers Association (NSTA), with funding and support from the National Science Foundation (NSF) and with advice from a number of experts in the field, designed and implemented two conferences that brought over 400 people together at an NSTA area convention in Seattle (September 2004) and another 350 people at the national convention in Dallas (April 2005). The goals of the conferences were to

- provide practitioners and policy makers with scientifically based research on the effective integration of literacy in the preK–8 science curriculum,
- describe potential roles of literacy in science instruction,
- illustrate effective strategies for linking science and literacy,
- highlight best practices in science and literacy integration, and
- engage the research and practice communities in dialogue and debate.

The last goal highlights one of the more serious problems in education: the gap between research and practice. The conference planners aspired to begin a dialogue between the research and development communities and the practice communities and provide an opportunity to build more bridges than we have now between visions, research, and reality.

This book takes another step toward meeting the goals of the conferences. The people whose work is presented here are leaders in the field who have had the opportunity to think about, write about, and practice ways of linking literacy and science that support both science and literacy learning. They come from classroom practice, research, development, and administration. They were asked to present their thinking, not necessarily (or along with) their results or answers. The intent of the conferences was not to present one coherent point of view; thus, what one writer says may conflict with the ideas of another. Readers of this book also will likely agree with some writers and disagree with others. The book will be a success if readers go away with ideas to ponder and strategies to adapt, as well as new questions, ideas, and ways of thinking. It will be a success if it stimulates continuing thinking, debate, and action among practitioners, leaders, developers, and researchers.

The book begins with a chapter on the nature of science inquiry and the vision of science teaching and learning that emerges from it. This vision with its set of beliefs and values about how our students should learn science is the foundation on which the book is crafted. All of the other writers, whether they come with a focus on science or literacy, assume a science instruction that is based in inquiry. This chapter also highlights another assumption of the conferences: that the link between science and literacy is an authentic characteristic of science and that appropriate use of literacy in science is needed to achieve deeper understanding of science and the ability to reason scientifically. Although we have chosen to start with this chapter on science inquiry and stay within a frame of inquiry-based science and the language that is essential to it, we also assume that there are many varied approaches and ideas within that frame and that there is no one way to teach and learn science, no single best curriculum or set of strategies.

Needless to say, there are other views about science and what students should know and be able to do, and there are other views about what is essential in literacy instruction. This results in many teachers being under pressure not only from NCLB but also from members of communities with varied values and beliefs. This book does not mean to exclude those who have a different point of view; but rather it is intended to encourage discussion about constraints in these contexts, areas of possibility, and varied strategies that can work.

All of the sections that follow the opening chapter begin with one or two case stories. As Wendy Binder, the author of the case stories, notes, these are "windows into K–8 classrooms from across the United States. It is in these classrooms where theory supporting science and literacy integration meets practice…. Each of the nine stories speaks to issues and challenges related to science and literacy integration in a unique setting…. They bring you moments, days, and sometimes weeks in the lives of dedicated professionals trying to create meaningful learning experiences for students using their current understanding of science and literacy integration strategies."

Further, the stories "illustrate the current state of science and literacy integration practice and are meant neither as exemplars nor as dilemma cases to be used in a professional development setting. Rather, [the] intent is that these cases…serve as catalysts for discussion of what-is and what-might-be in science and literacy integration among professional learning communities." To encourage and stimulate thought and discussion and make the link between theory and practice, the author of the case stories has provided several questions at the end of each case.

Sections 2, 3, and 4 of the book discuss each of the three language modalities: oral discourse, writing, and reading. But of course we cannot really separate literacy use into parts in this way, so if one reads the chapters in each section one will find that the reality is one of foreground and background. All have more breadth than is implied by their placement in a particular section.

Section 2 focuses on oral language, the role of discourse in writing and reading science, and how students develop the skills needed for oral discourse. There is only one chapter in this section along with the cases. Partly this is because oral discourse is so important to writing and reading science that it is integrated into many of the other chapters in Sections 3, 4, and 5. But partly it is because oral discourse often receives less attention in the science-literacy connection. We hope that the book may spur more writing in this area, particularly from the practice community. Section 3 is about writing and explores what kinds of writing opportunities are natural parts and extensions of science investigations. Science notebooks, which are becoming more and more prevalent in inquiry-based science instruction, are the focus of two chapters. And three others introduce different strategies for the scaffolding students need if they are to engage in rigorous science writing about their ideas and conclusions. In Section 4, the focus is on reading—exploring the roles books can play in inquiry-based science programs and the problem-solving approaches that inquiry and reading-comprehension strategies share.

Many of the chapters and cases in each section describe work with learners of diverse cultural and linguistic backgrounds. But in Section 5, the authors address cultural and linguistic issues directly and focus on specific strategies to ensure opportunities for English language learners in science. The authors also identify some of the things teachers need to know about language, culture, and science to teach effectively in diverse communities.

Finally, in Section 6 we turn from teachers and students in the classroom to a focus on administration and the curricular policy issues necessary for supporting the connections between science and literacy in the classroom.

It is our hope that educators at all levels and researchers will read this book and discuss it with others. We assume there will be challenges to the ideas presented here. There should be many questions raised: How do these ideas fit or not fit with the practice and policy worlds? What are the similarities and differences among science inquiry and literacy thinking skills? How can one approach be transformed to meet the realities of another community? We hope that readers will evaluate, filter, and come up with arguments, strategies, and ideas for moving forward in individual classrooms, schools, and districts.

The conferences and this book represent a strong commitment by NSF and NSTA to the science and literacy connection. As always is true, they would not have happened without the hard work of many people. But the two people who had the vision and did much of the hard work are Carole Stearns, former program officer at NSF, and Rowena Douglas, assistant executive director for professional development at NSTA. They were determined that we had to begin to bridge the gap between research and development and practice and, in doing so, send a strong message that without the knowledge, wisdom, and skill of practice—too often neglected—we will not meet the challenges of providing opportunities for all children to develop a rich and powerful relationship with science.

Linking Science and Literacy in the Classroom

CHAPTER 1

Visions of Inquiry: Science

Hubert M. Dyasi
City College of the City University of New York

S cience inquiry is about phenomena of nature, and phenomena of nature abound. All over the world, one can come across wind, clouds, rain, and different seasons of the year, so much so that just about everybody can rightfully claim to know a great deal about these phenomena. The same can be said about other phenomena, such as sound, light, darkness, rivers, oceans, mountains, cold, heat, leaves, flowers, grass, forests, trees, insects, dogs, cats, birds, and ourselves. People in general know enough about different phenomena to distinguish one from the other; for example, they know how dogs are different from cats, and trees from grass; and they can make finer distinctions within a single class of phenomena, such as distinguishing between maple and geranium leaves, and among flowers from different types of plants. At the broader end of the scale they can categorize phenomena as living or nonliving, thus seeing fundamental similarities among apparently disparate phenomena. But most people's knowledge of these phenomena can accurately be described as folk rather than scientific knowledge.

Over many years, people have used their knowledge of natural phenomena to "manufacture" tools and to create other phenomena such as houses, roads, bridges, boats, cars, trains, elevators, bicycles, pots, pans, eating utensils, the telephone, television, the radio, mirrors, the camera, the microscope, the telescope, the stethoscope, and rockets. To the extent that these artifacts satisfy the purposes for which they were designed and manufactured, they reflect their makers' knowledge and understanding of the characteristics of their constituent materials and of other phenomena surrounding their use. Once again, it would be fair to say that for many people there is no scientific understanding of the inner workings of these artifacts.

Science inquiry focuses on the development of a scientific understanding of phenomena of the world and on how scientists use the language of phenomena to gain that understanding. Immediately, we see, therefore, that the scope, practice, and precision of scientific inquiry are of a different pedigree and order from those of common sense. Scientific inquiry goes far beyond exploring phenomena using our unaided senses and leads to the development, documentation, dissemination, replication, and continual revision of detailed, scientifically verifiable facts, concepts, laws, and theories that explain and predict changes in phenomena and outcomes of interactions among phenomena. Unlike knowledge resulting from other kinds of inquiry, the veracity of knowledge developed through scientific inquiry is based on its degree of congruence with observed phenomena of nature and on whether it can be replicated through empirical investigations.

Thus, the bedrock of scientific inquiry is made up of a deep knowledge and careful applications of appropriate scientific ways of studying phenomena and of effectively and accurately communicating findings and understandings resulting from empirical studies. In this sense, scientific inquiry is a profound, tested way of developing literacy of the phenomena. Resultant scientific facts and concepts are important, but they are not worth much if there is no detailed description of the questions they answer, the kinds and sources and standards of evidence on which they are built, and the necessary scientific procedures, materials, and tools required to replicate them.

This chapter is centered on this view of science inquiry—that is, that science inquiry is about developing scientific literacy of the phenomena of the world. It is a view that regards science inquiry as equivalent to holding a sensible scientific conversation with a phenomenon, asking it questions in search of understanding, questions such as "What will happen if…?" and "How does … happen?" It is about taking scientifically oriented actions to obtain answers by following after and recording the phenomenon's responses to such questions, and by stringing together in a sensible manner the separate bits of information and data the phenomenon provides and making scientific sense of them. This process of question-and-action is an important pathway in science inquiry. It enables us to say scientifically what we know about the phenomenon, how we know it, and what makes us believe it. The answers provided by the phenomenon, however, are not terminal truths because further scientific inquiry may unveil more data that can lead to new scientifically testable conceptions and models that can explain and predict the phenomenon's behavior.

This chapter also advances the notion that scientific inquiry is not a solitary activity involving a single investigator and a single phenomenon, including in the K–8 education range, but rather a collaborative activity in which scientists often work in groups as science inquiry teams in pursuit of answers to questions about a phenomenon. In such work situations, facility with the spoken word is important as scientists discuss their questions, observations, and ideas. Almost invariably, during science inquiry activities, there is a need to measure quantities, compare sizes, and discover quantitative relationships; quantitative literacy, therefore, plays a significant role as well. Literacy of the phenomenon, therefore, is inextricably tied with literacies of the spoken and written word, number, and image. The written word, numbers, charts, and drawings are such an integral part of science inquiry that it is difficult to think of situations where they are not necessary; indeed, the science notebook has long been an essential tool for recording and organizing data, observations (including drawings), thoughts, and questions arising from scientific inquiry.

In elaboration of these two views, the chapter first looks at how science inquiry is viewed in the National Science Education Standards (NRC 1996). It then briefly describes some historical attempts to make science inquiry an important part of school science, discusses images of science inquiry, and concludes with a commentary on the relationships between science inquiry as literacy of the phenomenon on the one hand and literacy of the spoken and written word on the other.

Science Inquiry and the National Science Education Standards

Ten years ago, in 1996, the National Research Council[1] published the National Science Education Standards.[2] The Standards highlight science inquiry as an essential, fundamental component of science content, along with science subject matter of the various domains of science (e.g., physical science, life science, Earth and space science), science and technology, science in social and personal perspectives, and the history and nature of science. Although the various Standards are presented separately in the published version, they are intended to be viewed as an integrated whole that applies to each science topic chosen for study. Thus all the

Standards would simultaneously be applied to the study of motion, for example, instead of engaging students only in the study of the scientific facts, concepts, laws, and theories associated with the topic, as is often the case in school science.

According to the Standards, science inquiry is the "diverse ways in which scientists study the natural world and propose explanations based on the evidence derived from their work" (p. 23). In school science, it encompasses "activities through which students develop knowledge and understanding of scientific ideas and an understanding of how scientists study the natural world" (p. 23). Hence the Standards recommend that

> students at all grade levels and in every domain of science should have the opportunity to use scientific inquiry and develop the ability to think and act in ways associated with inquiry, including asking questions, planning and conducting investigations, using appropriate tools and techniques to gather data, thinking critically and logically about relationships between evidence and explanation, constructing and analyzing alternative explanations, and communicating scientific arguments. (NRC 1996, p. 105)

Science Inquiry and School Science: A Historical Perspective

Long before the National Science Education Standards came into existence, there were calls for the adoption of science inquiry as a controlling factor in the organization of school science. In the late 1950s, a nonprofit educational organization called Educational Services Incorporated (ESI) was created in Cambridge, Massachusetts. As part of its mission, ESI established the Physical Science Study Committee (PSSC) and a few years later it published a high school physics textbook, through which, according to Jerrold Zacharias, the group's leader, the committee hoped to give students "some kind of intellectual training that involved knowing [about] Observation, Evidence, the Basis for Belief" (Goldstein 1992). PSSC physics text writers planned to realize the hope by giving the ordinary student experiences in science inquiry that paralleled those of the scientist at work. As Zacharias put it,

> As scientists, we seek evidence before we try to create order, or orderliness, and we do not expect, nor even hope for complete proof.... We live in a world of necessarily partial proof, built on evidence, which although plentiful, is always limited in scope, amount and style. (Goldstein 1992, quoted in Hein 2005, p. 3)

Similar science teaching programs for the secondary school level were developed by other nonprofit and professional organizations in biology and chemistry.

Soon after PSSC, in 1962, ESI began development of an elementary school science program called the Elementary Science Study (ESS). These elementary school science learning materials centered on scientific inquiry:

Rather than beginning with a discussion of basic concepts of science, ESS puts physical materials into children's hands from the start and helps each child investigate through these materials the nature of the world around him. Children acquire a great deal of information, not by rote but through their own active participation. We feel that this process brings home even to very young students the essence of science—open inquiry combined with experimentation. (EDC 1970, p. 7)

Other science programs, for example, the Science Curriculum Improvement Study (SCIS), developed at the University of California at Berkeley, and Science: A Process Approach, developed by the American Association for the Advancement of Science, also produced investigations-based materials that were designed to help elementary school students to acquire scientific ideas based on understanding practical and intellectual processes of doing science. Similar developments occurred at the middle school level; for example, the stated purpose of the middle school Intermediate Physical Science program, developed in the early 1960s, was "to give all students a beginning knowledge of physical science and offer insights into the means by which scientific knowledge is acquired" (Hein 2005, p. 4).

A new wave of development of K–8 science education programs appeared in the mid-1980s. It also expanded the content of elementary and middle school science beyond subject matter concepts. For example, science teaching materials developed by Education Development Center (Cambridge, Massachusetts), the Lawrence Hall of Science (Berkeley, California), the National Science Resources Center (Smithsonian Institution and the National Academies, Washington, D.C.), and Technical Education Research Centers (TERC, Cambridge, Massachusetts) are built almost entirely on the notion that students learn science through hands-on experiences in the investigation of natural phenomena.

Images of Science Inquiry

As indicated earlier in this chapter, the National Science Education Standards view science inquiry in school science as involving more than developing knowledge of science subject matter; science inquiry also incorporates *knowledge of how* scientific facts, concepts, and laws are arrived at. For example, it is not sufficient to know that leaves of green plants contain starch, and that they use carbon dioxide, chlorophyll, water, and sunlight to produce it; one must also know how we know those facts and be able to check their veracity or engage in firsthand scientific inquiry into the phenomena themselves. The Standards also emphasize that successful engagement in that task demands acquisition of specific abilities, such as asking questions, planning and conducting investigations, using appropriate tools and techniques to gather data, thinking critically and logically about relationships between evidence and explanation, constructing and analyzing alternative explanations, and communicating scientific arguments.

A commonly held view of scientific inquiry, based on the experimental conception of science, is that scientists only do "controlled" investigations in which they keep all other things constant while they change one variable. In this kind of inquiry, the scientist collects data on the effects of changing one variable in the experimental setup (usually called the independent variable) on some other pre-selected variable or variables (called the dependent variable). In this situation, it is often necessary to simultaneously set up an identical investigation where all variables are kept constant. This double setup makes it possible to compare results from the former (experimental) setup to data from the latter (the control). A common example of this type of science inquiry in school science is an investigation of whether sunlight has an effect on growing green plants, such as beans. One set of green-leafed plants is provided with all the conditions necessary for its continuing growth except sunlight, and an identical set is grown in similar conditions and is exposed to light. The initial state and appearance of all the plants are examined and noted very carefully, usually on a two-column chart with one column used to record observations on one set and the other observations on the other set of plants. The plants are watered and observed regularly and all observations of the leaves and stem are dated and recorded. If, after a number of days of observations, discoloration of leaves and stem are observed only in the plants that were grown in the dark environment, it can be concluded that light is a factor in the production of the green color in plant leaves and stems.

The truth, however, is that there are several varieties of scientific inquiry, and they often overlap. Wynne Harlen, a highly respected science educator from the United Kingdom, has identified four general practices depending on the kind of question to be answered—namely, information seeking, action testing, pattern finding, and how-to-do-it investigations (Harlen 2001). Information-seeking inquiries are those where students primarily collect data only by making observations over time, without attempting to change the phenomenon under study. Questions that might lead to this kind of inquiry could be *I wonder what changes a bean plant undergoes from seed to maturity and to production of new seeds; I wonder what happens when water freezes; I wonder what happens when a candle burns.*

Action-testing investigations attempt to answer questions such as *I wonder what happens if….* To yield answers, the investigation requires the inquirer to make a change that might be expected to affect the phenomenon—for example, *I wonder what happens if we increase the number of flashlight batteries to light a flashlight bulb; I wonder what happens if we put dry ice in water at room temperature.* Sometimes there is a prior expectation of what might happen, sometimes not. If there is a prior expectation (or hypothesis), then the action could be rightfully interpreted as a test of the expectation, but only if it can be ascertained that the observed effects are the result of the change made and not the result of something else.

An elegant extension of this action-testing inquiry in the world of science is an investigation of mimicry that was carried out by two biologists and an undergraduate student at the University of North Carolina (Campbell and Reece 2005). Over the centuries, people have known situations in which a nonpoisonous or harmless kind of organism exists in geographical proximity with an almost identical but deadly poisonous one. In 1862, a British scientist named Henry Bates proposed a hypothesis that mimicry benefited the harmless organism because it makes potential predators avoid the harmless organism, confusing it with the harmful kind, which they have instinctively "learned" to avoid (Campbell and Reece 2005). The researchers at the University of North Carolina tested this hypothesis in 2001, taking advantage of a fortuitous geographical distribution of two almost identical kinds of snakes that inhabit North and South Carolina; one kind is poisonous and the other is not. The deadly poisonous eastern coral snake is characterized by "bold, alternating rings of red, yellow, and black," and the other, the nonpoisonous scarlet king snake, has an almost identical appearance and populates the same areas except that its distribution also extends beyond that of the coral snake (Campbell and Reece 2005, p. 22).

According to Bates's hypothesis, the scarlet king snakes would escape attacks by their predators because the latter confused them with the poisonous eastern coral snake. To test this hypothesis, the researchers made hundreds of two versions of artificial snakes, one resembling the king snakes and the other consisting entirely of "plain brown" members. Equal numbers of these two types of artificial snakes were placed in selected sites at areas inhabited by both coral and king snakes and also where only king snakes are found. "After four weeks, the scientists retrieved the fake snakes and recorded how many had been attacked by looking for bite or claw marks…. Compared to the brown artificial snakes, the ringed snakes were attacked by predators less frequently *only* in the field sites within the geographic range of the poisonous coral snakes" (Campbell and Reece 2005, p. 23; italics in original). These data supported Bates's hypothesis on mimicry. In this example, the experimental group is represented by the artificial snakes resembling the king snakes, while the plain brown variety was the control group. The design did not control all variables. The kind of predator, for example, was not a controlled variable, but its effect was canceled out by exposing both the experimental and control groups equally to all predators.

The extension of information-seeking and action-testing science inquiries can lead to pattern-finding investigations. Many scientific laws and generalizations are a result of pattern-finding investigations. For example, the period of the pendulum varies with its length; high-pressure air masses are associated with clear skies while low-pressure masses are associated with unsettled weather conditions. Some pattern-finding inquiries can result in findings that contradict intuitive knowledge; for example, the fact that heavy objects fall at the same velocity as lighter objects is counterintuitive.

In how-to-do-it investigations the object is to find ways of reaching a goal that has already been set. For example, students might be given the task of building a structure of a certain size and shape using a limited amount of construction materials, or they might be required to design and build an electrical device that can switch off electricity at specified time intervals or to create suitable growing conditions for plants.

An excellent illustration of a science investigation that cuts across the varieties of science inquiry described above is reported in *Inquiry and the National Science Education Standards: A Guide for Teaching and Learning* (NRC 2000). An elementary school class had conducted science investigations of seeds growing under different conditions the previous year. One day students noticed that among the three trees growing on the sloping school grounds, one had lost all its leaves, the middle tree had multicolored (mostly yellow) leaves, and the third "had lush, green leaves." They asked their teacher why the trees looked different, instead of looking the same, as they used to. The teacher capitalized on the students' curiosity and asked them to think of tentative explanations for the differences in the appearance of the trees. Students suggested causes such as the sunlight, too much water, change of season, difference in the ages of the trees, insects feeding on the leaves, and poison in the ground. The teacher had each student choose an explanation to test, and ended up with a "water group," a "seasons group," an "insect group," and so on. Each group had to plan and conduct a scientific inquiry that could generate evidence that answered the question of why the trees looked different.

In carrying out their investigations, students learned about the characteristics of the trees, including their ages, their life cycles, and their habitats. The group inquiring into age as a factor found out about the age of the trees from purchase receipts that showed age of the seedlings on the date of purchase, and they contacted PTA members who planted the trees to inquire about the date of planting. The water group decided to examine the ground every hour that they could and recorded their observations in their journals. They also read a pamphlet on healthy plants from a local nursery and learned that when plant roots are continuously submerged in water, they "drown." Occasionally, as the investigations continued (and at their conclusion) the various groups gave oral and written reports to the whole class. Evidence they generated showed that the tree without leaves was almost always standing in water, the middle tree was sometimes standing in water, and that the tree with green leaves was on damp ground but never stood in water.

Based on the evidence, students concluded that the leafless tree was drowning, that the middle tree was sort of drowning, and that things were just right for the third tree. With this evidence in mind, they examined the alternative explanations put forward earlier to judge whether they explained the observed differences among the trees. Since the students had found out that all the trees were the same type, the cause could not be attributed to difference in type of tree. It was possible, however, that some of the trees had a disease, because the evidence did not rule out that cause completely.

At the conclusion of their investigation, and at the encouragement of their teacher, the students wrote to the custodian apprising him of the findings of their investigation and their interpretation of the evidence. The custodian changed his tree-watering practices. To check whether the custodian's new watering system eliminated the problem, the students examined the trees the following year and found that all three bore lush green leaves.

A common thread of science inquiry described in the National Science Education Standards runs through all the varieties of science inquiry described above. Each illustration contains elements of "asking questions, planning and conducting investigations, using appropriate tools and techniques to gather data, thinking critically and logically about relationships between evidence and explanation, constructing and analyzing alternative explanations, and communicating scientific arguments" (NRC 1996, p. 105). For students to successfully enter and function in this culture of science inquiry, they need to learn science in educational environments that provide ample, generative opportunities for them to participate directly in science activities associated with scientific inquiry.

Science Inquiry and Literacy of the Spoken and Written Word

Science inquiry is typically a collaborative activity and as such involves teams of students in discussing, planning, and conducting investigations together and in sharing responsibilities for talking, reading, writing, and other kinds of presentations. Communication, therefore, plays a major role in science inquiry, and language is one of its central elements.[3] In science inquiry, however, communication involves simultaneous use of other forms such as pictorial and numerical representations. Teams of science inquirers talk about and write their questions, their tentative explanations, their plans, their data, their conclusions, and their reasons and judgments about relationships between evidence and explanations, and about how they make public presentations and scientific arguments in behalf of their work. It is in the context of this kind of scientific activity that students' literacy of the spoken and written word develops along with literacy of the phenomenon. It is also in relation to direct experiences in science investigations that words acquire nuances or "negotiated meanings"; inevitably, those meanings differ from meanings conveyed by the same words in ordinary speech. The following examples illustrate this point.

When students conduct investigations in electricity, they acquire context-based meanings of *voltage, current, resistance, electrical circuitry, conductors, insulators,* and *power.* They also learn about electrical tools and units of measurement and about distinctions between words that describe phenomena on the one hand and those that represent concepts and combinations of concepts. In investigations of motion, they learn meanings of descriptors (e.g., *displacement*) and operational meanings of words that express ratios and other kinds of relationships. The concept of acceleration, for example, is derived from concepts of velocity and time, and velocity in turn relates to displacement and time. Acquisition of the concept of velocity, therefore, is a precursor for a clear scientific understanding of acceleration, and an introduction of these terms to account for observed behaviors of phenomena during scientific inquiry enables students to grasp their special meanings. If, however, students encounter these terms in print without the benefit of firsthand engagement in relevant scientific inquiries, they are likely to experience immense difficulty deciphering literacy of the spoken and written word in the context of scientific inquiry. Jay Lemke, formerly of the City University of New York and now at the University of Michigan, included this kind of literacy of the spoken and written word in what he called the "hybrid speech" of science (Lemke 2004).

In 1992, Bill Aldridge, a former executive director of the National Science Teachers Association, made similar assertions in his article "Project on Scope, Sequence, and Coordination: A New Synthesis for Improving Science Education" (Aldridge 1992). According to Aldridge, science uses words as labels or descriptors of phenomena; but the labels themselves do not convey very much about the phenomenon unless one is already familiar with the phenomenon and the concepts embedded in the labels. Charles's law, that the volume of a gas is proportional to its absolute temperature if the pressure is held constant, sounds simple; but it would be difficult to grasp its meaning and relevance in a variety of situations unless one had already acquired the concepts of volume, temperature, and pressure. A further complication is that the concepts of temperature and pressure are themselves derived from other concepts. So, on close examination, an understanding of Charles's law involves prior acquisition of distinct concepts and then relating them to one another under special conditions. As student inquirers gain experience in scientific inquiry, however, they improve their facility with its hybrid language and grow to use it correctly when writing and reading their science notebooks and science journals and when reading appropriate published science print material.

One of the essentials of a learning environment that is favorable to the development of students' abilities to do science inquiry, therefore, is provision of ample opportunities and guidance for students to develop excellent oral and written skills using science inquiry activities so that they can talk, write, and communicate with clarity and precision to one another, their teacher, and others about their ideas and about their investigations. They also need ample opportunity to read with understanding what other inquirers have written about important aspects of the phenomena they inquire into, which may be preconditions for the advancement of their inquiries. Engagement in this kind of literacy of the spoken and written word gives students opportunities to test, rethink, and reconstruct their ideas, something that is of great value in the conduct of science inquiry (Harlen 1999).

Conclusion

There are five points to make here. First, science inquiry is a central element of science content and should, therefore, be an organizing feature of educational programs that purport to advance science literacy in students and that promote links between science and reading and writing.

The second point is that good science inquiry is not limited to circumstances where all variables can be manipulated at will. There are numerous instances where it is not possible to do so, and yet good science inquiry is carried out even under those circumstances. For example, it is not possible to manipulate movements of planetary bodies or change geological events of the past, but these phenomena have been the object of successful scientific inquiries.

The third and very important point is that science inquiry is an approach to the development of knowledge through repeated direct conversations with and interrogations of nature. Although questions about phenomena of nature come from people, answers come from inquiry into the phenomena themselves. In situations where direct interactions with phenomena are not possible, alternative mechanisms can be developed.

Fourth, science inquiry goes beyond development of practical skills such as observing, recording, classifying, and drawing conclusions. It also brings into play the development and application of high-level intellectual abilities, such as "identification of assumptions, use of critical and logical thinking [to connect evidence to explanations], and consideration of alternative explanations" (NRC 1996, p. 23).

Finally, the acquisition of science concepts as a result of participation in science inquiry carries with it an acquisition of the spoken and written word that goes beyond the decoding of symbols; it leads to comprehension of the substance represented by the "hybrid speech" of science.

References

Aldridge, B. 1992. Project on scope, sequence, and coordination: A new synthesis for improving science education. *Journal of Science and Technology Education* 1 (1): 13–21.

Campbell, N. A., and J. B. Reece. 2005. *Biology.* San Francisco: Pearson.

Education Development Center (EDC). 1970. *ESS reader.* Newton, MA: EDC.

Goldstein, J. 1992. *A different sort of time: The life of Jerrold R. Zacharias—Scientist, engineer, educator*. Cambridge, MA: MIT Press.

Harlen, W. 1999. *Effective teaching of science: A review of research*. Edinburgh: Scottish Council for Research in Education.

Harlen, W. 2001. *Primary science: Taking the plunge*. Portsmouth, NH: Heinemann.

Hein, G. E. 2005. Science education 1965 and 2005: Myths and differences. Paper presented at a symposium at the Museum of Science celebrating TERC's 40th anniversary, Boston.

Lemke, J. L. 2004. The literacies of science. In *Crossing borders in literacy and science instruction: Perspectives on theory and practice*, ed. E. W. Saul, 33–47. Newark, DE: International Reading Association.

National Research Council (NRC). 1996. *National science education standards*. Washington, DC: National Academy Press.

National Research Council (NRC). 2000. *Inquiry and the national science education standards: A guide for teaching and learning*. Washington, DC: National Academy Press.

Endnotes

[1] The National Research Council is a principal operating agency of the National Academies of Science and Engineering "in providing services to the government, the public, and the scientific and engineering communities." The development and publication of the National Science Education Standards were supported by the National Science Foundation, the U.S. Department of Education, the National Aeronautics and Space Administration, the National Institutes of Health, and a National Academy of Science president's discretionary fund.

[2] *National Science Education Standards*, or the Standards, is a comprehensive science education document that outlines "what students need to know, understand, and be able to do to be scientifically literate at different grade levels" (NRC 1996, p. 2). The document includes Standards for science teaching, professional development of teachers of science, assessment in science education, and science content; it also addresses Standards for science education programs and school systems.

[3] Drawings, graphs, or equations are usually included in reports on scientific inquiry in their own right as communication tools rather than as repetitions of accompanying text.

Case Stories
Introduction

Wendy Binder
Professional Development Division
National Science Teachers Association

C ase stories begin each section of this book. They are meant to be windows into K–8 classrooms from across the United States. It is in these classrooms that theory supporting the connection of science and literacy meets practice.

It was my privilege to get to know the dedicated subjects of each case story. Through a combination of site visits, interviews, phone calls, and videotapes, the practitioners shared their classrooms and schools with me. The evolution of the stories truly became a collaborative effort.

Each of the nine stories speaks to issues and challenges related to connecting science and literacy in a unique setting. Collectively, the stories describe a range of expertise and implementation levels. They bring you moments, days, and sometimes weeks of time in the lives of dedicated professionals as they use their current understanding of strategies for connecting science and literacy to create meaningful learning experiences. (The names of the schools and teachers are real; students' and parents' names are pseudonyms.)

The stories illustrate the current state of practice and are meant neither as exemplars nor as dilemma cases to be used in a professional development setting. Rather, my intent is that the cases and the questions that follow each one will serve as catalysts for discussion of what-is and what-might-be in science and literacy among professional learning communities. In sum, the stories are descriptive examples of the daily dilemmas faced by teachers and those who support them as they seek to connect science and literacy in a meaningful way, while staying true to both disciplines.

On Beyond Ordinary

Sandhills Intermediate School is located in Swansea, South Carolina, 20 minutes from Columbia, the state capital. Fifty-eight percent of the 560 fifth and sixth graders qualify for free and reduced lunch. In contrast with many high-poverty, rural areas in the state, 80% of the students are Caucasian and 20% are African American.

Jennifer C. and her friend Jennifer L. are students at Sandhills Intermediate. They begin class at 3:45 p.m. This would seem strange if the two Jennifers were in the fifth or sixth grade, but it is not so strange for a cadre of Sandhills teachers who become students in an after-school literacy study group that meets twice a month.

Recalls Jennifer C.:

When I came to this school, I was shocked that every teacher had a reading corner in his or her room. I thought, What is this? I realized then that part of my job at this school was going to be literacy even though I teach science. I felt professionally challenged. The teaching at the school was at a higher level than where I came from, and I realized I needed to be at that level too.

Then Mary Beth, the literacy coach, sent around a survey last spring describing her next South Carolina Reading Initiative (SCRI) study group. She described the group as one that would still be geared toward language arts teachers, but with a focus on how literacy strategies could be incorporated into other subjects. Jennifer L., who also teaches science, and I signed up.

I [Wendy Binder, author of the case stories in this book] am a student, too. I study the interaction and integration of science and literacy as it plays out in schools and classrooms across America. Over the last few years I have heard about the South Carolina State Department of Education's Mathematics and Science Unit (MSU) coaching initiative and was pleasantly surprised to hear that at Sandhills I could see for myself how a science coach and literacy coach were collaborating. I came to study this collaboration in action.

As I walk down the school's long hallways, I am struck by how young this teaching staff appears to be. Perhaps it is because the school was built and staffed only four years ago. I stop at room 219. I know this is the one I am looking for because the door is labeled with the school motto for excellence, "On Beyond Ordinary," with "Science" added to it. Lori, the science coach, introduces me to the school literacy coach, Mary Beth. I reacquaint myself with Cam, the MSU science specialist. We've worked together before. As we eat lunch and chat, I try to explain my role as "student." It's important in my work that they are comfortable with me so they will talk openly about how science and literacy intermingle in the school. I ask the coaches about their roles.

Mary Beth jumps in:

I am not here to fix people. I look for opportunities to provide professional development for the teachers and work with them in their classrooms. The ones in study group have homework that they try out in their classrooms like they would in any other grad class. Since every teacher is teaching something different, I don't focus on certain lessons, but rather on strategies they can take back and implement into their different lessons.

Lori responds as well:

Understanding my role has been my biggest challenge. I am not an administrator. Teachers used to say, "Hey, plan this for me." Cam helped me understand that a science coach supports the teachers and partners with them. When I work with teachers, they select a lesson that will go through a cycle of planning, observing, and reflecting. I try to respond to their needs.

Mary Beth and I were classroom teachers here and know each other well. So, when I became a coach I knew that I wanted to work closely with her. I recently presented a workshop to the school on implementing science notebooks. We talked about how she could support notebook use in study group and how we could work together to get the whole school using read-alouds.

After lunch, Lori takes me to Jennifer L.'s class. She is in her fourth year of teaching. As I enter Jennifer's classroom the students are reviewing prior work on simple machines. The class has already done an investigation in which students designed a machine to move sugar cubes a specific distance to build a pyramid. To apply their knowledge Jennifer shows a film clip from *A Bug's Life*, asking her students to identify all the machines they see in use. She then challenges the students to design and build a compound machine to perform a new task using only the items that are in a plastic bag. The class uses an anchor chart they generated that lists criteria they can refer to as they develop diagrams of their machines. Jennifer circulates, listens, and gives feedback as the groups use their class anchor chart to evaluate their models/diagrams.

The next morning I observe Jennifer C.'s classroom. She is in her second year of teaching. Jennifer begins with focus questions for her class: "How did the ancient Egyptians lift stones weighing several tons to a height of more than 400 feet without using modern machines?" "What is the difference between a picture and a diagram?"

Jennifer C. then does a shared reading on the age of pyramids. Before she reads, she does a "picture walk." She previews and discusses the pictures in the story with the class prior to the reading, reads the story, and then introduces a challenge (the students are to move a sugar cube a set distance). Jennifer C.'s class is a lesson or two behind Jennifer L.'s class. So this class has not yet developed its anchor chart. After comparing and contrasting a variety of diagrams, the class generates criteria for what a diagram should contain.

Before the study group meets that afternoon, I ask both Jennifers to talk about what they were doing to connect science and literacy before they joined the study group.

Jennifer L. begins:

I was doing occasional read-alouds but they weren't connected to the units. I did them just to say we read. I also used to have my students take out their science text to read because I was more comfortable with that. Now I push the book away and think, What else can I connect to the lesson?

Jennifer C. jumps in:

Yeah, two years ago I wasn't reading or writing in science. I would think to myself: A book in science? Let's not be funny!

I ask about how their taking on the role of student again has impacted their classroom practice. Jennifer L. replies:

Jennifer C. and I joined study group because we were asking ourselves, How can we make math and science more fun? We didn't want to just do read-

ing from a textbook, but we did want students to know how to read science text along with doing hands-on science.

Jennifer C. adds:

Now we are trying strategies like teaching about diagrams in the middle of this science lesson. Before study group I would never have thought about integrating these strategies. We have been taught in study group that if you do a read-aloud you should do something after it to keep the kids engaged in the book. I never would have known that.

I was reading a book over last night that I was to do a read-aloud on today. When I read through it, naturally for me as a reader I wanted to go ahead and look at the pictures first. I asked Mary Beth if that was OK. Mary Beth said I could do something called a "picture walk" with my class. Basically, I am supposed to look through and discuss the pictures with the class before I read so when I do read it they can focus more on the words. This strategy I tried immediately.

Before Lori's workshop I was doing science notebooks. Basically, my students had the space to write what was happening, their data, and a hypothesis. Now I realize the notebooks can be so much more!

Jennifer L. blurts out:

Well, at least you were using them! I wasn't. After the notebook workshop, I went right to the supply closet and filled my arms with composition books. Lori and Cam told us how important the ownership of notebooks is. Allowing the freedom to choose how to show their data by designing charts, tables, and/or diagrams is very empowering for students. My students feel such ownership they don't even want me to write in the notebooks, so I write my comments on sticky notes.

Jennifer C. adds:

I wanted some accountability with the notebooks, but Cam was saying we needed to help our students use them as a resource for class and self-assessments. We are trying to help students realize that the more they write and the more detail they include, the more of a help it will be when they need to apply the information.

Sometimes our homework in study group will be to pick one strategy we discussed in study group and use a Responsive Teacher Cycle (RTC) for-

in use. She then challenges the students to design and build a compound machine to perform a new task using only the items that are in a plastic bag. The class uses an anchor chart they generated that lists criteria they can refer to as they develop diagrams of their machines. Jennifer circulates, listens, and gives feedback as the groups use their class anchor chart to evaluate their models/diagrams.

The next morning I observe Jennifer C.'s classroom. She is in her second year of teaching. Jennifer begins with focus questions for her class: "How did the ancient Egyptians lift stones weighing several tons to a height of more than 400 feet without using modern machines?" "What is the difference between a picture and a diagram?"

Jennifer C. then does a shared reading on the age of pyramids. Before she reads, she does a "picture walk." She previews and discusses the pictures in the story with the class prior to the reading, reads the story, and then introduces a challenge (the students are to move a sugar cube a set distance). Jennifer C.'s class is a lesson or two behind Jennifer L.'s class. So this class has not yet developed its anchor chart. After comparing and contrasting a variety of diagrams, the class generates criteria for what a diagram should contain.

Before the study group meets that afternoon, I ask both Jennifers to talk about what they were doing to connect science and literacy before they joined the study group.

Jennifer L. begins:

I was doing occasional read-alouds but they weren't connected to the units. I did them just to say we read. I also used to have my students take out their science text to read because I was more comfortable with that. Now I push the book away and think, What else can I connect to the lesson?

Jennifer C. jumps in:

Yeah, two years ago I wasn't reading or writing in science. I would think to myself: A book in science? Let's not be funny!

I ask about how their taking on the role of student again has impacted their classroom practice. Jennifer L. replies:

Jennifer C. and I joined study group because we were asking ourselves, How can we make math and science more fun? We didn't want to just do read-

ing from a textbook, but we did want students to know how to read science text along with doing hands-on science.

Jennifer C. adds:

Now we are trying strategies like teaching about diagrams in the middle of this science lesson. Before study group I would never have thought about integrating these strategies. We have been taught in study group that if you do a read-aloud you should do something after it to keep the kids engaged in the book. I never would have known that.

I was reading a book over last night that I was to do a read-aloud on today. When I read through it, naturally for me as a reader I wanted to go ahead and look at the pictures first. I asked Mary Beth if that was OK. Mary Beth said I could do something called a "picture walk" with my class. Basically, I am supposed to look through and discuss the pictures with the class before I read so when I do read it they can focus more on the words. This strategy I tried immediately.

Before Lori's workshop I was doing science notebooks. Basically, my students had the space to write what was happening, their data, and a hypothesis. Now I realize the notebooks can be so much more!

Jennifer L. blurts out:

Well, at least you were using them! I wasn't. After the notebook workshop, I went right to the supply closet and filled my arms with composition books. Lori and Cam told us how important the ownership of notebooks is. Allowing the freedom to choose how to show their data by designing charts, tables, and/or diagrams is very empowering for students. My students feel such ownership they don't even want me to write in the notebooks, so I write my comments on sticky notes.

Jennifer C. adds:

I wanted some accountability with the notebooks, but Cam was saying we needed to help our students use them as a resource for class and self-assessments. We are trying to help students realize that the more they write and the more detail they include, the more of a help it will be when they need to apply the information.

Sometimes our homework in study group will be to pick one strategy we discussed in study group and use a Responsive Teacher Cycle (RTC) for-

mat to apply it. For the RTC we try the strategy, reflect on it, and explain if it worked or not and why [see Figure 1]. If it doesn't work, well, we try another approach!

FIGURE 1 Sample Responsive Teaching Cycle (RTC)

2/7

RESPONSIVE TEACHING CYCLE   *"A Bug's Life - Day 1"*

Observation	Meaning	New Plans
The students wanted to watch more of the movie. (Instead of just the clip)	1) They learn more from TV. 2) They didn't have to work as hard. 3) They liked the movie.	Use more video clips in my lessons, and see if there is a positive effect on their learning.
The students didn't finish writing down all of the vocabulary words.	1) Not enough time given. 2) Every student looked them up instead of working together. 3) The number of words (7) was too overwhelming.	Assign students in the group the words they will look up, and then have a transparency of all words for other group members that didn't get that word.
The students wanted to build right away. (Instead of waiting + drawing a diagram first)	1) The materials were left out. 2) They found it easier to build first. 3) Someone in the group grabbed the materials.	Don't allow students to touch materials until every student in the group has drawn a diagram and the group has chosen one.

Source: Adapted from Whitin, D., H. Mills, and T. O'Keefe. 1990. *Living and learning mathematics: Stories and strategies for supporting mathematical literacy.* Portsmouth, NH: Heinemann.

The anchor chart you saw in class yesterday was something we talked about in study group last Thursday. If I wasn't in study group I would have just said, "Go ahead and draw a diagram," not even thinking that the students might not know what I meant or how to start. Mary Beth said they need something to go back and refer to later, so she told us about using anchor charts. The students developed a list of what should be included in a diagram. We posted these criteria on the wall and students now refer to it throughout the year when they are drawing diagrams in their science notebooks. This way all students know what diagrams should include.

Jennifer C. continues:

Today you saw my class develop its anchor chart. I brought in different kinds of diagrams and compared and contrasted them with the class. I did that in study group when we had to write an "In the spotlight" article. Mary Beth brought in a bunch of articles and we discussed how they were alike and different. So I used that strategy to help develop our anchor chart on diagrams because it helped me so much with my writing in study group.

I am beginning to see that teachers who once again become students at this school have several teachers—Mary Beth, Lori, and Cam. How does this all end up working so fluidly?
Jennifer C. says:

It's so great how Lori and Mary Beth work together. Lori sits in on study group and adds things. Mary Beth comes to observe our class and also to team teach or model something. Lori does that too. When we started science notebooks she came to model how to get them going. So there is a lot of team teaching to help us. They always say, "Let's talk before the lesson and after." We get a lot of feedback; Lori will also sit and reflect on the lesson with us.

After talking with the Jennifers, I spent time with Lori discussing what her role would be in today's literacy study group.
Lori says:

Today in study group we are incorporating a science lesson. Mary Beth has covered many literacy strategies that can be used in math and science. Her focus for second semester is to pull in all curriculum areas so I will be helping more this semester than last.

Mary Beth always uses a read-aloud and a quick-write in class. Since the lesson today is about cholera, we brainstormed some read-alouds and decided on a poem. This will model the fact that read-alouds can be quick. I will facilitate the activity and incorporate the use of the group's notebooks. It's not written into this activity, so I decided where it would fit and ran it by Mary Beth. We discussed when to share the background knowledge on cholera and the timeframe for the activity, and we decided to end the lesson with a RAFT activity [see Figure 2]. A RAFT activity is a writing prompt that gives students a **R**ole, an **A**udience, a **F**ormat, and a **T**opic.

FIGURE 2 Jennifer C.'s RAFT Writing

RAFT Writing Assignment

You are Dr. John Snow writing a business letter to the Health Department of Sri Lanka following the tsunami advising them of possible health issues from the water based on your work in London.

> To: Health Department of Sri Lanki
>
> I am writing to inform you about a recent problem we've been having in London. Due to our untreated water, and pouring contaminated water into rivers, our water now has cholera throughout it. Because cholera is a bacteria, it has spread extremely fast, and we are having a hard time stopping it.
>
> Now that this natural disaster, Tsunami, has hit Sri Lanka, you need to be aware of how to treat your water. Find the source, and try filtering the water. Otherwise, many lives will be lost.
>
> Sincerely,
> Dr. John Snow

The group members are going to write a letter using information they get from the activity to inform tsunami victims of the threat of disease. Mary Beth will have a few more activities at the end to help "unpack" the strategies today, using a three-part framework, which the group members read about in one of the class texts for homework. The framework breaks a lesson into three parts:

Part One: Before Learning (activating knowledge)
Part Two: During Learning (the use of process checks and metacognitive strategies)
Part Three: After Learning (assessing to help make learning permanent)

After talking with Lori, I catch up with the Jennifers and head to study group. Of the 11 teachers, 3 are math and science teachers and 8 are self-contained (they teach all subjects). The assistant principal (who is also a regular member of the group) joins the teachers. As they go around and introduce themselves, I learn some are 17- and 18-year veterans; others are in their second year of teaching.

Mary Beth begins by reading a poem about success and asking the group to do a quick-write. Then Mary Beth continues:

Your homework reading focused on how we get kids to higher-level questioning based on the belief that if kids come up with their own questions they will care about answering them. I hope using the 3-2-1 format while you read (3 facts or quotes, 2 questions you have, and 1 thing you are left wondering about) worked for you as a learner [see Figure 3]. Today we want you to live out the process of the three-part framework and take the role of students.

For Part One (Before Learning), Mary Beth reads aloud a poem by Shel Silverstein to help activate prior knowledge about germs, diseases, and illness. Teachers then develop an "I Know/I Think" chart about how diseases are spread.

Then Lori facilitates a Poison Pump activity, which illustrates how diseases are spread. The groups write their thoughts and questions in their science notebooks as they read information from clue cards. Then they formulate their theories in writing before sharing ideas with the whole group, making sure they cite facts to support their thinking. Finally, "victim cards" are read and lines of learning are drawn out through discussion. All these processes demonstrate Part Two (During Learning) of the framework.

FIGURE 3 Jennifer L.'s 3-2-1 Response to *Teaching Reading in Social Studies, Science and Math*, Chapter 3, "Posing Questions"

3 key points	2 ways this type of learning benefits students	1 question I have
"The better students understand a concept, the greater chance they have of remembering, applying, and connecting this concept and new information to their learning." (p. 74)	Inquiry notebooks or "I Wonder" folders will help students expand their higher level thinking skills. This is an area where I am aiming to improve so setting aside time every few week for our I Wonder folders will help my students advance to a higher level.	If one of my goals is to help students with their higher level questioning skills, how do I go about doing this? Some of my students are ready for this type of responsibility and advanced questioning, but I also have students who struggle to ask and answer basic questions. Is there a happy medium? How can I inspire some students to go beyond and at the same time help other students keep their heads above the water?
Students should create and ask questions, not teachers.	By encouraging students to come up with the questions they will develop questions based on what they are interested in studying or what they are curious about. Allowing them to create their own questions will also inspire them to dig deeper and read different genres.	
"Students who are taught to generate questions acquire higher levels of questioning ability than those who receive no training." (p. 76)		

Part Three (After Learning) is done by asking the group to complete a written assessment in the form of a RAFT writing. Mary Beth and Lori then debrief the lesson using a pause-and-ponder prompt asking for insights, questions, and ideas for other literacy strategies that could have been pulled in (Figure 4). The study group ends with the teachers talking in pairs about their class applications of strategies they have learned.

FIGURE 4 Jennifer L.'s Pause and Ponder

Name ╳
Date 02/3/05

Pause and Ponder

"It's all about changing what's handed to you, about poking around a little, lifting the corners, seeing what's underneath, poking that. Sometimes things work out, sometimes they don't, but at least you're exploring."
~ Ann Martin, *A Corner of the Universe*

What are your major learning and insights today? How much of this framework learning have you done? What are obstacles in your way? What questions do you have?

it's a help

First of all, I've added several activities to my Poison Pump lesson and am so excited to do this again next year. I especially liked the T-chart idea to have thoughts that are facts vs. thoughts that are "I think" statements.

good

I have helped my students with anchor charts and that went well. I'm excited to try a T-chart or the 3-2-1 response sheet. And now that I've done an example of a RAFT I understand it better + am willing to try this with my students.

it's worth the time

I also love the assessment writing assignment. I do tests/quizzes because they're easy to grade I tend to stay away from written assessments due to the time involved. Great idea of integrating ELA with Science (business letter).

As I leave the group I am wondering how the teaching and learning in study group and in the classroom mutually support each other. I catch up to Lori and ask her.

Lori says:

Some of the ways we follow up on literacy strategies that are introduced to the group is through the RTC, observations in classrooms, conversations in study group, one-on-one conversations, and one-on-one planning conversations. I will be conducting a reflective conversation with Jennifer L. and Jennifer C. on the lessons we observed.

Epilogue

I am, of course, a very transient student. I come to a place like Sandhills and I go, but the learning there continues. After my visit, Lori and Jennifer L. met to reflect on the simple machines lesson I observed. Lori asked Jennifer L. to share her impression of how the lesson went, including application of the literacy strategy using anchor charts.

We just started the levers and pulleys kit. There is a huge difference from last year by introducing simple machines with Egypt and the pyramids as a real-life example. The kit went so much smoother and the students really understood more. I think having more background knowledge before they started the kit really helped their learning. The quality of the students' diagrams was higher because of the anchor charts. The student groups selected a diagram to build and were able to apply their knowledge designing and building a new complex machine.

Mary Beth and Lori also like being students. Lori has already completed over 100 hours of specialized training in content, pedagogy, and coaching techniques in her first eight months as a science coach. Through her school's partnership with South Carolina's Mathematics and Science Unit, she'll continue refining her coaching skills for another 27 months. Mary Beth has completed 675 hours of literacy coach training. Through SCRI she will continue to receive ongoing professional development for two more years.

Witnessing the relationship that the coaches at Sandhills have with each other and the teachers, as well as listening to the energetic voices of two young teachers, reminds me how vital it is for anyone's professional growth to be a learner again. Perhaps the best way to take learning on beyond the ordinary is with the help of a good coach…or two.

Resources

Billmeyer, R., and M. L. Barton. 1998. *Teaching reading in the content areas: If not me, then who?* Aurora, CO: McRel.

Harvey, S., and A. Goudvis. 2000. *Strategies that work: Teaching comprehension to enhance understanding.* Portland, ME: Stenhouse.

Hoyt, L. 2002. *Make it real: Strategies for success with informational text.* Portsmouth, NH: Heinemann.

Project WET (Water Education for Teachers) Curriculum and Activity Guide. *www.projectwetusa.org*

Robb, L. 2003. *Teaching reading in social studies, science, and math.* New York: Scholastic.

Tovani, C. 2004. *Do I really have to teach reading?* Portland, ME: Stenhouse.

Questions for Discussion

1. As described in the Local Systemic Change Initiative's Theory of Action (see Chapter 13), to improve instruction, and therefore student achievement, instructional leaders must combine high-quality instructional materials with sustained professional development. What evidence is there at Sandhills that this theory of action guides the efforts of classroom practitioners and those who support their work?

2. "While it seems possible on conceptual grounds to integrate disciplines while staying true to the key ideas of each, some previous efforts at integration have tended to give primacy to one of the disciplines, to the detriment of the other" (Chapter 13, page 369). What strategies have been put in place at Sandhills to address the challenges of staying true to the disciplines of science and literacy?

Science and Oral Discourse

Powering Oral Language With the Fuel of Science

Jane Yuster is in her third year of teaching. Her assignment at Hoover Middle School includes three sections of physical science, one section of English language development, and one section of social studies. All of Jane's students are eighth graders. This case story focuses on her physical science classes.

Hoover Middle School is located in Redwood City, California. The student population is 93% Latino, 3% Asian, 2% Caucasian, 1% African American, and 1% Pacific Islander. Eighty-six percent of Hoover's students are English language learners (ELLs). Nearly the same portion, 85%, is eligible for free or reduced lunch. Over 55% of Hoover's parents did not graduate from high school. Less than 4% of the parents hold a college degree.

Jane is speaking:

I went into teaching after retiring from the chemical and biotechnology industries. I was concerned that there is a growing shortage of scientists and frankly there are not very many women or minority scientists. I wanted to do something about this. I know from firsthand experience what it takes to be successful in a science career. The ability to communicate ideas is the cornerstone to success.

On the surface our class discussions in science seemed effective. The kids used the science vocabulary words, but it often felt very stilted to me. No enthusiasm. No begging for just a few more minutes. I assessed their knowledge both in oral and written form, but although the kids were interested and having fun with the investigations, the physics knowledge just wasn't being retained. I was really upset with myself. I realized that the kids were not sufficiently motivated to "fight" for conceptual understanding.

I went home one weekend and thought about my dilemma. I knew that if I was going to get them to communicate effectively, I was going to have to find something they wanted to talk about. The first challenge is to find curriculum so powerful that it motivates the students to want to learn about it and talk about their learning. The second challenge is to find information that is well written, interesting, and scientifically accurate. That's when I remembered rockets.

I was hooked on solid fuel rockets when I was in eighth grade, and I thought these kids might like them too. Who wouldn't want to talk about something that one builds, adds explosive to, and blows 1,000 feet into the air? That weekend I ordered the first rocket kits.

The group that would explore rocketry consisted of 12 special education students and 48 mainstream students. All of the students were English language learners, with most at the early advanced level. I call these students the "hump" kids because they often get stuck at this level of language proficiency and do not progress. I consider it my job to push them over the hump.

I had the kids work in cooperative groups to build solid fuel model rockets. I showed them all the safety precautions needed to launch. The excitement was fantastic. Some of the rockets went over 1,000 feet. They received the coveted "sick" rating from the kids. When we got back to the room there were lots of questions:

"Why do these rockets work?" "How do they work?" "What is the difference in the engines?" "What do the fins do?" "Is there some science here you are not telling us about?" "We want to do more." "Tell us about these things."

Step one complete. I had interest and it was high. I was ecstatic. Public communication is tough in eighth grade because the peer pressure says it is not "cool" to answer in class. This is what I had to overcome if we were going to make progress.

I found terrific curriculum from NASA on rockets that begins with a history of rockets and their earliest origins and goes right through all of the physics involved with rocketry. I read portions of the text out loud because most of my kids do not have the fluency required for a good read-aloud yet. I would read a sentence or two aloud and then I would think aloud with the class, helping them to come to understanding.

At one point in our reading we discovered that when rocket fuel burns the gasses expand and create a downward force. In direct response to this force and if the force is strong enough to overcome gravity, the rocket begins to rise. Not only did my kids understand this, they immediately said, "That's what happened when our rockets launched. We could see it." By relating their experience to the reading, my kids were actually discussing and making sense of the physics!

What I had not expected was that any of these kids would want to participate in the school Math, Science, and Technology Fair. I had introduced rocketry in an effort to ensure that they learned and retained the eighth-grade physics standards of force and motion. For these ELL students it was also important that I integrated the eighth-grade English standards relating to the reading of instructional materials and conducting research. The fact that two groups of students wanted to participate in the fair as a result of doing this unit was an unexpected and delightful surprise.

Eduardo, a special education student, and Miguel, a regular student, wanted to do a science fair project on model rockets. Both boys were English language learners with California English Language Development Test (CELDT) scores indicating overall language development at the high intermediate to low early advanced levels. Initially, Eduardo and Miguel thought they would just build a model rocket and that would be it. I really don't think they realized how much communication would have to be done and in what forms it would have to happen. The projects for the fair were going to be evaluated using rubrics I developed for the written and oral components (Figure 1). Both rubrics were reviewed and approved by our language arts teachers, and it is our language arts teachers who judged the projects using the Language Arts Rubric (Figure 2).

Until last year, there had never been a science fair in the 20-year history of the school. I don't think teachers believed that kids who were from low socioeconomic backgrounds and were English language learners could do this caliber of work. It is very difficult not to let go of the highest standards because the fight to get them can be very strenuous and time consuming indeed. I decided to forget about the time issue and support my students.

I decided to use the students' desire to do this project to integrate literacy objectives. For example, when I first started to talk with Eduardo and Miguel a typical conversation was like pulling teeth:

Ms. Yuster: Well, guys, what project so you think you'd like to do for the fair?

Miguel: Rockets.

Ms. Yuster: What about rockets would you like to study?

Miguel: Model rockets.

FIGURE 1 Science Fair Rubric

Science Fair Experiment: Judges' Form

Teacher Name: **Ms. Yuster**

Student Name: _____

CATEGORY	4	3	2	1
Display	Each element in the display had a function and clearly served to illustrate some aspect of the experiment. All items—graphs, etc.—were neatly and correctly labeled.	Each element had a function and clearly served to illustrate some aspect of the experiment. Most items—graphs, etc.—were neatly and correctly labeled.	Each element had a function and clearly served to illustrate some aspect of the experiment. Most items—graphs, etc.—were correctly labeled.	The display seemed incomplete or chaotic with no clear plan. Many labels were missing or incorrect.
Data Collection	Data were collected several times. Data were summarized, independently, in a way that clearly described what was discovered.	Data were collected more than one time. Data were summarized, independently, in a way that clearly described what was discovered.	Data were collected more than one time. Adult assistance was needed to clearly summarize what was discovered.	Data were collected only once and adult assistance was needed to clearly summarize what was discovered.
Conclusion/ Summary	Student provided a detailed conclusion clearly based on the data and related to previous research findings and the hypothesis statement(s).	Student provided a somewhat detailed conclusion clearly based on the data and related to the hypothesis statement(s).	Student provided a conclusion with some reference to the data and the hypothesis statement(s).	No conclusion was apparent, or important details were overlooked.

(continued)

FIGURE 1 (*continued*)

Diagrams	Provided an accurate, easy-to-follow diagram with labels to illustrate the procedure or the process being studied.	Provided an accurate diagram with labels to illustrate the procedure or the process being studied.	Provided an easy-to-follow diagram with labels to illustrate the procedure or process, but one key step was left out.	Did not provide a diagram, or the diagram was quite incomplete.
Overall Knowledge	Student clearly understood the subject matter and answered all questions asked without assistance.	Student understood subject, but needed some help to answer questions.	Student had some knowledge of subject, but could not answer questions well.	Student did not demonstrate knowledge of subject.

Ms. Yuster:	OK, good. Model rockets. What about model rockets?
Miguel:	Dunno.
Ms. Yuster:	Well, Miguel, let's ask your partner Eduardo for his opinion. [Eduardo is a really quiet kid. He is well-behaved and hopes that he can go unnoticed.] Eduardo, are you going to let Miguel make the decision for you?
Eduardo:	No!
Ms. Yuster:	Great! Why don't you two talk about what you might do and I'll just listen in if you do not mind. Is that OK with you?

Now there is silence as the boys hope that either I'll get bored and go away or that I'll get impatient and do the conversation for them. Once they start to talk, I applaud all of their efforts and then ask more questions.

Ms. Yuster:	What do you want to do?
Miguel:	We want to build model rockets.
Ms. Yuster:	Very nice. Could you give me more detail? Exactly what do you want to do with the rockets after you build them?

FIGURE 2 Language Arts Rubric

Research Report: Science Fair Project

Teacher Name: **Ms. Yuster**

Student Name: _____

CATEGORY	4	3	2	1
Organization	Information is very organized with well-constructed paragraphs and subheadings.	Information is organized with well-constructed paragraphs.	Information is organized, but paragraphs are not well constructed.	The information appears to be disorganized.
Paragraph Construction	All paragraphs include introductory sentence, explanations or details, and concluding sentence.	Most paragraphs include introductory sentence, explanations or details, and concluding sentence.	Paragraphs include related information but are typically not constructed well.	Paragraphing structure is not clear and sentences are not typically related within the paragraphs.
Quality of Information	Information clearly relates to the main topic. It includes several supporting details and/or examples.	Information clearly relates to the main topic. It provides 1–2 supporting details and/or examples.	Information clearly relates to the main topic. No details and/or examples are given.	Information has little or nothing to do with the main topic.
Mechanics	No grammatical, spelling, or punctuation errors.	Almost no grammatical, spelling, or punctuation errors.	A few grammatical, spelling, or punctuation errors.	Many grammatical, spelling, or punctuation errors.
PowerPoint	Presentation is well written, easy to read, and understandable.	Presentation is well written. Choice of background or fonts makes it harder to read. Material is understandable.	Presentation has errors. Background or font makes understanding difficult. Material is somewhat confusing.	Presentation contains many errors. Background and fonts are inappropriate. Material is not understandable.

Kids get so afraid of giving a "wrong" answer and looking foolish in front of their friends that they would rather not talk than answer incorrectly. This is the kiss of death if you are trying to encourage conversation. Therefore, it is imperative that every time you give an answer that has any possible negative connotations, you get confirmation from your students that shows they really understand what you mean.

Eduardo: What can we do?
Miguel: Ms. Yuster, can you give us a hint, please?
Ms. Yuster: I would love to. I just so happen to have several wonderful investigations with me. Why don't you take these, read them, and tomorrow tell me if you would like to try one of them.

I had come to this conversation with several investigations that I had already written up. They have to do with things like fin design, trying different fuels, and altering the amount of the same fuel put into the rocket. The boys are very excited, and as I leave to go to the next group they are already poring over the material.

From reading through the investigations I gave them, Eduardo and Miguel decided to test if the amount of fuel put in the rocket had an effect on how high it flew. Since we had started with the rocket curriculum, we had a good understanding of the physics, so we agreed that our new research should help us to expand that understanding even further. I asked questions on vocabulary and its meaning and overall conceptual meaning. They had to present me with a new piece of research they had done on the subject every week for the first six weeks of the project. We would all have to agree on whether or not we considered the information relevant. If we did, we kept it. If not, they needed two pieces of research for the next meeting. This procedure was followed for the experimental design, results, and conclusions sections of the report for the science fair.

After a few weeks of research, Eduardo and Miguel brought me an article on wind resistance and its relation to thrust. We had a good discussion about it.

Ms. Yuster: What do you have for me today?
Eduardo: We have some information about rockets. [Now you may not think this is much, but Eduardo says absolutely nothing in his other classes.]

Ms. Yuster: What kind of information?

Eduardo: About how they fly through the air.

Ms. Yuster: Wonderful! Can you tell me more?

Eduardo: It says that when the rocket tries to fly through the air that friction happens between the rocket and the air and when the scientists want to make the rocket fly they have to have good enough fuel.

Ms. Yuster: Good enough fuel to do what?

Miguel: To be better than the friction.

Ms. Yuster: Let me see if I understand. You learned that there is friction created when a rocket tries to fly through the air and that the rocket fuel has to be better than the friction.

Eduardo and
Miguel: Yes.

Ms. Yuster: OK, let's write this down in our lab notebooks.

I then ask Eduardo to read it and Miguel to listen and see if that is what they meant. I ask Miguel to listen because I know that Eduardo has an auditory processing difficulty and so having him listen will accomplish nothing except to get him frustrated. This way, he reads it, which he can do well, and he can look at it as well for errors. So, after Eduardo reads it, I get ready to ask a question, but Miguel says first, "That does not sound right." He immediately looks at what he has written down. Eduardo is also looking puzzled and is intently studying what he has written. I bite my tongue, hold my breath, and realize that something good may be about to happen.

Miguel: I am not sure that the part about the fuel being better is right.

Eduardo: Yeah.

Ms. Yuster: In what way? Do you think this is a question of word choice or is the idea wrong?

Eduardo: We get the idea, the words are wrong. They do not say what we want.

Miguel
agrees: We need better words.

Ms. Yuster: Where can you find them?

Eduardo: I get it! She wants us to look in the paper for a better word. Right, Ms. Yuster?

All I do is smile. The kids reread the article and suddenly they stop at one point.

| Miguel: | *Overcome*. Yeah, that's the word we want. |
| Eduardo: | Let's try it. The sentence is "Friction is created when a rocket tries to fly through the air and that the rocket fuel has to overcome the friction." |

The boys look triumphant.

During this discussion I knew in my mind exactly what the conversation should sound like for effective communication. So it became a question of patience and persistence to encourage the kids. I needed to take it one step at a time. I started with what they knew and tried to integrate science vocabulary one word at a time. I have learned to be patient and not forget to let my body language help when necessary. Over the course of the project and even to this day, the kids do not willingly use the science language first. I still have to ask questions in order to make it happen. The good news is that I now need to ask far fewer questions to get students to talk science!

During the project work, I noticed the kids became much more critical in their thinking. They began to bring me examples of things they found in research that they did not think were relevant and they could explain why. As they entered the writing phase, they began to help each other. They proofread each other's slides and introductions. I heard them correct each other's content knowledge. I even heard an argument break out as to whether something was really Newton's first law or not. They began to quiz each other when I was working with another group. I heard things like, "We could answer that better. We did not use the right words."

About a week before the fair, I prepped Eduardo and Miguel for their oral presentation portion. I asked questions like, "Why did you do this project?" "What did you learn from this project?" "What do you want others to know about your work?" "Please explain why this works or doesn't work."

Eduardo and Miguel created an excellent PowerPoint presentation (see Figure 3 for one of the slides). At the fair, they spoke with confidence and poise in Spanish and English. When we went outside, I heard squeals of delight as my rocket scientists launched air rockets again and again in the pouring rain because the younger students wanted to see if it was true that the harder you stomped, the higher the rocket went. My students engaged the young ones in discussion and even had them make a hypothesis before they launched the rocket because, as they explained, that is what all scientists do.

FIGURE 3 Sample PowerPoint Slide From Eduardo and Miguel's Project

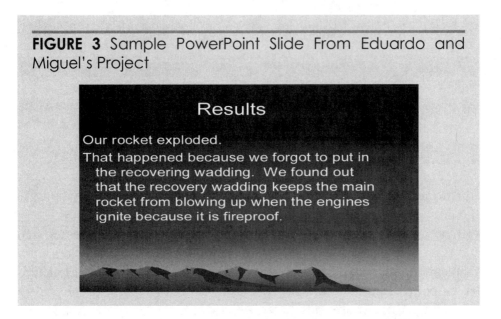

The fair had a huge impact on all of us. Our school received a great deal of positive press and reaction from our school board. Funds were allocated to build a science lab in our school and we have begun to assume a leadership role in science education in our district. We also have permission to purchase additional technology that will make our science program even stronger. Our students have more self-confidence and are more verbal than ever. I am delighted to see them learn the joy that is associated with the communication of results with others.

Resources

Berry, K. S. 1985. Talking to learn subject matter/learning subject matter talk. *Language Arts* 62 (1): 34–42.

Bertram, G. 2002. The importance of oral language in the school curriculum. English Online, *http://english.unitecnology.ac.nz/resources/resources/effective_communication.html.*

Holbrook, H. T. 1983. Oral language: A neglected language art? *Language Arts* 60 (2): 255–258.

Zhang, H., and N. K. Alex. 1995. Oral language development across the curriculum. *K–12 ERIC Digest.* ERIC Clearinghouse on Reading English and Communication. ERIC Identifier ED389029.

Questions for Discussion

1. What evidence is there that a classroom culture of inquiry and science discussion is present in Ms. Yuster's class? How could you strengthen the inquiry so it would be more student directed?

2. Using the Talking in Science chart on pages 49–51 of this book, identify and discuss some of the purposes, characteristics, and question/prompt types in Ms. Yuster's discussions with Eduardo and Miguel.

3. Productive questions are those that are cognitively demanding and generate student-to-student talk. What are some questions you might ask Eduardo and Miguel to facilitate a conversation about what they learned from their science fair experience?

CHAPTER 2

Talk in the Science Classroom:
Looking at What Students and Teachers Need to Know and Be Able to Do

Jeffrey Winokur and Karen Worth
Center for Science Education
Education Development Center, Inc.

In schools, talk is sometimes valued and sometimes avoided, but—and this is surprising—talk is rarely taught. It is rare to hear teachers discuss their efforts to teach students to talk well. Yet talk, like reading and writing, is a major motor—I could even say the major motor—of intellectual development.

—Calkins 2000, p. 226

L anguage and communication are central to the learning process. Researchers and practitioners alike have underscored the importance of language development and the impact it has on student learning. All modalities—reading, writing, and oral language—are important. This chapter focuses specifically on the role of oral language, one area that is less often discussed in science education. Yet the research suggests that it is talk that leads to understanding and helps us process what we are learning (Barnes 1993; Cazden 2001). Social constructivist theories based on the work of Lev Vygotsky (1934, 1978) suggest that learning and higher-level thinking are enhanced when students have opportunities to talk with peers and teachers about their ideas, and respond to and challenge the ideas of others (Almasi 2002).

Lauren Resnick (1999, Effort-Based Education and Learnable Intelligence: Principles for Teaching and Learning section, ¶8) expands on these basic ideas, suggesting that

> *not all talk sustains learning or creates intelligence. For classroom talk to promote learning, it must have certain characteristics that make it accountable. Accountable talk seriously responds to and further develops what others in the group have said. It puts forth and demands knowledge that is accurate and relevant to the issue under discussion. Accountable talk uses evidence in ways appropriate to the discipline (for example, proofs in mathematics, data from investigations in science, textual details in literature, documentary sources in history). Finally, it follows established norms of good reasoning. Accountable talk sharpens students' thinking by reinforcing their ability to use knowledge appropriately. As such, it helps develop the skills and the habits of mind that constitute intelligence-in-practice.*

For accountable talk to take place in the classroom, however, it is not enough to simply provide time for discussion and teach the appropriate vocabulary. The norms and skills that allow students to engage in such talk must be taught explicitly, yet this happens rarely.

The Role of Talk in Science Learning

This discussion of the role of talk in science learning is situated within the context of hands-on, inquiry-based science teaching, where students have opportunities to explore, question, and then investigate phenomena both firsthand and using secondary resources; gather their own data; and begin to construct ideas about the natural world. Talk plays a critical role in such science learning, not only because of the importance in science of communicating data, analyses, and ideas, but also because it is fundamental to the development of scientific reasoning skills and the construction of theories and explanations. As students talk about their experiences and the data they have collected and as they debate their ideas, they clarify their thoughts, generate conclusions, and develop new theories.

Anyone walking into an active hands-on science class at the elementary level will notice no dearth of talk as students work. But when gathered together in small or large groups, quiet descends and the teacher's voice emerges loud and clear: "Who will share their data?" "What did you learn today?" Often silence is the response. The excited chatter is gone and is replaced by teacher-led questions and responses with little real dialogue among students. The challenge for teachers is to create a classroom culture of science inquiry and to teach the skills and norms of accountable science talk so students can engage in rigorous discussions without losing the excitement and fluency of the talk they engage in as they actively investigate.

Language in Science Teaching: A Historical Perspective

Inquiry-based elementary science curricula developers have tended to underestimate the importance of talk in student learning. In the 1980s, as they began the process of developing new inquiry-based curricula, they were responding to a world in which much of the hands-on experiential side of science had vanished despite its strong presence in many of the programs of the sixties and seventies. There was a renewed concern about science learning in general, and a particular concern that science ought to be taught through inquiry and direct experience with phenomena. The thrust was to return hands-on science to the classroom. The developers of the inquiry-based programs also recognized that elementary teachers would require a good deal of guidance when it came to materials management and the science content of a particular module. They recognized the importance of providing carefully sequenced experiences to support the gradual development of conceptual understanding.

But, in retrospect, the developers did not think deeply enough about the bridge between direct experience and the understanding necessary to explain and theorize. They assumed it would happen and therefore provided relatively little guidance to teachers on how to support student reflection on ideas and the construction of explanations and theories based in the evidence they collected. It is now evident that building this bridge requires that students discuss their experiences with one another. Providing the opportunity for accountable talk is a vital component of science teaching and learning and many teachers need guidance if they are to make this happen.

In what follows, we assume that students are actively engaged in inquiry-based investigations and that language is a critical ingredient for developing the necessary scientific reasoning and conceptual understanding. We suggest ways that teachers can create the norms and teach the skills students need to think and communicate about their work with one another to reach new conclusions individually and as a group.

Developing and Supporting Student Science Talk

Conducting and facilitating fruitful discussions in science requires a great deal of thought and skill on the part of the teacher. Many teaching strategies and skills are the same as those used in comprehensive literacy programs and research-based mathematics programs. For example, in comprehensive literacy models, teachers first ask students to discuss a question with a partner before they ask for contributions to the full-group discussion. In many literacy programs, students learn, practice, and discuss specific skills, such as active listening, waiting their turn, and ways to add ideas to the thinking of others. Likewise in many mathematics programs, students learn to explain their thinking and how they arrived at a particular answer. *A Research Companion to Principles and Standards for School Mathematics* (Kilpatrick, Martin, and Schifter 2003) devotes a chapter to describing the thoughtful use of communication and language in mathematics teaching and learning.

But while there is much to transfer from literacy and mathematics discussion into science talk, teaching science talk requires specific attention to the

- science content and thinking goals that are the focus of the discussion,
- nature of a classroom culture of science inquiry,
- purpose of the discussion within an inquiry framework,
- stages of a discussion,
- guiding of a discussion, and
- recording of ideas and information.

The Thinking and Content Goals

Critical to effective facilitation of science discussions is the teacher's clarity regarding the content being discussed, the various ways students build their understanding of the science, and her or his explicit understanding of the learning expectations. Without this knowledge, it is difficult to determine a good question or prompt to start a discussion; to know which students' ideas to follow and when to refocus; and when to bring closure to a discussion. Though necessary for rich science discussions, how to go about building and deepening this knowledge is not the purpose of this chapter.

A Classroom Culture of Science Inquiry

We define a classroom culture of science to include norms of behavior, attitudes, and expectations. Teachers who provide students with direct experience often consider this hands-on exploration of materials to be the only place where science learning happens. They assume that the exploration of materials alone embodies the essence of a culture of science inquiry in the classroom. When pressed for time, they may skip over the discussions that precede or follow the experience. But those discussions are equally as important as the hands-on experiences and are where much of the rigorous scientific reasoning needed for understanding takes place. So a culture of science practice must include the expectations that

- discussion takes place,
- ideas and experiences are shared,
- all thoughtful and interesting ideas are valued,
- scientific reasoning is expected, and
- debate and argument are assumed to be part of science learning.

Along with an explicit set of expectations, students need to learn and practice basic discussion skills such as listening to one another, responding to one another's ideas, staying on focus, and supporting the participation of all of their peers. These skills need to be taught and practiced. For example, the teacher might introduce, describe, and demonstrate in a mini-lesson a discussion skill such as how to listen to others, much as she would do when conducting a literature circle or modeling for students how to use a magnifier. Once introduced, such a skill becomes a classroom norm to which students and teachers alike refer when engaged in a science discussion.

Other expectations focus more on the reasoning process itself. For example, evidence-based debate and argument are important to the development of science ideas and are both a part of accountable talk. Here, too, appropriate skills and behaviors need to be learned and practiced, including using data, disagreeing respectfully, and asking for clarification of someone's ideas. Mini-lessons can teach the use of specific language that makes this respect more explicit, such as "I have a different idea" or "Tell me why you think that."

If we were to drop in on a science discussion in a classroom where there is a culture that supports serious science discussion, we would likely notice most or all of the following common characteristics:

- The students are seated in a circle facing one another, making accountability more likely.
- There is a natural flow to the conversation with a good deal of student-to-student interaction rather than question and response with the teacher.

- The conversation is focused, and the students make connections to one another's ideas and linger on a particular idea.
- The conversation is not dominated by a single student or by the teacher.

Purposes of Discussions Within an Inquiry Framework

Science discussions can have a number of different purposes; each purpose influences the structure of the discussion and the roles of teacher and students. In an attempt to develop a framework for thinking about group discussions, we have identified a range of purposes for discussion (Figure 1). These include

1. to gather and take stock of ideas,
2. to plan an investigation, and
3. to develop conceptual understanding.

A discussion to *gather and take stock of ideas* is one in which students are encouraged to talk about what they know, describe experiences they have had, share ideas, and listen to the experiences and ideas of others. This kind of discussion often occurs at the beginning of a new topic or focus, when it is important for students to make explicit what and how they think about a topic. It also can occur after some initial direct experience to uncover the thinking the experience has sparked. For these discussions to be effective, basic norms for discussion must be in place, but rather than argument and lengthy debate, the discussion is one of brainstorming, speculation, and wondering.

As an example, consider this discussion from a third-grade class just beginning a study of water:

Teacher (T):	We're going to have a science talk as we begin a study of water. Let's remember that as we have this talk we want to listen to each other. Be sure to ask questions if you aren't sure about what someone means. What are some things you have noticed about water and what it does?
Maria:	It can push.
Tyrone:	Push? What do you mean?
Maria:	I saw it push leaves down the street when it was raining.
Joanne:	Oh yeah! I saw rain push a plastic bottle down the street!
T:	So some of us have seen water push. What else can water do?
Damien:	It can make sounds.

T:	Is anyone curious about what Damien is thinking when he says that?
Irina:	What sounds?
Damien:	Like when I was walking down the street yesterday when it was raining and when a car drove by it made a sound like water going sssssss….

FIGURE 1 Talking in Science: A Framework for Classroom Science Discussion

Purposes/Goals	Characteristics of Group Talks	Prompts/Questions
1. Gathering and Taking Stock of Ideas **Purpose** To take stock at a point in time of a group's experiences and ideas about an aspect of the science topic at hand. **Through** • activating prior knowledge; • capturing ideas, questions, and experience; and • generating hunches and wonderings.	• Focused on a topic or idea • Initiated with a statement and/or productive question • Open-ended • All ideas accepted • Limited challenge or disagreement • Dialogue around detail, understanding	**1. Setting the stage** (What are we wondering about?) Let's look at this X. • What do you notice? • What does it make you think about? • What do you wonder about? **2. Moving further** (What do we think/ speculate about this?) • What makes you think that? • That's an interesting experience. Can you tell us more? • Where did you find that out? **3. Bringing closure** (What are our collective experiences and ideas?) • You shared a lot of ideas. Some of you…. **Encouraging child-to-child discourse** • M, that's sort of like your experience. What do you think? • P, what do you think about H's idea? • Is there someone who has had a similar experience?

(continued)

FIGURE 1 (*continued*)

Purposes/Goals	Characteristics of Group Talks	Prompts/Questions

2. Planning an Investigation
 	
Purpose
To develop and/ or evaluate the particulars of a plan for an investigation, decide on "next steps," and understand why and how these next steps will help collect the data needed to pursue the question.
 	
Through
• focusing on a question,
• planning steps of the investigation,
• determining data to be collected, and
• determining recording structure.
	• Focused on a specific investigation
	• Initiated with a challenging question (make a plan)
	• Ideas backed by explanation
	• Dialogue for reasoning, clarity
	• Debate about effectiveness of the plan/step
		1. Setting the stage (What's the question?)
		  • Let's be clear on what our question is. What is it we want to find out?
		2. Moving further (How will we find out?)
		  • What data do we need to help answer the question?
		  • What do you think are some ways to get that data?
		  • What do you think that will tell us?
		  • What might we have to do first? next? finally?
		  • How might we record our data?
		3. Bringing closure (What do we predict?)
		  • Let's review the plan and be sure we have all the details.
		  • What do you think will happen?
		  • What do you think we will find out?
		
		Encouraging child-to-child discourse
		  • Do you have any questions for K about her suggestion?
		  • C, how can you add to D's idea?
		  • See if you can agree on what might be the best next step.

(continued)

This small piece of discussion displays some elements that are important to the class's study of water. It occurs in an environment in which students are learning how to listen and talk to one another, and in which the sharing of a range of ideas is encouraged. Because these ideas are based on the experiences of individual students, there is no need to challenge their ideas at this point. Instead, the teacher encourages students to ask questions about one another's ideas. The teacher recognizes that sharing prior experiences with water will help her students begin to think about what they already

FIGURE 1 (*continued*)

Purposes/Goals	Characteristics of Group Talks	Prompts/Questions
3. Developing Conceptual Understanding **Purpose** To develop and articulate the understanding that the group holds at a moment in time of a science idea or concept central to the current investigation, based on data collected by its members. **Through** • sharing data, • analyzing and discussing group members' evidence, • finding relationships and patterns, • coming to new conclusion/closure, and • raising new questions.	• Focused on data/evidence from a specific investigation • Initiated with a productive question • Meaning/theory oriented (What do we understand now?) • Ideas/theories based in evidence (notebooks, class data) • Debate and argument about interpretation, ideas, patterns, relationships	**1. Setting the stage** (What data do we have?) • We are going to be thinking about…. Let's gather all of the records we need to discuss X. • What does our experience/data tell us about X? **2. Moving further** (What do the data say? What claims can we make? What is the evidence to support them?) • What can we tell about X by looking at everyone's data? • How is the data from E different from the data from M? • How might we explain this to someone else? • What do you think is the relationship between X and Y? • What evidence do you have for that idea? **3. Bringing closure** (What can we conclude? What new questions do we have?) • What have we learned? • What do we need to check again? • What will we do next? **Encouraging child-to-child discourse** • R, what do you think about that? • E, listen to J's idea and see what you think. • J and you seem to have a similar idea. Why don't you two discuss it and come back? • J, what do you have to say to R about her idea? It's pretty different from yours.

have experienced, which will be a starting point for how they might begin to think about some of the properties of water.

A discussion to *plan an investigation* is one in which the class comes together to identify and/or clarify a question, focus on what is to be found out, and plan an appropriate investigation. It includes determining what data need to be collected, how to collect the data, and what to record. Once again, basic norms of discussion must be observed, but the goal usually is group consensus on what will be done.

Here, later in their water unit, we find the third graders sitting in a circle next to their working partners, making some plans.

T:	Yesterday we investigated drops of water on wax paper. Afterwards, Tyrone had an idea for what we might try today—what was your idea, Tyrone?
Tyrone:	I said, what if we tried to put drops on other things?
T:	Such as…?
Tyrone:	Aluminum foil, towels, raincoats…
T:	Yesterday each of your groups talked about what they might want to try today. So let's talk about what you think we should do and what we ought to look for. But before we go on together, I want each pair of you to talk together about this for a couple of minutes.

————

T:	OK, now let's talk about what you might do. Feel free to make suggestions to each other, but be sure to remember to wait until someone is through talking before you add or suggest anything. Luis, do you want to begin?
Luis:	Well, I think each group will have to have some of the same things and some different things to put the drops on.
T:	And what will we look for when we put the drops on different things?
Tanisha:	If it makes a circle.
T:	What do people think about what Tanisha said?
Maria:	Well, yeah, I agree, but it's a circle when you look down on it. But when you look at it from the side, it's different.
T:	Maria, do you mean you want to look at it from above and from the side just like we did with the wax paper?
Maria:	Yeah.

| Irina: | Then we can see if it looks the same or different than how it looked on the wax paper. |
| Maria: | If you make it a big drop it won't. |

Here the teacher is encouraging the students to talk to one another and to come up with some plans that will help them know what they might look for as they engage in the investigation. The students are free to challenge one another, but the group will be responsible for making a decision about how to proceed and what to look for. The teacher still is doing much of the talking, but she is trying to encourage others to share their ideas. It often takes a good deal of this kind of encouragement and direct teaching over the course of many discussions before students are able to take on more responsibility to respond to one another.

Finally, a discussion to *develop conceptual understanding*, the most difficult for teacher and students, is one in which data are analyzed, meaning is sought, explanations and theories are tried out, and argument and debate are encouraged. Here, too, the basic norms of discussion, as well as those for debate and argument, must be observed. In addition, there are expectations for the use of evidence and scientific reasoning as theories and explanations are developed.

Here are the third graders after they have had several experiences with looking at drops on different surfaces:

T:	So, we've looked at drops of water on wax paper and on a number of other surfaces. We have kept records of the drops in our notebooks with drawings and descriptions of what we have observed. We compiled some of the data about your predictions of what you would see and what actually happened from your notebooks onto the class chart yesterday. As we have this discussion, remember to use evidence to support your ideas. What kinds of ideas do you have about drops on different kinds of surfaces?
Tanisha:	It wasn't always in a circle.
T:	What is your evidence for saying that?
Tanisha:	On the chart, I saw that sometimes drops were in a circle and sometimes they weren't.
T:	You sound surprised. Did it surprise you that the drops weren't always circles?
Tanisha:	Yeah, it wasn't always like the wax paper. Only on some things.

T:	Were others of you surprised about the data we see on the chart? Michael?
Michael:	Yeah, I didn't like the aluminum foil.
Damien:	Me either.
T:	So what was it that you didn't like?
Michael:	I thought the aluminum foil would be like the wax paper, that the drops would look like half circles, but the drops spread out all over the place.
Damien:	That's what I thought, too. The foil is smooth like the wax paper but it kind of, like, melted.
T:	As I look on our chart I see that both Michael and Damien predicted that drops on foil would be like those on wax paper, and that in both cases the drops ended up looking very different. So what do people think makes them different? How might you explain what's happening?
Maria:	They aren't always the same.
Irina:	It depends on what you put them on.
T:	Do you agree with Maria and Damien or disagree? Why?

The teacher is now encouraging her students to use the class data chart to formulate some ideas about some factors that affect the shapes of drops of water. Students are using evidence to begin to analyze the patterns they might have observed. This teacher is certainly very present in the discussion, but her role is to generate conversation and thought rather than answer questions.

In the first two columns of Figure 1, we review the three purposes/goals of discussion and some key characteristics of each.

Stages of a Discussion

Clearly, the teacher's role in science discussions of all kinds is critical. As he or she guides a science discussion, the teacher must keep in mind the science concepts and skills that are the goals of the study and the particular discussion, and she must have a sense for the level of understanding to be expected of her students. With this in mind, she must orchestrate the discussion as a whole and manage a flow that proceeds through several basic stages:

- *Setting the stage:* How the teacher begins a discussion can deeply impact its success. The opening of a discussion also is the time for the teacher to establish with the students the purpose of the discussion, and to review the appropriate discussion norms and expectations.

- *Moving further:* This is the heart of the discussion. Teacher comments, questions, and prompts support rich discussion, maintain the focus as needed, and gently guide the thinking.
- *Bringing closure:* Depending on the purpose of the discussion, closure may be a review of ideas; a plan of action; a synthesis of ideas; or, indeed, an explicit statement or conclusion.

These stages appear in the third column of Figure 1.

Guiding a Discussion

Teachers generally see their role as question-asker. But in our experience, this often means that they ask many questions in a rapid-fire format, eliciting brief responses. Such a structure often does the thinking for students and rarely leads to the kind of reasoning and discussion that can result in new theories or explanations. Another common practice is to repeat what a student has said, making listening to one another unnecessary. Our experience suggests that one of the most difficult parts of guiding science discussions is determining the question(s), comment(s), and prompt(s) that will initiate and move a discussion forward. These must be specific enough to focus the thinking of the group yet open enough to invite thought. They must reflect student thinking and move the discussion toward common goals. They must encourage debate and argument yet stay focused on the ideas at hand.

Much is written about questions and questioning and how to categorize and describe different kinds of questions in terms of the responses they elicit. Here we have drawn from the work of Elstgeest and Jelly (found in Harlen 2001) to describe two basic categories of questions: unproductive and productive.

Unproductive Questions

Unproductive questions do not invite discussion. They include questions that ask for facts, definition, repetition, or rhetorical/information checks. They may be useful to the teacher to check for specific surface knowledge, vocabulary words, and definitions, but they do not generate the thinking that leads to deeper understanding.

Productive Questions

In contrast, productive questions do not presume a single, correct answer but, rather, offer more open-ended opportunities that lead to conjecture, dialogue, argument, and other types of science-based discussion. The focus of productive questions is clearly important for all involved, not just for the teacher. Productive questions open up student thinking rather than test student knowledge. Productive questions or prompts include language such as

- What do you notice…?
- What do you think will happen if…?
- What do you think we'll observe when…?
- How might you explain…?
- What connections can you make…?

Productive questions serve specific purposes during the course of a science experience or unit. For example, *prior knowledge questions* can be useful when probing students for what they already know about a topic. *Action questions* and *problem-posing questions* can be particularly useful during the investigation itself. *Reasoning questions* can be posed to begin group discussions when it is appropriate to process for some understanding of the implications of the investigation. The third column of Figure 1 provides examples of questions for different kinds of discussions and different stages of each.

In addition to focusing on the nature and specific substance of the question, teachers also consider how questions reflect what students know and what interests them. Eliciting student questions and selecting from them is one way to share the ownership of a discussion. A good discussion is often guided by a mix of questions, some that are teacher driven and, thus, very centered on the topic, and others that are offered by students, which can maintain a high level of student interest while not losing focus on important concepts and skills. As the teacher gains skill in posing and soliciting questions, he or she models important components of the inquiry process for the students.

Recording Ideas and Information
What happens to a discussion? How are interesting ideas preserved for future use? What record is there of the thinking of the group? It is common elementary teaching practice to record elements of classroom discussions—a brainstorm of ideas, vocabulary lists, descriptive phrases, class conclusions—on chart paper or on the board. These charts can play an important role in student learning, but it is vital to ask what purpose the recording

serves and what recording strategy might be most effective for this purpose. Some important purposes for recording include

- to display data from the whole group for group analysis. The data may be entered at the time of the discussion—if the focus is on the nature of the data gathering itself—or before.
- to record key ideas that emerge from an analytic/synthesizing discussion—a chart of progress.
- to summarize conclusions/essential ideas temporarily as the discussion proceeds—an anchor chart.
- to model what a notebook page, a set of notes, or any other kind of recording strategy can look like and sound like.

If the recording is done as the discussion proceeds for all to see, then the recording should not interrupt, slow, or distract attention from the discussion. The charts should remain visible to the class only as long as they play a role in the ongoing learning—as progress reports, as data collections, and as data for which there is likely to be some future need. They are useful if they are needed as learning tools, but not so if they are used as "displays."

As important as these charts can be in recording the development of ideas, they are not always recommended. Teachers may instead choose to take notes that are later turned into a sheet to be passed out to students or turned into a class chart. The teacher may use them to support summaries of what has been done or said, to refer students to what others have said, and/or to identify discourse patterns for discussion.

Rather than a class recording, in some cases students may record in their notebooks during or after a discussion. Again, this depends on the ultimate goal of the discussion. Taking time to record in notebooks can sometimes interfere with the discussion, so it is up to the teacher to decide if the recording will push the students' thinking as much as will participating in the discussion.

And finally, there are times when there is no need to record. There is nothing to be gained by recording everything for no apparent purpose. Even worse, excessive recording can actually interfere with student learning or, at least, send an inappropriate message about why this information is being recorded.

Conclusion

Talking is both an important component of the learning process and central to the culture of science. Discussions among students in classrooms and among colleagues in the science community serve to push thinking forward as well as to share experiences and ideas. Yet, classroom science discussions in which students are held to certain norms and are challenged to think deeply occur infrequently. There are a number of possible reasons for this. Time may be one, but if by neglecting these discussions students, in fact, learn less, then the time for discussion must be taken from some of the time set aside for the experience itself. A lack of understanding of the importance of discussion to inquiry-based science is certainly another reason for the infrequency of discussions. In this chapter we argue that carefully designed discussions are a critical part of science instruction, complementing, not replacing, the necessary direct investigation of phenomena, and providing the opportunities for students to come to a deeper understanding of science and a better understanding of the role of communication in science practice.

References

Almasi, J. F. 2002. Research-based comprehension practices that create higher level discussions. In *Improving comprehension instruction: Rethinking research, theory and classroom practice*, eds. C. C. Block, L. B. Gambrell, and M. Pressley. San Francisco: Jossey-Bass.

Barnes, D. 1993. *From communication to curriculum*. 2nd ed. Portsmouth, NH: Boynton/ Cook Heinemann.

Calkins, L. M. 2000. *The art of teaching reading*. Boston: Allyn and Bacon.

Cazden, C. B. 2001. *Classroom discourse: The language of teaching and learning*. 2nd ed. Portsmouth, NH: Heinemann.

Harlen, W. 2001. *Primary science: Taking the plunge*. 2nd ed. Portsmouth, NH: Heinemann.

Kilpatrick, J., W. G. Martin, and D. Schifter, eds. 2003. *A research companion to principles and standards for school mathematics*. Reston, VA: National Council of Teachers of Mathematics.

Resnick, L. 1999. Making America smarter. [Electronic Version] *Education Week Century Series* 18 (40): 38–40. Retrieved March 28, 2005, from *www.edweek.org/ew/articles/ 1999/06/16/40resnick.h18.html?querystring=L.%20Resnick%20Making%20America%2 0Smarter*.

Vygotsky, L. V. 1934. *Thought and language*. Moscow-Leningrad: Sokegiz.

Vygotsky, L. V. 1978. *Mind in society: The development of higher psychological processes*. Cambridge, MA: Harvard University Press.

Science and Writing

One Teacher's Rocky Road to Writing in Science

Katie Felix is in her second year of teaching fourth grade at Brichta Elementary School in the Tucson Unified School District (TUSD), Tucson, Arizona. The student population at Brichta is 66% Hispanic, 21% Caucasian, 6% African American, 5% Native American, and 2% Asian. Katie is a second-career teacher.

Katie is speaking:

It's 8:43 p.m. on a chilly Sunday night in January and I'm still working. In the next room I hear my nine-year-old son reading sweetly to my five-year-old daughter from a book I should be reading to them instead. My house is a mess. Wrinkled laundry lies untouched in the dryer, and the bills are piling up on the counter. I am grateful my husband likes to cook or we'd all be starving, too. Is it too early in the new semester to count the days until summer?

Think, Katie. Stop daydreaming. I need to complete these lessons. Anxiety fills my heart at the thought of my unfinished weekly parent newsletter.

Concentrate! I need to integrate expository writing with the scratch test in Investigation #2 of the unit on Earth materials, but how? Toni and Laura have given me some really good ideas, but what were they? Think like Laura…she showed you a graphic organizer. Was it a way to organize data about the scratch test? Maybe so. Four flaps, each one a different mineral, results on the inside. Would that be interesting to fourth graders?

My district standards say, "Expository writing includes nonfiction writing that describes, explains, informs, or summarizes ideas and content. The writing supports a thesis based on research, observation, and/or experience" (Tucson Unified School District Writing Standards, Fourth Grade).

I read through the student investigation booklet in the kit and learn that the scratch test is one technique geologists use to identify minerals. Hardness is a property they use to describe minerals but not rocks. I didn't know that. The big idea for this unit is for students to understand that hardness in minerals is relative. Do I give them this goal rather than let them discover it on their own? The booklet says, "It is important that students be given the chance to state, support, and argue their conclusions with data they have gathered." This is good; students can state the results of the scratch test as a thesis statement, and *thesis* is a good word to use as my language objective for my English language learners (ELLs).

A good student thesis statement would be the following:

During science, I conducted a scratch test on four different minerals in order to determine their hardness. My data show that mineral 2 can be scratched with my fingernail, minerals 3 and 1 with a penny, and mineral 4 only with the paperclip. Based on my results, I conclude that mineral 2 is the softest, minerals 3 and 1 are next, and mineral 4 is the hardest. The evidence I have to support my conclusion is....

This reads like the kind of report that comes back from labs that analyze water, soil, or homes. Great, I am starting to see a real-world connection. And the words *evidence* and *conclusion*—more language objectives! Yay! Using this thesis statement, I can make a nice graphic organizer (see Figure 1).

I switched to a teaching career last year, beginning with fourth grade, where I remain. I recently started connecting science and writing as a result of the phenomenal success other schools in our district have had. Not all teachers in my school are implementing this process, but several classes do integrate journals and science. My challenges are, first, to understand the writing process well enough to teach it effectively and, second, to calm the panicky feeling I get when trying to schedule all that is required.

OK, Katie, back to the objectives for tomorrow's lesson on the scratch test: "Students should understand that hardness is a property geologists use to identify minerals and should learn how to organize an expository paper that has three components: a thesis statement, research/data, and a conclusion." Armed with that graphic organizer I feel ready.

─────────

So, I teach the scratch test lesson. As usual, I end up making what could be an easy lesson so complicated. All the curriculum developer wanted the teacher to do is a simple scratch test. But that isn't good enough for me.

FIGURE 1 Graphic Organizer for Thesis Statement

Thesis statement: During science class, I conducted a scratch test experiment on four different minerals in order to determine their hardness. My data show that mineral 2 can be scratched with my fingernail, minerals 3 and 1 with a penny, and mineral 4 only with the paperclip. Based on my results, I conclude that mineral 2 is the softest, minerals 3 and 1 are next, and mineral 4 is the hardest.

Kinds of tests	Data gathered
Conclusions about data	Summarizing statement

Seizing the moment, I decide there is great value in pulling in a real-world situation. So I tie the scratch test to the mudslide in La Conchita, California. Here is how I begin:

> Today you are geologists who have to predict if the mountain in La Conchita is stable. There are four mineral samples pulled out of the mountain and you need to determine their relative hardness in order to predict the level of percolation possible if rain continues. The most abundant sample is #4, fluorite. Your team has been hired by the mayor of La Conchita and the governor of California.
>
> Your job is to conduct experiments on the mineral samples, gather data, formulate a conclusion from the data, and then write a thesis statement that summarizes your prediction about whether or not you think the mountain will slide again.

The students respond:

"Mrs. Felix, what does *abundant* mean?"
"Mrs. Felix, what do you mean 'formulate an opinion from data'?"
"Mrs. Felix, what the heck is a thesis statement?"

The ever-increasing weight of the mud that begins caking around my trembling ankles sucks my enthusiasm dry. The demons of my first year of teaching rise up to taunt me—*You should have quit these science kits last year! Go on; send 'em out for P.E. You know you want to.*

Rather than succumb completely, I let them begin to conduct the scratch test. Of course, I've forgotten to model the scratching technique or how to fill out the scratch test chart. So, I decide to model the process separately to six different teams.

My class is now happily working on their science investigations. Once the class determines the hardness, they take notes in their journals in the form of complete sentences to use in their report to the mayor and governor.

My naive plan is to model writing the thesis statement and then have my class write one. Nowhere in the district writing standards does it say, "And by the way, good luck trying to get your students to understand what a thesis statement is."

I write the lesson's objective on the overhead: "Today I will write a thesis statement." I have the students state the objective and write it on their paper. Then, I lead them through the scenario again.

We are a company of geologists who have been hired to determine if La Conchita will have another mudslide. We have studied samples of minerals and determined....

The students eagerly recount how they used various tools to scratch mineral samples to test them for their relative hardness. Most concur that fluorite is the hardest mineral and gypsum is the softest. A few have different results, and I reassure them that discrepancies happen in science, which is why a thesis statement is an educated opinion with observational facts thrown in. They stare at me blankly. However, the intensity of the overhead projector light has all but blinded me, and I miss their obvious plea for help. I then ask, "How does this connect to the La Conchita mudslide?" One student says, "If it rains too much, the ground gets saturated." An ELL student adds, "And you have to have percolation." When probed to explain, he adds, "It makes underground rivers."

I'm thrilled to see that they are using the vocabulary necessary to describe an important process that created the conditions that led to the mudslides. I lead them to the next step: "Based on what we have learned, what kinds of conclusions can we make about the mudslides in La Conchita?"

As the seconds tick by and not a hand goes up, my smile slowly melts into confusion, then panic. I try again. "You determined that fluorite was the hardest mineral from the samples studied. What does that tell you about the mudslides?" Nervously, they all look away, anywhere to avoid eye contact with me.

I move on. I tell them that in any piece of writing, we need to make sure the reader understands who, what, when, and where from the very start. I use the graphic organizer (see Figure 1) to help them organize their writing, but the writing does not come very easily. It takes us a few more class sessions to get some ideas written about the kinds of tests we performed and the results of our data, but neither the students nor I really understood how the hardness of minerals was connected to the mudslide in La Conchita. So, I called in Toni, our curriculum specialist, to help me figure out where we were and what I needed to do to complete the writing.

Trying to Dig Myself Out

Toni spent three planning sessions helping me understand the different modes of writing—procedural, persuasive, and recount—and the connection between evidence and inference. Evidence is what one observes and becomes one's fact. Inference is what one hypothesizes based on the evidence. Essentially, our thesis was that La Conchita would likely have another mudslide, but our evidence was theoretical based on my reading of news reports, not on direct scientific evidence. Toni suggested I call a professional geologist and ask what really happened, relay the conversation to the students, then use this as professional testimony from which we can make inferences.

The geologist I called told me the saturation/percolation theory was correct, although hardness of minerals is not what made the mudslide happen. The mountain was steep and the bedrock was actually a sedimentary rock that, when saturated, became extremely heavy and could not hold up its own weight. So gravity took over.

Toni offered to come teach evidence and inference, and facilitate an erosion experiment from the landforms kit to illustrate what the geologist meant.

By Toni teaching the erosion lesson, the students gained the missing link between our classroom experiments and understanding the situation at La Conchita. One boy said, "As the sand…uhm, you know…drank up all the water and it got…full and it couldn't take no more. And it fell apart." Though this student searched but could not find the words *percolation* and *saturation*, he improvised well enough to demonstrate that he understood the idea.

At this point I began to reflect on last year again, my first year of teaching. My first science unit was the very same kit on Earth materials I am using now. Last year, I looked at the manual and had no clue where to begin since I had not received training in it. I finally discovered that the investigations section told me what to do. I managed to figure out the part about copying the pages for student journals, though I struggled with the time and effort it took to put them together. That, combined with my general lack of knowledge about rocks, made the task seem overwhelming.

Challenges With Making Connections

In reflection, I think I know what makes teaching some of the science kits so difficult. For students to fully understand what they are learning, the teacher needs to be skilled at helping them construct their knowledge. Being handicapped by my inexperience and not innately prone to knowing how to construct knowledge, I rely on my scientific knowledge to get me through. However, my knowledge lies more in the life sciences than the Earth sciences. Without the tremendous support from the district science department, I would never have the strength to put student learning above my personal struggle to learn to teach.

This year I am adding the challenge of connecting science and literacy. Every quarter, we have a districtwide writing prompt focusing on a specific mode of writing. The point of the February prompt was to introduce students to persuasive writing, so I started to teach them how to write persuasively by connecting literacy to science. I started with the La Conchita mudslide paper, which was the thesis statement as well. However, trying to connect Earth materials to a persuasive writing sample was challenging.

Based on the student reactions, I think they were unable to distance themselves from feeling emotionally responsible for the lives of the people if they wrongly advised them. I did not expect this reaction from them. I thought they could differentiate between a made-up assignment that reflected a real situation and reality itself. I think I was wrong. So, I felt my class needed additional support in the science writing I was asking them to do. Modeling the thesis paper writing process with the whole group was the right way to go (see Figure 2).

I struggled to integrate writing into this unit. I tried to make sure the class understood the concepts, vocabulary, and technical aspects of the writing, including purpose, mode, and the six traits of writing I learned from Toni. Integrating takes a fair amount of time. Even though we had been through the persuasive process with the La Conchita paper, they still needed considerable teaching to understand how to structure a persuasive paper. To teach the concept of a persuasive piece, I gave them a scenario:

FIGURE 2 Two Student Thesis Papers

Mud Slide in La Conchita California.
2/16/05

By ▇▇▇▇▇▇▇
Our team of geologists, ▇▇▇▇▇▇▇, ▇▇▇▇▇,
▇▇▇▇▇ and I, studied the mudslide in La Conchita,
California in January of 2005 to determine if a
mudslide will happen again.

We got some evidents from four different minerals and
did scratch test to see which was the hardest. We used
a penny, tile, paperclip & fingernail to determine the
relative hardness of the minerals.

We found out that sample four, fluorite was the
hardest. Sample two, quartz was the softest.

We estimate, based on the number of samples pulled
out of the mountain, that florite was the most
abundant minerals.

We gathered evidence from two sources: a professional
geologist and our own experiments. The geologist told us
that gypsum was found in the soil. He also told us that
the soil was mainly clay, another fact he told us was
rain weighed down the clay until it was so heavy that
it got saturated, then gravity cleaved a chunk of the
mountain off.

Based on the experiments we did, we predict there
could be another mudslide in the future.

If rainfall is equal to percolation there should not be a
mudslide. How ever if rainfall is not equal to
percolation there could be another mudslide.

(continued)

FIGURE 2 (*continued*)

The California Mudslide

Our team of geologists studied the mudslide in La Conchita, California on January of 2005, to determine if a mudslide will happen again. Based on the experiments we did, we predict there could be a mudslide in the future.

We gathered evidence from two sources: a professional geologist and our own experiments. The geologist told us that gypsum was found in the soil. He also told us that the soil was mainly clay. Another factor he told us was, rain weighed down the clay until it was so heavy that it got saturated. Then gravity cleaved a chunk of the mountain off.

Our team then constructed our own experiment. First, we built a plateau in a sand tray. Next, we dripped water on the plateau simulating rain. Then, we observed the effect of water on the plateau, it caused the plateau to fall apart. Finally we think saturation of the soil combined with gravity caused the plateau to fall apart.

In conclusion, we think that if abnormal rainfall occurs in La Conchita again, there could be another mudslide.

You and your partner found a large sum of money. One of you is in favor of keeping the money and one wants to turn it in. The students then wrote a letter to their partners persuading them of their point of view (see Figure 3).

Last week the class had to respond to the district quarterly writing prompt. The prompt was to write a persuasive letter to the student body convincing them either to hire a restaurant to make our school food or to keep the cafeteria staff as is. I am eager to see if their understanding of persuasive writing transferred from the La Conchita assignment to a prompt they had to respond to completely unaided. The papers I looked at quickly were showing some tremendous growth in many of the students (see Figure 4).

Our district's next writing prompt introduces procedural writing, and I think this will be a concept my students will completely understand. Procedural writing is very easy to teach through science since the step-by-step process is an inherent part of science investigations. I am realizing that some modes of writing lend themselves to science better than others.

FIGURE 3 Persuasive Writing Sample

Febuary 22,20

Dear _____,

Remmember that day when we were walking from Walgreens and found the money? Well, I think you and I should keep it. And here are three reason why.

You and I could buy a lot of stuff like cars, houses, stores, mall, animals and candy. Or we could build houses and stores so we could get more money!

If we keep the money I could pay a professional basketball coach so I could become a great basketball

(continued)

FIGURE 3 (*continued*)

player, Because basketball
is my dream. I've been
playing for a long time and
I'd really like to go pro.

But if you want to
we could split the
money. And we could even
donate some money like
to the poor people, animals
or the tsunami people.

Actually I don't really
feel good about this so
I'm on your side. Let's
turn in the money.

Sincerely,
Your friend

FIGURE 4 District Writing Prompt Student Sample

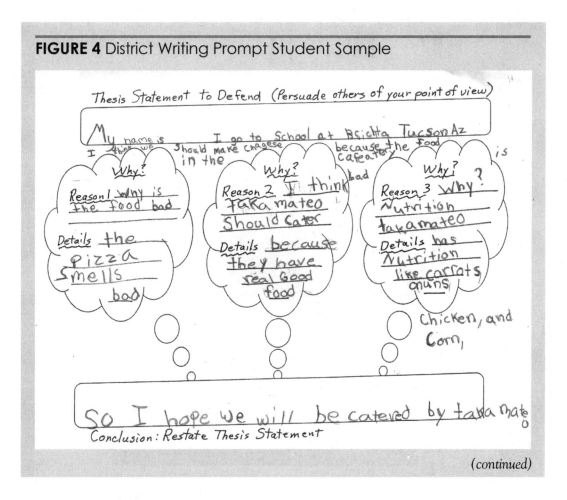

(continued)

Professional Development

What surprised me when I became a teacher was that 95% of most professional development I have been to is cheerleading. Presenters give data, facts, and evidence showing what we should be doing in the classroom without concrete strategies on how to accomplish the goal. I need concrete strategies to take back to the classroom. Novice teachers like myself are overwhelmed by the whole process and do not have time to really think about what works for them or how to make it work.

———

Well, it's another chilly Sunday night except it's March now. I haven't moved from my chair all day except to feed my starving children. I'm still in my pajamas and I still have to go to the market and take the videos back. Dinner will be late, the laundry isn't done, and neither are my lesson plans or my parent newsletter.

FIGURE 4 (*continued*)

February 23, 2005

I	O	V	WC	SF	C
4	4	3	3	3	4

Dear Student Body,

I am _____ a student at Brichita elementery in Tucson, Az. The food in the cafeteria is horrible!

Here are some resons why The pizza smells bad. The chicken is way to fatning, The chese chip are really burnt some times. Pizza has hair in it and pasta is Dryer then a desert.

I think Taxamateo Should Cater because they have awsome food like meat, vaggs, Seafood, and more. So I hope that this will convince you to be catered by Takamateo.

Sincerly

I'm reading the teacher's guide for the life science unit, wondering how I'm going to have the time to focus on this when the pressure of testing is mounting. Then, I come across something unexpected in the guide: four pages of writing connections, complete with performance objectives pulled straight out of the National Science Education Standards. Wow! Somebody's been working overtime. There are writing connections for every investigation.

Armed with these connections, I am determined to organize myself and my students this time to keep my sanity—and my students' sanity too!

Resources

Buss, K., and L. Karnowski. 2003. *Reading and writing nonfiction genres*. Newark, DE: International Reading Association.

Campbell, B., and L. Fulton. 2003. *Science notebooks: Writing about inquiry*. Portsmouth, NH: Heinemann.

Derewianka, B. 1999. *Exploring how texts work*. Sydney, Australia: Primary English Teaching Association.

Stead, T. 2002. *Is that a fact?* Portland, ME: Stenhouse.

Questions for Discussion

1. Think about the scaffolding process Mrs. Felix was using to help her students with writing thesis statements on the La Conchita mudslide. What are some strategies that might strengthen this process? How might you adapt the Science Writing Heuristic (SWH) (see Chapter 4) for this age level?

2. Mrs. Felix is in her second year of teaching inquiry science and is attempting to connect writing with science instruction. Based on the challenges she has articulated, what are some logical next steps in her professional development?

Writing and Science: The Perfect Chemistry

Jeannie Revello is in her fourth year of teaching for Seattle Public Schools in Seattle, Washington. This is her second year teaching fourth grade at Kimball Elementary School (K–5). This urban student population is 21% Caucasian, 13% African American, 59% Asian, 7% Hispanic, and 1% American Indian.

Jeannie is on her way to the district Lead Science Writing Teachers (LSWT) study group meeting. Jeannie and four other teachers will be planning instruction for integrating writing with a unit on food chemistry. This is her first year with the study group, but her third year integrating expository writing with science notebooks. Jeannie anticipates her time at the meeting:

> *I hope there is time to discuss ways to integrate literature resources with the inquiry-based science. But I am wondering how the other teachers did this. When and how do you introduce the readings and prevent students from "finding out" about the nutrients in foods? This knowledge somehow would invalidate their tests (or their sense of purpose or their "rigging" of the tests to get the results they think they already know). I don't think the other teachers have used the new food chemistry student book. If there is time today, I want to show the student book to them, and maybe together we could brainstorm ideas of how to integrate this.*

Jeannie is not sure what her role and responsibilities will be in the future, but she envisions becoming a facilitator for peer groups such as the LSWT meeting. This group is part of the district's peer process for analyzing student writing. Through the discussion of students' strengths and weaknesses in conceptual understanding, science skills, and expository writing, the teachers work together to develop strategies for improving science and writing instruction and providing constructive feedback to students.

Using the Protocol for Instructional Planning Meetings (Figure 1), Marcie, today's team facilitator, begins the discussion:

FIGURE 1 Protocol for Instructional Planning Meetings

Lead Science Writing Teachers
Protocol for Instructional Planning Meetings

The facilitator's role is to ensure that the protocol is followed.

For each lesson you are planning:
1. Reflect about the **"big idea(s)"** of the lesson and how it (they) relate to the conceptual story of the whole unit.
2. Think about **what we expect the students to know and be able to do** at the end of the investigation and reflection.
3. Consider the lesson's **focus question(s) and/or the reflective question(s)** to which the students may be responding in the entry.
4. Consider the **scientific skills and thinking** that may be involved in the investigation.
5. Discuss the **challenges** students could face in terms of the content.
6. Determine **what the teacher will need to model** before the lesson and/or the writing.

Agree what student work each member of the group will bring to the next meeting (e.g., samples from only one lesson? Multiple lessons? Each teacher's choice? How many samples from each teacher?).

Unit Title _____   Date _____

Lesson	Notes

Source: Copyright © 2003 Expository Writing and Science Notebooks Program. Seattle's K–5 Inquiry-Based Science Program. Reprinted with permission.

So what are the "big ideas" of the unit?

Well, says Natalie, *I think the big understandings are, one, the body is a system made of parts; two, foods are made up of multiple nutrients that support those parts of our body system; three, we are testing foods to determine their nutrients and if they are healthy or not healthy so we can make good informed choices about what we eat; and, four, the importance of recording data in a science notebook throughout an investigation.*

What skills will students be using? asks Marcie.

Natalie jumps in again:

Conducting tests, focusing on fair tests. There is also a lot of table design in this. We want students to understand that retesting is an option; they must recognize that there are variables and what to do about them.

Marcie summarizes:

OK, so creating tables; recording observations; drawing conclusions; obtaining varied results that can lead to conclusive and inconclusive tests; and developing the ability to make better decisions about food.

This unit gives students a lot of opportunity to improve their writing because many notebook entries are similar. By giving feedback in their notebooks early, we'll help students to know how they can improve their writing. We have the opportunity to develop their writing because they do not write one time; they write about a positive test many times.

Jeannie thinks to herself, *It's helpful to discuss the methodology, sequence, and purpose of the unit. I haven't taught the food chemistry unit yet, so I'm taking good notes on the other teachers' experiences with the unit.*

Natalie adds:

You need to give comments to strengthen their writing immediately. Any kid in class can improve that type of entry because they get to do the same thing again. They can increase detail in their observations and do a better job. They can write solid sentences and feel more confident in their writing, too. Having the templates makes a big difference. When students want to break from those writing frames they can. Some students will have to be weaned off of the frames.

Jeannie writes a note to herself to give feedback on sticky notes to each student after completing the first test. She is not clear, however, on when to read student notebooks and to give written feedback, other than through classroom-based assessments. She asks:

OK, but I am wondering what would be best modeled for students? What should students be able to develop on their own with some inquiry-based discussion?

Don't worry, says Marcie, showing them the writing frame (Figure 2) on the overhead, minus the example of a table, noting that the frame was all they needed to be successful with setting up their data-recording pages.

FIGURE 2 Writing Frame

Today we are testing for _____ . *We are using* _____ ,

which will _____ *if the nutrient is present.*

Then: In testing for _____ , *our results show conclusively that* _____

_____ .

However, some of our results are inconclusive because _____ . *I think these*

inconclusive results could have been caused by _____ .

Source: Copyright © 2003 Expository Writing and Science Notebooks Program. Seattle's K–5 Inquiry-Based Science Program. Reprinted with permission.

Natalie adds:

I have them create the table and I work them through it, asking things like, "If we are going to test this food what do we need to put in the table?" I basically facilitate the table making.

Jeannie makes another note to create a poster of a table for class data, but not to show it to students until after they have set up their own.

Let's think differently about our next session, which focuses on student work, says Marcie. I want to avoid the pitfall of having too much work to look at and end up feeling like we didn't get to everyone's concerns.

So, let's focus on the starch, fat, and protein tests. Bring student samples of data tables and comparison writing from one of those tests next time. Natalie, you bring a low ELL student's work. Jeannie, you bring a sample from a medium ELL student, and I will bring one from a high ELL student.

After the meeting Jeannie reflects on the discussion:

I left the session feeling confident to begin teaching food chemistry in a few days. I had a clear plan of what I wanted to prepare, with the intention of reviewing my meeting notes on the big ideas and skills we want students to gain from this unit.

I realize we spent almost the whole meeting discussing the writing protocol, which was entirely valuable, but I do feel like I'm on my own now to figure the other things out, as I am the only teacher at my school who is teaching food chemistry, and I won't meet with the group until we are nearly done with the unit. I do appreciate the focused writing protocol.

Across the district, 60 grade-level LSWTs meet monthly to focus on their current science unit. The first meeting in the rotation (fall, spring, or summer) is a planning meeting, which follows the protocol shown in Figure 1. During the second meeting, groups look at student work from one lesson that they chose during the planning session. (Jeannie's group chose to bring samples of tables and write-ups from the protein, starch, and fat tests to their second meeting.) In the final meeting of the rotation, the groups will look at evaluating entire student notebooks. These second and third meetings also have a specialized protocol to follow.

Inside Jeannie's Classroom

Since the first LSWT meeting, Jeannie has been teaching the food chemistry unit using the strategies for developing proficiency in expository writing from the Expository Writing and Science Notebooks curriculum provided by Seattle's K–5 Inquiry-Based Science Program (see Figure 3). Jeannie also is applying ideas that were shared and developed in the LSWT writing group as well as those learned from a grade-level writing class.

Jeannie began the food testing phase of the unit by facilitating a discussion with her class on how best to represent data from investigations and then she focused on test results:

My class came up with the idea of a table, and agreed on its important elements (easy-to-find information, title, labels for each column and row, and date). I then

FIGURE 3 Essential Components of Proficient Expository Writing (Expository Writing and Science Notebooks Program, Seattle's K–5 Inquiry-Based Science Program, 2002)

ESSENTIAL COMPONENTS OF PROFICIENT EXPOSITORY WRITING

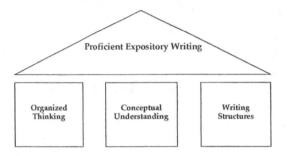

First, students need to begin to understand the <u>concepts</u> through inquiry.

As they are developing their conceptual understanding, they need <u>graphic organizers</u>, including <u>word banks</u>, to:

- Organize their thinking,
- Help them remember what they are learning, and
- Lead them to deeper levels of understanding as they construct and explain their own organizers (e.g., drawings, diagrams, tables, graphs, and models).

Finally, as they begin to write about their developing understanding, they need <u>writing structures</u> to:

- Help them remember what they need to describe and explain, and
- Help them communicate clearly, accurately, and in an organized way.

In addition to this support, they must have **ongoing** <u>modeling</u>, <u>practice</u>, and <u>constructive feedback</u>.

To help ensure the <u>quality of thinking</u> that should go into writing about scientific inquiry, teachers must ask themselves this critical question before students write an entry: *How will writing this notebook entry help develop the students' conceptual understanding and/or scientific skills and thinking?* This will focus their students' energy on creating meaningful writing.

modeled how to create the Table for Testing Liquids for Starch on the overhead. Students created their own, using the model as a guide. I showed them how to fold their notebook pages to make the table making efficient, and modeled how to leave the opposite page available for writing about their test results.

After the first investigations, I led a discussion about test results. I introduced the terms conclusive and inconclusive and had students interpret data verbally, using the vocabulary. After discussion and oral practice, I posted a writing frame (see Figure 2) from the Expository Writing and Science Notebooks curriculum to guide student writing. I talked them through how to use this frame to write about their investigations. Figure 4 shows an example of how one student used the frame.

FIGURE 4 Student Work Sample Using the Writing Frame

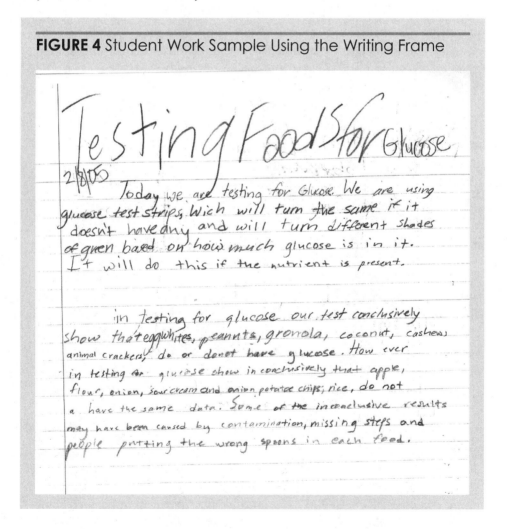

As a class we discussed how we knew the results were inconclusive (the class table showed disagreement), and we reread the test directions, looking for possible ways the results could have turned out differently.

Over time, Jeannie's students began creating tables during class writing time for the other food chemistry tests to allow for more time during science. The writing frames that had been posted were slowly taken down, and, with feedback from Jeannie, students began to write about their test results on their own.

I realized that the writing frame, as it existed, limited some students in their writing. They did not write about which results were positive or negative, or conclusive or inconclusive. The frame gave no structure for writing about how likely it is for a nutrient to be present. I want to discuss this at our second LSWT meeting when we analyze student work and plan for future instruction.

My discussion with the other LSWTs helped me decide when and how to use the suggested classroom-based assessment (CBA). I gave the first one—in which students are asked to compare and contrast fat and protein—with more structure than I did later, using the box and T-chart and associated writing frame. For the next CBA, in which they are asked to compare proteins and fats, I did not provide the instructions to use the box, T-chart, and writing frame (though they remain on the wall). I could assess their incorporation of the graphic organizer as a thinking map and how easily they use the frame as a language structure (see Figure 5).

One more thing I have been using, related to the writing curriculum, which was taken from the National Urban Alliance, is the Defining Format for taking notes on nonfiction reading (see Resources—Rothstein and Lauber 2000). This hasn't been discussed much in our LSWT group, as we haven't chosen student writing yet that reflects its use. I will probably suggest looking at some of these pieces at our next meeting. I have found that the Defining Format provides students with a structure to be successful in taking notes. Students are then able to write about what they have learned in complete, complex sentences. The Defining Format for describing nutrients consists of a double-page spread, with the name of the nutrient in column 1, categories of the nutrient in column 2, and characteristics in column 3, with seven guiding questions at the bottom (1. What does this nutrient do for the body? 2. When might you especially need it? 3. Does it come from plants or animals or both? 4. What foods contain it? 5. What other information is interesting about it?

FIGURE 5 Sample Student Box, T-Chart Notes, and Final Essay

3-9-05

they
Both

- Nutrients (Macro) ✓
- inside the body
- Get it from meat
- Dairy products
- from plants and animals ✓
- Give energy ✓
- peanuts contain both nutrients ✓
- Milk has both ✓

Fat	Protein
• Potects the bones and ✓ cushens the organs	• Repairs the body ✓
• You need it in a cold climate ✓ (mountains)	• Pregnate women and children need protein from babies to teenagers ✓ when growing
• Stain a paper bag that will be translucent when the nutrient is present.	• You test it with protein test strips called (compose blue paper
• corn oil contains fat	• egg white contains protein
• To much is dangerous	

(continued)

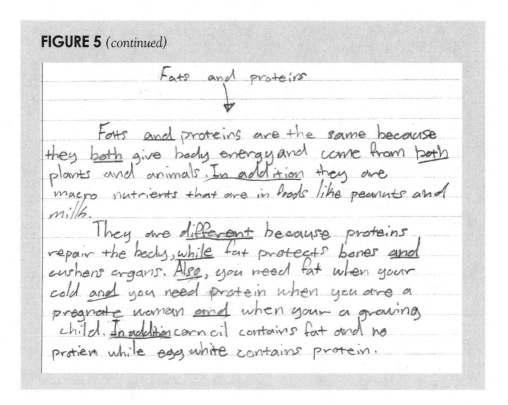

FIGURE 5 (*continued*)

Fats and proteins

Fats and proteins are the same because they both give body energy and come from both plants and animals. In addition they are macro nutrients that are in foods like peanuts and milk.

They are different because proteins repair the body, while fat protects bones and cushions organs. Also, you need fat when your cold and you need protein when you are a pregnate woman and when your a growing child. In addition corn oil contains fat and no protien while egg white contains protein.

6. How do you test for the nutrient? 7. What foods that you tested contain it?). I had students glue a model of this frame in their notebooks to refer to each time they read about a new nutrient.

After I read aloud, the students re-read independently and used the focus questions to record notes on the reading using the Defining Format. Students used these notes to write sentences (later, a paragraph) about the topic of the reading.

LSWT Meeting #2

The second LSWT meeting is focused on looking at single student notebook entries. Jeannie is bringing a sample from one of her ELL students of medium-low ability. The group will be following the protocol in Figure 6a. The protocol refers to "Criteria for Exemplary Science Notebook Entries" (Figure 6b) and the "Assessing Student Work and Planning Instruction" form (Figure 6c). Tim and Shauna, who missed the last meeting, are present at this meeting. Tim leads the group. They begin by discussing strengths of the writing sample (Figure 7).

Let's start with Jeannie's student sample.

Jeannie says:

Thinking about the student's strengths, I chose this sample because this student is obviously following what's going on. He is reporting his results and making sense of it. It's so great because he usually has low confidence in his writing. Writing frames are so useful with this type of kid. Can you imagine writing about science when it's your second language? But with recording data and using frames, students will eventually come up with it.

Tim comments:

I agree, Jeannie. The tests show conclusively that foods 4 and 5 don't have starch but one does—this kid gets it. His data table [not shown in Figure 8] is fairly well organized, and he is trying to explain inconclusive results and what a fair test is. That's a huge concept in fourth grade, in both science units. We want students to begin to think scientifically.

OK, what about the writing aspect of this sample? It is definitely organized using paragraphs and he uses the writing frame well. There are vocabulary and transitions in his writing. The content starts strong, referring to when a positive test is seen. I would say for early in this unit this is a fairly strong piece.

Moving to the next step in the protocol, Tim asks:

OK, so what are some weak areas that could benefit from improvement?

More clarity I think, says Natalie. I would ask the student to make sure he understood the reasoning for stating there are inconclusive class results. This child demonstrates that he knows that foods contain starch, which can be tested for by using iodine—he doesn't exactly explain why because it's not part of the frame.

Great! I really wanted to discuss this! says Jeannie.

Well, says Marcie, I put it in my frame. I add: "My results show conclusively that _____ because _____ and some are inconclusive because _____."
A struggle I have with the frames is that the kids stick to it even if they are

better writers. I tell my students to use the frame as a guide. Then some stick to it and some can add another sentence to it. I slowly wean them from the frames. I tell my students they can move away from using the frames when they can do as well on their own or better. For your student, Jeannie, another suggestion to give him is to also observe the control. He left out baseline data. I would like to see him mention which food had conclusive results and why.

Jeannie reflects on the study group meeting:

From the discussion of my student's work, and from hearing from teachers who have been using the frames longer, I learned that some adaptations need to be made. If emerging writers are going to use frames for the basis of their writing, the structure should not inhibit them from including more.

Back in Jeannie's Classroom

In preparation for writing comparison essays, my class brainstormed transition words (both, and, in addition, also, however, while, whereas, in conclusion, *and* another difference is…). *When the students finished the first comparison essay, I had them underline each transition word, and assign a point for each one. I challenged them to increase their "score" by revising, and including more transition words. I realized that the frames can provide essential support for some students to be successful with communicating their understandings, even in drawing and organizing their conclusions.*

Students use writing frames at different levels, from the struggling student organizing his ideas into a grammatically correct essay, to the more scientifically adept and fluent student gaining and expressing a deeper understanding of the scientific concepts and challenging him- or herself to organize the information in a clear and powerful way. Students tend to ease away from the actual wording of the frames and use them more as a guide or graphic reminder as they evolve as writers and gain confidence.

The frames also help me to assess what my students have learned. Today, as my students worked to fill in a box and T-chart (as a class) to compare fat and protein, they knew they couldn't write "gives you energy" on one side, without writing something about energy on the other side; they referred to their notes and came up with "gives you a lot of energy for a little while" and changed the first entry to "gives you energy that lasts longer." This strategy was useful when they wrote independently. (Figures 8a and 8b show comparison writing samples from an ELL student and a medium-high-level [not ELL] student.)

FIGURE 6a Protocol for Looking at Single Notebook Entries

Lead Science Writing Teachers
Study Group Protocol—Looking at Single Entries

The facilitator's role is to ensure that the protocol is followed.

1. **Briefly go over the guide,** *Criteria for Exemplary Science Notebook Entries,* which presents the standards we expect students to meet in the notebooks.

2. Silently, and fairly quickly, **read through the first sample without looking for anything in particular.**

   • The teacher who provides the sample should <u>not</u> explain anything about the student or the entry.

3. **Discuss the <u>strengths</u> of the sample** in terms of the standards (i.e., concepts; scientific skills and thinking; and three writing traits—Idea/Content, Organization, and Word Choice).

   • Do <u>not</u> mention any weaknesses or discuss any other criteria (e.g., neatness, Conventions).

   • List the strengths on the *Assessing Student Work and Planning Instruction* sheet.

4. **Discuss the <u>weaknesses</u> of the sample** in terms of the standards.

   • List weaknesses on the assessment sheet.

5. **Discuss and plan further instruction and feedback** that could build on the strengths and improve the weaknesses.

   • Make notes on the sheet regarding further instruction.

Note: If you think the Initial Use class and packet and/or the writing curriculum could be changed to better support the students in meeting the notebooks standards, please note the suggested changes on the feedback form for this session.

FIGURE 6b Criteria for Exemplary Science Notebook Entries

CRITERIA FOR EXEMPLARY SCIENCE NOTEBOOK ENTRIES

I. Conceptual Understanding	II. Scientific Thinking	III. Expository Writing
Understanding of "big ideas" of unit Demonstrates, through words and graphics, an accurate and quite full grasp of the major concepts that were introduced. *** May include one or more of the following: • Appropriate/accurate application of previous learning to new concepts and skills. • Extension of the new concept or skill to new problems or new phenomena.	Use of inquiry skills, processes Thorough and purposeful use of skills to advance learning—for example: • Makes accurate and full observations, with complete records. • Examines data and identifies results (e.g., by comparing different data points). • Asks own questions related to phenomena, evidence, problems. • Designs investigations to test questions. Use of evidence to draw inferences, support explanations Demonstrates understanding of relationship between data and inference: • Draws reasonable inferences from data. • Uses appropriate data fully to support explanations. Demonstration of discipline perspective, "habits of mind" Shows clear understanding of, for example: • Honest and accurate reporting; • Fair test; • Nature of variables, and their relationship to investigation and inference.	Idea/content (development) Has control of content: • States information or idea clearly. • Develops fully with relevant evidence, explanation, details. Organization (sequence) • Logically sequences or groups details. • Uses appropriate transition words to show logical connections. Word choice • Uses scientific vocabulary accurately. • Uses nonscientific vocabulary effectively to clarify, explain. ** These traits may be apparent: Voice (authority) • Has an engaged voice, showing confidence with scientific stance. • May include self-reflection. Sentence structure and variety Command of sentence style: • Can use multiple types of clauses and structures to clarify and develop ideas.

Source: Adaptation of work by Inverness Research Associates. July 2002. Expository Writing and Science Notebooks Program. Seattle's K–5 Inquiry-Based Science Program.

LSWT Meeting #3

The focus for the last LSWT meeting on food chemistry was on critiquing the whole science notebook. Jeannie was ill and missed this meeting. Tim and Marcie were the only two lead teachers who were able to meet. Tim took notes and shared them with Jeannie:

> We reviewed the major concepts (big ideas) of the food chemistry unit and the protocol for discussing student notebook entries [Figure 6a] that we will apply to the whole notebook.
>
> An important part of the review process is spending approximately 10 min-

---

FIGURE 6c Assessing Student Work and Planning Instruction

Assessing Student Work and Planning Instruction

1. Before assessing an entry, reflect on the:

❖ "Big idea(s)" of the lesson and how it (they) relate to the conceptual story of the whole unit;

❖ Lesson's **focus question(s) and/or the reflective question(s)** to which the student may be responding in the entry;

❖ **Scientific skills and thinking** that may be involved in the investigation.

2. Assess the entry using the attached guide for exemplary science notebook entries.

REMEMBER: Note the strengths first! Then discuss weaknesses and plan further instruction.

STRENGTHS	WEAKNESS(ES)	FURTHER INSTRUCTION

Source: Copyright © 2003 Expository Writing and Science Notebooks Program. Seattle's K–5 Inquiry-Based Science Program.

FIGURE 7 Student Sample From Jeannie's Class

1/25/05

Today we are testing starch. We are using iodine, witch will turn parple if the natrient is peresent

☒ In testing for starch our resalts show conclasically that corn oil, water, and milk don't have starc, and cornstarch does. How ever some resalts are inconclusive because there was postive notes on them, I think these incoclasice resalts could caused by people put more or less iodine in the liaidis.

utes independently reading one student's entire notebook. By doing this we are able to move into a discussion about the strengths of the notebook. What we noticed about this student's work was her knowledge of the role that test results can play in nutrient identification and the importance of supporting your results. We also identified that the student can explain her thinking, for example:

"Glucose and starch both give you energy but if you have a sport game right away you should eat something with glucose because glucose gives you energy. But if you have a game tomorrow you should eat starch because starch takes a little longer to make energy...."

Using the notebook protocol, we identified several other strengths in this student's notebook:

- Application of writing frames
- Conceptual understanding of conclusive versus inconclusive test results ("Our conclusive results also show that rice, apple, peanut, onion, coconuts test negative for protein. I know this because the test strip turned white. However, the results for flour were inconclusive. I think it's inconclusive because there is a lot of – and +.")
- Clearly recorded, accurate observations and results in student-created tables
We moved on to identifying one weak area:
- Sentence fluency hinders clarity ("The nutrient we are testing is protein. The test material we used are protein test strips. A positive is colored blue. Based on the class results, egg white has protein. I know this because the protein test strip stayed blue.")

The further instruction we agreed on that would help the student think about and improve her writing entries was to encourage rereading notebook entries to check for sentence fluency and edit to confirm and improve content. A possible activity we thought of was to have the student proofread, revise, and edit for 15–20 minutes once a week during writing time.

I hope this helps you, Jeannie, as you apply the protocol to your students' notebooks!

Jeannie later commented,

I felt so bad about missing the last meeting. It sounds like they spent most of the time looking at entire notebooks to assess overall conceptual understanding, and develop strategies for supporting student writing. I'm not sure about the idea of having students spend the time revising and editing. I've

FIGURE 8a Writing Sample (on Fat and Protein) From an ELL Student Who Has Been in the United States for Two Years

The The fat and protein are the same because they both are nutrient. In addition, they both come plant and animal.

They are difference because the fat make you fat and the protein help the baby for grown.

.Protein help you when you are pregnant, Also fat make you warm. You need protein when you are pregnant woman and you need fat when you are cold. You need to have paper bag for to test fat and you need coomessic paper for test protein.

FIGURE 8b Writing Sample (on Fat and Protein) From a Middle-High-Level (Not ELL) Student

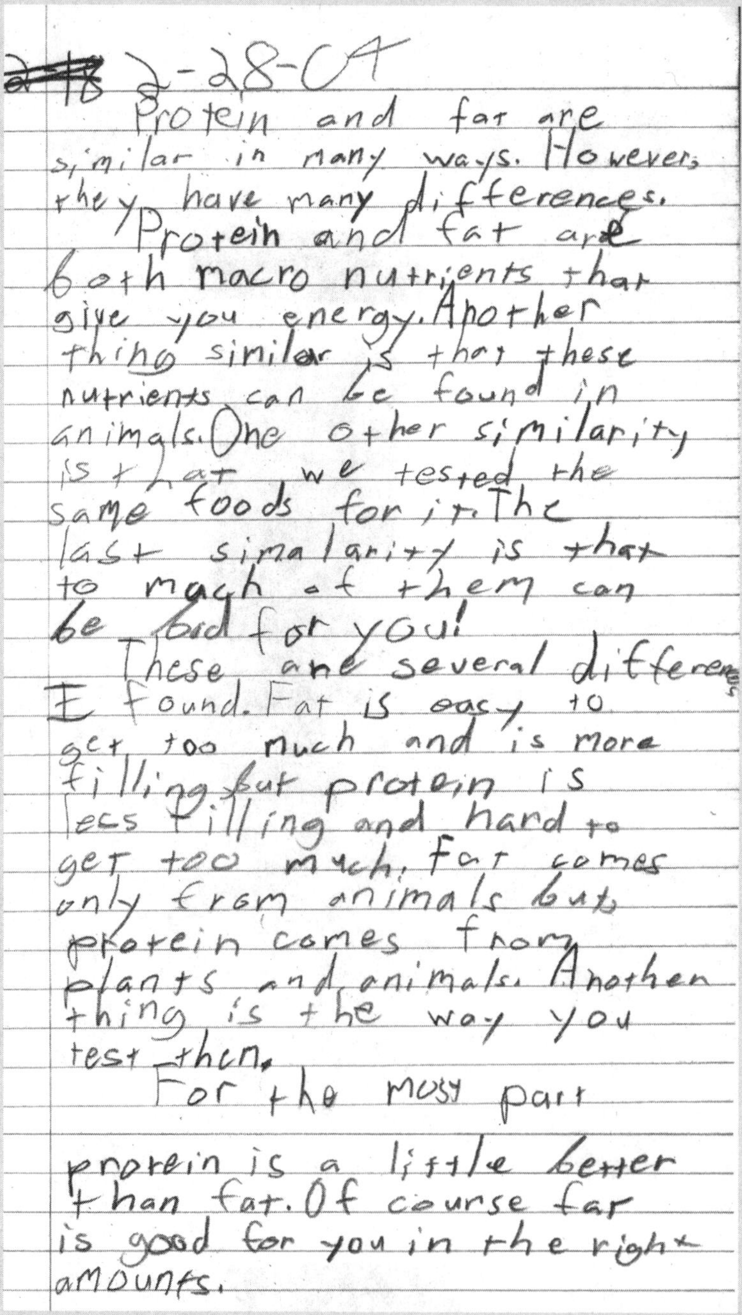

2-28-04

Protein and fat are similar in many ways. However, they have many differences. Protein and fat are both macro nutrients that give you energy. Another thing similar is that these nutrients can be found in animals. One other similarity is that we tested the same foods for it. The last simalarity is that to much of them can be bad for you!

These are several differences I found. Fat is easy to get too much and is more filling but protein is less filling and hard to get too much. Fat comes only from animals but protein comes from plants and animals. Another thing is the way you test them.

For the most part protein is a little better than fat. Of course fat is good for you in the right amounts.

always presented the science notebooks as tools they use as scientists—tools that would not be revised, edited, or published. I do emphasize that they need to write and record clearly, as they will use their notes, tables, and diagrams as data that could inform future investigations.

Jeannie's Reflections on Being a Member of the LSWT Study Group

I am really pleased with the LSWT group. Discussing student work with teachers who have more experience with the curriculum is so helpful to me. I enjoy the active involvement in a small group where I am comfortable candidly discussing my teaching and student learning. Working with my peers also builds my confidence and helps me feel that I am among a group who can and do make a difference in how students' writing and conceptual understanding in science are developing.

I in turn build my students' confidence by sharing that other teachers look at their writing to learn how to improve their teaching. Feeling important and motivated to learn is good for fourth graders and adults!

Resources

Harvey, S., and A. Goudvis. 2000. *Strategies that work: Teaching comprehension to enhance understanding.* York, ME: Stenhouse.

Nessel, D., and J. G. Baltas. 2000. *Thinking strategies for student achievement.* Arlington Heights, IL: Skylight Professional Development.

Rothstein, E., and G. Lauber. 2000. *Writing as learning: A content-based approach.* Arlington Heights, IL: Skylight Professional Development.

Questions for Discussion

1. Reflecting on your own context, how might incorporating an ongoing study group support your efforts to connect science and literacy?

2. What modes of writing, as outlined in Chapter 6, did the LSWT study group focus on, and what opportunities do you think there are to engage students in additional modes?

3. Based on the feedback strategies discussed in Chapter 5, what are some ways the LSWT group could help students do more self-assessment of their notebook entries?

Young Children's Own Illustrated Information Books:
Making Sense in Science Through Words and Pictures

Maria Varelas, Christine C. Pappas,[1]
and the ISLE[2] Team
University of Illinois at Chicago

Integrating science and literacy has been increasingly emphasized because scientists read and write as part of their scientific practices (Goldman and Bisanz 2002). They use and construct texts to inform and express the ideas that are integral to their inquiries. Young children learning science can develop these skills, too. In this chapter we focus on illustrated information books written by first, second, and third graders in urban classrooms as a culminating activity of an integrated science-literacy unit on matter. We discuss what we have learned as we explored the content and the language (of words and of pictures) of books written by young children.

---

[1]Joint first authorship of the two main authors.

[2]The ISLE (Integrated Science Literacy Enactments) Team consists of the two main authors; Chicago Public School teachers Anne Barry, Begona Cowan, Sharon Gill, Jennifer Hankes, Ibett Ortiz, Amy Rife, and Neveen Keblawe-Shamah; and, at the time the chapter was written, research assistants Eli Raymond-Tucker, Uma Iyer, and Eunah Yang.

The language of science texts is specific to science. That is, because science as a discipline represents certain ways of thinking and knowing, scientists use a certain type of discourse that linguists call scientific *registers* or genres (Gee 2004; Halliday and Martin 1993; Lemke 1990). Several distinctive linguistic features are realized in scientific writing and information books (Pappas et al. 2003). These features are understood best by contrasting them to linguistic features usually found in the storybook genre.

First, different kinds of nouns (and referent items) are used in the two genres. Typical stories use particular characters, objects, and places. Referent items (pronouns—e.g., *he, she, you, my, I, they, them, it*—and the definite article *the* plus a noun construction) refer to the particular characters, objects, and places. In typical information books, particular animals, objects, and places are not realized but instead *classes*, via *generic nouns*, are. Thus, "a squirrel" found in the beginning of an information book on squirrels is not placing a character on stage but rather is introducing the class or topic to be covered. Referent items (but not usually personal pronouns such as forms of *I, you, he, she,* and *they*) may be used. Singular forms such as "a squirrel" and subsequent singular referent items ("*the* squirrel," "he," or "it") may occur in information books, but plural forms (e.g., *squirrels, insects, tunnels, robots, zoos, planets*) as well as nouns relevant to our Matter unit (e.g., *clouds, storms, solids, liquids, gases)* are much more prevalent (including the plural pronouns that refer to them).

Another difference between storybooks and scientific information texts is verb tense. Storybooks most often use the past tense (except in quoted dialogue). Information books most often use the present tense. Other aspects of verbs also differ in the two genres. For example, mental process verbs—verbs of cognition denoting thinking, knowing, and understanding; verbs of affection denoting liking, fearing, and hating; and verbs of perception denoting seeing and hearing (Eggins 1994; Halliday 1985)—are prevalent in storybooks because they express characters' feelings, intentions, and motivations. Such verbs are rarely found in information books. Instead, there is a density of two other verb types. There are *relational verbs*, such as *is, are, has, have,* and *resembles,* that express characteristics of a class, classify members, or define parts or aspects of them, and there are *material verbs* of doing, usually the concrete actions related to the topic being addressed in an information book—the typical behaviors of animals, the processes involved in a phenomenon, and the actions that are parts of an experiment.

Finally, the vocabulary of the genres differs. Storybooks typically use the vocabulary of everyday objects or places—words that children are likely to know because of their life experiences. Information books use more technical terms. Indeed, a major function of information books is to describe and explain entities in the world and the conventional names given to their parts and processes. All the six children whose work we explore in this chapter used the typical linguistic features—the registers—of science described above.

Another feature of scientific informational texts is that they include a range of visual designs or images (Lemke 1998, 2004). When young children interact with such texts through reading and writing, they make meaning in a range of modes of communication including visual images (Kress 1997). According to Kress and van Leeuwen (1996), "children actively experiment with the representational sources of word and image, and with the ways in which they can be combined. Their drawings are not just illustrations of a verbal art, not just 'creative embellishment'; they are part of a 'multimodally' conceived text, a semiotic interplay in which each mode, the verbal and the visual, is given a defined and equal role to play" (p. 118).

When children compose pictures, they employ visual-design features to express understandings. For example, they use color, size, shape, and position of objects to express or distinguish important concepts and to depict action, perspective, and salience. As we discuss the scientific content and language of the six children's books, we will also explore how their ideas and language are related to their illustrations.

The Integrated Matter Unit

In the Matter unit, the children explore the three states of matter (solids, liquids, and gases); their characteristics; examples of everyday substances in each of the three states; changes of states, such as freezing, melting, evaporation, and condensation; and the water cycle. For grades K–3, the National Science Education Standards (NRC 1996) recommend developing young children's observational skills and abilities to notice and describe patterns in data. Theorizing, engaging with ideas, generating interpretations, and developing explanations/conceptions about how the world works is reserved mostly for older children, starting in the middle grades. Science, however, is the dance between data and ways of understanding data. And, although early-elementary-grade children may not be ready to develop sophisticated ways of thinking and talking about some science topics, we believe they must be given opportunities to engage in observing and experimenting and in developing ways to understand and explain what is going on in the world. Thus, in the Matter unit, we introduce students to the idea of matter consisting of molecules that behave differently in different states—an idea that explains the various characteristics of the different states. We also explore with students the phenomena of evaporation, boiling, and condensation that sometimes are considered sophisticated topics necessitating cognitive differentiations that primary school children may not be ready for and may not be able to construct. Our goal is not mastery of these ideas, but rather to offer the children opportunities to engage in looking at evidence and to *begin* to theorize about phenomena that they experience in their everyday lives.

Throughout the unit, children write and draw in their science journals, make predictions regarding some of their hands-on explorations, and contribute ideas to a semantic map (or concept map) that the teacher keeps on a trifold poster board. The unit consists of approximately 20 lessons that last from 45 minutes to one hour. We start by asking children to think about and write/draw in their journals about three questions:

1. Where does rain come from?
2. What are clouds made of?
3. How are clouds made?/Where does the water in the clouds come from?

Then we have two read-alouds, *What Is the Weather Today?* (Fowler 1991) and *When a Storm Comes Up* (Fowler 1995), followed by starting a weather chart the children work on for five days. Two more read-alouds follow: *What Do You See in a Cloud?* (Fowler 1996) and *It Could Still Be Water* (Fowler 1992). Then the children start their first hands-on exploration. They work in groups, fill a graduated cylinder with water, and put it at a particular location. They keep track of the water level in a data table over a period of two weeks. At the end of this time, each group makes its own graph, or the teacher makes the graphs using the children's data.

We read aloud pages 1 through 17 of *What Is the World Made Of?* (Zoehfeld 1998), which talks about states of matter, not changes of states. This is followed by the second hands-on exploration in which the children work in groups to classify objects, such as a drinking straw, a closed empty water bottle, clay, a pencil, a helium balloon, a can of soup, a bar of soap, liquid soap, an uninflated balloon, salt in a Baggie, shaving cream in a Baggie, a Baggie puffed up with air, and a sponge. We then spend a bit more time on one of the states of matter, gases, which is the most elusive for children. We read aloud *Air Is All Around You* (Branley 1986), and we stop to have the children do the hands-on exploration shown in the book—stuffing a paper towel at the bottom of a plastic cup and submerging it upside down straight into a bowl of water, and then submerging it on a tilt—and then finish the read-aloud.

The several hands-on explorations that follow give the children opportunities to explore changes of states of matter. First, children working individually try to melt an ice cube in a Baggie as fast as they can. Then we perform a class experiment—dropping one ice cube into a cup of cold water and another ice cube of the same size into a cup of hot water and recording the time it takes for the ice cube to melt in each cup. Another class experiment follows. We set three wet pieces of paper towel on a surface—one flat, one hanging down, and one crumbled up in a ball shape—and the class records the times it takes for each of the pieces to dry up. Then, in groups, children observe a frozen, sealed water bottle and explain why they see water on the outside of the bottle. Finally, we conduct a class demonstration by boiling water on a hot plate and placing a cold cookie sheet some distance from the boiling water. The children observe and discuss why water drops form on the cookie sheet. After all these hands-on explorations, we read aloud the rest of *What Is the World Made Of?*

The children then act out how molecules behave inside solids, liquids, and gases. They enact the three molecular characteristics—speed, closeness, and bonding strength—that are different among the three states. Exploring the CD-ROM *States of Matter* (New Media 1997) comes next, followed by reading aloud *Down Comes the Rain* (Branley 1983). This book goes home to the children's families, along with materials needed and a blank booklet for children to write in, for a "home project."

In the final hands-on exploration, groups of children watch a drop of food coloring diffuse in a clear plastic cup of room-temperature water, and draw what they see at 0, 30, 60, and 90 seconds. Then the teacher does a similar class demonstration, dropping a drop of food coloring in a cup of cold water and then a cup of hot water, and the children observe. As the unit is coming to an end, groups of children read a book of their own choice in literature circles and present to the rest of the class something they found interesting from their book. The literature circle book choices include *Feel the Wind* (Dorros 1989); *Snow Is Falling* (Branley 1986); *Weather Words and What They Mean* (Gibbons 1990); and *What Will the Weather Be?* (DeWitt 1991).

The unit ends with children writing their own illustrated information book on a topic of their choice that is related to the ideas discussed in the Matter unit. The directions for this activity include the following:

- Write about a part of what we have studied in the unit—something that other first graders (or second graders or third graders) who haven't studied this unit would like to read.
- Include both writing and drawing in your book. Your book should be like the books we read that have print and pictures.
- Make this book your *own* book on a topic that you are interested in, not something that you have copied from books. You can look at our semantic map, the books we read, and other things we created during the unit to get you started.
- Decide on what part of the unit to write or draw about, because you won't be able to write/draw about everything we studied.
- Decide what ideas you want to explain in writing and what ideas you want to explain in pictures.

After the children have finished their books, we have individual book conversations with them. We ask them to share their book with us, to read page by page and to explain their pictures (what the different elements are, why they decided to draw these pictures, and why they used particular sizes, colors, and shapes). These books, and the conversations about them, offer us an opportunity to explore how children think and communicate (in other words, how children "mean") in science, both in words and in pictures, because each mode affords different ways to further express and develop their ideas.

Different Ways to Express and Depict Meanings

Our analysis of the six books created by two first, two second, and two third graders (all children's names are pseudonyms) includes examples of pages of their books and excerpts of the conversations we had with these young authors/illustrators around their books. (Unfortunately, due to budget constraints, the examples of the book pages could not be printed in color. In Figures 1–6, therefore, we inserted boxes indicating the colors that the children used in their drawings.) The four first and second graders were in four different classrooms, and the two third graders were in the same classroom. Each of the five classrooms had a single grade. The books reveal a range of understandings and relationships between words and pictures. The following questions guided our analysis of, and our discussion about, the children's books:

- How do children make sense and express ideas linguistically and visually?

- How are their writing and drawing related, and how are they redundant and/or complementary?
- How do writing and drawing capture approximations in developing understandings?
- Is there a different type of precision in language than in images?
- How are the children's writing and drawing related to the linguistic and visual elements of other texts (defined broadly) available to them, such as read-aloud information books, books used in literature circles, the class semantic map, and hands-on experiences?
- In what ways does children's talk about their writing and images provide insights into their science understandings and how to express them in language and visual images?

Ernesto

First-grader Ernesto wrote a book about different types of storms and titled it *The Storms*. He had 10 pages in addition to the front and back covers. Each of the first seven pages was devoted to one particular type of storm—tornado, hurricane, thunderstorm, hailstorm, flood, snowstorm, and rainstorm. In his last three pages, Ernesto recapped in pictures the various types of storms, putting two or three storms on each page and mostly repeating the major parts of drawings he had on the previous pages. This particular illustration feature of his book—called the *recapitulation element* (Pappas, forthcoming)—is sometimes seen in informational books written by children's literature authors. For example, four of the read-aloud books in the unit were written by Fowler, who ends his books with major words from the text accompanied by small versions of the photographs that were used in the text. When asked how he got his idea for the recapitulation, Ernesto said that "some books have ... features like [his] book."

For his first three types of storms he wrote about what each type "causes." Tornadoes "cause strong wind," "hurricanes cause trouble," and "thunderstorms [with a picture depicting lightning] cause fire." For the last four types of storms, Ernesto defined each of them: "hailstorms are tiny pieces of ice falling from the sky," "floods are a bunch of water that makes floods," "snowstorms are a lot of snow," and "rainstorms are a lot of water that falls." For the first three types, he wrote about the damage these storms produce—they "destroy houses" and "take houses," he wrote, or they destroy "a farm," as he called a structure he had drawn on the tornado page. Although for thunderstorms he wrote only that they cause damage, he showed a house being hit by lightning in his picture. Similarly, on the floods page, he did not mention "house" in his text, but he depicted a house that is flooded and a boy with a "house on top of him so he can't escape." Thus, we see houses as being very salient in Ernesto's mind when it comes to damage by storms.

Focusing on the relationship between text and picture, we find that many aspects of Ernesto's pages are text-picture redundant—that is, the meanings that were expressed in his verbal text were also depicted in his pictures. For some pages, however, his talk about his pictures revealed that the pictures reflected ideas not covered in his text. The "extra" meanings centered on Ernesto's consideration of the impact of storms on people (or animals, as in the case of the cow that was included on the tornado page). This was especially clear on the flood page, where he showed a boy trapped in the water who Ernesto said "can't breathe any more" and "like he is screaming," and another boy who "is trying to save him." Similarly, on the hailstorm page, a boy and girl depicted in the pictures "are running from the hail," and on the rainstorm page, a boy is also "running," holding an umbrella for protection from the storm. And, on the snowstorm page (see Figure 1), Ernesto showed a "guy … who keeps trying to move" and the wind, shown by the spiral lines, "is pushing him back." Ernesto had drawn the person's head leaning forward to balance the wind resistance ("that is why I put his face like that"). Only the hurricane page lacks depictions of particular houses or people. Here the effect of the storm is directed to the whole state of Florida. During the conversation, however, Ernesto explained that above the Earth that he had depicted in his picture there was "like the satellite [with] like the radio signal sending into the radio station" letting people know that "there is gonna be a hurricane." Considering the words and pictures together in Ernesto's book, we realize that the major theme of his book was the damage and harm that storms may cause.

Angela

First-grader Angela called her book *States of Matter and How the Molecules Move*. The second part of her book's title specifies the content boundaries of her book. The first part of the title may imply characteristics of the three states, but Angela presented only ideas about the molecules inside the states of matter. More specifically, she wrote about how close molecules are in each of the three states, namely, that molecules are "close" in liquids, "very close" in solids, and "very far" in gases. Although the focus on the relative distance among molecules in the various states does not fit with the second part of her title, which implies a focus on how molecules move inside the three different states, she implicitly addressed movement

FIGURE 1 Ernesto's Snowstorm Page

- Brown face and hat
- Red cape and hands
- Yellow body with blue decorations
- Purple legs
- Black small lines representing snow and larger coil-shaped lines representing wind
- Black snowflake in the left margin

of molecules in her book. Angela devoted two pages to each state of matter (first liquid, then solid, and finally gas). One page consisted solely of illustrations, and the other page included text and pictures. On pages with text, Angela wrote about the effect of temperature on molecule movement by repeating "if it is heated the molecules will move faster." This seemed to be a salient idea in Angela's mind that fit her book title. When she was presenting her book, she explained that she got her idea for her title from the CD-ROM on states of matter that the class had used. "I made the title by watching the computer … and I wrote how … all of the molecules move when they are heated because the heat makes them move faster."

Angela's text and picture pages expressed similar meanings in each mode. Her picture-only pages elaborated some of her ideas. For example, on the left-hand page on the topic of liquids (see Figure 2), the text and the picture expressed roughly the same ideas. Angela left the molecules uncolored and close together in the midst of blue-colored water. She indicated

FIGURE 2 Angela's Liquids Pages

that the cup on the right-hand page was heated by putting a candle next to it and she showed fewer molecules. Angela explained, "This is the cup with a candle by it and … it's kind of moving faster." This picture captures the same ideas that we find in her text: "The molecules of a liquid are close together and if it is heated the molecules will move faster." Our talk with her revealed, however, that the right-hand page—a picture-only page—depicted extra meanings. The pictures on this page represented "some more stuff … that is liquid. These are clothes hanging to get dry and there's … liquid going up into the air…. This [pointing to the blue squiggly lines coming from the brown clothesline], this is water vapor. It always goes up into the sky." Later, pointing to another picture next to the hanging clothes' picture on this picture-only page, she said that "the water goes up into the cloud and then … when it gets too heavy it starts to rain … it goes up even if it is raining even if it is snowing…. And when the cloud gets too heavy uh the water vapor … the water vapor is water so that's why clouds are made of water." These pictures capture Angela's concept of evaporation and her idea of the continuous cycle that produces rain. She drew water vapor blue, as she said, because this is water. Although her talk on these pictures does not tell us whether she realizes that water vapor is a gas that is different from liquid water, looking at other parts of her book gives us this sense. More specifically, her cover shows examples of the three states of matter—a cup with spilled liquid, a door with a person knocking representing a solid, and the same kind of picture, with clothes hanging and water vapor coming from them, that she had inside her book representing a gas.

Celina

Second-grader Celina focused on only one of the three states of matter discussed in the unit in her book titled *The Book of Solids*. In each of the three pages, Celina wrote only about solids, but she brought in other big ideas of the unit by linking them with solids. On her first page, Celina wrote about where solids are found ("all around"), gave examples of solids (trees, beds, pillows, TV), and made sure that she presented properties of solids ("they can be hard or soft"). On the second page, Celina presented her understanding of changes of states of matter—"Water that we drink can become a solid. When it freezes it turns into a solid." She also continued offering properties of solids—"Every solid has its own shape." And for her last page, Celina showed that she knew that "molecules are close together and only move a little" in solids. Thus, she wrote about two molecular characteristics of solids, referring to the proximity of the molecules and their low speed. On that last page, she also repeated two properties she had referred to in her previous two pages—namely, that solids are hard or soft and that they keep their shape. However, she wrote about the latter in a different way—"A solid can only change if you do something to it."

Examining Celina's text-picture relationships, we find that Celina tended to elaborate ideas in her text and to use her pictures as illustrations of some of her textual points. During the presentation of her book, Celina said that "if they [the readers of her book] don't understand this [referring to her text] they can look at the picture." For example, Celina's illustration on the second page of her book (see Figure 3) does not capture all the points she wrote about, but it does show her understanding about the relationship between liquid and solid water, even depicting an idea not explicitly presented in her text. Her picture shows that the "water that we drink" takes the shape of the pitcher, and the drops, which fall in the ice-cube-tray squares, take the shape of the tray, freeze (which means "turns into a solid" and a solid "has its own shape"), and become "ice" (the label that Celina used near the small square above the ice tray).

FIGURE 3 Celina's Freezing Page

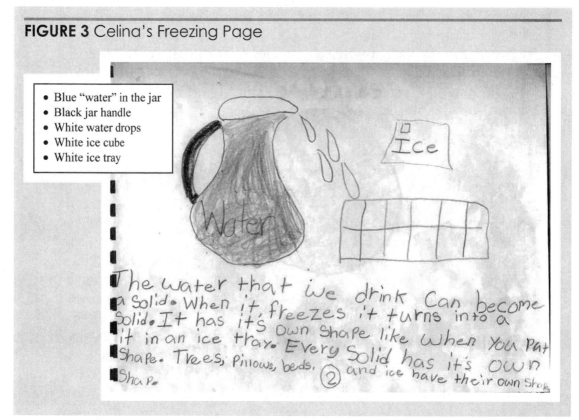

- Blue "water" in the jar
- Black jar handle
- White water drops
- White ice cube
- White ice tray

Ice

Water

The water that we drink Can become a Solid. When it freezes it turns into a Solid. It has it's own Shape like when you Put it in an ice tray. Every Solid has it's own Shape. Trees, Pillows, beds, ② and ice have their own Shape.

Pablo

In contrast to Celina, second-grader Pablo presented all three states of matter in his book, which he called *Matter*. At the end of his book Pablo included his semantic map (similar to the ongoing semantic map his class created during the unit) that he had made before he composed his book. In the four pages of his book, Pablo addressed all the initial ideas depicted on his map plus a few more.

He first presented gases. He offered some important properties of gases—"gases don't have their own shape" and "gases are always invisible." He also addressed where they can be found—"all around you." An example of gases, vapor, was also mentioned. On the right-hand page that went along with his first page, he showed that he knew that in gases "the molecules have too much space to move in," thereby referring to both proximity of molecules and movement at the same time. Then Pablo wrote about solids. He again shared properties: "It never changes unless you do something to it," "it's hard to break it or smush it," and "a solid has a shape or some don't." His last state-ment seems contradictory, but it is not. It became clearer during his presentation when he talked about the pictures he had drawn on this page—a key, a flag, a kid, and a dog—all of which were examples of solids. The key and the flag were solids that keep their shape, whereas in talking about the kid and the dog, Pablo said they do not have their own shape; they move, and thus they change shapes. For solids to have their own shape, according to Pablo, all the parts of a body together—rather than each part separately—had to be considered. On this page, Pablo also brought in molecular characteristics—"the molecules doesn't have too many space to move in"—again referring to both proximity of molecules and movement. Finally, Pablo expressed his ideas about liquids. He included two properties of liquids—"all liquids feel like water" and "liquids always take the shape of the container they're in." But, he also wrote about a change of state—"some liquids turn into vapor."

Most of Pablo's pages had picture-text redundancy. As we talked with him about his pictures, however, he revealed finer understandings but also struggled with concepts and how to express them. For example, on his first page (see Figure 4), he represented vapor as blue circles that spread all over the available space (top picture). When he talked about this picture, he said, "I know that water is blue, so maybe the vapor will be blue." But he also said that he thought that vapor is white. In fact, it seemed that Pablo had considered the color of water vapor at various points while making his book, and he was leaning more toward white. However, when he was discussing his pictures of liquids—on the page where he wrote "some liquids turn into vapor"—he remarked that white crayon does not show on white paper, so he drew them blue.

The rest of his drawings depict his interesting ways of showing something that "you can't see." He first showed the gases with specks of blue crayon, because, as he said, "you can't see as they are little." But, eventually, to make sure his readers knew that gases are "invisible," he made his "little dots" in the bottom picture with a pencil instead of a crayon. He explained: "I don't want it to show because blue is kind of dark." At that point, considerations about size seemed to take over in Pablo's mind. He did not worry about the color of the gases he was writing about. He only considered that his pencil would give him tinier dots that would fit with his textual point that "gases are always invisible."

Nadia

Third-grader Nadia made a long book called *Clouds*. She started with the composition of clouds—"clouds are made of water." She then addressed evaporation in her next two pages: "water evaporates," "vapor is like a gas

FIGURE 4 Pablo's Gases Page

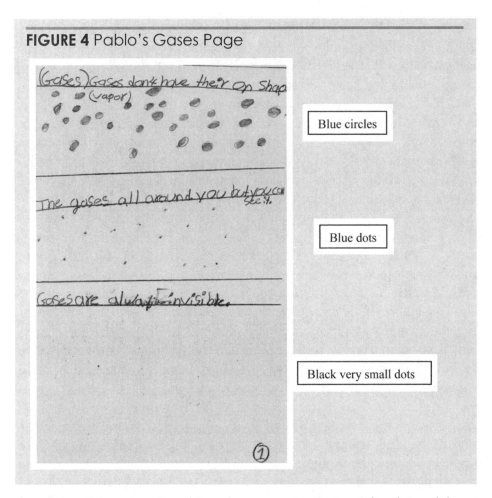

that comes from water," and "water vapor goes up into the sky and forms into a cloud." Then in the next two pages, Nadia addressed cloud movement and types of clouds: "wind blows clouds across the sky" and "clouds can be gray or white or blue." In the following three pages, Nadia presented a potpourri of ideas related to clouds. She first wrote about the Sun coming out when it stops raining and drew a rainbow. Having just addressed rain, she then addressed hail as something coming out of clouds too. According to Nadia "hail is little grains of ice coming from a cloud," referring to its solid state of water as opposed to the liquid and gaseous states she had referred to previously in her book. Finally, she presented fog as something "above the ground" and "something really thick." For her last five pages, Nadia focused on relationships between rain and clouds. For her, dark clouds bring rain, rain comes out of clouds, the rain comes from "the water from the oceans, lakes, and rivers [that] evaporates to the sky," then "when it finished raining the clouds turn gray to white," and finally full circle back to the fact that "clouds hold rain."

Studying Nadia's picture-text relationships, we realized that Nadia's book is predominantly split between pages that are text-picture redundant and pages that contain text elaboration. An interesting feature is that in every picture she labeled all or most of the entities she depicted, such as cloud, water vapor, wind, ocean, evaporation, tree, and fog.

Nadia also made some interesting distinctions in expressing ideas in both words and images. On page 10 of her book (see Figure 5), Nadia wrote "rain comes out of clouds" and showed a cloud outline that she had left uncolored with small vertical blue and black lines dropping from it. In her text, "rain" is the actor of the action "comes out of," with the location of the action being "clouds." Except for the possible significance of the different colors of rain (blue and black) in her picture, the text ideas are consistent with those depicted in the picture. Both express that rain coming out of clouds makes the clouds become "empty." In talking about the two colors

FIGURE 5 Nadia's Rain and Clouds Pages

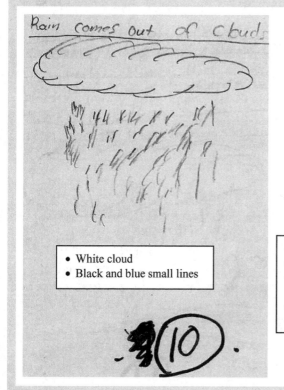

- White cloud
- Black and blue small lines

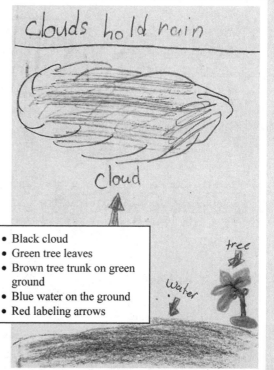

- Black cloud
- Green tree leaves
- Brown tree trunk on green ground
- Blue water on the ground
- Red labeling arrows

of rain in the picture, Nadia explained: "I made it [blue] because that's why the raindrops are blue because it comes from the water, the ocean." However, as we found out, the black lines shown in her picture representing rain did not have any intended meaning for Nadia—they were just traces of her first sketches of rain before she colored it in. On page 13, similar scientific meanings are expressed as those found on page 10—"clouds hold rain." Here, however, "clouds" is the actor of the action "holds," and "rain" is the goal or object of this holding action. Her picture showing a cloud colored in with horizontal black lines is different from the picture on page 10. It includes a cloud filled with rain, matching her textual message.

An earlier page in Nadia's book (not included here) is also of interest. In her picture on that page, Nadia depicted an outline of an "empty" or white cloud, and also included a multicolored rainbow and green grass. Her picture and text on this page ("When it stops raining the sun comes out") seem quite complementary. Text and picture do not communicate identical ideas, but they present ideas that fit with each other. That the pictured cloud would be "empty" makes sense if it had rained (and stopped), and her explanation in sharing her book somewhat underscored this idea in that when it is raining the cloud is gray and "when it stops it turns white." Prompted further to say whether water is in the white cloud, she said that there is no water in there and that the cloud has "like gas" inside it. Nadia seemed to struggle to make sense of the idea of clouds still existing after the rain, which they had held, came out of them. Sometimes it is necessary to explore with students, especially those such as Nadia who write longer texts, several pages of text and pictures to get more sense of the scientific understandings these children are trying to express—and how they are doing so.

Roberto

Third-grader Roberto focused his book on snow, which he appropriately titled *Snow*. Roberto was sure about the value of his book. He started out on his first page writing "this book will teach you about snow." On the same page he also presented two big ideas—composition of snow and impact ("snow is made out of water" and "snow can cause accidents and injuries"). He continued on the next page writing about properties of snow related to its temperature ("snow is very cold" and "snow can never be warm") and its behavior ("snow is also kind of sticky") and expressing ideas about how dangerous snow and ice can be ("you can slip on snow," "or someone can throw a big piece of ice at you"). On his third page, Roberto addressed that it is fun playing with snow and specified that snow is falling in winter. He elaborated more on this idea on his next page, which presented how snow is formed and revealed that he seemed to mix in his mind hail with snow. Both his text and the top part of his picture showed that first "rain falls down from the sky." Then he stated "since the air in the sky is cold the raindrops freeze"—depicted in the middle part of his picture by wavy blue lines (with the label "cold air") and small blue circles (with the label "rain freezing"). On the lower part of the page, his text included "the raindrops then become snowflakes," with a picture showing small uncolored, white circles and the label "snow."

On his next page he presented more details on snowflakes. Roberto knew that snowflakes have different shapes and that the instrument used to detect these shapes is a magnifying glass. Roberto's following page included three ideas—two new (people go ice-skating on ice and a blizzard is a snowstorm "when a lot of snow falls down from the sky") and one he had already presented. He reiterated his statement that snow is made of water, this time writing "snow is water," but he also noted a change of states of matter, "when snow melts it is a liquid." After elaborating on blizzards for two pages, he proceeded (see Figure 6) with more references to changes of states of matter—first about melting ("snow melts in spring") and then about evaporation ("when the snow melts the water from the snow evaporates"). Moreover, he also included the impact of melting—"snow can cause floods." On his last page, Roberto recapped that his "book was about snow … about snowstorms," and he reiterated the value of his book: "This book taught you about snow."

The text and pictures in Roberto's book are often complementary in nature. That is, although he has ideas in the text that are also depicted in his illustrations, he also expressed different ideas in words and/or pictures. Figure 6, discussed above, is an example of such a complementary page. Roberto specified in his text that "snow melts in spring"—a season that is known for weather warmer than that in winter—and he showed the Sun—the source of heat—that melts the snow. He also showed flowers growing as a result of snow melting. He explained during the conversation on his book that "when snow is melting, flowers are growing," demonstrating that his picture included ideas not expressed in his text. In contrast, in his text he wrote about a different effect of snow melting—"snow can cause floods"—but floods were not depicted in his illustrations. As indicated above, he also had text-picture redundancy. For example, Roberto presented both changes of states of matter—melting and evaporation—in both modes. He depicted evaporation with blue curvy lines because as he said, "water is colored blue and it's going up." He depicted wind with a curvy line of different color and

FIGURE 6 Roberto's Changes of States of Matter Page

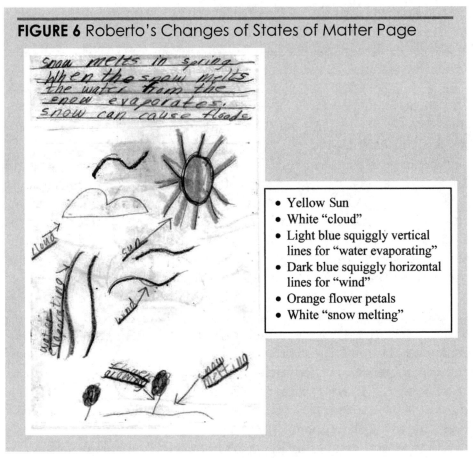

- Yellow Sun
- White "cloud"
- Light blue squiggly vertical lines for "water evaporating"
- Dark blue squiggly horizontal lines for "wind"
- Orange flower petals
- White "snow melting"

orientation so that it would not be confused with water evaporating. He also had a cloud in his picture. Thus, this page of Roberto's book is a rich example of the various ways that children make sense and communicate via both words and images.

Writing and Drawing in Elementary Classroom Science

The information books that the six children wrote revealed much about their understandings of the science concepts and processes that the unit centered on, and they gave us a strong sense of the meaningful ways in which young children compose informational text and visual images. We will recap four major ideas that the analysis of these six books brought up.

First, these books showed the various similarities and differences that young children's books may have. Certainly, in a unit as multifaceted as the Matter unit, we would expect a range of topics that children could choose to focus their books on. But what is particularly interesting is how thematically coherent the children's books were and how they were different from each other. Each book had a clear theme, and each book's pages related to that theme. Most of the time there was a progression of ideas from page to page, a flow that made sense for the science ideas presented. This does not mean, however, that all the books portrayed scientifically accepted points of view. Some children struggled with various ideas—liquid water being blue or white instead of clear, clouds having gases inside them after rain, and snow being formed from freezing rain. Despite these scientifically problematic ideas, the children constructed some profound understandings— about molecule positioning and movement, about properties of different states of matter, about changes of states and factors that affect them, and about various types of storms, their origins, and their impact.

Second, the children's drawings show the sophisticated ways that children think about ideas. There are pages on which texts and pictures were redundant and others on which they complemented each other, as well as pages where either the text or the picture elaborated on ideas. All of the children except first-grader Angela included labels in their pictures, but the third graders included them most frequently. Labels or captions, as minor text, are a typical feature of adult scientific multimodal texts (Lemke 1998, 2004; Unsworth 2001), but also a feature of several of the children's informational books used in the Matter unit, including dialogue bubbles (Kress and van Leeuwen 1996; Unsworth 2001) that two of the children (Celina and Pablo) also used. Children were concerned about the size, the color, the position, the look of the entities in their pictures, but this was not always clear from just looking at their pictures. Our conversations with them revealed and untangled some of their meanings behind their pictures—illustrating the importance of teachers' asking children about their pictures in the same way they might ask about their written text.

Third, it is important to underscore that all the children—at all grades— used the linguistic registers of science, even though none of their teachers explicitly taught these linguistic features. That is, the children used generic nouns, present tense verbs, relational and material verbs, and the scientific vocabulary or technical terms of the unit. We believe that their books reflected this typical science discourse because the children were immersed in many authentic ways of "sciencing." They were read children's informational books that reflected these linguistic patterns, and they had many opportunities to write in scientific ways in their journals or to engage in creating class charts or semantic maps, all of which were integrated with their hands-on explorations.

Finally, during their conversations with us, we asked the children to identify the part of their book that they thought other children at their grade level might find interesting. Children chose parts of their books for reasons that seemed to fall into three different types. One type of reason was to teach other kids something they probably would not know. Nadia, for example, chose the page on which she presented that hail, which she defined as "little grains of ice," comes out of clouds because as she said, "some [third graders] don't even know that hail is like circles and it's like you kind of can't see it sometimes and that it's like crunched up." Pablo chose the page that focused on the ample space among the molecules inside a balloon filled with air, because, as he said, "I don't think they know the molecules have too much space to move in."

The second type of reason was selecting parts that showed something that other children could associate with and that they might like. Roberto chose the page on which he had written that "snow is a lot of fun to play with," including building a snowman and having a snowball fight. According to Roberto, others would find this page interesting because "they like to play with snow."

A third reason was to present something—a picture, an idea—that the particular author of the book liked or found interesting. Ernesto chose his tornado page "because this has the tornadoes and tornadoes are cool." Celina chose the page with water that can turn into ice when it freezes "because it's showing like you pour water on the tray." Unfortunately the bell rang and Celina had to leave so she did not finish her thought, but she seemed to have started sharing that the reason was that she, herself, liked the drawing on the page. Finally, Angela identified two ideas in her book. She chose: "The solid has the most particles, the gas has the less particles." These ideas are found on two different sets of pages in Angela's book, and they are ideas that she herself found most interesting.

We believe we still have a lot to learn about the ways young children think about scientific ideas, concepts, processes, and phenomena and about how they express their meanings when they are offered opportunities to do so as authors of authentic illustrated information books. As teachers and researchers continue to work together to explore children's writing and drawing, we may come to appreciate and understand more of children's intriguing ways with words and pictures.

Acknowledgment

The project is funded by a three-year (2004–2007) National Science Foundation ROLE grant (REC-0411593). The data presented, statements made, and views expressed in this chapter are solely the responsibilities of the authors.

References

Eggins, S. 1994. *An introduction to systemic functional linguistics.* London: Pinter.

Gee, J. P. 2004. Language in the science classroom: Academic social languages as the heart of school-based literacy. In *Crossing borders in literacy and science instruction: Perspectives on theory and practice,* ed. E. W. Saul, 13–32. Newark, DE: International Reading Association.

Goldman, S. R., and G. L. Bisanz. 2002. Toward a functional analysis of scientific genres: Implications for understanding and learning processes. In *The psychology of science text comprehension,* eds. J. Otero, J. A. Leon, and A. C. Graesser, 19–50. Mahwah, NJ: Lawrence Erlbaum.

Halliday, M. A. K. 1985. *An introduction to functional grammar.* London: Edward Arnold.

Halliday, M. A. K., and J. R. Martin. 1993. *Writing science: Literacy and discursive power.* Pittsburgh, PA: University of Pittsburgh Press.

Kress, G. 1997. *Before writing: Rethinking the paths of literacy.* London: Routledge.

Kress, G., and T. van Leeuwen. 1996. *Reading images: The grammar of visual design.* London: Routledge.

Lemke, J. L. 1990. *Talking science: Language, learning, and values.* Norwood, NJ: Ablex.

Lemke, J. L. 1998. Multiplying meaning: Visual and verbal semiotics in scientific text. In *Reading science: Critical and functional perspectives on discourses of science,* eds. J. R. Martin and R. Veel, 87–113. London: Routledge.

Lemke, J. L. 2004. The literacies of science. In *Crossing borders in literacy and science instruction: Perspectives on theory and practice,* ed. E. W. Saul, 33–47. Newark, DE: International Reading Association.

National Research Council (NRC). 1996. *National science education standards.* Washington, DC: National Academy Press.

Pappas, C. C. Forthcoming. The information book genre: Its role in integrated science-literacy research and practice. *Reading Research Quarterly.*

Pappas, C. C., M. Varelas, A. Barry, and A. Rife. 2003. Analyzing young urban children's written illustrated information books: Insights into emergent scientific understandings and linguistic registers. Paper presented at the Annual Meeting of the American Educational Research Association, Chicago.

Unsworth, L. 2001. *Teaching multiliteracies across the curriculum: Changing contexts of text and image in classroom practice.* Buckingham, UK: Open University Press.

Children's Literature and CD-Rom References

Branley, F. M. 1983. *Down comes the rain.* New York: HarperCollins.

Branley, F. M. 1986. *Air is all around you.* New York: HarperCollins.

Branley, F. M. 1986. *Snow is falling*. New York: HarperCollins.

DeWitt, L. 1991. *What will the weather be?* New York: HarperCollins.

Dorros, A. 1989. *Feel the wind*. New York: HarperCollins.

Fowler, A. 1991. *What's the weather today?* New York: Children's Press.

Fowler, A. 1992. *It could still be water*. New York: Children's Press.

Fowler, A. 1995. *When a storm comes up*. New York: Children's Press.

Fowler, A. 1996. *What do you see in a cloud?* New York: Children's Press.

Gibbons, G. 1990. *Weather words and what they mean*. New York: Holiday House.

New Media. 1997. *States of matter, multimedia CD-ROM for pc and Macintosh*. New York: Facts on File.

Zoehfeld, K. W. 1998. *What is the world made of? All about solids, liquids, and gases*. New York: HarperCollins.

CHAPTER 4

Using the Science Writing Heuristic to Promote Understanding of Science Conceptual Knowledge in Middle School

Brian Hand
The University of Iowa

Middle school is the time when science becomes a much more prominent subject than it was in elementary school and when students' ideas about science are cemented. It is important for middle school students to participate in science activities that reflect the nature of science rather than simply complete replication activities. Thus, inquiry-based activities need to be a critical component of middle school science. Such activities require that students be actively engaged in thinking through, and building on, the major concepts of a unit. The Science Writing Heuristic (SWH) is an inquiry-based approach developed by Hand and Keys (1999) that provides a scaffold for implementing inquiry activities based on the use of critical-thinking and reasoning skills. These skills require that students constantly negotiate meaning throughout the inquiry process as a way to construct rich understandings of the topic.

The Science Writing Heuristic (SWH)

The SWH (see Figure 1) has been designed in two parts: The *teacher template* shows what teachers need to do when using this inquiry-based approach; the *student template* helps students to build a scientific argument through a structured, critical-thinking process. We know that scientists use a traditional laboratory report format consisting of hypothesis, procedure, observations, results, and discussion when reporting the results of their research. However, this structure does not necessarily represent the actual process that scientists go through in terms of the negotiations and debates that naturally occur during research. The SWH reflects the need for students to have to negotiate their understandings of a science topic in small groups, in whole-class settings, and in writing assignments. Writing is a negotiation process; that is, in writing up the laboratory activity using the SWH template, students need to determine, or negotiate with themselves, what they believe is essential and needs to be written down. The negotiation process is an essential part of building conceptual understanding.

Implementing a Science Unit Based on the SWH Approach

A number of important issues have to be addressed when implementing an inquiry-based science unit. Given that science inquiry should be based on student-centered learning strategies, teachers need to undertake the following activities prior to beginning to teach a unit:

- *Identify the unit's big ideas.* To ensure that teachers have an understanding of the conceptual framework for the unit, they should begin by constructing a concept map of the topic. Teachers' understanding of the core concepts of a unit is critical, especially later, when students raise issues or suggest inquiries.
- *Have a range of student activities available that address the major concepts of the unit.* Materials necessary for the topic should be readily available to students—maybe on a cart or laid out in the storeroom.
- *Conduct an activity that uncovers what the students know about the topic.* Teachers can find out what students already know about the topic through a hands-on activity, a writing activity, or small-group and whole-class discussions.
- *Plan a pathway for the unit after completing the first activity.* Having found out what the students know, the teacher plans a possible pathway for the unit. However, given that the SWH inquiry approach encourages students to pose questions, teachers need to be flexible in their planning to allow student input to have meaning.

FIGURE 1 The Science Writing Heuristic: Teacher Template and Student Template

Science Writing Heuristic, Part I Teacher Template (Activities Designed to Promote Laboratory Understanding)	Science Writing Heuristic, Part II Student Template
1. Exploration of pre-instruction understanding through individual or group concept mapping or working through a computer simulation.	1. Beginning ideas—What are my questions?
2. Pre-laboratory activities, including informal writing, making observations, brainstorming, and posing questions.	2. Tests—What did I do?
3. Participation in laboratory activity.	3. Observations—What did I see?
4. Negotiation phase I—Writing personal meanings for laboratory activity (e.g., writing journals).	4. Claims—What can I claim?
5. Negotiation phase II—Sharing and comparing data interpretations in small groups (e.g., making a graph based on data contributed by all students in the class).	5. Evidence—How do I know? Why am I making these claims?
6. Negotiation phase III—Comparing science ideas to textbooks or other printed resources (e.g., writing group notes in response to focus questions).	6. Reading—How do my ideas compare with other ideas?
7. Negotiation phase IV—Individual reflection and writing (e.g., creating a presentation such as a poster or report for a larger audience).	7. Reflection—How have my ideas changed?
8. Exploration of postinstruction understanding through concept mapping, group discussion, or writing a clear explanation.	8. Writing—What is the best explanation of what I have learned?

- *Develop a range of conceptual questions for the pretest and posttest.* An important component of any unit is the testing of student knowledge. Given that the SWH inquiry approach is based on building students' conceptual understandings rather than factual knowledge, teachers need to use extended-response questions that require students to engage in higher-order thinking.

Understanding the Relationship Between Claims and Evidence

In using the SWH inquiry approach with students, I and the teachers I work with focus on helping students to understand the value of making claims based on evidence. It is essential that students are able to make the distinction between these two concepts and have practice with them. Many different scenarios can be used to achieve this. For example, a game of Clue can stimulate discussion about what is a claim and what is evidence. We have also used a mystery scenario that was developed by a former graduate student, James Rudd (Figure 2). We ask students to work in small groups to solve the mystery and present their solutions along with their evidence. An interesting part of the exercise, which the students get very involved in and excited about, is that there is no solution; that is, there is not enough evidence to support any claim. However, this does not prevent students (or adults) from coming up with a variety of intriguing solutions. The trouble is that the students cannot support their claims with evidence. This immediately provides a very good opportunity for a rich discussion about claims and evidence and the interplay between the two.

FIGURE 2 Solving a Mystery: Observations, Claims, Evidence, and Conclusions

You and your partner are private detectives who have been hired to investigate the death of the wealthy but eccentric Mr. Xavier, a man who was well-known for his riches and for his reclusive nature. He avoided being around others because he was always filled with anxiety and startled easily. He also suffered from paranoia, and he would fire servants whom he had employed for a long time because he feared they were secretly plotting against him. He would also eat the same meal for dinner every night: two steaks cooked rare and two baked potatoes with sour cream.

Upon arriving at the tragic scene, you are told that Mr. Xavier was found dead in his home early this morning by the servants. The previous evening, after the chef had prepared the usual dinner for Mr. Xavier, the servants had been dismissed early so that they did not have to go home during last night's terrible storm. When they returned in the morning, Mr. Xavier's body was found face down in the dining room.

(continued)

FIGURE 2 (*continued*)

Looking into the room, you start your investigation. The large window in the dining room has been shattered and appears to have been smashed open from the outside. The body exhibits laceration wounds and lies face down by the table, and there is a large red stain on the carpet that emanates from under the body. An open bottle of red wine and a partially eaten steak still remain on the table. A chair that has been tipped over is next to the body, and under the table is a knife with blood on it.

Based on these preliminary observations, please work with your partner to draw initial conclusions about what happened. Please provide as much evidence as you can to support each conclusion you make.

Using the SWH Inquiry Approach in a Unit on Classification

The unit on classification described below was taught using the SWH inquiry approach with seventh-grade students. The teacher involved worked with me and carried out the planning process as described above. Three concepts were chosen as being critical for students' understanding of the purposes of a classification system:

1. A classification system is a system of sorting based on similarities.
2. Organisms are classified by their structure and function.
3. Organisms are classified into seven levels.

While a large number of factual items were required to understand these three concepts, the teacher was able to frame the unit around these basic ideas.

Finding Out What Students Know

To introduce the concept of classification and to begin using the SWH, as well as to find out what the students knew, the teacher used a practical activity. Working in small groups, students were given a box of small objects and asked to divide them into two groups, with two subgroups within each group. While this may appear to be a simple activity, it served to build students' use of the scientific argument and of the terms *claims* and *evidence*. Also, students' definitions of *classification* became public, and students engaged in the dialogical interaction necessary for replicating the work of scientists. Most important, students began to understand that teaching was not about information transfer from the teacher to them—they were required to use the SWH format to make claims, produce evidence, check what others said, and then reflect on how their ideas changed. The teacher was able to determine if the students understood the concept of classification as a system of sorting based on similarities.

Laboratory Activities

Three other laboratory activities were built into the unit. Each of these used an SWH format. The first was a standard dichotomous-key activity with sharks that is found in many textbooks. However, students were required to justify their choices based on the evidence that was supplied by their information sheets.

The second activity required each small group to produce their own dichotomous key based on their own interests. For example, one group produced a key for determining the classification of their CD collections; another group that happened to be all girls produced a key for their Care Bears collections. The emphasis was on understanding how to set up a system of classification. As students worked with the traditional classification system, they were building a conceptual understanding of the purposes for the system and the confidence to use it.

The final laboratory activity was a dissection of an invertebrate (earthworm) and a vertebrate (frog). The dissection gave students an opportunity to explore the differences between these types of animals.

Writing Activities

The teacher had the students complete three writing activities as part of the unit. The first was to create a mnemonic for the levels of classification; that is, the students had to come up with their own mnemonic to help them remember the levels of classification used in the world of biology.

The second activity was a descriptive writing task involving specimen identification. Specimens from the storeroom were placed around the room. Each student then generated a specimen card such that his or her peers could identify the particular specimen. The labels on the jars were then covered up, and students placed their cards into the same pile from which they also chose a card (obviously not their own). They were then required to find the particular specimen using the information on the card they had chosen.

The last major writing activity was a unit summary in which the students wrote a letter to Aristotle explaining the modern classification system. The intent of the summary letter was for the students to explain what a classification system is, using both biological examples and nonbiological examples they may have generated.

Unit Test

One of the critical outcomes of the SWH approach is for students to be tested in a way that reflects the cognitive work they have undertaken. In the SWH approach, students are constantly being required to argue for a position, defend their ideas, and reflect on changes in understanding. These activities require that they engage in cognitively demanding work—thus, it is folly to test them using memory games and fill-in-the-blank type items. Having recall of science facts must not be overlooked; however, if we ask students to think critically during the course of a unit, we need to test them in ways that reflect this emphasis.

The teacher involved with this unit of classification constructed a number of conceptual, or extended-response, questions. These questions were intended to have the students reason through an explanation, with the experience being a further writing-to-learn opportunity. Two questions used by the teacher were the following:

1. Taxonomists classify animals down to the level of species. Argue why they should do this, rather than only classify down to the genus level. Give examples when necessary.
2. Why do scientists find it useful to have a consistent system for classifying living things? What might occur, if it was not consistent?

Does the SWH Inquiry Approach Work?

We have used this approach with many different teachers (Greenbowe and Hand 2005; Hohenshell and Hand, forthcoming; Hand, Wallace, and Yang 2004). Table 1 compares student performance data (from the Iowa Test of Basic Skills) for the students of the teacher described above (Teacher 1) and those of the other seventh-grade teacher in the school (Teacher 2). Teacher 1 engaged the students in much dialogue, recognized the need for students to have control of knowledge, and focused on dealing with the major ideas that were framing the topic. Teacher 2, on the other hand, did not generate much student dialogical interaction, was not prepared to allow students to have control of the knowledge in which they were engaged, and did not focus on the major ideas of the unit; instead, he was more concerned with the content knowledge of the unit and controlling all the activities in the classroom. Students who worked with Teacher 1 had Iowa Test of Basic Skills scores in science that were much higher than those in any other subject areas and almost equivalent to Teacher 2's students, who routinely scored much higher in all subject areas.

TABLE 1 Student Scores for Two Teachers on the Iowa Test of Basic Skills

Teacher 1 Iowa Test of Basic Skills Data		Teacher 2 Iowa Test of Basic Skills Data	
Reading total	61	Reading total	70
Language total	57	Language total	74
Mathematics total	67	Mathematics total	78
CORE total	61	CORE total	75
Social Studies	62	Social Studies	76
Science	76	Science	78

We have replicated these results in classrooms from sixth grade through university freshman chemistry classes.

Summary

To implement the SWH approach, teachers must become aware of, and be prepared to use, writing-to-learn strategies. Although implementation of the negotiation phases shown in the SWH teacher template appears to be straightforward, it should be noted that it calls on teachers to adopt a variety of different strategies and approaches. Most important, dialogical interaction does not occur if all the questions must be addressed by the teacher (the favored approach of students attempting to become teacher pleasers). Teachers need to encourage students to judge the merits of their comments among themselves. This traditionally is a very difficult thing to do because teachers have been locked into a particular pattern of questioning; to shift to a new way of interacting in the classroom is not easy. Writing-to-learn strategies do not simply ask students to write. The function of the SWH is to provide students with opportunities to explore, talk, and write in a structured framework so the benefits to be gained are related to conceptual understanding and not just science facts.

References

Greenbowe, T. J., and B. Hand. 2005. Introduction to the science writing heuristic. In *Chemists' guide to effective teaching*, eds. N. J. Pienta, M. M. Cooper, and T. J. Greebowe. Upper Saddle River, NJ: Prentice Hall.

Hand, B. and C. Keys. 1999. Inquiry investigation. *The Science Teacher* 66 (4): 27–29.

Hand, B., C. Wallace, and E. Yang. 2004. Using the science writing heuristic to enhance learning outcomes from laboratory activities in seventh-grade science: Quantitative and qualitative aspects. *International Journal of Science Education* 26: 131–149.

Hohenshell, L., and B. Hand. Forthcoming. Writing-to-learn strategies in secondary school cell biology. *International Journal of Science Education*.

CHAPTER 5

Comprehension Strategies and the Scientist's Notebook:
Keys to Assessing Student Understanding

Ronald D. DeFronzo
East Bay Educational Collaborative

If your school district is anything like the districts that we at the East Bay Educational Collaborative (EBEC) of Rhode Island work with (and I suspect it is), then you are probably struggling with many of the same questions that they have regarding the role of science in the elementary curriculum:

- How can our district respond to the ever-increasing challenge of meeting state and national standards in science, while at the same time improving students' literacy skills?
- How can we use what cognitive scientists have discovered about the ways students learn to improve literacy and science comprehension?
- What does the research have to say about best practices in the teaching and learning of science, as well as literacy (reading, writing, speaking, and listening), and, more important, how can we apply what the research has to say? [Figure 1 lists many of the research findings that have guided EBEC's attempts to connect reading and writing with inquiry science.]

- How can we sort through all the research on the effectiveness of programs and practices to identify what is really important?

FIGURE 1 Research That Has Guided Our Practice
in Rhode Island

- Research findings that support the inquiry approach:
  - Understanding science is more than knowing facts.
  - Students build new knowledge and understanding on what they already know and believe.
  - Students formulate new knowledge by modifying and refining their current concepts and by adding new concepts to what they already know.
  - Effective learning requires that students take control of their own learning.
  - The ability to apply knowledge to novel situations, that is, transfer of learning, is affected by the degree to which students learn with understanding. (NRC 2000, pp. 116–119)
- Elementary students need to have a purpose to their reading, writing and communicating, and science can provide that purpose. (Akerson 2001, pp. 42–47)
- The reading process parallels the process of scientific inquiry—both areas require skills in questioning and setting a purpose, analyzing and drawing conclusions, and communicating results. (Yore, Craig, and Maguire 1995, pp. 24–27)
- When students had more opportunities to read and teachers integrated literacy instruction in the content areas, the result was increased reading comprehension, conceptual knowledge, problem-solving skills in science, and motivation to read. (Guthrie, Schafer, and Huang 2001, pp. 145–162)
- Integrated reading should begin before 4th grade…. [B]eginning readers can and do extend their knowledge from meaningful books. If children do not encounter meaningful content in books until 3rd or 4th grade, the major message they may be learning in the meantime is that reading lacks purpose. (Chittenden, Salinger, and Bussis 2001, p. 72)
- If our goal in education is to produce fully literate citizens, then convergence of subject content is fundamental. This idea is not new. As early as 1916, John Dewey cautioned that isolation in all forms should be avoided, and we should strive for connectedness. (Dewey 1936, pp. 71–73)

(continued)

FIGURE 1 (*continued*)

- Recent brain research tells us that long-term memory depends upon learning experiences that make sense and are relevant to the learner. We now know that without making connections among the subjects, students struggle to understand unrelated topics and to memorize isolated facts. (Wolfe 2001, p. 48)
- We should not wait to address this problem (many children and adults struggle to comprehend informational text) until children reach late elementary, middle, and high school when learning from text is a cornerstone of the curriculum. Four strategies can help teachers improve K–3 students' comprehension of informational text. Teachers should
  - Increase students' access to informational text
  - Increase the time students spend working with informational text in instructional activities
  - Explicitly teach comprehension strategies
  - Create opportunities for students to use informational text for authentic purposes (Duke 2004, pp. 40–44)

These questions and supporting research have been the focus of our attention at EBEC since 1991, as we have attempted to write our own story of science education reform in the communities along the eastern shores of Narragansett Bay. It is our story that I will attempt to tell in this chapter—not as a sequence of historical events but rather as a synthesis of what we've learned as we've studied the research and examined practices that work. Two proponents of those practices, Stephanie Harvey and Anne Goudvis (Harvey and Goudvis 2000), make the point that the "reader writes the story." That is, when a person reads a piece of text, an inner conversation takes place in the reader's mind that is unique to him or her—just as that person draws from a unique set of prior experiences or background knowledge. We all bring something different to the reading of information, and we construct meaning based on the building of connections between our personal schema and the new information.

So it has been with our journey of deciphering the research, making personal and collective meaning of it, and finding ways to apply it to our own practice. This story will draw heavily from the works of Stephanie Harvey and Anne Goudvis, Suzanne Zimmerman and Chryse Hutchins (2003), Ellin Oliver Keene (1997), and their colleagues at the Public Education and Business Coalition (PEBC) of Denver, Colorado. Indeed, I will draw on one of the PEBC's "7 Keys to Comprehension"—that of "determining importance"—to scale down the scope of the research that has influenced us to those few key ideas that, for us, have had the greatest impact on student learning.

The Research

Considerable research has emerged in the last decade that supports the connections between reading and content-area instruction. In fact, cognitive scientists tell us that we learned more about how the brain works between 1990 and 1995 than in the previous 100 years. We have learned a great deal about purpose, making meaning, opportunity and motivation, meaningful content, connectedness and relevance, and authenticity—ideas that are key to developing our students' powers in scientific literacy and literacy in general.

So where to begin? With the advent of information technology, it is all too easy to get lost in a sea of data. I was pleasantly reassured by what the editors of *How People Learn: Brain, Mind, Experience, and School* (Bransford, Brown, and Cocking 2000) had to say: "What is perhaps most striking is the…ways in which evidence from many different branches of science are beginning to converge" (p. 3). Finally, for us at least, the messages are beginning to converge, and we have identified a few promising practices that have proven to be extremely effective with students in other parts of the country.

In our effort in Rhode Island, we draw from the practical experience of two groups that are building connections between science and reading/ writing in their own work and that have greatly influenced our thinking:

1. the Vallé Imperial (California) Project in Science (VIPS), and in particular the use of scientist's notebooks, which we have carried out through a partnership with Michael Klentschy, superintendent of schools in Imperial County's El Centro, California. The research/work conducted by Klentschy and his colleagues was funded by the National Science Foundation (Klentschy and Molina-De La Torre 2004).

2. the efforts of teachers and literacy specialists who work together under the umbrella of the PEBC. In this chapter we draw especially from the PEBC's *7 Keys to Comprehension: How to Help Your Kids Read It and Get It!* (Zimmerman and Hutchins 2003).

Scientist's Notebooks[1]

Let's look at how we have synthesized these bodies of information. I begin with the work of Michael Klentschy in the use of science notebooks with the

---

[1] In El Centro, the notebooks are called "science" notebooks. In Rhode Island, we use the term "scientist's" notebooks to reinforce to students that they themselves are scientists and are keeping a notebook just as scientists do.

students of El Centro, California. A first question might be, Why should we in Rhode Island be interested in what this small community on the Mexican border, 2,600 miles away, has accomplished? One reason is based on data from the University of California (Figure 2), which annually reports the eligibility rate of students who apply for admission to the state university system—in particular, the underrepresented populations. During a five-year period—the academic years 2000–2001 through 2003–2004—El Centro's eligibility rate rose from 4% to over 12% (Imperial County Office of Education 2004) while the state's average remained level at just under 4%. For the longest time in our work, we were looking for similar evidence that inquiry science had an impact on student learning—data that we could use to garner business and parental support for our own science reform effort. Up until 1999, all we had

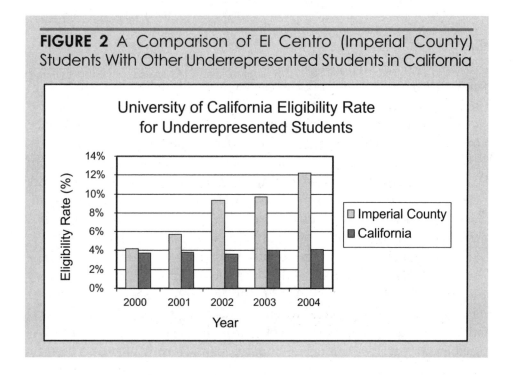

FIGURE 2 A Comparison of El Centro (Imperial County) Students With Other Underrepresented Students in California

to go on was our intuitive feeling that we were on the right track, with little more than anecdotal evidence that we were making a difference.

In 2000, Klentschy presented data to the science education community indicating that student achievement in both science and literacy rose as a result of combining inquiry science and literacy instruction in a mutually

FIGURE 3 National Percentile Rank (NPR) Comparison of the Science Scores of Students Who Participated in an Inquiry Program (VIPS) With Those in a Traditional Program

Vallé Imperial Project in Science
Stanford 9 Achievement Test: Science Scores
1998–99 NPR (%)

	Grade 4	Grade 6
Mean NPR	36	40
Participating NPR	43	49
Nonparticipating NPR	25	31

Source: Amaral, O., L. Garrison, and M. Klentschy. 2002. Helping English learners increase achievement through inquiry-based science instruction. *Bilingual Research Journal* 26 (2): 213–239.

beneficial approach. Two cohorts of students were studied over a period of five years—those who had participated in an inquiry science program, and those who had not. The study showed a significant difference in the science scores of students who had been part of the inquiry program over those who had not, as measured by the Stanford 9 Science Achievement Test (Figure 3). Moreover, scores in the areas of writing and reading for these students increased significantly over those who were not in the inquiry program (Figure 4 and Figure 5). And these results were cumulative; that is, the more years a student was in an inquiry program, the better he or she did.

Prior to coming to El Centro, Klentschy served as an assistant superintendent in Pasadena, California, and worked with Laurie Thompson, literacy specialist and director of the CAPSI (Caltech Precollege Science Initiative) project. This project brought together university scientists from Caltech with school administrators and teachers to implement a program of teaching elementary science through an inquiry approach with a focus on literacy. Klentschy and his team of science and literacy specialists have identified at least one reason for the increase in student achievement—the use of science notebooks by every student, in every school, every day. That was the expectation set by the superintendent—that every student would be engaged daily in reading and writing in the content areas, especially science. The expectation was made clear to every principal and every teacher in the district. My own hypothesis is that the success of the VIPS is due in large part to the consistent use of a common language and practice for every teacher and student across all grades from K to 8.

Klentschy's team developed a set of six components that form the basis of what they call the science notebook's "blueprint" (see Figure 7, column 1). At first glance, these components are no surprise—in fact, they mirror pretty closely the guidelines for scientific inquiry as outlined in the National Science Education Standards (NSES) (NRC 1996). But when we began using these elements as practiced in El Centro, we noted two that seemed to be especially important—"claims and evidence" and "making meaning conference." Indeed, according to *Inquiry and the National Science Education Standards* (NRC 2000) the learner should be able to "use data to construct a reasonable explanation" (p. 19) and "give priority to evidence in responding to questions" (p. 29).

But it wasn't until we saw the idea applied in practice that it came to life for us. During the course of an inquiry investigation, students collect data (evidence). In the course of their discussion with one another and the teacher, the students collectively begin to make sense of this data. This sense-making activity culminates in what Klentschy calls a "making meaning conference." During this whole-group activity, the teacher conducts a conference to draw out the collective understanding that the students have gained as a result of their investigation. Through careful

FIGURE 4 Passing Rates for the El Centro District Writing Proficiency

El Centro District Writing Proficiency Spring 1999 Results—Grade 6

Cumulative Pass Rate	71%
Participating Classes Pass Rate	89%
Nonparticipating Classes Pass Rate	58%

Source: Amaral, O., L. Garrison, and M. Klentschy. 2002. Helping English learners increase achievement through inquiry-based science instruction. *Bilingual Research Journal* 26 (2): 213–239.

FIGURE 5 National Percentile Rank (NPR) in Reading Scores Sorted by the Number of Years in VIPS

Vallé Imperial Project in Science Stanford 9 Achievement Test: Reading Scores 1998–99 NPR—Grade 4 Sorted by Years in Program

Years	LEP*	EO*
0	21	30
1	22	39
2	39	51
3	34	57
4	49	64

*Limited English proficiency
*English speaking only

Source: Amaral, O., L. Garrison, and M. Klentschy. 2002. Helping English learners increase achievement through inquiry-based science instruction. *Bilingual Research Journal* 26 (2): 213–239.

questioning and guidance, the teacher leads the class to a common under-standing of the fundamental idea of the lesson. If misconceptions persist, the teacher can have the students return to the investigation and test their ideas. When the teacher is satisfied that they "get the big idea," the students can then move on to consolidate this new learning in their conclusion and reflection. It is an amalgamation of the teaching of science content, peda-gogy, and assessment of student learning. It's really a thing of beauty to see how the parts fit together. There is probably no better way to assess student understanding than to look at what students write in their conclusions (see samples of student work, Figure 6; all student names are pseudonyms).

FIGURE 6 Samples of Student Work

Michael–Kindergartner
- Planning and conducting simple investigations
- Creating sensory images

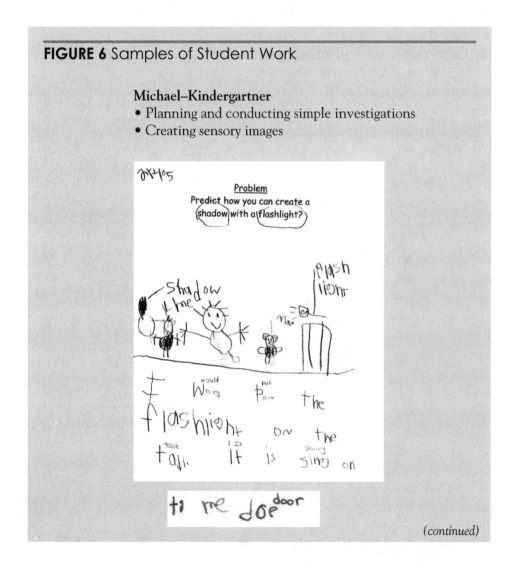

(continued)

FIGURE 6 (*continued*)

Lynn–Third grader
- Claims and evidence
- Determining importance

Claims	Evidence
Water can go through a paper towel.	If you do it there is water underneath.
Water is absorbed by wax paper.	Water leaves a mark on wax paper after awhile the H_2O will absorb.
When you put H_2O on copy paper it doesn't absorb at that moment.	after a while the water will absorb.

- Communicating investigations and explanations

Reflection: If you have a piece,a big piece of foil,you made a hill,then you put twelve drops of H_2O on the hill,would it fall down or would it stay up?

Patrick–Third grader
- Prediction

	Big Question	Prediction
Part 1	What happens to water when it's placed on a slide?	-Slide down in a sqiggeley on wax paper

(*continued*)

FIGURE 6 *(continued)*

Jennifer–Second grader
- Relating new to known (schema)
- Asking questions about objects, organisms, and events in the environment

1/28/05

How do axles help whells?
I think if I push the axle it
will move the whells.

Maria–Fourth grader
- Planning and conducting simple investigations

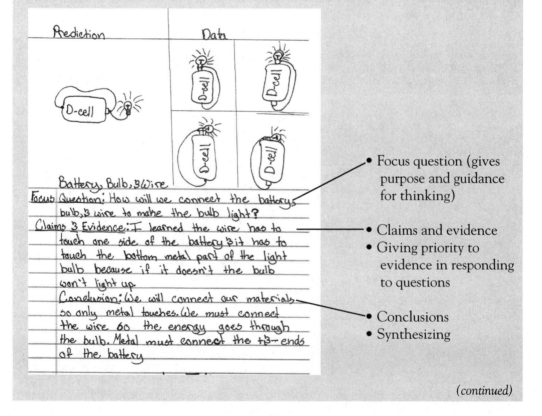

Prediction   Data

Battery, Bulb, 3 Wire

Focus Question: How will we connect the battery, bulb, 3 wire to make the bulb light?

Claims 3 Evidence: I learned the wire has to touch one side of the battery 3 it has to touch the bottom metal part of the light bulb because if it doesn't the bulb won't light up.

Conclusion: We will connect our materials so only metal touches. We must connect the wire so the energy goes through the bulb. Metal must connect the +3 ends of the battery

- Focus question (gives purpose and guidance for thinking)

- Claims and evidence
- Giving priority to evidence in responding to questions

- Conclusions
- Synthesizing

(continued)

FIGURE 6 (continued)

Susan–Eighth grader

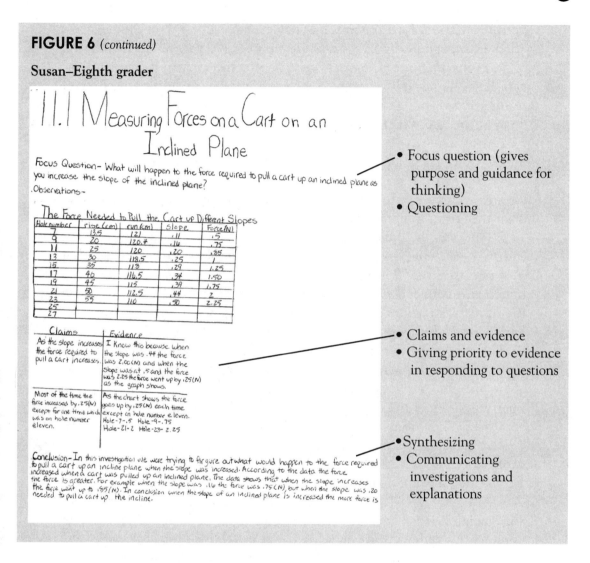

11.1 Measuring Forces on a Cart on an Inclined Plane

Focus Question- What will happen to the force required to pull a cart up an inclined plane as you increase the slope of the inclined plane?

.Observations-

The Force Needed to Pull the Cart up Different Slopes

Hole number	rise (cm)	run (cm)	slope	Force(N)
7	13.5	121	.11	.5
9	20	120.7	.16	.75
11	25	120	.20	.85
13	30	118.5	.25	1
15	35	118	.29	1.25
17	40	116.5	.34	1.50
19	45	115	.39	1.75
21	50	112.5	.44	2
23	55	110	.50	2.25
25				
27				

Claims	Evidence
As the slope increases the force required to pull a cart increases.	I know this because when the slope was .44 the force was 2.00(N) and when the slope was at .5 and the force was 2.25 the force went up by .25(N) as the graph shows.
Most of the time the force increased by .25(N) except for one time which was on hole number eleven.	As the chart shows the force goes up by .25(N) each time except on hole number eleven. Hole-7-.5 Hole-9-.75 Hole-21-2 Hole-23- 2.25

Conclusion- In this investigation we were trying to figure out what would happen to the force required to pull a cart up an incline plane when the slope was increased. According to the data the force increased when a cart was pulled up an inclined plane. The data shows that when the slope increases the force is greater. For example when the slope was .16 the force was .75 (N), but when the slope was .20 the force went up to .85(N). In conclusion when the slope of an inclined plane is increased the more force is needed to pull a cart up the incline.

- Focus question (gives purpose and guidance for thinking)
- Questioning

- Claims and evidence
- Giving priority to evidence in responding to questions

- Synthesizing
- Communicating investigations and explanations

Our task in Rhode Island has been to make this model our own, so we are working with templates that our teachers are using to scaffold student work (see Appendix).

Comprehension Strategies

In the area of reading, we defer to those whom we consider to be practitioner experts in the field—folks like Stephanie Harvey, Anne Goudvis, and so many others too numerous to mention here by name, but who work collectively through the PEBC. One of them, Ellin Oliver Keene, co-author of *Mosaic of Thought*, recently spent a day with teachers in our districts. During her presentation, Keene pointed out that many state literacy frameworks are the size of phone books—one state has over 400 pages in its framework. With everything else a teacher has to do in the course of the day, how can she or he possibly determine what is important about the teaching of reading and writing from such a voluminous document? Keene went on to describe the research of David Rumelhart. As a result of decades of study on reading comprehension, Rumelhart isolated six elements that must be attended to at each grade level, K–12. Three of these deal with what he terms "surface structure systems" of text, and three others address "deep structure systems" of text. Keene pointed out that to teach kids to truly comprehend what they read, teachers need only to attend to these six things, and do it well. And that we have 13 years to do it! Now that's manageable. From the deep structure systems, Keene and her colleagues have developed what they refer to as the "7 Keys to Comprehension." The magic for us has been to build the connections between the scientist's notebooking strategies and the thinking strategies of the literacy experts. Figure 7 illustrates the parallel process skills involved in both.

The thinking strategies in Figure 7 go beyond reading and writing—they cut across the boundaries of all content areas. Our focus has been to apply these ideas to the teaching and learning of science. For instance, in inferring the intention of an author, "readers have to amass the evidence and draw conclusions for themselves" (Zimmerman and Hutchins 2003, p. 106). In science, students use the strategy of hypothesizing to create an explanation for a given set of data.

The thinking skills required are the same. "Synthesizing" a text passage and drawing a conclusion in science are corollary skills. "Determining importance" and "monitoring for meaning" in reading are parallel cognitive processes to using "claims and evidence" in science and "making meaning" of our world. The strategies that enable kids to read with understanding are the same for science or, for that matter, for all content subjects. We in Rhode Island have become vociferous students of and advocates for the 7 Keys to Comprehension, not only for what they bring to student understanding, but for their ability to help us focus on how we are learning. It is not enough simply to use a particular comprehension strategy. We need to take our students to that next, metacognitive step: having them consider how a particular strategy helps them to remember and understand more deeply. With the strategy in place, they can then apply it to new areas of interest. The strategies must be explicitly taught so that students can construct knowledge for themselves and understand how the processes work together. They need to take a metacognitive approach.

FIGURE 7 A Comparison of the El Centro Model for Science Notebooks and the Public Education and Business Coalition's (PEBC) 7 Keys to Comprehension

El Centro Model for Science Notebooks	PEBC 7 Keys to Comprehension
Engaging Scenario (what Madeline Hunter [1984] called "an anticipatory set")—a mental set that causes students to focus on what will be learned.	1. Relating new to known (schema)—Proficient learners connect information from text and other learning experiences to schemata in long-term memory. Information is learned, remembered, and reapplied because it is linked to other learned information. 2. Creating sensory images—Proficient readers spontaneously and purposefully create mental images while and after they read. The images emerge from all five senses and from the emotions and are anchored in a reader's prior knowledge.
Focus Question (gives purpose and guidance for thinking)	3. Questioning—Proficient readers use questions to focus their attention on important components of the text; they understand that they can pose questions critically.
Hypothesis/Prediction—students create a plausible explanation for a given set of data or observations or predict a new outcome.	4. Inferring—*Inferring* refers to the process of creating a personal meaning from text. It involves a mental process of combining what is read with relevant prior knowledge (schema).
Claims and Evidence	5. Determining importance—Students should be able to articulate how they make decisions about what is important in a given context and how those decisions enhance their overall comprehension of the piece.
Making Meaning Conference	6. Monitoring for meaning—Proficient readers monitor, evaluate, and make revisions to their evolving interpretation of the text while reading.
Conclusions	7. Synthesizing—A synthesis is the sum of information from the text, other relevant texts, and the reader's background knowledge, ideas, and opinions produced in an *original way*.

I think Larry Lowery, Principal Investigator for the Full Option Science System (FOSS) Program, says it best:

The new consensus on the nature of learning helps educators understand what fosters learning and gives us ideas for improving those aspects of teaching that are ineffective or detrimental to learning. It supports the intuition of our most thoughtful teachers and it describes how learners best move from being novices to becoming experts. The view is expressed simply:
* *Learners construct knowledge for themselves*
* *To understand is to know relationships*
* *Knowing relationships depends on having prior knowledge*
                                    (Lowery 1998, pp. 26–28)

Just how does one "construct knowledge"? Glynn and Muth (1994) developed a conceptual model that makes this construction come alive for me (Figure 8). In this powerful metaphor for making meaning, the process begins as the student encounters a phenomenon from the real world through one of the five senses, or "windows to the brain." As Glynn and Muth point out, this new information comes into the brain to our short-term or working memory—a place in the brain where meaning is made. It is a place where all the higher-order thinking skills come to play (e.g., analyzing and synthesizing). If the brain were a computer, this would be the CPU—central processing unit. Whenever the brain encounters new information, the first thing it does is to go to the long-term memory to find out what it already knows about the particular phenomenon. The computer equivalent would be the hard disk memory storage. Since the brain is an eminent sense-making device, it immediately compares the new information from the external world with the prior or background knowledge from long-term memory. The process is really much more complicated, of course. Our long-term memory represents the sum total of all our experiences. Using countless billions of neural connections, our brain calls upon our long-term memory to make meaning out of new experiences by comparing those with prior experiences.

The process is iterative—the brain seeks out new information from the senses and draws from our ability to apply science process skills to deepen our picture. The brain brings in reading skills to enlarge our understanding and writing skills that require that we synthesize the ideas so as to make them understandable to someone else. Even speaking and listening come into play, especially for those

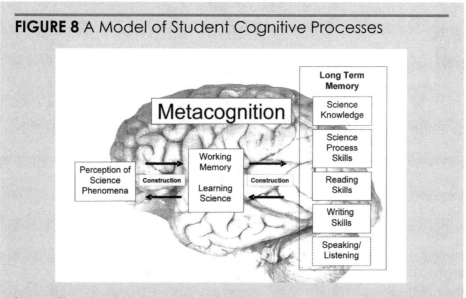

FIGURE 8 A Model of Student Cognitive Processes

Source: Glynn, S., and D. Muth. 1994. Reading and writing to learn science: Achieving scientific literacy. *Journal of Research in Science Teaching* 31 (9): 1057–1073. Reprinted with permission.

students who may not yet have developed a fluency in written information. In this wonderful dance between the realms of the external world and of long-term memory, the brain "constructs" new understanding, which will ultimately be stored in long-term memory, ready to be used in future problem solving.

Many researchers have commented on the links between literacy and science:

- "By their very nature, reading and writing activities can play a vital role in achieving a minds-on emphasis in the learning of science. Reading and writing activities can serve as conceptual tools for helping students to analyze, interpret and communicate scientific ideas." (Holliday, Yore, and Alvermann 1994, p. 877)
- "These activities can help engage in students' minds the complex reasoning and problem solving processes that scientists use in the course of their work. Meaningful learning is the process of actively constructing conceptual relations between new knowledge and existing knowledge…." (Glynn 1991, p. 222)
- "Students should learn concepts as organized networks of related information, not as lists of isolated facts." (Glynn and Muth 1994, p. 1060)

These ideas are reinforced by Donovan and Bransford (2005) in *How Students Learn: Science in the Classroom*:

(1) Students come to the classroom with preconceptions about how the world works. If their initial understanding is not engaged, they may fail to grasp the new concepts and information, or they may learn them for the purposes of a test but revert to their preconceptions outside the classroom. (2) To develop competence in an area of inquiry students must (a) have a deep foundation of factual knowledge, (b) understand facts and ideas in the context of a conceptual framework, and (c) organize knowledge in ways that facilitate retrieval and application. (3) A "metacognitive" approach to instruction can help students learn to take control of their own learning by defining learning goals and monitoring progress in achieving them. (p. 1–2)

Feedback and Assessment of Student Comprehension

Finally, how can we know if we as teachers have been successful? More important, how can we help students to know when they have been successful? In *Classroom Instruction That Works*, Marzano, Pickering, and Pollock (2000) offer some thoughts about setting goals and giving students feedback to help them assess their own learning. About feedback, they say,

1. Feedback should be corrective in nature
2. Feedback should be timely
3. Feedback should be specific to a criterion
4. Students can effectively provide some of their own feedback

They also note that teachers should provide students with clear assessments of their progress on each learning goal and that students can assess themselves on these goals and compare these assessments with those of the teacher.

The El Centro notebook model offers at least three powerful opportunities for assessment. First, the "making meaning conference" allows the teacher to have a conversation with his or her students about the ideas they are developing as a result of the lesson. During this time of formative assessment and feedback, the teacher can judge the readiness of the students to move on to the next portion of the lesson. Once the teacher is satisfied that the "claims and evidence" have been established, the students can then move on to formulate their own explanations of the concepts in the conclusion of the investigation. This is the second opportunity to assess the students' understanding. The students begin by restating their focus question as a topic sentence, and then present the claims and evidence in their own words.

The student notebook then becomes a portfolio of performance assessments. In this third way to assess student growth, the notebook becomes a powerful tool to assess the progress of a student over time and is particularly valuable for student/parent conferences. We have been experimenting with a variety of feedback forms for different age levels. For example, students can assess their own work using sticky-note flags, color-coded to certain performance criteria. In this case, students are asked to place a flag in their notebooks where they feel they have made their best observations, drawn their best diagram, created the best conclusion based on evidence, and done their best overall work. As their work improves, they can make judgments about when and where to move their sticky notes to the better work. Our experience has been that students place a very high intrinsic

FIGURE 9 Feedback Form Developed by El Centro School District

Student Self-Assessment	Teacher Feedback and Comments	Proficiency Criteria
		Focus Question • Relate it to the "Big Idea" • Use your own words
		Hypothesis/Prediction • Make a hypothesis or prediction • Explain why you think this will happen
		Planning • Describe the steps you take so someone else can repeat the experiment and get the same results
		Data/Diagrams • Organized • Clear • Accurate • Diagrams follow criteria chart (labels, title, details)
		Claims and Evidence • A "claim" is a statement about what you observe to be happening in this experiment. For each claim, you should give the evidence from the experiment that supports it. • Claims should be related to the underlying principles • "Evidence" includes what works and what doesn't work when appropriate
		Conclusion • Begin with an appropriate topic sentence that puts the focus question into a sentence format • Use words from the "word wall" appropriately • Refer to the evidence you gathered to support your claims • Show the connection to the focus question • Show the connection of the Big Idea to the "real world"
		Next Steps • What new thoughts or questions do you have? • Describe a "Wow" factor

value on their notebooks—they hang onto the notebooks after the school year has ended and want to make sure they get their notebooks back if a teacher asks to keep them for a while. This sense of ownership attests to a high degree of authenticity in the work found there.

The feedback form developed by El Centro (Figure 9) lists the key elements of the notebook blueprint, with a place for the student to self-assess and for the teacher to write comments.

Summary

Our work in Rhode Island is certainly not unique. All across the country, educators are striving to build on the natural connections between science and literacy. Our own work has brought together the best thoughts from two key efforts. One is the scientist's notebook model developed by the El Centro School District, which focuses on making meaning of the phenomenon being investigated and giving priority to evidence in responding to questions. The second is a way of having students take responsibility for their own learning through the explicit teaching of literacy strategies in the content areas. Both efforts are tied to the ways of thinking about thinking—metacognition.

If what we learned between 1990 and 1995 represents a doubling of the previous 100 years, then I am personally excited about what the next 5 years will bring. As I think about the strategies on which we are currently focused, I am struck by how much sense they make. In retrospect, it seems that we should have know about them all along. It's like coming home for the first time. We look forward to joining with teachers all across the country in striving to make a better way for kids to learn.

Appendix

Student Guide to Use of Scientist's Notebooks

Title of Lesson_____

Focus Question (Big Idea)
- What do you have to investigate or figure out in this lesson that is related to the big idea?
- What will be the main question that will guide your learning? (What..., How..., Does... are good beginnings.)

Prediction/Hypothesis
- What do you think will happen (Using Prior Knowledge)? Create a plausible explanation for the phenomenon (e.g., If I do...then...will happen because... OR I think... because...).

Planning
(Don't rewrite procedures. Use if you need to design a procedure.)

Data
- Record the data in a way that will make sense to you later—use paragraphs, bullets, tables or charts, drawings, graphs, and so forth.
- Be sure to title and label diagrams and pictures.
- Measurements should be specific and accurate and units should be labeled.

Claims and Evidence

Claims	Evidence

- State your claim based on your evidence (data collected from observations).
  - What do you claim to be true?
  - How can you prove what you are stating? Back it up. Use sentence such as *I know this to be true because I observed…* OR *I claim that when…, then… (happens)*.

Making Meaning Conference
- Make your thinking public in a class discussion.
- Turn and Talk.

Conclusion/Reflection
- Restate the focus question as a topic sentence:
  - In this investigation…
  - In this inquiry…
  - I (we) learned that…
- Use data from your claims and evidence chart to answer the focus question. Every claim must be supported by evidence.
- Refer back to your hypothesis:
  - My hypothesis was correct/incorrect because…
  - I (we) liked/did not like…because
  - My (our) prediction that…was…because…
  - This reminds me (us) of…because…
  - I (we) discovered that…
  - Now I (we) think that…because…
- What were your thoughts after the experiment (understandings, likes, related thinking, connections)?

Questions
What new questions do you have to extend your learning?

References

Akerson, V. 2001. Teaching science when your principal says "teach language arts." *Science and Children* 20: 42–47.

Amaral, O., L. Garrison, and M. Klentschy. 2002. Helping English learners increase achievement through inquiry-based science instruction. *Bilingual Research Journal* 26 (2): 213–239

Bransford, J., A. L. Brown, and R. Cocking, eds. 2000. *How people learn: Brain, mind, experience, and school.* Washington, DC: National Academy Press.

Chittenden, E., T. Salinger, and A. Bussis. 2001. *Inquiry into meaning: An investigation of learning to read.* New York: Teachers College Press.

Damian, C. 2002. The power of convergent learning. *ENC Focus Magazine* (Nov. 2): 1.

Dewey, J. 1916. *Democracy and education.* New York: Macmillan.

Dewey, J. 1936. Rationality in education. *The Social Frontier*: 71–73.

Donovan, M. S., and J. D. Bransford, eds. 2005. *How students learn: Science in the classroom.* Washington, DC: National Academies Press.

Duke, N. 2004. The case for informational text. *Educational Leadership* (March): 40–44.

Glynn, S. 1991. Explaining science concepts: A teaching with analogies model. In *The psychology of learning science*, eds. S. Glynn, R. H. Yeany, and B. K. Britton, 219–240. Hillsdale, NJ: Lawrence Erlbaum.

Glynn, S., and D. Muth. 1994. Reading and writing to learn science: Achieving scientific literacy. *Journal of Research in Science Teaching* 31 (9): 1057–1073.

Guthrie, J., W. Schafer, and C. Huang. 2001. Benefits of opportunity to read and balanced instruction on the NAEP. *The Journal of Educational Research* (Jan./Feb.): 145–162.

Harvey, S. A., and A. Goudvis. 2000. *Strategies that work: Teaching comprehension to enhance understanding.* Portland, ME: Stenhouse.

Holliday, W. G., L. D. Yore, and D. E. Alvermann. 1994. The reading-science-learning-writing connection: Breakthroughs, barriers, and promises. *Journal of Research in Science Teaching* 31: 877–893.

Holloway, J. 2002. Integrating literacy with content. *Educational Leadership* (Nov.): 87–88.

Hunter, M. 1984. Knowing, teaching, and supervising. In *Using what we know about teaching,* ed. P. Hosford, pp. 169–192. Alexandria, VA: Association for Supervision and Curriculum Development.

Keene, E., and S. Zimmerman. 1997. *Mosaic of thought: Teaching comprehension in a reader's workshop.* Portsmouth, NH: Heinemann.

Klentschy, M. P., and E. Molina-De La Torre. 2004. Students' science notebooks and the inquiry process. In *Crossing borders in literacy and science instruction: Perspectives on theory and practice,* ed. E. W. Saul. Newark, DE: International Reading Association.

Lowery, L. 1998. How the new science curriculums reflect brain research. *Educational Leadership* (Nov.): 26–28.

Marzano, R., D. Pickering, and J. Pollock. 2000. *Classroom instruction that works: Research-based strategies for increasing student achievement.* Alexandria, VA: Association for Supervision and Curriculum Development.

National Research Council (NRC). 1996. *National science education standards.* Washington, DC: National Academy Press.

National Research Council (NRC). 2000. *Inquiry and the national science education standards: A guide for teaching and learning.* Washington, DC: National Academy Press.

Rumelhart, D. 2004. Toward an interactive model of reading. In *Theoretical models and processes of reading,* eds. R. Ruddell and N. Unrau. Newark, DE: International Reading Association.

Wolfe, P. 2001. *Brain matters: Translating research into classroom practice.* Alexandria, VA: Association for Supervision and Curriculum Development.

Yore, L., M. Craig, and T. Maguire. 1998. Index of science reading awareness: An interactive-constructive model, test verification, and grades 4–8 results. *Journal of Research in Science* Teaching 35 (1): 24–27.

Zimmerman, S., and C. Hutchins. 2003. *7 keys to comprehension: How to help your kids read it and get it!* Three Rivers, MI: Three Rivers Press.

Writing to Learn: Science Notebooks, a Valuable Tool to Support Nonfiction Modes/Genres of Writing

Marleen Kotelman, Toni Saccani, and Joan Gilbert
Tucson, Arizona, Unified School District

As teachers across the content areas build their repertoires of and expertise in writing instruction, students have more opportunities to develop, strengthen, and deepen their writing skills, as well as to understand content. Writing skills have become gateways to academic success, from young children learning how to write a personal narrative, to older students writing persuasive text to influence societal issues. Students must be involved in writing every day. As Zinsser (2001) states, "You learn to write by writing" (p. 49). And students must be familiar with multiple genres (or modes) of writing in order to select a mode that will suit their purpose for writing.

As is well-known today, students' writing skills across the nation are dismal. According to *Reading Today* (IRA 2003), National Assessment of Educational Progress (NAEP) results indicate that virtually one student in five, in grades 4, 8, and 12, produces completely unsatisfactory prose, about 50% meet "basic" requirements, and only one in five can be called "proficient." Strong recommendations are outlined in *The Neglected "R": The Need for a Writing Revolution* (National Commission on Writing 2003) report; the amount of time and money devoted to writing must be dramatically increased, and writing must be required in every curriculum at all grade levels. The NAEP findings necessitate compelling measures to change the status quo, with increased professional development that provides teachers at all grade levels with skills to teach writing across content areas. Unacceptable achievement in writing should drive all educators to work toward change.

The change that is most needed comes in the realization that writing improves learning in all areas. When students increase their writing abilities, they increase their ability to think and reason. McLaughlin and Vogt (2000) state it well:

> [W]riting is considerably more than a way to record and demonstrate knowledge. Writing is, most importantly, a way of knowing, a way of working through confusion and fuzzy ideas and moving toward clarification and articulation of knowledge. Writers literally achieve insight in the act of writing; new ideas come as we write and from what we write. (p. 283)

For students to have a deep understanding of science content, it is imperative that they develop and refine thoughts through their writing.

With the urgent need to provide writing opportunities in all content areas, teachers may ask what writing opportunities are natural parts of science investigations. How do students engage with scientific learning in a written form? As demonstrated in the real world, scientists have many opportunities for writing. In fact, there are virtually no instances when scientists do not write in some form or fashion. Field notebooks documenting observations, journal articles citing research and new questions, lab reports that outline specific procedures—all these are authentic writing activities natural to science.

Science notebooks are an integral component of a successful science program. Recent research shows that student understanding and literacy skills improve when doing hands-on, minds-on science and using notebooks to make sense of their science (e.g., Klentschy 2005). Writing in notebooks allows students to explore their own thinking as they describe, explain, formulate, persuade, and question scientific experiences and phenomena.

CHAPTER 6

In Tucson Unified School District, where K–8 classrooms use a hands-on program, teachers find notebooks do indeed support student understanding and literacy skills. Using predominately FOSS (Full Option Science System) curriculum, students combine notebook use with the investigations to plan, organize, and record information in a variety of formats.

With the various interpretations of what a science notebook is, clarification is needed. A science notebook is a tool that provides students a place to record their thinking and their learning before, during, and after a science investigation. It reflects a chronological accounting of the progression of an investigation as the student records questions, materials, procedures, observations, data, explanations, and reflections. It is a silent companion, a "back pocket" tool that can be referred to and reread throughout a unit of study. As a working document, the science notebook is a rough draft whose primary audience is the student. Notebooks are essential for students to "mess about" with their thinking which then leads to learning. Learning comes from the processing of experience rather than the experience itself (Garmston 1997).

Science notebook writing allows children to communicate their observations and ideas while building and reinforcing their understanding of key science concepts. It is a tool students can use to

- organize thoughts and information,
- reflect,
- refer to (available for recall and later use in reporting and discussions),
- self-assess,
- view their developmental progression through an investigation,
- record ideas and questions for future study or inquiry,
- use as a resource for the creation of a final product or presentational writing, and
- develop a habit of mind in using writing as a thinking tool.

Science notebook entries provide opportunities for writing in various modes while learning science. While these nonfiction modes should be explicitly taught during language arts, they are reinforced in the context of doing science, giving meaning and purpose to the writing. This chapter will use descriptive, explanatory, procedural, recount, and persuasive modes to describe the modes of science writing.

When Do Various Writing Opportunities Occur in Science?

Most educators are comfortable with students recording data and writing conclusions. A few still view writing opportunities in the science notebook in the traditional lab format of the "scientific method." Those are but a few of the opportunities for students to use writing as a thinking and learning tool. Table 1 lists writing opportunities and strategies from lessons and investigations that were created by teachers. The lists are lengthy but not exhaustive. Writing opportunities are virtually endless depending not only

TABLE 1 Writing Opportunities and Strategies in Science

Before an Investigation	During an Investigation	After an Investigation
• Activate current knowledge and make personal connections (Quick Write*, Carousel Brainstorming*, Sort Cards or Pictures*, KWL*)	• Data	• Findings/Results
	• Observations	• Conclusions
	• Lists	• Summaries of Learning (3..2..1*, Ticket to Leave*, The Important Thing*)
	• Drawings	
• Set a purpose for learning (Anticipation Guide*, inquiry/investigation question, and student questions)	• Descriptions	• Reflections
	• Questions	• Further Questions
	• Notes	• Graphic Organizers
• Predict what will happen and why	• Graphic Organizers	• Presentational Writing
	• Reflections	• Reports
• Record ideas while messing about with the materials or a phenomenon connected to the investigation		• Letters
		• Poetry, Songs
• Plan and develop procedures		

* Indicates that the strategy is described in the Appendix on pages 159–160.

on the student's learning of science but also on the teacher's awareness and use of the science experience to provide writing contexts.

What Modes Are Reinforced When Writing in Science?

The status of writing at the national level, as reported in *The Neglected "R"* (National Commission on Writing 2003), is reflected similarly at the state level, prompting many states to revise writing standards, placing a heavier emphasis on nonfiction writing. Researchers have found in their work that 86% of reading and writing used each day to access and communicate information is nonfiction (Duke and Bennett-Armistead 2003). This focus on nonfiction writing in state standards will better prepare students for the kind of writing they will use daily as adults.

Mirroring the type of writing that scientists do, students engage in a variety of nonfiction writing modes when writing in a science notebook. Nonfiction texts have a recognizable structure and language that changes according to the social purpose of the text (Derewianka 1999). The guiding principle in determining the mode of writing is purpose. Helping students become familiar with the structure and language of the various modes will support them as they write in their science notebooks.

The Descriptive Mode

Just as scientists write technical descriptions, students write descriptions based on their observations. Whether describing the rock samples they are studying, or plant growth, students record factual information when systematically describing things.

Descriptive writing in science can be used to create a vivid impression of an object, event, or phenomenon. In terms of structure, this mode of writing begins with an opening general introduction. A body composed of various aspects of the topic follows this. It often concludes with a summarizing comment. The language of descriptive writing is generally present tense, does not use chronological order, focuses on generic participants, and depends on the use of precise and factual, rather than imaginative, vocabulary. It allows the writer to show rather than tell about a thing (see Figure 1).

The Explanatory Mode

Students use an explanatory mode of writing in their notebooks when giving an account of how something works or why something happens. Fifth graders studying landforms write explanatory text discussing why they

---

FIGURE 1 Student Sample of Descriptive Writing

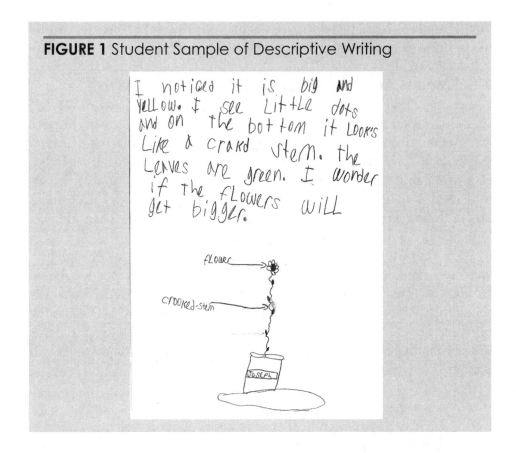

think the river flowed the way it did (their claim or inference) based on evidence (observations) they have gathered during the investigation. They build their explanation based on a sequence of events that support the cause-and-effect relationship that they have determined exists.

In scientific writing nothing is more important than the quality of explanatory writing. An explanation provides an objective, balanced, and factual response to the questions "how" and "why." It answers the questions in sufficient detail, with clarity, and often in a logical sequence. Scientific explanations usually begin with a definition or statement about the phenomenon. The second part of the explanation explains the how or why. It may end with a summary statement. Language features of an explanatory text include generalized nonhuman participants, cause-and-effect relationships, time relationships, and action verbs that convey material processes (see Figure 2).

FIGURE 2 Student Sample of Explanatory Writing

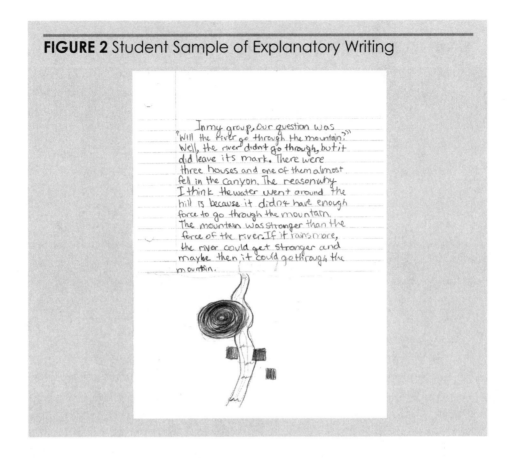

The Procedural Mode

Procedural writing occurs when students develop plans to carry out investigations to answer their questions. First they list materials they will use; then they write out their plans as a sequence of actions or steps they will follow. A fourth-grade student's question about crayfish habitat preferences will lead to writing a procedural text in which students will outline the actions that will be taken to investigate the question.

Procedural writing in science—telling how to follow a set of procedures—needs to be clear, concise writing that is accurate and gives specific information. The information in procedural writing is presented in a logical sequence of events that is broken up into small sequenced steps. The first part of a procedural text states what is to be achieved. A listing of materials needed follows. A series of sequenced steps or instructions is next. There may be a final step, which is how to evaluate whether or not the procedure was successful. Features of the language of the procedural mode

FIGURE 3 Student Sample of Procedural Writing

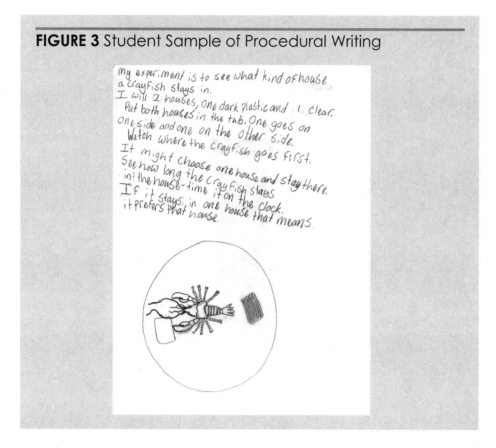

> My experiment is to see what kind of house a crayfish stays in.
> I will 2 houses, One dark plastic and 1 clear.
> Put both houses in the tub. One goes on one side and one on the other side.
> Watch where the crayfish goes first.
> It might choose one house and stay there.
> See how long the crayfish stays in the house—time it on the clock.
> If it stays in one house that means it prefers that house.

include generalized participants, simple present tense, mainly action verbs, and linking words having to do with time (see Figure 3).

The Recount Mode

Recount, a form of narrative writing, is probably the most commonly used form of writing for beginning young scientists. Starting from a very young age, students naturally favor the personal narrative mode of writing. In fact, there is a natural tendency when writing about an investigation in science notebooks for students to basically retell what happened during the investigation. Following an orderly sequenced structure, a second-grade student writes what he did *first, next,* and then *finally,* when, for instance, investigating air using a vial, paper towel, and tub of water.

There are different types of recounts. In science writing students generate factual recounts, retelling in chronological order an event or series of events that took place during their science investigation. A recount begins with an opening statement that provides background information. Events

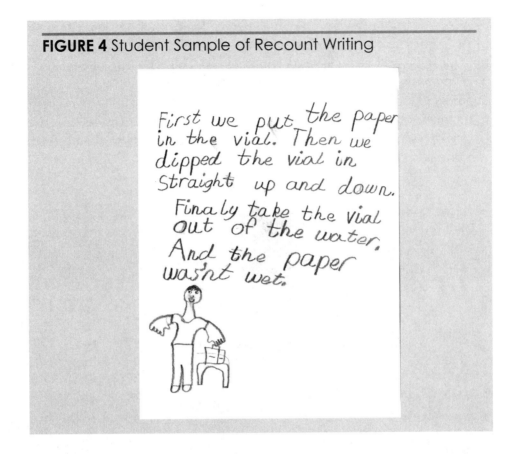

FIGURE 4 Student Sample of Recount Writing

that occurred are described in sequential order. The ending may describe the outcome of the investigation. Recounts are written in the past tense. Events are described using action verbs and words that link events in time (see Figure 4).

The Persuasive Mode

Scientists use persuasive writing to convince their readers that their claims are supported by evidence and are therefore reasonable. Students use observations (qualitative and quantitative data) from their science notebooks as evidence to develop a logical argument that justifies their claim. By providing supportive factual evidence, students hope to convince the reader to think in a certain way. Second graders studying air and weather write a persuasive text to convince readers that they know air takes up space (their claim or inference), based on evidence (observations) they gathered during a series of investigations.

When writing persuasive text in science, logical reasoning is the main focus. To present a logical argument from a particular point of view, students must develop and provide supporting details. The structure of persuasive writing consists of an opening statement of position, followed by a series of points supported by evidence. The writing concludes with a summary or restatement of the opening position. Persuasive text is generally written in timeless present tense, the focus is on generalized participants, and strong effective adjectives are used (see Figure 5).

FIGURE 5 Student Sample of Persuasive Writing

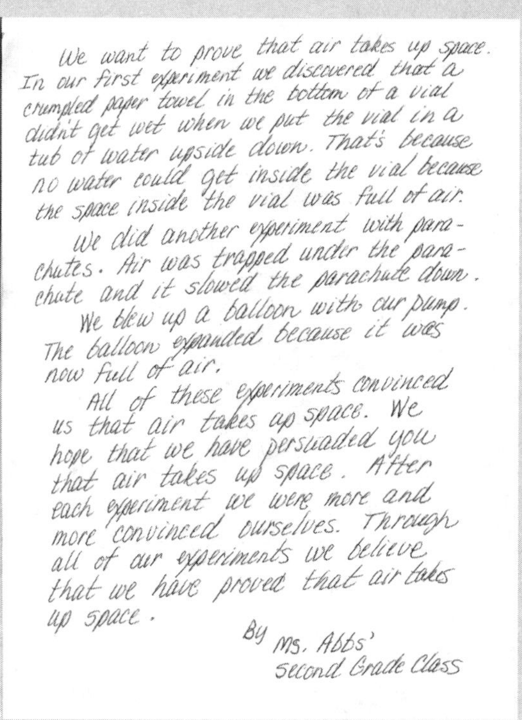

We want to prove that air takes up space. In our first experiment we discovered that a crumpled paper towel in the bottom of a vial didn't get wet when we put the vial in a tub of water upside down. That's because no water could get inside the vial because the space inside the vial was full of air.

We did another experiment with parachutes. Air was trapped under the parachute and it slowed the parachute down.

We blew up a balloon with our pump. The balloon expanded because it was now full of air.

All of these experiments convinced us that air takes up space. We hope that we have persuaded you that air takes up space. After each experiment we were more and more convinced ourselves. Through all of our experiments we believe that we have proved that air takes up space.

By Ms. Abbs' Second Grade Class

Yore (2004) writes, "Scientists as writers are involved in a variety of writing tasks to meet their responsibilities and purposes..." (p. 80). To model the writing practices of scientists, it is important to have students engage in similar writing practices. Understanding and using the structure and language of the various tasks (modes) help students clearly express their thinking. Science notebooks provide an ideal place for students to practice writing modes in an authentic context.

How Can Teachers Ensure That Students Learn the Different Modes of Writing?

Because elementary students have limited experience with nonfiction modes of writing, it is of critical importance that these modes are systematically and explicitly taught during language arts. An approach to teaching nonfiction writing to students revolves around a supportive structure called *scaffolding* (Wood, Bruner, and Ross 1976). Scaffolding is a support to student learning that involves actions and structures that are intentional, temporary, and flexible. The amount and nature of the support teachers offer students will enable students to develop confidence and competence as they gradually begin taking on more responsibility for their own learning.

Scaffolding begins with modeling, followed by guided practice, leading to independent practice and finally student independence. This support structure begins with modeling because as Scott (1993) writes, "The modeling of various language forms in science helps students not only gain scientific knowledge, but also gain knowledge of how language works, and how to use language to write and learn" (p. 42).

Writing in science using the various nonfiction writing modes requires a way of thinking that may be entirely new to students. Teachers wanting students to write, for example, a thorough explanation of a science investigation will have better results if they have first modeled this type of writing for their students. The next step is for students and teacher to construct explanations together through shared writing. When students begin to demonstrate an understanding of the language and structure of this mode of writing, they are then ready to write independently.

Appendix
Writing Strategies in Science

Quick-Write
The teacher poses a question, problem, or prompt and students write for a short, specific amount of time, perhaps several minutes, about a designated topic related to the lesson.

Carousel Brainstorming
Prompts or questions related to the topic of study are placed on charts on the walls around the room. In groups, with each group using a different colored marking pen,

students rotate around the room brainstorming and writing responses to each posted question or prompt.

Sort Cards or Pictures

Working with 6–12 teacher-selected words/pictures from an investigation to be completed or a text/article to be read, students (with a partner or in groups) classify or group the words/pictures in any way they think they relate or go together. Students take turns sharing a group of words/pictures and explaining why they put them together. Then students engage in the investigation and/or read the text, then re-sort their words/pictures if necessary.

KWL

- To activate prior knowledge, students ask themselves, "What do I know?"
- To set a purpose, students ask themselves, "What do I want to know?"
- To reflect on new learning, students ask themselves, "What did I learn?"

Anticipation Guide

The teacher reads four to six statements about a topic the students will be investigating. Working with a partner or in a group, after each statement is read, the students react and discuss in their group (or with a partner) whether the statement is true or false. Before the teacher reads the next statement, students share out their thinking (and their reasons for thinking that way). Finally, students engage in an investigation, then read the follow-up text to corroborate their pre-investigation/reading stance for the statements.

3...2...1

At the end of an investigation, students write three facts they've learned, two terms they want to remember, and one question they have.

Ticket to Leave

Upon the conclusion of an investigation, on a half sheet of paper that looks like a ticket, students write something about the lesson just taught—a summary statement, a reflection, a question, or a point that was confusing. Then this information can be used as a review at the beginning of the next investigation.

The Important Thing

At the completion of an investigation, students record several facts they learned. As in Margaret Wise Brown's *The Important Book*, they then identify one fact as the "most important (significant) thing" to remember.

References

Derewianka, B. 1999. *Exploring how texts work*. Sydney, Australia: Primary English Teaching Association.

Duke, N., and S. Bennett-Armistead. 2003. *Reading and writing informational text in the primary grades: Research-based practices*. New York: Scholastic.

Garmston, R. 1997. Presentation at Conference on Cognitive Coaching, Tucson, AZ (Feb.).

International Reading Association (IRA). 2003. Report calls for "a writing revolution." *Reading Today* 20 (6).

Klentschy, M. 2005. Science notebook essentials: A guide to effective notebook components. *Science and Children* 43 (3): 24–27.

McLaughlin, M., and M. Vogt. 2000. *Creativity and innovation in content area teaching*. Norwood, MA: Christopher-Gordon.

National Commission on Writing. 2003. *The neglected "r": The need for a writing revolution*. Available at *www.writingcommission.org*.

National Assessment of Educational Progress (NAEP). *Nation's report card*. Available at *www.nces.ed.gov/nationsreportcard/naepdata*.

Scott, J. 1993. *Science and language links: Classroom implications*. Portsmouth, NH: Heinemann.

Wood, D., J. Bruner, and G. Ross. 1976. The role of tutoring in problem solving. *Journal of Child Psychology and Psychiatry* 17: 89–100.

Yore, L. D. 2004. Why do future scientists need to study the language arts? In *Crossing borders in literacy and science instruction: Perspectives on theory and practice*, ed. E. W. Saul, 71–94. Newark, DE: International Reading Association.

Zinsser, W. 2001. *On writing well*. New York: HarperCollins.

Practitioner Resources

Brown, M. W. 1977. *The important book*. New York: HarperCollins.

Buss, K., and L. Karnowski. 2002. *Reading and writing nonfiction genres*. Newark, DE: International Reading Association.

Campbell, B., and L. Fulton. 2003. *Science notebooks: Writing about inquiry*. Portsmouth, NH: Heinemann.

Stead, T. 2002. *Is that a fact? Teaching nonfiction writing K–3*. Portland, ME: Stenhouse.

CHAPTER 7

Supporting Middle School Students in Developing Scientific Explanations

LeeAnn M. Sutherland, Katherine L. McNeill, and Joseph S. Krajcik
The University of Michigan
Kalonda Colson
Detroit Public Schools

To participate fully in scientific inquiry, students must be able to engage in a variety of practices. Among them, students must be able to ask researchable questions; generate hypotheses; collect, represent, and analyze data; interpret results; use evidence to construct and evaluate explanations; and communicate findings.

In the context of a large urban school district, our team of university researchers and classroom teachers has undertaken a collaborative effort to support students as they engage in these practices. Scientific explanation has been one focus of our work in an effort to help students think more deeply about science concepts and to communicate their understanding in writing. Elsewhere (Moje et al. 2004; Sutherland et al. 2006; Sutherland et al. 2003; McNeill and Krajcik, forthcoming; McNeill et al., under review), we have outlined a systematic approach to teaching middle school students to construct scientific explanations that include appropriate claims, relevant evidence, and logical reasoning. In this chapter, we illustrate that approach using examples from a seventh-grade chemistry curriculum, "How can I make new stuff from old stuff?" Although our research is done in the context of curricula we have created and professional development activities we have conducted, we have also found the framework to be useable by other teachers, in other classrooms, using other curricula, as well.

The Role of Scientific Explanation in Inquiry

Historically, science has been portrayed in classrooms as a body of facts to be memorized. In reality, science is not only a knowledge base but also a way of thinking and reasoning about the natural world (Alberts 2000). Incorporating scientific inquiry into classroom science encourages this shift away from memorization to a focus on scientific practices and discourse. Driver, Newton, and Osborne (2000) indicate that having students engage in practices that align with those of real scientists not only provides students with a more accurate image of science, but it can also benefit their learning of science concepts and processes. A core activity of scientists, as the authors describe, is the construction of scientific arguments or explanations.

In *Science for All Americans*, the American Association for the Advancement of Science (AAAS) argues that "[t]here are…certain features of science that give it a distinctive character as a mode of inquiry. Although those features are especially characteristic of the work of professional scientists, everyone can exercise them in thinking scientifically about many matters of interest in everyday life" (1990, p. 4). Specifically, in its *Benchmarks for Science Literacy*, AAAS indicates that while not all scientific inquiry is undertaken in an identical manner, "Scientific investigations usually involve the collection of relevant evidence, the use of logical reasoning, and the application of imagination in devising hypotheses and explanations to make sense of the collected evidence" (1993, p.12). The National Research Council's (NRC) National Science Education Standards also indicate that students must be able to "Think critically and logically to make the relationships between evidence and explanation" (1996, p. 145). In particular, "Scientific explanations emphasize evidence, have logically consistent arguments, and use scientific principles, models and theories" (1996, p. 148). Although the NRC and AAAS envision a scientifically literate nation, and they provide some guidelines for how that might be achieved, it is classroom teachers who must make that vision a reality.

Developing scientific explanations is difficult work for students. They need to learn science content at the same time that they learn how to reason and to write in new ways. In an effort to reduce the complexity of the writing task (Quintana et al. 2004), we have designed a framework for students' construction of scientific explanations. We have also developed guidelines for teachers that include strategies for teaching explanations. Herein, we describe a systematic approach to teaching scientific explanations that has been successfully used with students across a range of achievement levels in rural, urban, and suburban schools.

The student examples used in this chapter are taken from the seventh-grade chemistry unit test on which students are given a data table containing information about the density, color, mass, and melting points of four unknown liquids. The question tests students' understanding of *substances* and *properties* as revealed in their response to an open-ended item: "Write a *scientific explanation* that states whether any of the liquids are the same substance" (see Figure 1).

FIGURE 1 Data Table from a Seventh-Grade Chemistry Unit Test

Instructions: Examine the following data table. Then, write a **scientific explanation** that states whether any of the liquids are the same substance.

	Density	Color	Mass	Melting Point
Liquid 1	0.93 g/cm3	no color	38 g	–98°C
Liquid 2	0.79 g/cm3	no color	38 g	26°C
Liquid 3	13.6 g/cm3	silver	21 g	–39°C
Liquid 4	0.93 g/cm3	no color	16 g	–98°C

Components of a Scientific Explanation

Our guidelines for creating explanations specify three components that a writer must include in a scientific explanation: 1. Make a *claim* about the problem, 2. Provide *evidence* for the claim, and 3. Show *reasoning* that links the evidence to the claim. One student's response to the test question, shown in Figure 2, illustrates what we consider to be a strong effort. In the following section, we describe each component of a scientific explanation in greater detail, using this student's work to anchor the discussion.

FIGURE 2 Example of Strong Student Explanation

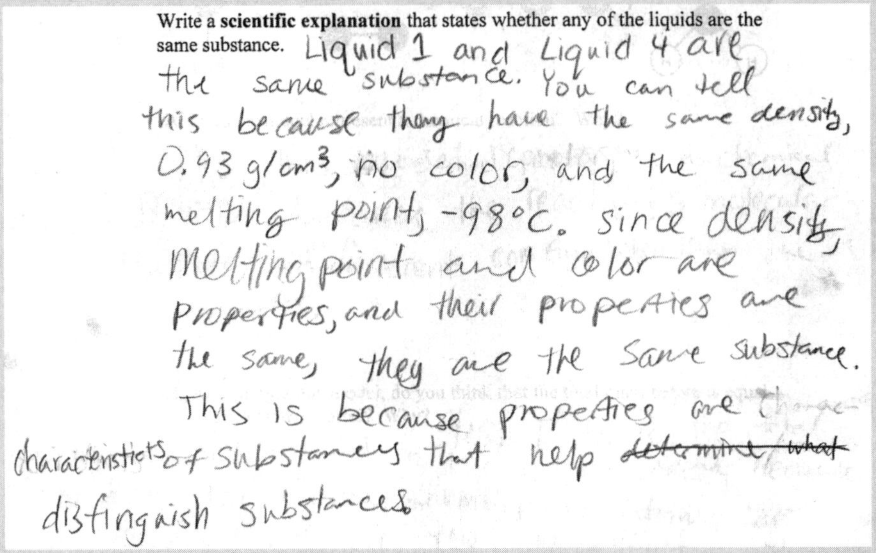

Write a **scientific explanation** that states whether any of the liquids are the same substance. Liquid 1 and Liquid 4 are the same substance. You can tell this because they have the same density, 0.93 g/cm³, no color, and the same melting point, −98°C. Since density, melting point and color are properties, and their properties are the same, they are the same substance. This is because properties are those characteristics of substances that help ~~determine what~~ distinguish substances

The Claim

We define *claim* as a statement of one's understanding about a phenomenon, about the results of an investigation or experiment, or about other data. A claim can be stated in a complete sentence. In order to make the teaching of this process easier for students, teachers initially teach that the claim must be the first sentence in an explanation. When a specific question is asked, the claim is likely a response to that question. When an investigation has independent and dependent variables, the claim must describe the relationship between those variables. In the example given, the student is asked whether any of four unknown liquids, whose properties are described in a table, are the same substance. After analyzing the data presented, he concludes that "Liquid 1 and Liquid 4 are the same substance." This statement is his claim.

Evidence That Supports the Claim

Raw data, whether generated by students or by another source, become evidence when they are used to support a particular claim. Data can originate in investigations one conducts or observations one makes, or in reports of research others have done. The earliest, simplest explanations students encounter as they learn to write explanations purposefully have very limited evidence, such as the observations made in a single experiment or a simple demonstration. Although simple activities have been found to be helpful as students learn the process of writing a scientific explanation, they learn in time that one piece of evidence, such as a single trial in an experiment, is insufficient for scientists to make and defend a claim.

In fact, *sufficiency* and *appropriateness* are key aspects of the evidence component of a scientific explanation. The student responding to the test question above provides a relatively complete statement of the evidence: "You can tell [two liquids are the same substance] because they have the same density, 0.93 g/cm^3, no color, and the same melting point, –98°C." Had the student written only about the two liquids' density, the evidence would have been appropriate for the claim, but not sufficient. Had the student written about mass as an indicator that the liquids are the same substance, the evidence would not have been appropriate, as mass is not a characteristic property of substances. Had the student indicated that Liquid 1 has a density of 0.93 g/cm^3, no color, and the same melting point, –98°C, and Liquid 4 has a density of 0.93 g/cm^3, no color, and the same melting point, –98°C, the data would have been appropriate (the "right" data to answer the question) but not sufficiently marshaled as evidence for the claim.

We teach students that data must be interpreted, not simply translated from chart or graphic form into sentence form. It is not sufficient to list data without making clear what those data mean in relation to the original question and to the claim. Because the test question asks students to compare four liquids in a chart, the student must tell what the data mean in relation to that question, as this student does when he makes the comparison, "they have the same [density, color, and melting point]."

It is also important to note that as students are asked to conduct increasingly complex inquiry activities, it is likely that not all data they generate, nor all data represented in a table or graph they are asked to interpret, relate to the original research question posed, hypothesis put forth, or the claim being made. In such cases, only *some* data are relevant to a particular claim. Students need a great deal of practice marshaling data as evidence, however, before they encounter intricate data sets.

Reasoning That Links the Evidence to the Claim
Reasoning is complex and is consistently the most difficult aspect of explanation writing to teach. It is through reasoning that an individual justifies the data used to support the claim, and in so doing, the data become evi-

dence. Reasoning involves building a logical argument about the relationship between the claim and evidence, showing how the connections follow logically from scientific principles.

What does this mean for seventh graders, and how does a teacher support middle school students in developing this understanding? We break reasoning down into two parts. First, reasoning requires relating *scientific principles*—accepted understandings in science—to the question the student is answering or investigating in order to show how the data support the claim. In the example above, the student employs the scientific principle "Properties are characteristicts of substances that help distinguish substances" as the understanding that undergirds his decision to focus his explanation on *properties*. Reasoning also requires showing *how* a particular principle connects particular evidence to a particular claim. The student does this when he writes, in addition to the above, "Since density, melting point and color are properties, and their properties are the same, they are the same substance." The quality of a student's reasoning is evident in both the manner in which he or she constructs an explanation and in the content of that explanation.

Many teachers in our work have found the word *reasoning* to be difficult language for their students. When teachers first taught reasoning as a way to *link* the evidence to the claim, several found that the change in word choice did not significantly improve students' understanding of *reasoning*. Teachers then tried the analogy of reasoning as a *bridge* that connects the evidence to the claim. Most report that their students better understand the function of reasoning in an explanation when they think of it as making a bridge, yet some still find *linking* or *connecting* more useful. Regardless of the language used by the individual teacher, who can best adapt the framework to his or her own students, most important is that students understand how a claim, evidence, and reasoning work together in a well-constructed scientific explanation.

Other Aspects of Writing

Other aspects of writing to which many teachers attend are not components of scientific explanations per se but are important in all scientific writing. It is essential, for example, that writers use precise and accurate scientific language. Writing "It went from 96 to 100" is not as precise and scientifically accurate as "The temperature increased from 96° to 100° Fahrenheit." Another aspect of all writing that can be honed as students write scientific explanations is attention to audience. Explanations should be detailed

enough that someone not present at the time of an investigation could understand, at least on a cursory level, what took place. In its most simple sense, this requires attention to pronoun use. In the example, "It went from 96 to 100," the word "it" does not clearly signal to an audience unfamiliar with the investigation that the numbers refer to temperatures. Without such precision, a reader might imagine the numbers to represent a 1–100 scale, to represent volume, or to represent area.

Students must use the language of science in order to develop facility with that language. Explanation writing is one way in which they can attend to scientific language closely and can practice using it in written form. In our work, teachers are consistently encouraged by the progress of each individual student. Even those students who initially struggle to write a sentence or two learn to generate clearer sentences within more coherent paragraphs.

Looking at the Components in the Context of Weaker Explanations
During the time of our research project, we have consistently seen that students learn to write claims relatively easily. Standardized test questions, which often ask, "What can you conclude?", are one context in which writing only a claim is an important skill. But a complete explanation involves more, and it is the other components that are the most difficult to teach and to learn. Below are examples of two students' weaker explanations (Figures 3a and 3b), also written in response to the test question in Figure 1.

Both examples contain an adequate and appropriate claim: Liquid[s] 1 and 4 are the same substance[s]. The first example, however, does not include appropriate data as evidence. The student indicates that having the same properties means that two unknown substances must be the same substance, but his explanation, as written, does not incorporate the appropriate data from the table, such as melting point or density. The student's response suggests an understanding that even though the mass of the two liquids is different ("mass changes"), it is not important for determining whether the two liquids are a substance. But the response does not tell the teacher whether the student thinks mass is a property, whether he thinks mass must be different for two substances to be the same, or what he actually understands a property to be. The student's understanding of the applicable scientific principle—substances have characteristic properties that help to distinguish one substance from another—is evident to some degree in his statement: "Substances are anything made of

FIGURE 3a Example of Weaker Student Explanation

Write a **scientific explanation** that states whether any of the liquids are the same substance.

Liquids 1 and 4 are the same substances. Substances are anything made of 1 material throughout. I know they are the same substances because their properties are the same. I also know that they are the same substances because there mass is different and mass changes. Therefore, two of the liquids above are the same.

FIGURE 3b Example of Weaker Student Explanation

Write a **scientific explanation** that states whether any of the liquids are the same substance.

Liquid 1 and 4 are the same substance. they are the same substance because they have the same density, which is .93g/cm³. Both substances also have the same melting point which is -98°C.
My reasoning for stating this is because Liquid 1 and 4 have the same density + melting point.

1 material throughout. I know they are the same substances because their properties are the same."

In the second example, the writer provides appropriate data from the table, and her explanation likely illustrates an understanding that an explanation must incorporate more than one piece of data as evidence for a claim. However, we would consider the evidence insufficient because the writer does not talk about color, and information about color is available in the table. The writer has also not shown that she understands the applicable scientific principle. A teacher might assume from the statement "My reasoning for stating this is because Liquid 1 and 4 have the same density and melting point" that the student understands density and melting point to be significant in distinguishing substances. Yet the teacher cannot assume that the student understands "all substances have characteristic properties," which is a key learning goal of the unit as specified in national science education standards.

It should be noted that many of the students in the classrooms in which we work write explanations that are far weaker than either of these examples. These were taken from posttest responses, written after several weeks of writing explanations. It may be that a teacher looks at the examples we have identified as "weaker," and thinks, "I'd be happy if my students wrote like these weaker examples!" Many students, in fact, do not write explanations of this caliber even at the end of the school year. However, regardless of the relative strength or weakness of the explanations they write, students who are taught using this framework *improve* their understanding and their ability to communicate that understanding in writing.

Supporting Students' Construction of Scientific Explanations

Most of the middle school students with whom we work find constructing scientific explanations difficult. They require support in terms of when and how to use the claim/evidence/reasoning framework. Rooted in learning research, literacy research, and teachers' experience with this framework, a number of instructional strategies have been shown to help students gain facility with this inquiry practice. To support students in developing scientific explanations, researchers and classroom teachers developed a series of what we call "guidelines for teaching scientific explanations." Those guidelines and a number of strategies are the focus of this section.

Access Students' Prior Knowledge About Explanations
Students are aware of many instances in which people are called upon to explain. It is important to use what students know about everyday uses of

explanation to help them think about what distinguishes *scientific explanations*. Teachers who have used this process begin by asking students to think about and describe instances that they need to explain in their everyday lives. Students must explain to a parent why they are arriving home later than the curfew, or they sort out a misunderstanding with a friend by explaining what happened from their perspective. They might explain how to play a new videogame or how to do story problems as they help a younger sibling with math. Because students already have an everyday meaning for *explain*, they fit scientific explanation in that framework. If a teacher can help students to analyze those everyday explanations, to think about which ones require facts or other evidence, to think about how an explanation typically begins, and to think about which are considered "good explanations" and which are not, they can help build a foundation from which to construct an understanding of explanations as having particular requirements in scientific discourse.

This step primarily involves *conversation* about explanations and may be done in a single class session. It is also an ideal conversation in which to distinguish opinion-based from evidence-based explanations. "Here's why I think Singer X is better than Singer Z" relies on opinion. One could argue, based on CD sales or concert attendance, that Singer X seems to be more popular, but that does not make him or her "better." Automobile B might get better gas mileage and higher scores on safety tests than Automobile D, but I still might consider Automobile D better because it's far more comfortable for me to drive. Many teachers create such examples as an opportunity to help students think more deeply about what distinguishes fact from opinion, to think about what counts as "fact" in science, and to consider what kind of claim can be legitimately made based on particular data.

Generate Criteria for Explanations

Although teachers have in mind the claim/evidence/reasoning framework, many guide students to generate those components inductively, by considering multiple explanations and determining "what counts" in a scientific explanation. The claim/evidence/reasoning framework can be given to students without involving them in generating it collectively; however, students have a deeper understanding of why the components matter, and they have more buy-in to the importance of the components when they have worked to generate them as a class. Students will likely generate names for the components other than *claim*, *evidence*, and *reasoning*, and the teacher can either suggest these words by linking them to those the students generate or choose to use different words instead. Whether students learn to "make a statement about the problem or the question" or to "write a claim" is less important than that they understand why this component is essential in a scientific explanation.

Make the Framework Explicit

Teachers typically post a description of the three components in their classrooms for ongoing reference during instruction. One caveat inherent in teaching the components, however, is that it is easy for students to lose sight of explanations as a *whole*. Explanation writing could become a simple algorithm, a series of formulaic steps that, completed in sequence, create an explanation. Writing an explanation might also become a sentence completion activity (e.g., "My claim is…") in which students do not learn to think about how an explanation, as a whole, serves to answer an initial question, to speak to a hypothesis, or to communicate findings. Instead, they only learn that they need to write about three different parts. While naming and describing the components guides students in construction, and the quality of each individual component can be evaluated, it is important for teachers to help students move (cognitively) back and forth between the parts and the whole of scientific explanation. Teachers need to encourage evaluation, for example, of how a piece of written text—as a whole—functions as an explanation of a particular phenomenon.

Model the Construction of Explanations

Wherever possible and appropriate, teachers should create opportunities to model explanation construction orally and in writing. A think-aloud process that makes a teacher's thought processes visible helps students to understand what a writer does as she constructs an explanation. For example, after completing an investigation to determine whether boiling water is a chemical reaction, a teacher can demonstrate appropriate scientific explanation construction orally, in writing, or both. She might write an explanation on an overhead transparency, verbalizing what she is thinking as she writes. She might say aloud, "Well, I know it isn't a chemical reaction because a chemical reaction means I would have different substances, but I don't. I had H_2O molecules in the form of liquid water when I started, and the liquid I collected after I boiled it was still water because it was still made of H_2O molecules all the way through. Now, how do I write that as an explanation? First, I need to say that boiling water is not a chemical reaction [writing 'Boiling water is not a chemical reaction' as she talks]. That'll be my claim. Now, what's my evidence?" This kind of talk can easily move between the whole (the "big picture" of the investigation) and the components (naming each as it is written), modeling for students how to think about an investigation, how to think about and incorporate scientific principles, and how to construct a scientific explanation that communicates one's understanding to others.

It is also important for students to see models of good explanations so that they know the goal toward which they are aiming. Often, teachers are hesitant to give models (examples) because they do not want students simply to mimic the examples as they write. However, there are particular rules for many types of writing (e.g., a lab report or a newspaper story), and it is important not only to learn the rules but to see what writing looks like when it is done effectively. Students need to see models of good explanations so that they can have a sense of both the components and a sense of how they should work together as a whole.

Provide Students With Practice Opportunities

Practice is essential, and many students will need a great deal of practice to become proficient explanation writers. In fact, although students will end the school year better writers than they were when they began, different content, different types of data, and different types of problems or questions will require somewhat different shaping of an explanation. Students are differently successful in applying the framework across contexts. Teachers should consider explanation writing as a long-term process that will likely require more than one unit and, in fact, may require an entire school year in order for some students to develop relative proficiency.

There are many ways to provide practice opportunities. Students can be encouraged to use explanations in their oral responses, whenever appropriate. During class discussions, teachers can ask students to provide evidence and reasoning to support any claims they make. A number of the teachers with whom we work use bellwork, journal time, or "do nows" at the beginning of the class period as a way to focus students' attention on the work of the day or to review previous work. Such activities provide opportunities to practice explanations or any component of explanations. For example, many teachers provide graphs or tables on the overhead and ask students to use the data to make a claim. Teachers may write a claim and ask students to describe the appropriate and sufficient evidence from a table or graph provided. Explanations actually written by students, displayed anonymously, are an excellent source of examples for critique, as described below.

Practice Critiquing Explanations

Although students may be accustomed to revision as they undertake process writing in their English language arts class, they may not see revision as something to be done in science class. Whole-class, teacher-led critiques of examples enable students to see that written explanations can also be revisited, rethought, and revised. Think-alouds are an effective way to model reasoning that students sometimes have in their heads, but do not adequately transfer into their written explanations. Initially, the teacher can create sample explanations for purposes of critique. Once students have written explanations themselves, anonymous student responses can be used for whole-class review. Other examples of scientific explanations can be taken from websites, newspapers, or magazines and critiqued using the claim, evidence, and reasoning framework.

After a teacher has done think-alouds to model the critiquing process, teacher-guided critique, in which the teacher asks students probing questions, is an important next step. When a student says about a sample explanation, "It doesn't have good evidence," a teacher might ask questions such as: "What do you mean by *good evidence*? Why isn't this evidence good? What is it about the evidence that isn't good? Is it that there isn't enough evidence? Is it that the evidence doesn't fit the claim?" Following this discussion, she might also ask, "What could we say to the writer to help him improve this explanation? How could we describe the problem with the evidence so that a writer would understand what we mean?"

In any critique, both strengths and weaknesses should be highlighted, and concrete suggestions for improvement should be offered. Attention should be focused on the written product rather than on the writer. Teachers should model the language they want students to use for feedback: "These data come from the table, but it's really just a list of numbers; it doesn't show how the numbers are related to each other." This kind of talk surpasses, "You didn't show how the numbers are related to one another," which feels to a writer more like criticism of himself than objective critique of a written product. Once students have practiced teacher-led critique, they can exchange with a peer and critique one another's written explanations. Critique is not always criticism. Critique is a form of analysis through which the class may determine, in fact, that everything about an explanation under review is well done. Good examples should be shown and critiqued, as well.

Provide Students With Feedback

The above critique process can be augmented by teacher feedback to individual students. Teachers can provide feedback on the quality of the explanation as a whole, as well as on the quality of the individual components. The type of feedback that teachers provide is very important and should focus specifically on ways to improve (Black 2003). Comments such as "Be more specific" or "Use appropriate evidence" are very difficult for students to translate into meaningful revision. It is far more helpful to offer comments, guiding questions, or alternative examples of wording that help students to know precisely what they need to do to improve their work. For example, given the explanation:

> *Liquids 1 and 4 are the same substances. Substances are anything made of 1 material throughout. I know they are the same substances because their properties are the same. I also know that they are the same substances because their mass is different and mass changes. Therefore, two of the liquids above are the same.*

a teacher might write (or review with a student orally) something like this:

> *[Student name]: This claim is right on target! It answers the question clearly. I see reasoning when I read that the properties of substances are important for making this claim. But there are data in the table about properties that this explanation doesn't use. Look back at the properties in the table. How can the data about properties be used as evidence to support the claim in this explanation? Also, I don't understand how this explanation is using mass. If two substances have different mass, what does that tell me about those two substances? I need to know more about why this explanation is using the data about mass to support the claim. Work some more on the evidence, to see if you can make the explanation show more of what you know about substances and properties.*

Only after a significant amount of this kind of oral or written feedback might language such as "use appropriate evidence" become class shorthand for revision steps that students can take on their own. It may be that "look at the data again" or "what's your evidence?" or other language is useful for an individual teacher and the students in his or her class. What is important, initially, is that students hear and read this kind of feedback and see

revision based on this type of feedback modeled before a simple phrase will effectively guide meaningful revision.

One tool for guiding feedback is a rubric. Whether drafted collaboratively or created by the teacher and given to students, a general or base rubric such as that shown in Figure 4 has been used successfully by teachers incorporating explanation writing into their classroom instruction. This rubric can (and should) be adapted to the particular task, creating what we refer to elsewhere as a *specific rubric* (Harris et al., forthcoming). Because a specific rubric aligns with a particular learning goal, it can provide teachers with formative feedback both in terms of students' understanding of

FIGURE 4 Rubric for Scientific Explanations

Component	Level 1	Level 2	Level 3
Claim: A statement that responds to the question asked or the problem posed.	Does not make a claim, or makes an inaccurate claim.	Makes an accurate but incomplete claim.	Makes an accurate and complete claim.
Evidence: Scientific data used to support the claim.	Does not provide evidence, or only provides inappropriate evidence (evidence that does not support the claim).	Provides appropriate, but insufficient, evidence to support the claim. May include some inappropriate evidence.	Provides appropriate and sufficient evidence to support the claim.
Reasoning: Using *scientific principles* to show *why data count as evidence* to support the claim.	Does not provide reasoning, or only provides reasoning that does not link evidence to the claim.	Provides reasoning that links the claim and evidence. Repeats the evidence and/or includes some scientific principles, but is not sufficient.	Provides reasoning that links evidence to the claim. Includes appropriate and sufficient scientific principles.

scientific explanation (e.g., whether they include evidence) as well as their understanding of science content (e.g., whether they understand that mass is not a property).

The various levels of the rubric can be assigned scores, points, or qualitative descriptions in language a teacher finds useful for his or her own students (e.g., "good attempt," "almost there," "nailed it!"). The rubric shown in Figure 4 reveals one way to tease apart the components, which is especially useful as the teacher is trying to determine what students are "getting" and what they are still struggling with in their writing. A teacher may wish to give feedback to students in this manner, or give feedback on the overall explanation, or do both. A teacher may also wish to provide feedback only on one component for a period of time. The rubric can and should be adapted to the learning goals, the particular task, and the students' developing facility with explanation writing.

Provide Opportunities for Revision

As indicated, and as is well-established in research in the English language arts, writing is a process of drafting, receiving feedback, and revising. The number of revisions and the amount of feedback depend on the students' growing abilities, the time teachers wish to devote to scientific explanations, and the purposes of each writing activity. A teacher may wish to focus only on evidence, for example, when she identifies it as a common problem across the class or a consistent problem for an individual student.

In other words, teachers do not need to make suggestions about claim, evidence, and reasoning when it makes more sense to only provide feedback on one or two of those at a time. In a second round of revision, after a student has clearly represented appropriate and sufficient evidence for a claim, a teacher could provide feedback such as: "The evidence in this explanation now really helps me to see what you are thinking about these data and how they relate to the two liquids. These are great revisions! Now, let's try one more round of making this explanation even better by thinking about the reasoning...." Be sure that throughout a revision process, students save their drafts so that they can see how they are improving in their ability to write scientific explanations. Drafts are a fabulous tool not only for the student and for the teacher's own collection of examples to be used for modeling, but for use with parents at conferences or in other contexts. Drafts clearly communicate each student's developing understanding of complex science concepts and his or her competence with writing as a way to make sense of those concepts and to communicate understanding.

Conclusions

Constructing scientific explanations allows students to take part in an important inquiry practice and promotes greater science literacy. Because previous research has shown that students have difficulty engaging in this practice, the framework and the teaching guidelines help teachers to successfully incorporate explanation writing into their classrooms.

Although the guidelines appear as a list of steps in a linear process, they do not, in fact, occur only in that order. Nor do teachers need to move through the steps only one time in order to have students learn to write explanations. In other words, although a teacher models explanations early in the process, he may need to model again and again. Explanations in some units look quite different from those in other units, although the concept of making a claim and supporting it with appropriate, sufficient evidence crosses science disciplines and units. In one unit, for example, data may be presented in table form. When students move into the next unit, they may obtain data from graphs or representations that are increasingly complex. A teacher will again need to model making a claim and marshaling evidence when the data look different from those with which the student is familiar. When tables contain more data than are needed to answer the question being asked, teachers need to practice think-alouds so that students learn how to make a decision about which data are appropriate to use as evidence for particular claims.

Another aspect of explanations with which students will need modeling and practice is considering alternative explanations of the same phenomenon. The National Science Education Standards state, "Scientists evaluate the explanations proposed by other scientists by examining evidence, comparing evidence, identifying faulty reasoning, pointing out statements that go beyond the evidence, and suggesting alternative explanations for the same observations" (NRC 1996, p. 148). We have chosen not to focus on alternative explanations in the seventh grade because we want students to first understand explanations as a whole—and claim, evidence, and reasoning as parts of that whole—on a deep level. We have found the above framework for students and guidelines for teachers to be an appropriate way to scaffold students as they learn to write scientific explanations. We have found that learning to write explanations in chemistry, biology, and Earth science units across a single school year is enough of an undertaking when students are introduced to this practice, so we do not introduce the evaluation of alternative explanations until students have first developed facility with these. We purposefully reduce the complexity so that seventh graders can take part in what is a demanding yet important inquiry practice. It may be, however, that this practice can be expanded in other classroom contexts. Teachers should similarly scaffold students' consideration of alternative explanations when they judge it an appropriate time to do so.

The amount of time a teacher devotes to each step in the guidelines depends on the teaching/learning context, students' prior understanding, and the learning goals of the task. Students' writing performance and their ability to revise according to feedback, for example, are dependent on other experiences they have had with process writing. The classroom context also matters. The time devoted to explanation writing and revising, the nature of the conversations around explanation, and the talk about the role of explanation in science that permeates the classroom will shape students' understandings and their needs.

Supporting students' construction of scientific explanations is a time-consuming process. However, working through that process results in students' enhanced understanding of science as an inquiry process, in deeper understanding of complex science content, and in improved science literacy as students congruently develop thinking and writing skills in the context of project-based scientific inquiry.

Acknowledgments

The research reported here was supported in part by the Collaborative Research: Developing the Next Generation of Middle School Science Materials—Investigating and Questioning Our World through Science and Technology project (NSF-ESI 0439352); the Center for Curriculum Materials in Science (NSF-ESI-0227557); and the Teaching Strategies to Promote the Construction of Science Understanding in Urban Schools project (NSF-REC-0106959). Any opinions expressed in this work are those of the authors and do not necessarily represent either those of the funding agency or the University of Michigan.

References

Alberts, B. 2000. Some thoughts of a scientist on inquiry. In *Inquiring into inquiry learning and teaching in science*, eds. J. Minstrell and E. Van Zee, pp. 3–13. Washington, DC: American Association for the Advancement of Science.

American Association for the Advancement of Science (AAAS). 1990. *Science for all Americans*. New York: Oxford University Press.

American Association for the Advancement of Science (AAAS). 1993. *Benchmarks for science literacy*. New York: Oxford University Press.

Black, P. 2003. The importance of everyday assessment. In *Everyday assessment in the science classroom*, eds. J. M. Atkin and J. E. Coffey, pp. 1–11. Arlington, VA: NSTA Press.

Driver, R., P. Newton, and J. Osborne. 2000. Establishing the norms of scientific argumentation in classrooms. *Science Education* 84 (3): 287–312.

Harris, C. J., K. L. McNeill, D. L. Lizotte, R. W. Marx, and J. Krajcik. Forthcoming. Usable assessments for teaching science content and inquiry standards. In *Assessment in education: Practical experiences and education research.* Arlington, VA: NSTA Press

McNeill, K. L., and J. Krajcik. Forthcoming. Middle school students' use of appropriate and inappropriate evidence in writing scientific explanations. In *Thinking with data: The proceedings of the 33rd Carnegie Symposium on Cognition*, eds. M. Lovet and P. Shah. Mahwah, NJ: Lawrence Erlbaum.

McNeill, K. L., D. J. Lizotte, J. Krajcik, and R. W. Marx. Under review. Supporting students' construction of scientific explanations by fading scaffolds in instructional materials.

Moje, E. B., D. Peek-Brown, L. M. Sutherland, R. W. Marx, P. Blumenfeld, and J. Krajcik. 2004. Explaining explanations: Developing scientific literacy in middle-school project-based science reforms. In *Bridging the gap: Improving literacy learning for preadolescent and adolescent learners in grades 4–12*, eds. D. Strickland and D. E. Alvermann. New York: Teachers College Press.

National Research Council (NRC). 1996. *National science education standards.* Washington, DC: National Academy Press.

National Research Council (NRC). 2000. *Inquiry and the national science education standards: A guide for teaching and learning.* Washington, DC: National Academy Press

Quintana, C., B. Reiser, E. A. Davis, J. Krajcik, E. Fretz, R. Golan, E. Kyza, D. Edelson, and E. Soloway. 2004. A scaffolding design framework for designing educational software. *The Journal of the Learning Sciences* 13 (3): 337–386.

Sutherland, L. M., A. Meriweather, S. Rucker, P. Sarratt, Y. Hines-Hale, J. S. Krajcik, and E. B. Moje. 2006. *More emphasis* on scientific explanation: Developing conceptual understanding and science literacy. In *Exemplary Science in Grades 5–8: Standards-based success stories*, ed. R. E. Yager, 99–113. Arlington, VA: NSTA Press.

Sutherland, L. M., E. B. Moje, D. P. Brown, P. C. Blumenfeld, J. S. Krajcik, and R. W. Marx. 2003. Making scientific explanations: The development of scientific literacy in project-based science classrooms. Paper presented at the 53rd Annual Meeting of the National Reading Conference, Scottsdale, AZ (Dec.).

Science and Reading

Science and Reading

"Is This Science or Reading, Mrs. Heying?"

Donna Heying has been teaching reading for 15 years and science for 12 years in Garnavillo Elementary School. This is a small school in rural Garnavillo, Iowa, in the Clayton Ridge School District. Ninety-eight percent of the 85 students in her school are Caucasian. This year she teaches 15 students in fourth grade and 17 students in fifth grade. Her assignment includes language arts as well as science. Six years ago Donna's school went to block scheduling. This structure allows her to teach science and language arts in two 80-minute blocks.

Donna is speaking:

While we were putting our "shaken out" words into categories for our rain forest Picture Word Inductive Model (PWIM) (see Figure 1, pp. 186–191), one student offered the category of "words that are verbs." We had been talking about verbs the week before, and it was wonderful to hear him making the connection to the words from our poster.

> *There are lots of action words up there, Mrs. Heying, like* pouncing, climbing, flying, crawling, *and* jumping.

The PWIM is a language arts strategy I use with two or three units a year. I put up a picture or poster that relates to the topic the class is discussing. As a group, students say words that come to mind when they look at the visual (called "shaking out" the words). The words are posted next to the visual. I "shake out" words two or three times during a unit, hoping for more specific vocabulary each time.

I also go back to the list of words many times during the unit, maybe

FIGURE 1 Picture Word Inductive Model (PWIM)
Implementation Log

/ DeeAnn + Judy both observed 1st day

Picture Word Inductive Model
Implementation Log

School or Agency: Garnavillo   Name: Donna Heying

Grade level/Position: 4th   Beginning date of PWIM Cycle: 11-10-04

Description of Class (grade level, number of students, special needs):
A 4th grade class with 15 students - 4 female and 11 male
1 student has an IEP
4 are entitled to Title I services

A. Describe your picture.
The poster we used was an animated picture of a rain forest section. There were many plants and animals in the picture doing various things. This poster is very colorful and eye catching.

B. List of words shaken out of the picture:

beauty	understory
amazement	canopy
life	forest floor
color	people
trees	wild boar
moth	lizard
toucans	vines
butterfly	hummingbird
banana trees	ferns
jaguar	monkey
roses	parrots

We had some extra time after our lang. lesson on verbs, so we listed the verbs we saw in the picture.

spying	pointing	flying
searching	growing	climbing
thinking	sneaking	walking
watching	sitting	looking
running	prowling	hanging
making	hiding	kneeling
feeling	learning	standing
petting	experimenting	

Words added to the picture word chart and word sets after the first round:

snail	carbon dioxide	trunks of trees	animals
air	oxygen	stems	frogs
glory	chlorophyll	branches	rubber tree
wonder	photosynthesis	mammals	seeds
amphibians	transpiration	insects	flowers
marsupial	transportation	leaves	plants
wonderful sight	respiration	dirt	reptiles
the sky	evaporation	creatures	emergent layer

C. Examples of categories of words or phrases generated by students:
animals, plants, verbs

(continued)

Source: Adapted from Calhoun, E. F. 1999. *Teaching beginning reading and writing with the Picture Word Inductive Model.* Alexandria, VA: Association for Supervision and Curriculum Development.

"Is This Science or Reading, Mrs. Heying?"

Donna Heying has been teaching reading for 15 years and science for 12 years in Garnavillo Elementary School. This is a small school in rural Garnavillo, Iowa, in the Clayton Ridge School District. Ninety-eight percent of the 85 students in her school are Caucasian. This year she teaches 15 students in fourth grade and 17 students in fifth grade. Her assignment includes language arts as well as science. Six years ago Donna's school went to block scheduling. This structure allows her to teach science and language arts in two 80-minute blocks.

Donna is speaking:

While we were putting our "shaken out" words into categories for our rain forest Picture Word Inductive Model (PWIM) (see Figure 1, pp. 186–191), one student offered the category of "words that are verbs." We had been talking about verbs the week before, and it was wonderful to hear him making the connection to the words from our poster.

> *There are lots of action words up there, Mrs. Heying, like pouncing, climbing, flying, crawling, and jumping.*

The PWIM is a language arts strategy I use with two or three units a year. I put up a picture or poster that relates to the topic the class is discussing. As a group, students say words that come to mind when they look at the visual (called "shaking out" the words). The words are posted next to the visual. I "shake out" words two or three times during a unit, hoping for more specific vocabulary each time.

I also go back to the list of words many times during the unit, maybe

FIGURE 1 Picture Word Inductive Model (PWIM)
Implementation Log

DeeAnn + Judy both observed 1st day

Picture Word Inductive Model

Implementation Log

School or Agency: Garnavillo   Name: Donna Heying

Grade level/Position: 4th   Beginning date of PWIM Cycle: 11-10-04

Description of Class (grade level, number of students, special needs):
A 4th grade class with 15 students - 4 female and 11 male
1 student has an IEP
4 are entitled to Title I services

A. Describe your picture.
The poster we used was an animated picture of a rain forest section. There were many plants and animals in the picture doing various things. This poster is very colorful and eye catching.

B. List of words shaken out of the picture:

beauty	understory	We had some extra time after our lang. lesson on verbs, so we listed the verbs we saw in the picture.
amazement	canopy	
life	forest floor	
color	people	spying / pointing / flying
trees	wild boar	searching / growing / climbing
moth	lizard	thinking / sneaking / walking
toucans	vines	watching / sitting / looking
butterfly	hummingbird	running / prowling / hanging
banana trees	ferns	making / hiding / kneeling
jaguar	monkey	feeling / learning / standing
roses	parrots	petting / experimenting

Words added to the picture word chart and word sets after the first round:

snail	carbon dioxide	trunks of trees	animals
air	oxygen	stems	frogs
glory	chlorophyll	branches	rubber tree
wonder	photosynthesis	mammals	seeds
amphibians	transpiration	insects	flowers
marsupial	transportation	leaves	plants
wonderful sight	respiration	dirt	reptiles
the sky	evaporation	creatures	emergent laye

C. Examples of categories of words or phrases generated by students:
        animals, plants, verbs

(continued)

Source: Adapted from Calhoun, E. F. 1999. *Teaching beginning reading and writing with the Picture Word Inductive Model.* Alexandria, VA: Association for Supervision and Curriculum Development.

FIGURE 1 (*continued*)

Picture Word Inductive Model

Implementation Log

...continued

D. Examples of categories or concepts selected by you for instructional emphasis:

Phonetic Analysis Categories or Concepts –

compared
ne two → Words with double vowels, making one sound.
  ex. beauty, jaguar, toucan, snail, people, air, leaves

Words with double vowels, making two sounds
  ex. marsupials, amphibians, hyena

How some vowels are long and short.

Structural Analysis Categories or Concepts –
verbs
words with prefixes/suffixes

Content Categories or Concepts –

Parts of a Rain forest	Plants of the Rain Forest	Animals of the Rain Forest	Plant Processes
Canopy	roses	jaguar	respiration
Understory	rubber tree	toucans	transpiration
Forest Floor	banana tree	monkey	photosynthesis
Emergent Layer	trees	humming bird	evaporation
	ferns	wild boar	life
	vines	lizard	
		butterfly	

Other –

Thoughts of Rain Forests
wonder
wonderful sights
color
glory
amazement
beauty

snail
parrots
people
frog
moth
kids

Species of Animals
marsupials
mammals
insects
reptiles
amphibians

Plant Parts
leaves
seeds
branches
stems
flowers
trunks of trees
chlorophyll

spores
roots air
oxygen
CO₂

(*continued*)

FIGURE 1 (*continued*)

Picture Word Inductive Model

Implementation Log
...continued

E. Examples of titles generated by students:

From the Picture – Day 1   "Rain Forest"
                              "Jungle"
                              "Plants and Animals of the Rain Forest"

From the Picture Word Chart –

Our Jungle   Wildlife
The Rain Forest
Our 4th Grade Jungle
Nature
Rain Forest and Its Animals
A Wonderful Place
Life in a Rain Forest
Rain Forest Amazement
Amazing Things in the Rain Forest
What Lives in the Rain Forest
The Outdoor's Beauty

From Sentence Groups or Categories –

The Variety of the Rain Forest ← (the group liked this
Layers of a Rain Forest   one the best)
Rain Forests are Always Different
Rain Forests are Always Changing

(*continued*)

FIGURE 1 *(continued)*

Picture Word Inductive Model

Implementation Log
...continued

F. Examples of sentences generated by students:

Copies attached to form

G. One of the informative paragraphs composed by you from student ideas:

Copies of <u>student</u> informative paragraphs
attached to form.

Be sure to do a Composing Think-aloud with your students about how you put the ideas together to convey your message.

(continued)

FIGURE 1 (*continued*)

Picture Word Inductive Model

Implementation Log
...continued

H. Sample(s) of Student Work:

You may want to simply attach examples of student work to the implementation log.

Be sure to take samples of student work, when they are available, to your sessions with your Peer Coaching partner and to designated sessions with the rest of the staff as a learning community. You may take work from your whole class or group; however, I suggest you take for collective student, the work of six students whose responses you are monitoring more formally and maybe more analytically than those of the whole class.

I. If you used trade books with PWIM cycle, list the title and author of the best trade books used:

	Title	Author	NF or F	Strategy (Read-aloud, Talk-aloud, Think-aloud, Explicit Instruction)
1.	A Walk in the Rain Forest p 5-7, 10-13	Rebecca L. Johnson	NF	Read-Aloud
2.	A Walk in the Rain Forest p. 17-45	Rebecca L. Johnson	NF	Think-Aloud / Read-Aloud
3.	What is a Hyrax? p. 19-24	Edward R. Ricciuti	NF	Read-Aloud
4.	A Walk in the Rain Forest	Rebecca L. Johnson	NF	Talk-Aloud
5.	Floratorium p.4	Joanne Oppenheim	NF	Talk-Aloud
6.	Floratorium p.16-17	Joanne Oppenheim	NF	Think-Aloud / Talk-Aloud
7.				
8.				
9.				
10.				

(*continued*)

FIGURE 1 (*continued*)

Picture Word Inductive Model
Implementation Log
...continued

Strategies	Total #
Read-aloud	3
Talk-aloud	3
Think-aloud: Reading	2
Think-aloud: Composing	—
Explicit Instruction	

Comments and Reflections:

This was a very interesting and fun experience for the students and myself. I was pleasantly surprised to see all the words shaken out of this picture. Many of the words were new vocabulary from units earlier in the year, and many students made connections. The students were also very excited about doing something "new" and different with a poster.

As we progressed through this PWIM, I realized that I have done many of these same things with other posters and diagrams, but have not done it this formally or organized.

Questions:

Number of lessons/days in PWIM Cycle: __14__

Ending date of PWIM Cycle: __11-25-04__

Number of times you planned with your Peer Coach in this PWIM Cycle: __4__

Number of times you demonstrated with your Peer Coach in this PWIM Cycle: __2__ looking at phonetic structures of words, parts of speech, prefixes, and suffixes. You can integrate a variety of language concepts that align with the topic you are exploring. The words are eventually categorized (that's the inductive part) and read aloud over several days. Then the students write sentences using the words. The sentences themselves are then categorized and formed into paragraphs. Toward the end of the PWIM cycle, the students are doing a lot of writing both as a group and individually.

One fourth grader, Kenneth, transferred here last year while he was in third grade. When he came he hardly said one word during class. He is of average ability, but his writing skills were way below average for a fourth grader. As you can see from his writing in Figure 2, he uses upper- and lower-case letters at random in his writing and struggles to form letters. His writing used to have no capitalization or punctuation, but he would leave space at the end of each sentence to signal it was the end. Some of the skills I have been working on with Kenneth are sentence structure issues, such as basic letter formation; correct use of upper- and lowercase letters; spacing between words; and punctuation and capitalization. As you can see from his writing sample, we have a long way to go, but we have already made some significant progress. Kenneth volunteers quite a bit during class now, which is something that didn't happen at the beginning of the year.

Like Kenneth's writing sample, the other samples in Figure 2 really show the impact connected instruction can have on students who struggle academically for a variety of reasons.

Emily reads at about a second-grade level, and her writing skills are about at that level, too. She really likes the PWIM activities because we do a lot in groups and we don't use a textbook that she has to read out of. Emily can choose books to read and explore that are at her grade level.

Todd is a very bright boy, but is a classic case of hyperactivity. Hands-on investigations are excellent learning opportunities for him. The PWIM activities are as well because kids can sit on the floor and move around somewhat.

I attribute success with my students to the new strategies the teachers in my school are using that allow for student input into the topics we will be discussing and writing. Getting the students involved with deciding what we were going to study this year began very simply. I asked the students what questions and/or topics they wondered about and wanted to study. As a group, we took these lists and put them into categories according to topics. One category that aligned well with our science units was "Animals and why they do the things they do."

FIGURE 2 Three Samples of Student Writing Based on the PWIM Activity

Kenneth's Writing

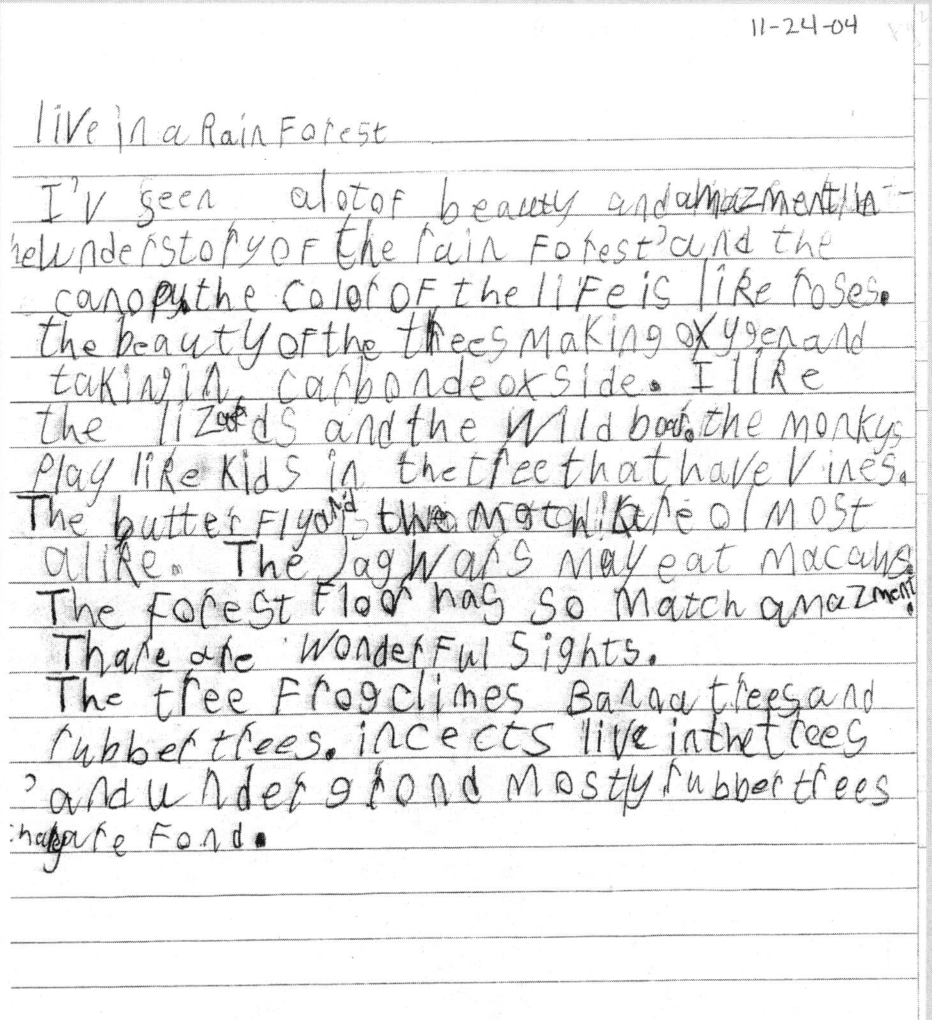

11-24-04

live in a Rain Forest

I'v seen alotof beauty and amazment in the understory of the rain Forest and the canopy the color of the liFe is like roses. the beauty of the trees making oxygen and takin in carbondeoxside. I like the lizerds and the wild boor, the monkys play like kids in the tree that have vines. The butterFly and the moth are almost alike. The Jagwars may eat macaws The forest floor has so match amazment Thare are wonderful sights. The tree frog climes Banaa trees and rubber trees. incects live in the trees and underground mostly rubbertrees are Fond.

(continued)

FIGURE 2 (*continued*)

Emily's Writing

11-24-04

Life in a Rain Forest

The toucan can fly and hang on branches. The toucan probaly catches prey from the ground. It likes to fly in the canopy and that would be pretty high in the air and it would hurt if you fell on the ground. Even toucans live in trees. I wish I was a toucan.

Todd's Writing

11-24-04

Animals of the Rain Forest

A lot of animals live in the rain forest. The monkeys are wild and climb like me. The jaguars hunt for meat in the rain forest. The lizards are green just like the trees. The butterflies are colorful. The toucan is like a rainbow.

Animals and Their Adaptations

This is a very rural community, so the majority of students are exposed to a variety of animals every day. Because of this, the students could answer many of each other's questions about domesticated animals and provide some proof for some of their claims. Thus, I decided that we would focus on animals from other areas of the world, such as from a rain forest. One of our science units is on living things and how they survive, which aligns with our district science and language arts standards and benchmarks, so it was perfect.

I began the unit with a pre-assessment of what the students already knew about animals and how they survive. I had students respond to a writing prompt that asked them to explain to their grandmothers about some of the animals they might find in their backyards and what adaptations allow these animals to survive there. I was pleasantly surprised at how much content the students shared. This told me that many of them have a good knowledge base about animals and gave me an idea where to start with instruction.

I started the unit as I usually did by reading aloud a book and then discussing it with the class:

> Today, we are going to be reading the book called The Great Kapok Tree, by Lynne Cherry. When sharing read-alouds with you, I usually choose books that are nonfiction, but today I chose a fictional book that we are going to discuss some real things about.

I read from the book. When I finished, I asked,

> Why would these animals survive well in the rain forest and not in Garnavillo, Iowa?

Immediately my students chime in:

> It's not hot enough here!
> We don't have enough trees for them.
> We don't have their food here.
> Iowa has winter.
> They could live here in the summer, then migrate south in the winter.
> We don't have palm trees.

I ask,

How would cutting down this kapok tree have affected each of the animals in the book?

The students respond:

The monkeys couldn't swing from branches.
The sloth would fall to the ground.
The birds would lose their nest.
The anteater wouldn't be able to find as many ants.

As I probed with these questions, the idea of animals and their adaptations for survival emerged.

The teachers in our district are required to keep logs and have to turn in two of each read-aloud (Figure 3 shows one read-aloud implementation log), think-aloud (Figure 4), or talk-aloud (Figure 5) each month. Our district has a reading team consisting of our curriculum director, our principal, and a member of the statewide reading team from our area education agency (AEA). This team reads and critiques our logs.

Even though the logs are a lot of work, by using them I can see a big improvement in how students find information and comprehend what they read. Students are now also much more likely to pick up a nonfiction book dealing with science content.

The next day I tried another read-aloud using the book *What on Earth Is a Hyrax?*, which is about an unusual animal that none of the students have heard of.

As I read, listen for things about the hyrax that make it possible for it to survive where it does. This could include things about its body, what it eats, how it has young, or anything else you hear.

I read the book, and then recorded the students' thoughts on chart paper.

"The Hyrax and How It Survives":
It has suction cups on its feet to help it jump up on rocks and run away.
It's hairy to keep warm.
It looks fat.
It has big teeth to kill other animals.
It's a mammal.
It has long claws to dig holes with.

FIGURE 3 Nonfiction Read-Aloud Implementation Log

The Nonfiction Read-aloud
Implementation Log

Review:

A Read-aloud is simply reading aloud to your students. Read-alouds of information, expository prose can be very brief, sharing as little as a sentence and illustration, or a single paragraph. When you are looking for good models to share and discuss with your students, look for: a) passages that address concepts that fit into curriculum content across discipline; and b) passages that are well-written, especially in terms of how the author(s) announced and supported his/her major points. One of the major instructional purposes of the nonfiction Read-aloud is to provide an opportunity for students to learn science, social studies, mathematics, and other curriculum concepts. Our long-term goal, however, is for students to use similar text as learners and independent readers.

Implementation Information:

___X___ I am using this log to plan or record notes for my lesson.

_____ I am using this log as I observe my peer coaching partner: _____

_____ I am using this log as I observe a live or videotaped demonstration during

staff development: _____

Date: *11/16/04*_____School Organization: *Garnavillo Elem.* _____

Name, Grade Level or Role: *Donna Heying – 4th Grade – Science/Reading*_____

Title of Nonfiction Book Used: *The Great Kapok Tree* Pages *whole book*

Author(s): *Lynne Cherry* _____

Source of Book: Public_____ School_____ Classroom *X* AEA_____ Other_____

1. Concepts addressed from social studies, science, mathematics, other:
Standards: Standard #5: Understands the structure and function of cells and organisms
Benchmark: Knows that plants and animals have features that help them live in different environments.
Standard #6: Understands relationships among organisms and their physical environment
Benchmark: Knows that living things are found almost everywhere in the world and that distinct environments support life of different types of plants and animals.

2. Language arts concepts and processes represented in the text selection:
Standard: Uses reading skills and strategies to understand and interpret a variety of literary and informative texts. (Getting the meaning)

Source: Adapted by Guttenberg Community Schools, 2003, from Calhoun, E. F., The Phoenix Alliance, Every Child Reads/Reading First Initiative.

FIGURE 4 Think-Aloud Implementation Log

The Think-aloud

Implementation Log

Review:

Think-alouds provide an opportunity to **share with students your use of comprehension processes or strategies as you gather meaning from and use written text.** *This may include how you determine main idea or the author's purpose, use the author's organization of text, access and use prior knowledge, and how reading often creates new questions for us to answer. Essentially, you are* **modeling for students how you gather meaning from text, explicitly telling/modeling for students the comprehension process or strategy you are using to understand the author's message.** *This also includes how you think about or approach the task of gathering meaning using that strategy. One of the major instructional purposes for using nonfiction Think-alouds is to model the use of reading comprehension processes and strategies for students; however, our long-range goal is to have students use these processes and strategies themselves. In order to do this, they may need many practice opportunities doing their own Think-alouds across a wide range of text.*

Implementation Information:

_____I am using this log to plan or record notes for my lesson.
_____I am using this log as I observe my peer coaching partner.
_____I am using this log as I observe a live or videotaped demonstration during staff development: _____

_____

Date: _____   School/Organization: _____

Name, Grade level or Role:_____

Title of Nonfiction Book Used:_____ Pages: _____

Author(s): _____

1. Concepts addressed from social studies, science, mathematics, other:

2. Language arts concepts and processes represented in the text selection:

Process Modeled _____

3. How does the teacher model the comprehension processes or strategies?

Moves:
1. Introduction – announce the reading comprehension process or strategy and its purpose.

(continued)

Source: Adapted by Guttenberg Community Schools, 2003, from Calhoun, E. F., The Phoenix Alliance, Every Child Reads/Reading First Initiative.

FIGURE 4 (*continued*)

2. Read passage

3. Set up demonstration – describe again the process or strategy you will be modeling

4. Demonstrate using the reading process or strategy

5. Review why the process or strategy is useful

6. Student application activity

5a. Reflections on the attributes of the Think-aloud and organization of the lesson:

5b. Reflections on student response:

Please include a copy of the passage used for your Think-aloud.

Implementation Data

In the last 5 days, have you worked with your peer coaching partner/s to select and rehearse Think-alouds?

_____Yes   _____No   If "Yes", how many times? _____

In the last 5 days, have you demonstrated a Think-aloud (with students) for your peer coaching partner?

_____Yes   _____No   If "Yes", how many times? _____

FIGURE 5 Talk-Aloud Implementation Log

The Talk-aloud
Implementation Log

Review:

*Talk-alouds provide an opportunity to model the reading/writing connection so students can "see" and hear how an experienced and skillful reader relates to and uses what the author has provided. The text used may be only an illustration, a sentence, or several pages. Talk-alouds often include **mentioning something you noticed or appreciated about the text**. Comments may include discussing **what you noticed** about the relationship between the cover, the title, and the first line, and how they all worked together to announce the primary message of the book. Or, you might address **what you noticed about how the author organized the text** to get across the message. It is during Talk-alouds that we can address anything that relates to the communication loop between the author and the reader (the reader/writer connection). Our long-range instructional purpose for Talk-alouds is to have students be aware of and use the reader/writer connection themselves. Thus, while every teacher Talk-aloud does not need to be followed by student Talk-alouds, enough practice must be provided so that students learn to use the strategy themselves.*

Implementation Information:

    X   I am using this log to plan or record notes for my lesson.

    _____ I am using this log as I observe my peer coaching partner: _____

    I am using this log as I observe a live or videotaped demonstration during staff
    development: _____

Date: *12/1/04* _____ School Organization: *Garnavillo Elementary*_____

Name, Grade Level or Role: *Donna Heying – 4th Grade – Science/Language*_____

Title of Nonfiction Book Used: *Invertebrates*_____Pages _____

Author(s): *Gareth Stevens*_____

Book # *103086* _____   Quality fiction/non-fiction + -

Source of Book: Public_____ School_____ Classroom_____ AEA *X* Other_____

    1. Concepts addressed from social studies, science, mathematics, other:
Standard 5: Understands the structure and function of organisms.
Benchmark: *Knows that living organisms have distinct structures and body systems that serve specific functions in growth, survival, and reproduction. (e.g. various body structures for walking, flying, swimming, surviving)*
    2. Language arts concepts and processes represented in the text selection:
Standard: Uses reading skills and strategies to understand and interpret a variety of literary and informative texts. (Getting the meaning)
Benchmark: Students can understand stated information they have read.

(continued)

Source: Adapted by Guttenberg Community Schools, 2003, from Calhoun, E. F., The Phoenix Alliance, Every Child Reads/Reading First Initiative.

FIGURE 5 (*continued*)

3. How does the teacher model his or her use of what the author(s) provided in the text?
    1. *Earlier, we had been talking about a couple of new terms about animals. Those new words were vertebrates and invertebrates. We had some discussion about what we think these words mean, but some of us still weren't sure what type of animals these were, so I found a book called <u>Invertebrates</u> that I want to share with you as a Talk-Aloud today. In this book the author did a really nice job of using text and pictures to help me understand what an invertebrate is and how it is different from a vertebrate.*
    2. *Read pages from book*
    3. *Discuss how the author used bold-faced words to help me understand what they meant, and how context clues were used in many of the paragraphs to help me understand what new words meant. The author gave me a much clearer understanding about what an invertebrate is by the text and the use of pictures of various animals that are invertebrates to see what some of the characteristics of an invertebrate is. The author also did a comparison of the similarities and differences between animals that are vertebrates and those that are invertebrates.*

    4. What, if any, student application activity was used?
    Now we are going to go back to the animal books and search for some more information about vertebrates and invertebrates, as well as some examples of animals that are each kind. When we are finished exploring the books, we'll share our information and list it on some chart paper. Then in groups, we'll complete a Venn Diagram comparing the similarities and differences between vertebrates and invertebrates.

5a. Reflections on the attributes of the Talk-aloud and organization of the lesson:
This Talk-Aloud tied in very well with what we are discussing in Science. The Read-Aloud that I did with another book about animal adaptations and the student application activity somewhat lead us to this talk-aloud because of some of the new vocabulary terms they had found in the books.

5b. Reflections on student response:
The students responded to this talk-aloud very well. They really did a nice job of finding other examples of how authors used bold-faced words to help them understand what they were reading and how context clues helped them to figure things out. They also found many interesting facts about invertebrates that they shared

Please include a copy of the passage used for your Read-aloud.

Implementation Data:

In the last 5 days, have you worked with your peer coaching partner to select and rehearse Talk-alouds?

X __ Yes   _____No   If "Yes," how many times? *1* _____

In the last 5 days, have you demonstrated a Talk-aloud (with students) for your peer coaching partner?

____ Yes   *X*____No   If "Yes," how many times? _____

When we finished with our chart, I brought out two boxes of nonfiction books about animals that I got from our AEA.

Now let's explore some books to see if we can find some more animals that interest you. We want to find out some things about these animals that help us understand how and why they live where they do.

The students went to the books very enthusiastically. As they read, I circulated and learned about their discoveries:

The happy face spider has a smiley face on its bottom!
A snow leopard is almost all white.
I can't see those goats in that picture because they are camouflaged.
An eagle's nest weighs more than I do.
Bears and squirrels don't really sleep all winter when they hibernate.

When the students had finished exploring books, each student talked about one of the animals he or she had read about and the students asked each other questions. Many new vocabulary words were added to our word wall, such as *instinct, migration, hibernation, cold-blooded, warm-blooded, vertebrates,* and *invertebrates.*

New vocabulary led to new explorations. For example, we wanted to further explore and compare the characteristics of vertebrates and invertebrates. So we observed earthworms and completed a class Venn diagram comparing worms to people. After we completed the diagram, each student created three complete paragraphs about what we found out. One paragraph was on characteristics of worms, one on characteristics of people, and one on characteristics that worms and people share.

To show how informational text can help readers find out more about invertebrates, I used a talk-aloud to model what I am thinking as I read:

We have been talking about a couple of new terms about animals. Those new words were vertebrates *and* invertebrates. *We had some discussion and exploration about vertebrates and invertebrates but some of us still aren't sure what type of animals these are, so I found a book called* Invertebrates *that I want to share with you as a talk-aloud today. In this book the author did a really nice job of using text and pictures to help me understand what an invertebrate is and how it is different from a vertebrate.*

I began to read from the book and talk aloud as I made sense of what I was reading.

"An invertebrate is an animal without a backbone." Ah! The author put the word invertebrate *in bold print and the sentence the word is in must be its meaning! By bolding the word in the sentence that tells me the sentence is describing that word. That's how the author helped me to find what the word meant.*

In the next paragraph I find the word arthropod. *I am not sure if I have ever heard that word before. Well, it is in bold print, too. So I know it must be an important word. But that sentence didn't tell its meaning so I am going to read on to see if the next sentence will explain what it means. "An arthropod is an animal with an exoskeleton." The word* exoskeleton *is also in bold print! So words that are bolded mean they are important or new vocabulary. The sentence they are in doesn't always give the meaning of the word. Sometimes the meaning is in the next sentence or two.*

"An exoskeleton is a skeleton on the outside of the animal's body." OK, again the author put the word in bold print to make me recognize that it was an important word, and helped me understand its meaning by also putting the meaning of the word in the next sentence. Great! I have a much clearer understanding about what an invertebrate is and I learned two new words!

Now let's go back to the animal books and search for some more information about vertebrates and invertebrates, as well as some examples of animals that are each kind. When we are finished exploring the books, we'll share our information and list it on some chart paper. Then as a group, we'll complete a Venn diagram comparing the similarities and differences between all vertebrates and all invertebrates.

This talk-aloud tied in very well with what we were discussing in science. The students really did a nice job of finding other examples of how authors used boldfaced words to help them understand what they were reading and how context clues helped them to figure things out. They found many interesting facts about invertebrates that they shared with the group.

Feathers and Beaks

A few days later we were talking about birds' feathers and how some are different from others. We investigated why there are different types and the different jobs that feathers do for the birds. We also talked about what had happened to the birds' feathers that we had read about in the book *Sea Otter Rescue*. The birds and other animals in this book were affected by the oil spill of the *Exxon Valdez*.

While observing a variety of feathers, one of the students asked, "Why don't birds have teeth?" We discussed this a little bit, and some of the student's theories were that

They don't need them for eating squishy worms.
Their mouth is too small.
It would make them too heavy to fly.

This led into talking about different kinds of beaks that various birds had. We looked at some pictures of different birds from the books we had in the room. We then used Popsicle sticks, glue, and clothespins to investigate how the different beaks helped different types of birds get their food. The challenge was to create three different types of beaks that can pick up different-shaped objects. Students recorded what happened on their log sheets.

I could see and hear how students understood the different characteristics and adaptations of animals. I was hearing a lot of new vocabulary being used, and as I read their writing, I could see them using the vocabulary in the correct context. This told me that they understood the words and how to use those words.

We did several more investigations as we progressed through the unit. Students loved going to the park to plot out a square foot of ground, examine all of the life in that plot, and discuss why they thought those living things survived where they did.

If my students, especially those with learning difficulties, had been asked to find out all of this information by reading a textbook, I am quite sure they wouldn't have learned as much content, or had as much fun learning it. Many of the students commented that they liked learning information from the investigations and the "real" books rather than their textbooks.

Reflections

I am so fortunate that teaching science with reading and vice versa are encouraged by the administration. In fact, that was part of the rationale for block scheduling. It tied in so well with the Reading First initiative and our desire to have the students read more nonfiction, content-based books.

Initially, I was worried about what the parents would think about combining science and reading but there have been no problems. In fact some students with learning disabilities have told their parents that mixing the subjects is easier for them.

My other concern has been the challenge of *time*. A wide gap in academic levels as well as maturity levels exists, especially with the fourth-grade group. I have some students that read at a first- or second-grade level and some that read at an eighth-grade level. Finding interesting materials suitable for all of these students is sometimes a challenge, but I have access to a variety of materials, including sets of books that align with our science units. I have to give myself enough time to go through the books and materials to make sure what I choose aligns well with the lessons, and writing up read-aloud logs, talk-aloud logs, and think-aloud logs takes an enormous amount of time!

I don't always get done what I want to, but taking time to connect reading and science makes my job a lot easier when I'm teaching kids. When I see how some of my struggling students learn new concepts and vocabulary and apply them with confidence when working with their groups, it's all worth doing.

Is this science or reading, Mrs. Heying?

What do you think this is, Brad?

Well, kind of both I guess, Mrs. Heying.

Do you think your parents have a certain time of day that they do science, reading, math, or social studies on their jobs or at home?

No, well, my mom reads at different times of the day.

Yeah, Mrs. Heying, my dad reads the paper in the morning, and then at work I think he writes.

In real life, you don't separate your day into reading, language, science, social studies, and math. So, I thought I needed to get you ready for the real world by connecting your subjects up at school.

Oh, I get it— so, what are we going to do now, Mrs. Heying?

Resources

Cherry, L. 1990. *The great kapok tree*. New York: Harcourt, Brace, Jovanovich.

Ricciuti, E. R. 1998. *What on Earth is a hyrax?* Woodbridge, CT: Blackbirch Press.

Smith, R. 1993. *Sea otter rescue*. New York: Harcourt, Brace, Jovanovich.

Stevens, G. 2002. *Invertebrates*. Discovery Channel School Science: Plant and Animal Kingdom Series. Milwaukee, WI: Gareth Stevens.

Questions for Discussion

1. Compare and contrast the science-literacy workshop model outlined in Chapter 9 with the science-literacy strategies Mrs. Heying implements in her classroom. In what ways could you apply the science-literacy workshop model to strengthen the inquiry and enhance learning in both subjects?

2. The think-aloud, read-aloud, and talk-aloud strategies that Mrs. Heying uses help students construct meaning from text. How could you apply strategies discussed in the chapters in this section ("Science and Reading") to extend the inquiry investigations of the outdoor plot and engage students in reading and writing texts to support their investigations?

Treasures From Home

Nancy McDonough teaches second grade at Walter Stillman School in Tenafly, New Jersey. This is a suburban school with a large multilingual population that is 63% Caucasian, 32% Asian, and 5% Hispanic. Nancy's class consists of 7 girls and 13 boys. Two students are classified with learning disabilities. Four children receive basic skills instruction, and two attend ESL classes.

I figured out, Eli told his fellow second graders, *that if you look through this part of the magnifier* [pointing to the high magnification lens] *you can see the tentacles on the coral better.*

Eli had been carefully observing the live coral housed in our class's marine aquarium. Then, taking out a drawing pad, Eli opened to a page posted with a fluorescent green sticky note. Eli continued,

Here is a picture of the coral [Figure 1]. *I labeled the parts and I showed the tentacles in this magnified drawing. I wrote about it, too.*

Eli reads aloud the paragraph that swirls down the right-hand side of his page:

"Coral is what makes a coral reef. There are a lot of fish in a coral reef. Some starfish, like the Crown of Thorns, eat coral."

The rest of my class listens attentively as Eli talks about endangered reefs and pollution, and then they join in the conversation. They ask questions and contribute information, sharing Eli's enthusiasm about his "Treasure From Home" (my version of show-and-tell, which is always linked to our topics of study). The children had been studying ocean communities for six weeks now, so they have a lot to say!

FIGURE 1 Eli's Coral Picture

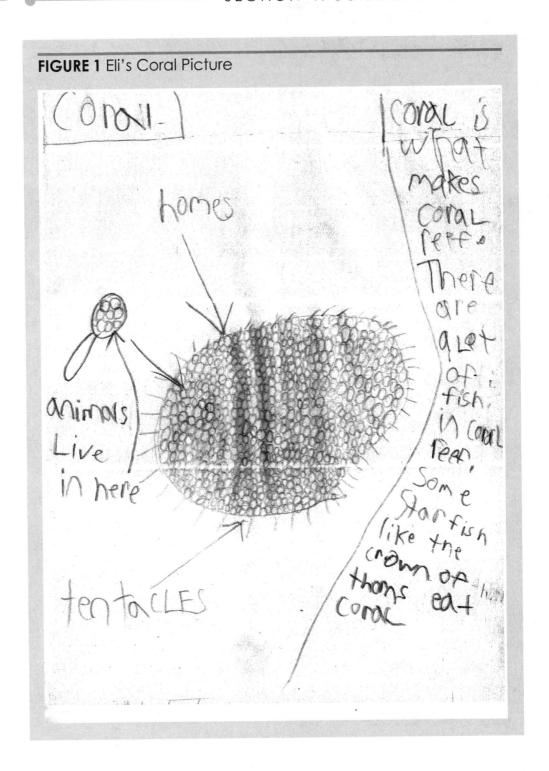

Preserving My Sanity

I smile and think back to my personal curriculum catharsis about 12 years ago. It was right after a particularly brutal day. My second-grade children and I had all worked mightily for six hours and yet nothing was finished! Our day was spent doing a little of this and a little of that—and at the end of the day, it all added up to a little of everything, and a lot of nothing.

So, I took a hard look at my schedule:

9:00–10:45 Reading Block (three groups reading fiction 85% of the time)

10:45–11:45 Writing Block (conferences yielding narratives 80% of the time)

12:00–1:00 Lunch

1:00–2:00 Math

2:00–2:45 Social Studies, Science, Birthday Parties, Announcements, etc.!

The problem was apparent immediately. Trying to crush all of my content areas into the last 45 minutes of the day was just unworkable. No wonder I couldn't "cover the curriculum." I realized that I had only two choices: one, work faster or, two, begin teaching more than one subject at a time. I determined that both the children and I were already working just about as fast as we could, so in order to "fit it all in," I would have to connect the curriculum areas.

Now, a dozen years later, I preserve my sanity by putting science content at the core of my teaching. I unify knowledge, skills, and processes by wrapping them around and through science concepts and processes. The unifying concept must allow me to connect all the content parts, while at the same time attend to the basic language arts components that lie at the heart of primary instruction. All the units in my curriculum have the same simple structure: They are a series of connected micro-units. A micro-unit, lasting from several hours up to several weeks, focuses on a smaller component of the large unit. A few of the micro-units that were part of the larger Oceans unit this year were Sharks, Sea Mammals, Kelp Forests, Frozen Oceans, and The Depths. The sequence of instruction in each micro-unit is always the same:

1. Build background knowledge (usually orally to "lighten the cognitive load")
2. Gradually release control (usually a combination of reading or writing supported by talk; often in pairs)

3. Independent study (which sometimes continues long after the unit has ended or reappears after long periods of dormancy; sometimes is shared in Treasures From Home; sometimes just done for the fun of it)

All units grow from what preceded them and lead to what will follow. Nothing but math stands alone. We have no distinct reading or writing "time"—we read when we have something we need to learn and write when we have something to say. Based on the unit content, I then decide what language arts skills and science process skills the children will need to be able to do. Woven through it all is talk, and we talk when there is something to share. For example, as the kids are learning about sea turtles or oak trees or monarch butterflies, I'm teaching main ideas or classification or topic sentences. The children are motivated because the content is inherently interesting and "talk" is a natural part of what we do; therefore, discussions emerge spontaneously and often.

I pack units of study with ideas and information designed to capture the attention of 20 eight-year-old scientists, but I also invite the children to develop those skills and habits of mind used by all active learners: the ability to read with good comprehension, to write with clarity, to observe carefully, to find information efficiently, to exchange ideas openly in conversation, and to build purposefully on prior knowledge. I want my second graders to wonder, to infer, and to ask questions. In short, I aim for *understanding*.

It was in this instructional context that Eli offered the class his picture and thinking on coral reefs. The conversations that ensued sparked the interest of his classmates, and they, in turn, wanted to learn more about reef communities. My job was to plan the micro-unit that would both support and be supported by our ongoing study of oceans. I was delighted to do so.

I began by having the kids do as Eli did and re-view the coral in our class's aquarium (which also contains sea stars, anemones, shrimp, sea cucumbers, snails, urchins, crabs, clams, and mussels). The kids have been observing the aquarium for a few months. They have had experience organizing their thinking using an O-W-L chart (a three-column graphic organizer: Observe, Wonder, Learn). To do a formal observation, they gather around the aquarium in small groups for 15-minute sessions. Their task is to watch generally and then to focus their attention on a specific animal. They then sketch, ask a question, and comment about the day's viewing (Figure 2).

The kids spontaneously talked about the animals, especially the coral, and their underwater lives. As with Eli's observations, these conversations lead to questions that, in turn, lead to further investigation.

FIGURE 2 Three Student O-W-L Charts

O-W-L Chart

OBSERVE	WONDER	LEARN
	I wonder why they have holes naw I now why. animals live in it.	I learnd that there are little doors so nothing eats them.

O-W-L Chart

OBSERVE	WONDER	LEARN
coral	Does coral have a brain?	createns Live inside the corals holes.

(continued)

FIGURE 2 *(continued)*

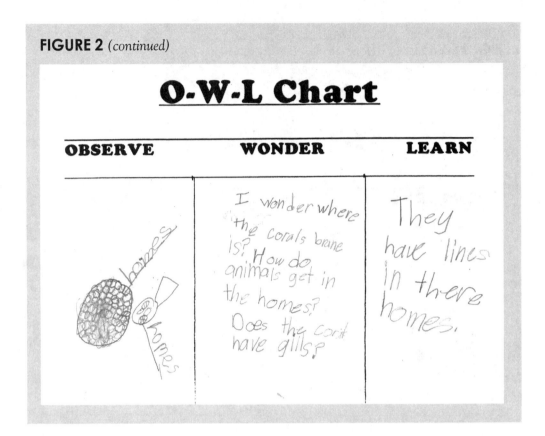

O·W·L Chart

OBSERVE	WONDER	LEARN

In listening to the children's conversations, I realized that they had come to believe that *all* coral looked like the species in our aquarium. So rather than beginning our study in the usual way, which is by sharing some of our beloved books, I decided that we must first observe a living coral reef. The closest we could come to that direct experience was to watch a video. I chose Reading Rainbow's *Dive to a Coral Reef,* in which my students could see a huge variety of coral and more accurately picture the habitat we would read about together later in the day. Our discussion after the video focused on getting an accurate mental picture of a coral reef and preparing to use that image to enhance further understanding.

An Interactive Read-Aloud

My next step was to engage the children in an interactive read-aloud. The interactive read-aloud is a new feature—I've been working on it for a year now. I have glorious, informative science trade books, and I wanted the kids to experience them more actively. But, with the price of picture books, there was no way I could afford to purchase more than one copy of each book, so the question became how could I use single copy texts more effectively and, at the same time, get students to work orally on comprehension strategies (always an eye toward instructional efficiency!). I certainly do not do extensive lessons with every book I read aloud, but I do regularly choose "benchmark texts" and spend quality time working on them with the kids.

I choose my read-aloud books carefully. They are always related to our unit of study, but they are more difficult than the kids can read on their own, in terms of either vocabulary or content. They must have challenging text supports and engaging pictures to develop visual literacy and hold attention—and I must love them! After years of experience, I have learned that primary children are eager to hear and to read informational text.

Today we are going to read At Home in the Coral Reef. *During the read-aloud we will be stopping and talking and having a summary circle at the end. First, let's remind each other what we already know about how a coral reef grows. Turn to the person next to you and share how a coral reef grows for a few minutes.*

OK, who wants to share what you discussed with your partner?

Now, our book today is about how a coral reef is born.

An interactive read-aloud differs from other read-alouds because, as the name suggests, the students are actively and overtly involved in processing information through conversations with each other and with me. The partner discussions we had that reviewed how coral grows is the type of talk that helps students access vital background knowledge and invites them to begin processing it so they can understand the topic under study. It is this preparation that readies young scientists to proceed independently in their reading and in their continued study.

The second type of talk that takes place next during the interactive read-aloud is directed toward generalized reading comprehension strategies: recall of detail, sequencing, questioning, determining main ideas, summarizing, using text supports, and predicting. As I read the book to the class, I keep my tone conversational and my questions exploratory. I assess the children's current level of understanding, and we lay the groundwork for more independent inquiry and reading.

At the end of the next page I want you to be ready to ask a question that can be answered by information on that page. Half of you will get a chance to ask the question and the other half will be ready to answer them! "Once a year, coral polyps have babies…." OK, who has a question for the class based on the page I just read?

What is a baby polyp called?

If you can answer that question raise your hand.
Planula!

What would be another question? Think about who, what, where, why, or how.
What might eat the planula?

Great questions—now let's continue reading. "The water in the lagoon is calm…." Anyone remember the word that means animals that make their own light?
Bioluminescence!

Turn to your partner—remind each other of something you remember about bioluminescence.

Let's share out what you discussed with your partner.

Here comes the summary page in the book that will help you with summary circle.

We are now going to do the Stop Reading. What Are You Thinking? Summary Circle. Please make a circle. Now it's time to share something you were thinking while I was reading or connections you were making…. Matthew is ready to go—I am going to be as quiet as I can. Matthew, go ahead and start the conversation.

My class talked with each other for five minutes—sharing thoughts, adding on to each other's comments, answering each other's questions. Their science talk included comments about how sand is made, feelings about polluted coral reefs, and the "coolness" of the mazes in brain coral. They speculated about what animals might do in the case of the destruction of a reef—would they be willing to share homes or would they all have to seek new ones? Their conversation with each other was amazing! At one point a question sparked Elizabeth to think about symbiosis and that brought Matthew to think about the relationship between jellyfish and algae, a topic we read about weeks ago in *Jellies*, a book by Twig George. The summary circle continued the development of crucial knowledge, interweaving new information with old.

During the interactive read-aloud, I used four procedures, all of them familiar to my students For general comprehension I used (1) Clarify Vocabulary and Paraphrase and (2) Ask a Question. For developing background knowledge I used (3) Think, Pair, Share and (4) Stop Reading. What Are You Thinking? Summary Circle.

The read-aloud served its purpose: Kids practiced their reading comprehension skills by manipulating the information they were gathering about coral. Though this leg of the study was "teacher controlled," it set up the next sections of reading and conversation that are student dominated.

Gradual Release of Teacher Control

So, now that the kids have added to their background knowledge about coral reefs, I begin the gradual release of control. After the read-aloud, the kids did a "partner read" and completed a double entry entitled "I Used to Think…But Now I Know…." The purpose of the organizer is to help children talk about how their thinking is changing as a result of study. The procedure is simple. I pair readers and together they choose a text from a collection of books. They complete the organizer together, each writing in only one of the columns. (The two handwritings ensure that both kids are participating. The written document serves as assessment.)

As I listened to the conversations each pair of children was having, I was struck by how often they used prior knowledge to interact with the text. I also noticed that having knowledge in common gave them plenty of topics to discuss—there was no feeling of "what can I say next?" Reading and talking are mutually supportive, particularly with very young children who are just becoming fluent readers. Several of the kids who had some difficulty speaking during my read-aloud (some shy, some language disabled) were more chatty during the book work and made insightful comments. I was delighted by two students asking to do "extra credit" (you can see some examples of it in Figure 3). It is never hard to motivate kids who are interested in the topic and have experienced the pleasure of knowing something really well.

The students often demonstrate their thinking in a concrete fashion— for example, projects, posters, drawings, books, written reports, and artifacts. These in turn spark conversation and congratulation, which then ignite future learning, some of it in class (like the coral micro-unit) and some independent. This snowball effect is indicative of the critical role that oral presentation plays in science learning for young children.

FIGURE 3 Student Work—"I Used to Think But Now I Know"

We, ————————— and ——————————,
read Life In A Coral Reef.

I used to think…	But now I know…
that sea cucumber had nothing to do with a coral reef	a sea cucumber spits sand at cracke near the coral reef
that thair was only a few fish at a coral reef	that there zolions of fish at the coral reef
that Parrot fish just went to sleeip	that they cover their self with slimy mucus bags befor going to bed

✓++
great observations
and
extra credit

(continued)

FIGURE 3 (*continued*)

We, —————————— and ——————————,
read Life in the coral reef .

I used to think…	But now I know…
that Sea Star had no thorns.	that some seastars have thorns like the crownofthorn sea star.
that coral had parents	that thay have no parents.
Sea otter eat urchin and clams	Sea otters also eat celp.

√x

(*continued*)

FIGURE 3 (*continued*)

We, _____ and _____,
read coral _____.

I used to think…	But now I know…
all coral was hard / coral was not a live	that some are soft they are a live.
that coral reef are plants	thay are animals
that fan coral was not flat.	that it is flat and it looks like a leaf.
if coral brocke the peas of coral coral well die.	it dose not die it stay alive

√++
(extra credit!)

During Treasures From Home time at the end of the coral micro-unit, Jeffrey and Eli raise their hands to share a treasure with the class. As you recall, it was Eli's Treasure that got this whole coral study underway. Eli is profoundly dyslexic. But because of his rich spoken vocabulary, developed through doing and talking about science, his reading is improving. Though Eli is out of the room daily for special reading instruction and twice a week for speech therapy, he never misses a beat. His reentry into the classroom is facilitated by the connected day. It's not as if he leaves when we are doing social studies and returns when we are doing writing.

Nancy:	Eli and Jeffrey, what do you have to share with us today?
Eli:	We looked at books and drew these [Figure 4] by looking at the books. I drew from a scientific book on sharks. We labeled its eyes and dorsal fin—we looked for all kinds of fins.
Jeffrey:	Some sharks like 90 degree water….
Eli:	Shark jaws are the most powerful jaws on Earth….
Nancy:	So, you formed a committee and studied this on your own, comparing your books?
Eli and Jeffrey:	Yeah!
Nancy:	Class, any questions about sharks or something to add about sharks?

FIGURE 4 Student Drawing of a Squid, Jellyfish, and Great White Shark

Resources

Block, C., and M. Pressley, eds. 2002. *Comprehension instruction: Research-based practices.* New York: Guilford.

Farstrup, A., and J. Samuels, eds. 2002. *What research has to say about reading comprehension.* Newark, DE: International Reading Association.

Harvey, S., and A. Goudvis. 2000. *Strategies that work: Teaching comprehension to enhance understanding.* York, ME: Stenhouse.

Pearce, C. 1999. *Nurturing inquiry: Real science for the elementary classroom.* Portsmouth, NH: Heinemann.

Routman, R. 2003. *Reading essentials.* Portsmouth, NH: Heinemann.

Saul, W., and S. Jagusch. 1991. *Vital connections: Children, science and books.* Portsmouth, NH: Heinemann.

Questions for Discussion

1. What evidence is there that the classroom culture supports science and literacy?

2. Mrs. McDonough uses text to connect firsthand observations of coral made by students in her class to information about other coral colonies not observable in class. Examine Table 1, "Illustrations of the Shared Cognitive Functions of Inquiry and Comprehension Strategies," on page 234 of Chapter 8. How could these strategies be applied in Mrs. McDonough's classroom so that firsthand inquiry remains closely integrated with secondhand or textual inquiry as defined in Chapter 10?

Reading and Writing in the Service of Inquiry-Based Science

Gina N. Cervetti and P. David Pearson
University of California, Berkeley
Marco A. Bravo
San Francisco State University
Jacqueline Barber
Lawrence Hall of Science, University of California, Berkeley

As literacy educators venturing into the world of science curriculum, we have been guided by two assertions, one a statement of fact and the other an aspiration.

- The fact: State and federal policies have, for better or worse (mostly worse), marginalized disciplinary curricula, including science, in deference to a massive, almost manic, devotion to literacy teaching and learning.
- The aspiration: In a perfect (or at least a better) world, language and literacy—like learning—would be regarded as a means to learning in the disciplines rather than an end unto itself.

In that vein, the guiding principle in our work has been to lead with science and follow with literacy. In other words, we try to make the knowledge, skills, and dispositions of inquiry-based science the "end" of our work; then we position language and literacy as a part of the array of means that can help students achieve that end. For too many years, educators and policy makers have regarded literacy as an end unto itself, as a curricular enterprise on a par with science, social studies, art, or mathematics. As a result we have created curricular structures (e.g., standards, assessments, and mandated curricula) that undercut both disciplinary learning and, ironically, the acquisition of higher literacy skills, such as comprehension, critical literacy, and strategic reading. Only when we return to a more functional view of the role of language and literacy in supporting disciplinary learning can we achieve our goal of an informed citizenry who can use their literacy skills to think critically and flexibly across many domains of knowledge and inquiry. Applying language and literacy tools to science learning, we think, provides precisely the right opportunity for promoting these lofty but essential educational goals.

We have mixed feelings about making yet another contribution to the very enlightening, interesting, and even provocative—but largely "data free"—conversation about the science-literacy connection. On the one hand, we believe that we have a genuine contribution to make to this conversation. On the other hand, we believe that all of us who care about this interface, ourselves included, need to move beyond theoretical ruminations about the benefits of integration to tough-minded empirical examinations. We are pleased to report that we are in the process of gathering evidence that speaks directly to the science-literacy connection, and we will share some of our preliminary results, but our work is still too preliminary to allow us to speak with great confidence about instructional implications and recommendations that could assist teachers in promoting synergy between science and literacy.

Nonetheless, we do have a message in the form of a model that might guide teachers and curriculum developers, as it has guided us, in shaping an appropriate and supportive role for text and for literacy practices in inquiry-based science. What we have are some very good hunches that come with several sources of support, none of it definitive but all of it consistent in pointing to these synergies. First, there is some good theory about the efficacy of integrated curriculum.[1] Second, we can take some guidance from a body of loosely related cognitive research and an even smaller corpus of solid instructional research.[2] Third, we have much to draw from in careful accounts of the professional wisdom of experienced teachers embodied in what we have come to call "best practices" research.[3] Fourth, and most important in shaping this chapter, we have been forced (whether we wanted to or not), as we have tried to achieve this integrated approach, to develop insights about what works, what doesn't, what is easy to achieve, and what is very, very hard.

CHAPTER
8

Our journey into the interface of science and literacy begins with a description of the context in which we have conducted our conceptual and empirical work on the science-literacy connection, followed by a brief review of the science-literacy perspectives that have guided us. Next, the heart of the chapter unfolds as a set of insights we have developed as we have carried out our work, and this leads to the finale—a promising, but cautiously proposed, set of implications for teaching integrated science-literacy curriculum.

Context for Our Work

Our understanding of the science-literacy interface has developed in the context of our work on a National Science Foundation–funded curriculum development and research project, Seeds of Science/Roots of Reading, a joint effort of the Graduate School of Education and the Lawrence Hall of Science (LHS) at the University of California, Berkeley. The goal of the project is to transform existing inquiry-based science units from the Great Explorations in Math and Science (GEMS) curriculum series developed at LHS into materials that help students make sense of the physical world through firsthand experiences while addressing foundational dimensions of reading, writing, and language.

Seeds/Roots has assembled science and literacy experts to study, enact in the form of curriculum, and test the limits and potential of the science-literacy interface. The questions that have guided the effort are the following:

- How can reading and writing be used as tools to support inquiry-based science learning?
- What benefits accrue to reading and writing when they are embedded in an inquiry-based science curriculum?
- What skills, strategies, and processes are shared by these two curricular domains?

During the first two years of the project, we have built a model of science-literacy integration, applied that model to the development of three integrated units for second- and third-grade students, and carried out a nationwide field test of these units in 87 classrooms in 21 states. We have also initiated a series of qualitative and quasi-experimental research studies designed to inform our curriculum development work and answer foundational questions about both science and literacy learning in the context of an integrated curriculum. While complete results are not yet available, we can and will share some early findings and some insights from our reflections on the entire experience to date.

Related Literature: Relevant Work on the Science-Literacy Interface

Our work draws in part on literature from the 1980s and early 1990s examining the overlapping cognitive demands of science and literacy. For the most part, this work is more conceptual and theoretical than empirical or pedagogical in orientation and consists largely of insights into the shared demands and processes of thinking in science and literacy. For example, Padilla and his colleagues (Padilla, Muth, and Padilla 1991) suggest that discovery science and reading emphasize a shared set of intellectual processes (e.g., observing, classifying, inferring, predicting, and communicating) and that the very same problem-solving processes are used "whether [students are] conducting science experiments or reading assigned science texts." Others connect reading and science through metacognition (thinking about our thinking), arguing that science and literacy share a concern with fostering independent learning. Baker (1991), for example, suggests that, while metacognition ("the awareness and control individuals have over their cognitive processes") is widely recognized as an essential component of reading, its connection to science has not been explored even though many science process skills can be regarded as highly metacognitive (e.g., formulating conclusions, analyzing critically, evaluating information, recognizing main ideas and concepts, establishing relationships, and applying information to other situations). Baker contends that attention to metacognition in science can help teachers foster independence through "lectures, discussion, laboratory work, and hands-on activities."

Our work also relies on existing, empirically based models of science-literacy integration. Palincsar and Magnusson (2001) have contributed greatly to our understanding of this integration process; among their most important contributions, in relation to our work, is their distinction between first- and secondhand investigations. In their approach, literacy engages students in secondhand investigations for one of three purposes:

1. To bolster and reinforce learnings from firsthand investigations
2. To take students on vicarious journeys (deep in the ocean, far into outer space, or inside a volcano) that cannot otherwise be taken in our classrooms
3. To provide students with an opportunity to apply the inquiry-based skills and processes acquired in firsthand investigations to new do-

mains of inquiry (e.g., drawing conclusions based on reading an account of an investigation)

Romance and Vitale (1992) take us in a slightly different direction. They were among the first to design and empirically test a science-literacy integrated curriculum that attempted to use vicarious text-based experiences as a "test bed" for applying knowledge and reasoning skills that students were supposed to have gained in firsthand science investigations. Students in their integrated approach outperformed the control group (side-by-side but thoroughly encapsulated science and literacy curricula) students on standardized measures of reading and science, and they displayed more positive attitudes toward science.

Guthrie and his colleagues (e.g., Guthrie and Ozgungor 2002; Guthrie et al. 1998) have approached the integration of science and literacy from the reading side of the curricular integration and, equally as important, from a perspective that pays as much attention to engagement as it does to cognitive learning. Concept-Oriented Reading Instruction (CORI) places emphasis on providing a rich and compelling context for teaching reading strategies. Inquiry science (or other subject matter foci) serves as the real-world interaction ingredient for the CORI model. In the early phases of CORI, Guthrie and colleagues were able to show impressive advantages over conventional approaches on measures of reading comprehension and engagement but failed to examine conceptual learning of science. In their later work, they added conceptual science learning to their portfolio of outcomes and found positive results for science as well as literacy.

These few studies are the most notable exemplars in a much larger body of work that has guided our entry into the science-literacy interface. They represent at least a few of the points along the broad continuum of views about the ideal relationship between science and literacy. In this work, and among scholars in both science and literacy education who are concerned about the disciplinary interface, there is broad acknowledgment that the work of scientists is reliant in part on their literacy skills, particularly in accessing ideas from text and communicating results. Yore and his colleagues, as well as Kamil and Bernhardt, recognize the active role that reading and writing play in the everyday work of science and scientists.[4]

Despite this recognition that text is a fundamental part of the scientific enterprise, there is at the same time strong apprehension about the use of text in school science, particularly in the inquiry science tradition and particularly with younger students. Three concerns seem to predominate.

First, as Yager (2004) has noted, science texts are more often "declarations of 'fact'" than real representations of the "heart and soul of the scientific enterprise" (p. 95). Second, science texts, particularly trade texts, often include misinformation, exaggerations, and other misrepresentations that can interfere with the development of science concepts. Third, text can eclipse scientific discovery, taking the place of observation and experimentation and supplanting children's involvement in inquiry with passive reception of ideas.[5]

Given these pervasive concerns, it is not surprising that text has been largely absent from inquiry-based science or that, where text is part of the curriculum, it has been relegated to a peripheral position. Even in programs like those of Romance and Vitale and Guthrie and colleagues, where science and literacy are given comparable status, the firsthand experience component of the integrated curriculum always precedes the text component.

Insights From Our Work in Seeds of Science/Roots of Reading

In investigating the natural convergences between science and literacy, we found a great deal of evidence for mutual support, and none was more central than our understanding of the way in which text can support rather than supplant inquiry-based science learning—and appropriately that is our first insight. But as we planned our instruction, as we looked more closely at elements like concept development and vocabulary, comprehension and inquiry skills, visual displays, and talk about text and science, we came to understand that, in some important respects, science and literacy are more than supportive and synergistic, that they are in fact *isomorphic*—that is, they have an inherent similarity of form and appearance, like two ancestrally related organisms or two different substances that share the same crystal structure. A careful analysis of which strategies and cognitive processes are shared between science and literacy, and which are domain specific, led us to four conclusions: comprehension strategies *are* inquiry strategies; words *are* concepts; science *is* discourse; and literacy *is* visual literacy. These principles have guided our model of science-literacy integration as we continue to seek strategic opportunities to help students develop their ability to use these common strategies and cognitive processes in both domains. Seeds/Roots instructional materials explicitly make the connection between science and literacy strategies and provide time for students to reflect on how those similarities can make their learning more effective.

Insight #1: Texts Can Support Scientific Inquiry

In the inquiry tradition of science education, inquiry is often equated with firsthand involvement in investigations. Secondhand investigations, such as "accounts" of scientific inquiry encountered in text, are generally regarded as poor substitutes for the real thing. And when teachers adopt a strict inquiry approach, text may play little if any role in science learning. As members of the literacy education community, we recognize that there are serious limits to what students can learn about science through text, but just as surely there are limits to what students can learn through an exclusively firsthand approach. Not everything we want students to learn about science can be observed or manipulated in the classroom (and some not in the natural world!). In addition, as Palincsar and Magnusson (2001) point out, it is unlikely that children will come to meaningful understandings in science solely by interacting with materials and phenomena in a firsthand way. Osborne (2002) elaborates on the limits of the laboratory and how "engaging in the discourse of the scientific community requires scientists to engage in both reading the work of others and writing to communicate their own findings." Indeed practicing scientists would be the first to admit that text plays a significant role in the development of their own learning, theory development, and methodological expertise. They learn about and come to understand the natural world through text as well as firsthand experience. So too can students, or at least that is our claim and our goal.

Our experience suggests that text can serve a number of roles that are supportive of inquiry science—before, during, and after firsthand investigations. In laying out these roles, we once again remind readers of our basic commitment to leading with science and allowing literacy, including texts, to play the supportive role of assisting students in acquiring and organizing facts, concepts, and patterns into networks of meaningful relations (see Guthrie et al. 1998).

Providing Context

Facts, concepts, and patterns—the stuff of scientific learning—are grounded in contexts; contexts include the discipline in which the learning is situated, the real-world context in which the scientific phenomena operate, and the specific experiential/instructional context in which the learning occurs. And contexts provide a natural link to the knowledge and experience that students bring to both first- and secondhand investigations. Text can support firsthand inquiry by providing an invitation for students to engage with the scientific context and content. Text can prepare students for inquiry by inspiring students to wonder about science. In a study by Anderson and colleagues (Anderson et al. 1997), students read books to provoke their wondering about a scientific topic, asked questions about the topic, and engaged in investigations to answer their questions. Students selected books by asking, "Is this interesting? Does it make us wonder about science things? Do we want to talk about these wonderments with our friends?" Collectively, they found many books that prompted "wonderments," which were sufficiently engaging to lead the students to substantive explorations at a later point.

Text can introduce the scientific domain and invite students to engage with the context. Texts that serve this introductory or invitational function may engage students by representing new ideas or phenomena in interesting ways or by presenting the familiar in a new, scientific frame—"making the familiar strange," if you will. We developed a book for a physical science unit on mixtures that engages students in thinking about the relationship between properties, materials, and human-made objects by exploring imaginary and imaginative mismatches, such as rain boots made of paper and frying pans made of rubber. The students subsequently think about the relationship between properties and materials as they design new mixtures. Franklyn M. Branley's *What the Moon Is Like* invites students to view the Moon up close as an astronaut would. The book offers a variety of perspectives on the Moon, from the aesthetic to the scientific, and shows the Moon from Earth and up close. We cannot arrange classroom trips to the Moon, but this book might set the context for study of the Moon or solar system involving more inquiry-oriented, firsthand investigations.

Text can connect firsthand investigations to the world outside the classroom. Students studying life science may never encounter many of the habitats they study. Books can situate their learning and connect firsthand investigations in the classroom to the environments in which the phenomena operate in the world outside of school. Melvin Berger's *Oil Spill* describes the aftermath of the 1989 *Exxon Valdez* spill. It can be used to support students' firsthand investigations of oil spills by connecting that firsthand experience with the causes and consequences of a real oil spill in the ocean.

Delivering Content

Text can deliver (some of) the "goods." Text can present scientific concepts, facts, and patterns to students. This is the most traditional role for text in science. And, as Palincsar and Magnusson (2001) suggest, it is an authentic role: "[T]he notion that inquiry must be exclusively activity based is problematic because, in fact, much of what we know about scientific reasoning has been acquired through the thinking and experiences of others; that is, through learning in a secondhand way. Frequently, although not exclusively, this secondhand learning can be facilitated with the use of text" (p. 152). Most science texts deliver science information. Some present scientific content incidentally as they, for example, discuss the work of particular scientists. Other books are designed principally for delivering information, including reference readers (e.g., encyclopedias, field guides, and dictionaries) and "all about" books (e.g., a book all about plant roots that students might read after they have observed and compared several root structures firsthand). The delivery of information can connect, supplement, and extend, not supplant, students' firsthand investigations.

Texts can make the obscure accessible. Text can provide information about, and even illustrate, phenomena that would otherwise be unobservable in a classroom context. Sometimes objects and phenomena are actually unobservable; other times they are practically unobservable. Phenomena may be unobservable because they are too small, too big, too hidden, or too distant for us to see firsthand or because they are too expensive to recreate in classrooms. In Ann Earle's *Zipping, Zapping, Zooming Bats*, students can seek out information about internal and external structures of a bat. Few students will see a bat close up, and fewer will be able to examine its internal structures in a firsthand way.

Modeling

Both implicitly and explicitly, texts can model important processes in both literacy and science. The models range from inquiry, to reading and writing, to the nature of science itself.

Texts can model inquiry processes. Text can provide rich models of scientific inquiry skills, including what careful observation involves, how to compare and classify things, and how to make inferences and explanations based on evidence. In Irene Brady's *Wild Mouse*, students can read a true account of a writer who discovers that a mouse has nested in the drawer of her desk. The writer makes systematic observations and drawings of what turns out to be a pregnant mouse every day for a month. This book models careful observation and description and the use of drawings to amplify particular parts of the text.

Texts can model literacy processes. Just as the stories students read provide models for their own narratives, so science texts can provide models of how particular text genres are constructed, how data are recorded, and how scientists read and make sense of scientific information. Text can model scientific modes of communication, including evidence-based explanations and argumentation. In one of our units, we use a story about a boy who consults his older sister at every stage of the process of preparing a report for his science class. Importantly, scientific texts can provide students with practice reading informational scientific text, so rarely encountered in the early grades. The scientists' notebooks texts developed by Palincsar and Magnusson for their Guided Inquiry supporting Multiple Literacies (GIsMl) project are good examples of text models of literacy processes (and of secondhand investigations); they provide students with models of scientists writing and reading about scientific investigations.

Texts can illustrate the nature of science. Text can provide insights into the scientific enterprise and scientific dispositions. Text can model the wondering, exploration, and hypothesis testing that are the heart of scientific literacy (Yager 2004). Books can model missteps and dead ends, as well as successes of science and the application of scientific work to everyday dilemmas. Text can demonstrate human and commercial uses for science. There are many examples of high-quality trade texts that focus on the life and/or work of a particular scientist, books in which scientists describe their interest in science, demonstrate scientific habits of mind such as persistence and curiosity, share aspects of their work, and model excitement, passion, and commitment.[6]

Supporting Secondhand Inquiry

Texts provide experience with data. Text can provide data on which the reader is challenged to draw conclusions and develop claims. Secondhand investigations can allow students to investigate phenomena that are not easily modeled in classrooms. Texts can also provide additional practice with especially challenging inquiry skills, such as making sense of data and drawing conclusions. Palincsar and Magnusson's scientists' notebooks texts provide an opportunity for students to make sense of data collected by an invented scientist. In Steve Jenkins and Robin Page's *What Do You Do With a Tail Like This?*, students draw conclusions about the function of specific animal structures based on illustrations of those animal structures. On one spread, students are presented with illustrations of various animals' feet and asked, "What do you do with feet like these?" Without making direct observations of various animals' feet, students are challenged to make inferences about the form-function relationships in nature.

Supporting Firsthand Inquiry

Texts provide information that facilitates firsthand investigations. Texts can help students make sense of their firsthand investigations and draw conclusions about their data. They can provide an opportunity for students to support and/or revise their thinking based on the addition of new information in text. They can address misconceptions that might arise in the conduct of firsthand investigations. Reference readers are often useful for this purpose. For example, a reference guide that pictures and describes Earth minerals might be used to help students find information related to the composition and formation of the sand as they investigate real sand samples.

Texts support students in making sense of firsthand investigations. Texts can provide information that brings meaning to firsthand investigations. Leslie Dendy's *Tracks, Scats and Signs* provides students with a field guide they can use to identify evidence of animals they see on a nature walk. A book such as this can encourage students to be careful, motivated observers—to take on a scientific stance—and it can help them make sense of the things they observe.

Texts can inspire firsthand investigations. Students can be inspired to engage in firsthand investigations by the texts they read. One of the books in a unit on designing mixtures, *Jess Makes Hair Gel*, prompted more than one group of second-grade students to design their own hair gel and send us pictures of the results.

Insight #2: Comprehension Strategies Are Inquiry Strategies

The model of science-literacy integration that guides our work relies on a recognition that science and literacy share a set of core meaning-making strategies. Comprehension strategies and inquiry strategies represent accepted problem-solving and meaning-making strategies in literacy and science respectively. Inquiry is the approach that scientists use to pose questions, investigate phenomena, and make meaning. Comprehension strategies similarly represent an approach to questioning and making sense around text. As the domains of meaning making in reading and science, comprehension and inquiry share a set of important functions and strategies that, at least in second and third grade, are identical.

Some Shared Functions

- *Metacognitive regulation.* Comprehension strategies and inquiry strategies share a concern with promoting self-regulation. That is, comprehension

strategies and inquiry strategies are both designed to help students monitor their learning—to help students plan an approach to the task ahead,
evaluate the outcomes of their efforts, and revise them as needed.

- *Acquiring information.* Comprehension strategies, particularly in informational and content-area literacy, support students' efforts to acquire information. Inquiry shares the goals of gathering and making
sense of information in order to construct more complex and complete understandings.

- *Solving problems.* Problem solving is all about managing complexity. We
take a complex domain and make it manageable by attacking one aspect of the problem at a time. Then we piece the steps and chunks back
together. Comprehension and inquiry strategies structure, systematize,
break down, and then re-synthesize aspects of reasoning about text or
experience in exactly this way. And save for the fact that the information that drives the process comes from different sources (text versus experience), the overall process looks and feels the same across domains.

- *Making connections.* Comprehension and inquiry strategies help students
bring together diverse sources of information—including text-based information, experience, and personal knowledge—to make judgments
and draw conclusions. Comprehension requires a reader to both understand ideas from the text ("Oh, I get it!"), build a coherent account of
the full array of ideas the text offers ("Oh, I see, this goes with this."),
and connect them with other experiences and ideas already available
in schema-like structures in long-term memory ("Oh, this is sort of
like…"). Inquiry requires a scientist to see steps as well as the relationships among the steps of any particular inquiry process and to compare
them to previous experiences with similar inquiries.

All of these functions come together to support meaning making. While
the "doing"/activity element of reading and scientific inquiry look quite different, the meaning-making elements share powerful commonalities and can
look very much the same. As Pratt and Pratt (2004) note, while the source
of learning differs (natural phenomenon as object versus text as object),
both "call for the construction of meaning from experience" (p. 396).

Shared Strategies

Comprehension strategies and inquiry not only share overlapping goals
and functions, they also share common strategies—strategies that support
the construction of meaning. Our emphasis is on encouraging students to

engage in meaning making around their firsthand experiences and their reading and to be both active and strategic as they do so. We want to help students connect the strategies to the doing. We find these strategies in both science and literacy activity:

- *Activating prior knowledge*. When we read, just as when we do scientific investigations, it is essential to think about what we know. Activating prior knowledge prepares students to make connections, draw conclusions, and digest new ideas (Barton, Heidema, and Jordan 2002). In our work, we connect literacy and science by encouraging students to activate their knowledge from text experiences, hands-on experiences, and out-of-school experiences. We also emphasize reviewing prior knowledge in light of new information.
- *Establishing purposes/goals*. In both reading and science inquiry we set explicit goals for what we want to learn and we identify strategies to help achieve those goals.
- *Making/reviewing predictions*. Prediction builds purpose in either domain; you read on or work on to see whether your prediction turns out to be accurate. Prediction builds commitment by giving readers and scientists a stake in the outcome.
- *Drawing inferences and conclusions*. An essential goal of science education is to encourage students to weigh evidence and reach defensible conclusions (Watson 1983). In reading, drawing conclusions is a valued high-level interpretive skill. In both instances, using evidence to warrant claims is the heart of the activity.
- *Making connections/recognizing relationships*. When reading and engaging in inquiry, we want students to broaden and deepen their understandings by making connections across a range of experiences and information and by discerning relationships of various kinds, including cause and effect relationships and comparison/contrast relationships, among others.

Table 1 illustrates what each of these important strategies looks like when it is exemplified by a prompt designed to provoke students to be more strategic *both* when reading and when engaging in inquiry.

Insight #3: Words Are Concepts

To have active control of a word is to know more than its definition; it is also to know how the word is used in different contexts and where it fits in

TABLE 1 Illustrations of the Shared Cognitive Functions of Inquiry and Comprehension Strategies

Shared Strategy	Common Questions	Example in Science	Example in Literacy
Activating prior knowledge	• What do I already know? • What do I know now that I didn't know before?	Students use an anticipatory chart to monitor their growing knowledge of shorelines and the organisms that live on shorelines.	Before reading a book about earthworms, students discuss what they have learned from their hands-on observations of earthworms.
Establishing purposes/goals	• Why am I reading/doing this? • What am I trying to learn? • What information am I seeking?	Before engaging in guided investigations of their shoreline organisms, students write about what they want to learn through their investigations.	Having investigated the effects of oil spills through a series of hands-on science activities, students discuss what they still want to know before reading a book about a real oil spill.
Making/reviewing predictions	• What do I think is going to happen?	Students continually make, review, and revise their predictions about what will happen in a worm bin—and they document the growing evidence that soil is being made.	Students make predictions about what a habitat scientist is and does before reading a book about a habitat scientist; they review and revise those predictions during and after reading.
Drawing inferences and conclusions	• What does this mean? • How do I explain x?	Students gather evidence from a bucket of beach sand to answer the question, "What is sand made of?"	Students use a scientist's sand journal to make inferences about the origins of sand samples.
Making connections/recognizing relationships	• What caused x? • How are x and y related? • How is x like/unlike y?	Students compare the adaptations of different isopods.	Students use a reference reader about substances to select ingredients that will help them make paint with specific properties.

a rich network of related concepts. Word knowledge is multidimensional (Nagy and Scott 2000). At its most basic, knowing a word involves knowing how the word sounds or looks when it is written. More sophisticated knowledge of a word might involve knowing its definition. Even more sophisticated knowledge might also involve things like its syntactic register, its context of use, and its association with other words.

In this sense, word knowledge at its most mature is conceptual knowledge—it involves understanding of words as they are situated within a network of other words and ideas (what psychologists have called *paradigmatic* relations) and their relationship to other words in spoken or written contexts (what psychologists have called *syntagmatic* relations).

We suggest that, from this perspective, word learning in science can and should be approached as conceptual learning. Even though it is true that words are labels for concepts, it is better to think of them as inherently conceptual in order to prevent ourselves from teaching them as a set of labels and definitions. If we assert that words are concepts, we are more likely to help students understand how they connect to other concepts to form rich conceptual networks.

Vocabulary instruction in science has sometimes been reduced to recall or definitional knowledge of a large number of words. Indeed some science textbooks introduce more new vocabulary than foreign language textbooks! However, vocabulary instruction at its most complex focuses on a targeted number of words and approaches a depth-of-knowledge criterion that is comparable to that of science conceptual learning. In science (as in other domains), "students should learn concepts as organized networks of related information" (Glynn and Muth 1994, p. 1060).

We know from a substantial body of research that effective vocabulary instruction integrates new words with other word knowledge. We also know that word learning requires multiple exposures in meaningful contexts. As Stahl and Stahl (2004) suggest,

> For each exposure, the child learns a little about the word, until the child develops a full and flexible knowledge about the word's meaning. This will include definitional aspects, such as the category to which it belongs and how it differs from other members of the category…. It will also contain information about the various context in which the word was found, and how the meaning differed in the different contexts. (p. 63)

In many ways, science is an ideal context for developing rich conceptual networks of words. Science provides natural opportunities for authentic, repeated, and varied encounters with these new words/concepts—during firsthand experiences, through texts, and in discussions and written activities. All of these contexts provide students opportunities to practice using the words in appropriate ways.

In our work, we create opportunities for students to encounter and use a focused set of core concept words in discussion and in print. [All of the words in italics below are core concepts for the science unit. Students encounter and learn these words as a connected set of ideas.] For example, students are introduced to the concept of *habitat* as they simulate a forest floor habitat in building their own terrariums. Students discuss the various elements of a habitat (food, *shelter*, water, air, light) for the *organisms* (plants and animals) they will introduce to the *terrarium*. Further discussions take place about the *soil* the organisms will require and the *nutrients* and *moisture* that the soil will provide the habitat.

Students also read about the concept of *habitat* in the *Talking With a Habitat Scientist* book, where they learn that a habitat is a place where plants or animals live and find everything they need to *survive*. The book explains how plants and animals *depend* on each other and the *prey/predator* roles they play in the *environment*. Through print, discussion, and firsthand experiences, students learn about the concept of *habitat* in relation to a conceptual network of other important science words.

Insight #4: Science Is Discourse

Science is an academic language, a way of communicating about the natural world. In this fourth synergy, we recognize that in addition to being a discipline, science is a social context in which the language used is a powerful and specialized way of talking about the world, writing about the world, and even "being" in the world of scientists (Gee 2004). The specialized language of science, which linguists call a discourse, has its own vocabulary and organization, which are embodied in the ways scientists communicate about their work. Postman (1979) emphasized this point by claiming that "biology is not plants and animals. It is language about plants and animals.... Astronomy is not planets and stars. It is a way of talking about planets and stars" (p. 165).

This is very different from older views that treated science and language as existing in separate domains where science was about experience—thinking about or doing science—and not about language at all. Science, in fact, is a highly communicative field with established ways of talking and writing. Lemke (1990) puts the proposition in bold terms: "Learning science is learning the language of science." Postman and Weingartner (1971) state it quite practically: "What is biology (for example) other than words? If all the words that biologists use were subtracted from the language, there would be no biology...." For example, the need for precision motivates scientists to exchange the vocabulary of everyday language for specialized words that will be clear to other scientists (but are likely to be obscure to the average person). Scientists make predictions rather than guesses, they observe rather than see, and they talk about habitats rather than homes and properties rather than qualities.

But the discourse of science is more than specialized words; it is also about organizing claims and evidence into arguments expressed in a scientific way of "talking" or "writing." The language of science is evident in the way scientists debate and discuss scientific concepts and in the ways they approach investigations and negotiate meaning by questioning and posing alternative solutions during scientific discourse. Argumentation plays a major role in the social construction of scientific knowledge. Language mediates this process of "supporting, criticizing, evaluating, and refining of ideas, some of which may conflict or compete, about a scientific subject" (Kuhn 1992).

While this specialized discourse serves the interests of the scientific community, it is generally inaccessible to outsiders, including students in our schools. Yet, the language of science is part and parcel of doing science, and it is one of the many academic discourses that students are expected to understand and use when encountering texts and tests in school. And, talking about science is critical to the social activity involved in science—observing, describing, questioning, evaluating, concluding, arguing, classifying, comparing. In other words, students must learn the various, often complex, scientific discourse styles, including the vocabulary necessary to share, clarify, and distribute knowledge among peers. For many students, these special discourses become a catch-22. They don't come to school with the discourse of science already under control, so it is hard for them to just jump in and do and talk science. But unless they just jump in, they are not likely to get better at doing and talking science. We are committed to demystifying the language of science so that students can embrace it in the science classroom. We do students a disservice if we do not help them acquire this tool kit for doing science.

One strategy for dealing with the obscurity of scientific discourse is to avoid it or at least delay its use until middle or high school. Our experience with inquiry-based science for young learners suggests, to the contrary, that they benefit from thoughtful immersion in and exposure to the language of science early and often. Just as students deserve a chance to acquire the firsthand tools of inquiry-based science, so too do they deserve a chance to acquire its discourse. Science is a powerful discourse that, among other things, will support their entry into valued disciplines of academic learning. In our own work, we have found that even second- and third-grade students can appropriate the discourse as they participate in firsthand science if the curriculum is focused and systematic in scaffolding the language use to fit the science goals and processes.

We are committed to a four-pronged approach:

First, we create an environment for science instruction that is replete with the discourse of science. Students encounter the words and linguistic structures of science through books, student sheets, visual displays, and teacher talk.

Second, we have chosen core scientific terms to emphasize both within and across domains. Thus, within the domain of Earth science, in a unit on habitats, core words include *habitat, decomposition, adaptation, ecosystem, evidence, investigate, observe,* and *classify*. Notice that the first four words are crucial to the domain of life sciences and will be essential to classroom talk about the activities of the creatures in the terrariums the students have built. The last four words are not unique to life science; students will encounter them in units in physical science and Earth science.

Third, we use students' existing understandings about language and the world to support their development of scientific language. As we mentioned above, we use everyday language as hooks on which students can "hang" new scientific language. But we also help them understand why and how it makes a difference when you say *observe* rather than *see* or *look,* or when you talk about your data as *evidence* rather than *clues*.

Finally, we view firsthand investigations as the glue that binds together all of the linguistic activity around inquiry. The mantra we have developed for ourselves in helping students acquire conceptual knowledge and the discourse in which that knowledge is expressed (including particular vocabulary) is "read it, write it, talk it, do it!"—and in no particular order, or better yet, in every possible order.

Insight #5: Literacy Is Visual Literacy

Text, particularly in science, refers to more than words on the printed page. Science relies heavily on the use of visual elements to represent and convey information, and these visual elements are an essential component of science text (Kress 2000). In science, the diversity of visual elements extends from photographs to highly complex charts, tables, graphs, and diagrams. These visual representations often carry new information that supplements and supports printed text, and sometimes they literally offer *re*-presentations of textual information in a visual format. Both forms of representation—visual and print—are used to communicate complex arrays of ideas, evidence, and claims about natural phenomena. But visual representations also serve three special functions that support students' ability to recognize relationships, solve problems, and draw conclusions:

1. They can condense large amounts of information in ways that facilitate drawing of conclusions.
2. They can represent relations among facts, concepts, and patterns in a way that increases the likelihood that students will develop a rich and elaborate set of connections among these elements.
3. They make transparent what can otherwise be obscure; this is the maxim that a picture is worth a thousand words.

But these functions apply to more than pictures. A graph, for example, makes the magnitude of a linear relationship between two variables immediately apprehensible in a way that even the most well-crafted sentence cannot. These three functions make problem solving and conceptual understanding all the more likely.

Visual displays also bring variety to the representation of complex ideas and data, increasing opportunities to access that information. In our work, we have been able to identify key roles for at least the following types of visual displays—maps, charts, graphs, and diagrams; moreover, each of these major types has its own subcategories (e.g., within diagrams, we have cross-sectional, Venn, and flow).

Despite the centrality of visual information to science, students are often not taught to "read" and interpret these displays. As Lowe (2000) suggests, successful reading of scientific representations requires different skills from those required for reading other, more "everyday," photographs and illustrations. To "read" visual elements in science requires an understanding of their form, purpose, and function. While we might be more inclined to surround print texts with comprehension instruction and assessment, the centrality of visual texts in science invites an equally strong emphasis on both literal and interpretive comprehension tasks. Either can be examined at "face value" (akin to a literal reading) or from a more interpretive perspective (e.g., How does this display change how we think about X?) (Lowe 2000).

In our work, we teach students to read visual representations, connect them to information provided in the print text (i.e., words arrayed in sentences and paragraphs on the page), and create their own representations as they conduct and communicate their firsthand investigations. For example, in each book that students encounter in our curriculum, teachers are encouraged to provide students with explicit instruction and opportunities to practice reading illustrations, diagrams, and tables. Our book on snail investigations, for instance, distills large amounts of data from the investigations of several students by placing data in table format. To help students gain access to this information, teachers are asked to explain the function of tables (make connections between various pieces of information) and how to read the table (the role of row and column headings and how to trace certain findings using these two elements). Students are then encouraged to make conclusions about the investigation outcomes and connect this information to the printed text. Understanding the form and function of tables helps students to use tables to record the outcomes of their own investigations.

Taking Stock

We are very excited about our work and fully committed to seeing it through to the end, or at least to the point where we have lots of empirical data, of both a qualitative and quantitative character, to test the efficacy of our insights. The early returns from our first year of field trials is very encouraging. On measures of science learning, vocabulary acquisition, and reading comprehension, an approach that integrates literacy (both reading and writing) and oral language activities into inquiry-based science units elicits significantly greater growth than does either a strict inquiry-only approach or a text-only approach (Pearson and Cervetti 2005). Thus even at this early point in the research process, the evidence we do have points compellingly to this integrated approach and to some highly plausible principles to guide us in our quest to improve both literacy and science learning by capitalizing on what each has to offer the other.

Use text, don't avoid it. We are not afraid of using text to support inquiry-based science. We understand—and share—the fear that many science educators have that text will supplant experience as the primary medium for learning science. Our experience tells us that in spite of a dismal history in its support of science learning, if we can keep our wits about us text needn't be regarded as an alternative to science. Instead, it can be a powerful support to inquiry by extending firsthand into secondhand investigations, by helping students travel into spaces where experience cannot easily take them, and by providing an integrative fabric to weave together experiences that might otherwise remain discrete and disconnected.

Celebrate the synergies and isomorphism. At the level of activity and cognitive process, science and literacy are much more alike than different. One of the dangers in offering a separate curriculum for each discipline is that students will learn that it is better to encapsulate the insights from each rather than to search for common processes, strategies, and understandings. Our experience tells us that both literacy and science are supported by integration and shortchanged by encapsulation. While we have emphasized in this chapter the ways in which literacy can support inquiry-based science, we could just as easily have emphasized the ways in which learning literacy is enhanced by situating it in the science classroom. Literacy learning benefits when it is enacted as a means to an end rather than an end unto itself. The stuff of science, both content and process, gives meaning and motive to literacy activity.

Emphasize the authenticity of embedding literacy within science. We are convinced that when reading and writing and text are put to service in the interests of acquiring scientific knowledge, they become appropriately contextualized in a school setting. When literacy is encapsulated in its own curricular space (often for 120 to 150 minutes per day because of Reading First), it runs the risk of becoming the curricular "bully" in today's schools, gobbling up so much of the curricular time and space as to effectively eliminate science, social studies, and the humanities as viable enterprises. The early evidence suggests that both literacy and science benefit when the former is embedded in the latter. We want to opt for the metaphor of literacy as a critical friend (one that can provide support and a lens for reflection). In short, literacy can be a curricular "buddy" rather than a curricular "bully." To move from one to the other requires only a small phonological shift!

References

Anderson, T. H., C. K. West, D. P. Beck, E. S. Macdonell, and D. S. Frisbie. 1997. Integrating reading and science education: On developing and evaluating WEE Science. *Journal of Curriculum Studies* 29 (6): 711–733.

Baker, L. 1991. Metacognition, reading, and science education. In *Science learning: Processes and applications*, eds. C. M. Santa and D. E. Alvermann. Newark, DE: International Reading Association.

Barton, M. L., C. Heidema, and D. Jordan. 2002. Teaching reading in mathematics and science. *Educational Leadership* 60 (3): 24–28.

Gavelek, J. R., T. E. Raphael, S. M. Biondo, and W. Danhua. 1999. *Integrated literacy instruction: A review of the literature.* Report: Ciera-2-001.

Gee, J. P. 2004. Language in the science classroom: Academic social languages as the heart of school-based literacy. In *Crossing borders in literacy and science instruction: Perspectives on theory and practice,* ed. E. W. Saul. Newark, DE: International Reading Association.

Glynn, S. M., and K. D. Muth. 1994. Reading and writing to learn science: Achieving scientific literacy. *Journal of Research in Science Teaching* 31 (9): 1057–1073.

Guthrie, J. T., and S. Ozgungor. 2002. Instructional contexts for reading engagement. In *Comprehension instruction: Research-based best practices,* eds. C. C. Block and M. Pressley. New York: Guilford Press.

Guthrie, J. T., P. Van Meter, G. R. Hancock, S. Alao, E. Anderson, and A. McCann. 1998. Does concept-oriented reading instruction increase strategy use and conceptual learning from text? *Journal of Educational Psychology* 90 (2): 261–278.

Hapgood, S., S. J. Magnusson, and A. S. Palincsar. 2004. Teacher, text, and experience: A case of young children's scientific inquiry. *The Journal of the Learning Sciences* 13 (4): 455–505.

Kamil, M. L., and E. B. Bernhardt. 2004. The science of reading and the reading of science: Successes, failures, and promises in the search for prerequisite reading skills for science. In *Crossing borders in literacy and science instruction: Perspectives on theory and practice,* ed. E. W. Saul. Newark, DE: International Reading Association.

Kress, G. 2000. Multimodality: Challenges to thinking about language. *TESOL Quarterly* 34 (2): 337–340.

Kuhn, D. 1992. Thinking as argument. *Harvard Educational Review* 62: 155–178.

Kuhn, D. 1993. Science argument: Implications for teaching and learning scientific thinking. *Science Education* 77 (3): 319–337.

Lemke, J. L. 1990. *Talking science: Language, learning, and values.* Norwood, NJ: Ablex.

Lowe, R. 2000. Visual literacy and learning in science. *Eric Digest,* Report EDO-SE-00-02.

Nagy, W., and J. Scott. 2000. Vocabulary processes. In *Handbook of reading research, Vol. 3,* eds. M. Kamil, P. Mosenthal, P. D. Pearson, and R. Barr, 269–284. Mahwah, NJ: Lawrence Erlbaum.

Osborne, J. 2002. Science without literacy: A ship without a sail? *Cambridge Journal of Education* 32 (2): 203–218.

Padilla, M. J., K. D. Muth, and R. K. Padilla. 1991. Science and reading: Many process skills in common? In *Science learning: Processes and applications,* eds. C. M. Santa and D. E. Alvermann, 14–19. Newark, DE: International Reading Association.

Palincsar, A. S., and S. J. Magnusson. 1997. The interaction of first- and secondhand investigations in guided inquiry science teaching. Paper presented at the Annual Conference of the National Reading Conference, Austin, TX.

Palincsar, A. S., and S. J. Magnussen. 2000. The interplay of firsthand and text-based investigations in science class. Ann Arbor, MI: CIERA Report 2-007. Retrieved June 2, 2005, from *www.ciera.org/library/reports/inquiry-2/2-007/2-007.pdf.*

Palincsar, A. S., and S. J. Magnusson. 2001. The interplay of firsthand and text-based investigations to model and support the development of scientific knowledge and reasoning. In *Cognition and instruction: Twenty-five years of progress*, eds. S. Carver and D. Klahr, 151–194. Mahwah, NJ: Lawrence Erlbaum.

Peacock, A., and S. Gates. 2000. Newly qualified primary teachers' perceptions of the roles of text materials in teaching science. *Research in Science & Technological Education* 18 (2): 155–171.

Pearson, P. D., and G. N. Cervetti. 2005. Reading and writing in the service of acquiring scientific knowledge and dispositions: In search of synergies. Paper presented at the Reading Research 2005 preconvention of the International Reading Association, San Antonio, TX (May).

Postman, N. 1979. *Teaching as a conserving activity*. New York: Delacorte.

Postman, N., and C. Weingartner. 1971. *Teaching as a subversive activity*. New York: Delacorte.

Pratt, H., and N. Pratt. 2004. Integrating science and literacy instruction with a common goal of learning science content. In *Crossing borders in literacy and science instruction: Perspectives on theory and practice*, ed. E. W. Saul. Newark, DE: International Reading Association.

Pressley, M., R. Wharton-McDonald, J. Rankin, J. Mistretta, L. Yokoi, and S. Ettenberger. 1996. The nature of outstanding primary-grades literacy instruction. In *Balanced instruction: Strategies and skills in whole language*, eds. E. McIntyre and M. Pressley. Norwood, MA: Christopher-Gordon.

Rice, D. C. 2002. Using trade books in teaching elementary science: Facts and fallacies. *The Reading Teacher* 55 (6): 552–565.

Rice, D. C., and A. D. Rainsford. 1996. Using children's trade books to teach science: Boon or boondoggle. Paper presented at the Annual Meeting of the National Association for Research in Science Teaching, St. Louis, MO.

Romance, N. R., and M. R. Vitale. 1992. A curriculum strategy that expands time for in-depth elementary science instruction by using science-based reading strategies: Effects of a year-long study in grade four. *Journal of Research in Science Teaching* 29 (6): 545–554.

Stahl, S. A., and K. A. Stahl. 2004. Word wizards all! Teaching word meanings in preschool and primary education. In *Vocabulary instruction*, eds. J. F. Baumann and E. J. Kame'enui. New York: Guilford Press.

Watson, F. 1983. On the drawing board: A 21st century curriculum. *The Science Teacher* 50 (3): 62–63.

Yager, R. E. 2004. Science is not written, but it can be written about. In *Crossing borders in literacy and science instruction: Perspectives on theory and practices*, ed. E. W. Saul. Newark, DE: International Reading Association.

Yore, L. D., B. Hand, S. R. Goldman, G. M. Hildebrand, J. F. Osborne, D. F. Treagust, and C. S. Wallace. 2004. New directions in language and science education research. *Reading Research Quarterly* 39 (3): 347–352.

Endnotes

[1] There are several good starting points on integrated curriculum, such as Gavelek et al. (1999) and Yore et al. (2004).

[2] The work of Guthrie (e.g., Guthrie and Ozgungor 2002) and Palincsar (e.g., Hapgood, Magnusson, and Palincsar 2004) is most relevant to this issue.

[3] The most relevant work on best practices in literacy comes from Pressley and his colleagues (e.g., Pressley et al. 1996).

[4] Yore and his colleagues (2004) note that "scientists rely on printed text for ideas that inform their work before, during, and after the experimental inquiries" (p. 348). Kamil and Bernhardt (2004) further suggest that "anyone lacking literacy skills will be unable to access [the scientific] body of knowledge and data" (p. 126).

[5] Rice makes the point about the misinformation rampant in science texts (Rice 2002; Rice and Rainsford 1996), and many have noted the damage to inquiry inflicted by assuming that text is "all knowing," that is, the ultimate authority for content (e.g., Palincsar and Magnusson 1997; Peacock and Gates 2000).

[6] Jane Goodall's *Chimpanzees I Love: Saving Their World and Ours* is a good autobiographical example. We have also written several biographical books, not limited to lives of a few famous scientists but including scientists in different stages of their careers, in different disciplines, and from a diverse array of ethnic backgrounds.

Constructing Science-Literacy Workshops:
The Journey From Powerful Ideas to Classroom Practice

Joan Armon
Regis University
Linda Morris
Jefferson County Public Schools, Golden, Colorado

In Mr. Plock's third-grade classroom, children peer through hand lenses at wriggling caterpillars, enter questions and observations in notebooks, and argue about the significance of their caterpillars' colored flecks. Internet or book searches confirm, extend, or change children's thinking during their investigations. The school day closes with presentations by three-student teams to explain findings or raise new questions.

This is a science-literacy workshop in which Mr. Plock overlaps science investigation, oral language, reading, and writing as children raise and pursue questions about phenomena (see Figure 1). He uses inquiry-based instruction (Bennett et al. 2004) in which he draws out students' assumptions as starting points for construction of new knowledge. Beginning with students' existing knowledge, Mr. Plock supports students in generating questions, actively seeking answers and explanations, as well as examining and changing faulty assumptions. It was the powerful ideas and practices of

Saul (2002) and colleagues that deepened his implementation of science inquiry in the context of reading and writing workshops (Calkins 1994; Harvey and Goudvis 2000). Features of literacy workshops that he and his students rely on as they read, write, speak, and investigate phenomena include strategies that extend thinking, such as predicting; questioning; making connections to their own experience and other texts and/or events; visualizing; summarizing; inferring; and synthesizing.

FIGURE 1 Constructing Science-Literacy Workshops: The Journey From Powerful Ideas to Classroom Practice

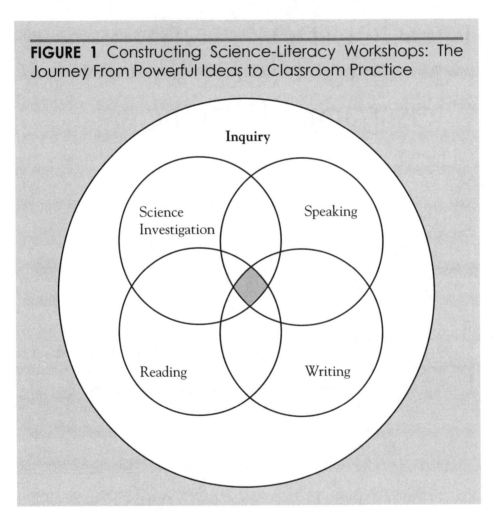

Within a workshop structure, Mr. Plock presents a focus lesson about content or process in literacy and science, models strategies for inquiring into that content, orchestrates guided and independent practice, and facilitates sharing among students about their discoveries, further questions, or ideas.

Workshops in his classroom continue to evolve as he overlaps these literacy strategies and workshop structure with features of science inquiry. Students' inquiry into phenomena involves the following activities, which are adapted from the work of the National Research Council (2000). Students

- state and/or write questions, predictions, ideas, and inferences;
- observe to collect and record evidence (through, for example, writing, charting, drawing, and graphing);
- state and/or write explanations from evidence;
- state, read, and/or write explanations that connect to scientific concepts; and
- communicate and justify understanding to others.

The science-literacy workshop occurs during the literacy and/or science blocks in his schedule.

Our purpose in this chapter is to report why and how educators in one school district integrated science and literacy. The following three questions guided that effort:

1. How might educators bridge science and literacy in an inquiry context to enhance learning in both subjects?
2. How does such integration look?
3. What roles do elementary teachers, administrators, curriculum specialists, and instructional coaches play?

These questions frame the chapter. In the first section, we discuss the background of the project and a rationale for bringing science and literacy together. The second section describes how Mr. Plock meshes science and literacy, with particular emphasis on overlapping reading comprehension strategies and science inquiry within a science-literacy workshop. In the final section, we report the significant roles key people played to initiate and sustain changes in two schools, changes that continue to surface in other schools within the district.

Bridging Science and Literacy in an Inquiry Context to Enhance Learning in Both Subjects

Project Background

The initiative to link science and literacy began with an invitation from Wendy Saul, author of books such as *Science Workshop: Reading, Writing, and Thinking Like a Scientist* (Saul 2002) and principal investigator of a study on the linkages between science and literacy funded by the National Science Foundation. The invitation was to participate in an examination of how science-literacy linkages look in varying school districts around the nation. Educators in Jefferson County Public Schools in Golden, Colorado, accepted the invitation and began by reading publications such as Saul's *Science Workshop*.

Readings, discussions, and website explorations prepared six representatives from Jefferson County Public Schools to join other educators from around the country at an August 2003 conference in Baltimore, Maryland, hosted by Saul and her colleagues. The purpose was to learn more about theory-to-practice efforts linking science and literacy and to construct goals and strategies compatible with each district's needs and existing programs. The Jefferson County educators included two classroom teachers from a middle-class suburban school, three curriculum and content specialists from literacy and science departments, and one administrator from the English Language Arts Department. (The two authors of this chapter were two of the curriculum and content specialists.) Shortly after the conference, a third teacher from a suburban Title I school joined the project. The three teachers participated in the project based on principal recommendations.

To learn how best to implement and evaluate science-literacy workshops, we (the authors of this chapter) observed and videotaped classroom teaching and learning on a regular basis throughout the year. We also interviewed teachers and administrators, facilitated professional dialogue to analyze teachers' instruction and students' writing and speaking, and clarified our thinking by preparing and presenting the project to teachers at a local science conference.

Reasons for Overlapping Science and Literacy

Among an array of reasons for overlapping science and literacy, three points emerged as key considerations. Educators involved in the project wanted to (1) increase the amount of time spent on elementary science instruction, (2) expand classroom use of informational texts, and (3) build on existing curricular initiatives. We discuss each of these points below.

1. Time spent on elementary science instruction in the district had dwindled over the past few years as teachers responded to state testing mandates. In our roles as curriculum and content specialists working in schools

throughout the district, we learned that teachers were eliminating science instruction so they could devote increased amounts of time to the heavily tested subjects of literacy and math. As Saul (2004) points out, this is a phenomenon occurring in other communities as well. Because we perceived science as an essential component of the curriculum that promotes not only content knowledge and skills but also a way of complex thinking, we decided to investigate approaches that supported teachers in making a place for science in their instruction.

2. Primary-grade teachers were becoming aware of the importance of informational texts to provide foundational knowledge and skills students needed to transfer learning to content texts in later grades (Duke 2000; Duke and Bennett-Armistead 2003). Teachers were therefore eager to learn about and integrate informational science trade books into science investigations. Moreover, the emerging science assessments in our state involved significant amounts of informational reading and writing, and teachers wanted students to have more experience with science reading and writing.

3. Existing district initiatives represented a third aspect of our rationale for linking science and literacy. Educators at all levels in the district had already spent considerable amounts of time and energy on developing expertise in using effective literacy strategies in a workshop format (Allington and Johnston 2002; Clay 2002; Calkins 1994; Fountas and Pinnell 1996, 2001; Pressley et al. 2001). It therefore made sense to build on that understanding and expertise rather than add a professional learning requirement disconnected from previous initiatives. And, in science, professional development efforts had also been underway. Literacy strategies meshed well with the BSCS Science T.R.A.C.S. elementary school materials already implemented in the district.

As classroom examples in the next section reveal, Mr. Plock constructed his science-literacy workshop deliberately, embedding literacy instruction within science investigations as well as aspects of science investigations within literacy instruction. This approach provided a meaningful context for reading and writing and highlighted the significance of communication tools in science. He also assessed students' work in both science and literacy.

How Science-Literacy Integration Looks:
A Classroom Close-up

Mr. Plock adapted a writer's workshop format based on the work of Calkins (1994) to foster a gradual release of responsibility from teacher to student. Ideas from Saul (2002) about a science workshop also informed his thinking and practice. The result was a science-literacy workshop that supported students as they engaged in inquiry learning during both the literacy block and science block.

As the free- and reduced-lunch rate in Mr. Plock's school approached 50% with increasing numbers of students learning English, the science-literacy workshop reinforced salient learning strategies while supporting students' success throughout the day. He found that the workshop approach engaged all students, including his bilingual speakers who built on strategies they already used in their home lives such as making connections to prior experiences as they drew inferences (Jiménez 2001).

One Example of a Science-Literacy Workshop Lesson

Components of Mr. Plock's workshop from a lesson in an April life cycles unit appear below. Students were familiar enough with the workshop process that Mr. Plock was able to focus on multiple aims, including development of their questions, observations, record keeping, and explanations based on evidence.

Focus Lesson (Whole Class)
Mr. Plock:
- Reviewed how students used questioning as a reading strategy
- Explained questioning that a scientist uses to begin, continue, or end an investigation
- Formulated a question about the caterpillar in front of him
- Demonstrated how to enter a question in his science notebook page on the overhead, leaving space to write tentative and/or confirmed answers
- Explained how the question serves as a tentative guide for his observations, recording, and explanations based on evidence
- Recorded observations and explanations based on evidence in his science notebook with comments on how specific observations and explanations might address his question
- Raised and recorded additional questions

Guided Practice (Three-Person Teams)
Students:
- Interacted with Mr. Plock as he listened, asked questions, and redirected, if necessary, while students formulated and recorded questions, observations, and explanations with their own caterpillars

Independent Practice
Students:
- Generated and recorded questions, observations, and explanations based on evidence in science notebooks. Examples include the following:
  - *How does a caterpillar make a chrysalis?*
  - *My caterpillar is 1″ long.*
  - *My caterpillar has grown a lot since I saw him. I also think he is dead because he is crumpling up.*

Presentation of Findings, Questions, Next Steps (Whole Class)
Mr. Plock and Students:
- Took turns presenting questions, observations, and explanations based on evidence (researchable questions such as "Where is their natural habitat?" or testable questions such as "How can we tell if they [the caterpillars] are growing?")
- Responded with questions or suggestions for fine-tuning information presented

Closure
Mr. Plock:
- Recapped lesson purposes
- Reviewed questioning and observations strategies
- Highlighted successes and comments about next steps

Confidence blossomed as students learned about the routine regarding sequenced events and use of materials, the roles of all participants, the level of support to give or expect from team members, and opportunities to work and think independently.

During one science-literacy workshop lesson on life cycles, Mr. Plock overlapped literacy and science questioning. The lesson began when Mr. Plock held a book with a centipede on the cover, asked students to look at it as he walked around the room, and started a discussion.

Mr. Plock:	What is something a good reader does?
Lena:	Predict.
Mr. Plock:	Yes, good readers predict what they think the book is going to be about. What's the first thing good readers do?
Elizabeth:	Question.
Mr. Plock:	Yes, good readers question. What's a question a good reader might ask?
Adam:	I wonder if centipedes can bite.
Mr. Plock:	Perfect. Did you hear those words, "I wonder"?

[Several other students raised questions.]

Mr. Plock:	What's something good scientists do?
Adam:	If you're studying a life cycle, don't take it and tap, tap, tap.
Mr. Plock (smiling):	That's right. Treat these critters with respect. Let's think back to what we talked about.

The above interchange was one example of Mr. Plock's heartfelt acceptance of the thinking students expressed, acceptance that fostered his third graders' confidence to communicate their ideas. Such acceptance was the norm he established as students presented and listened to peers. The discussion continued as Lena returned to Mr. Plock's earlier question.

Lena:	They ask good questions.
Mr. Plock:	Yes, they ask good, solid questions. That's what we'll focus on today.

For several days before this lesson, Mr. Plock talked about the thinking that led to his own question, modeled writing it in his science notebook, and demonstrated how he used that question to guide his thinking, observations, recording of data, explanations, and further questions about a caterpillar. That day students were ready to work in teams as they pursued investigations guided by their own questions. Toward the end of the lesson, he invited students to share questions they wrote in their science notebooks.

Lena:	Where is their natural habitat?
Dominique:	Where does the silk come from?
Mr. Plock:	Where does the silk come from? What makes you think it's silk?
Dominique:	Because it can't be like a web because if it was a web, there would be a spider there and there is not a spider.
Mr. Plock:	You can't call it a spider web because there is no spider in there. So you're calling it caterpillar's silk, I suppose. All right. Adam?
Adam:	Why is there a web of silk around the jar? I have an answer for it. Maybe he's making a cocoon.
Mr. Plock:	You asked a great question, Adam. And you're taking the next step. Who noticed what Adam did after he asked a question?
Conner:	He tried to answer it.
Mr. Plock:	Yes, you gotta come up with a plan to answer it.
Mr. Plock:	What is something we can do to try and answer these questions? What are some of the possibilities we can do? Cody?
Cody:	Predict.
Mr. Plock:	Off of a question you can make predictions, that's true. However, if we want an answer to the question, what do we continue to do? Sammy?

Sammy: Observe more.

Mr. Plock: That's great, Sammy said to observe more…. OK, by doing what Sammy says, if we observe and look at these throughout time we might be able to answer some of those questions. That's a great connection there. What is something else you can do to answer questions? Dominique?

Dominique: You might look in books and go on the internet.

Mr. Plock: Perfect, do research about it. Yeah, you can go to the internet and check out books about it. That's a great thought. Does anyone have any other questions they would like to ask?

Adam: I have an answer to Lena's question for where their natural habitat is.

Mr. Plock: Great, fire away.

Adam: Caterpillars' natural habitat is where there is mostly leaves and grass because they mostly eat leaves and grass but not in like Asia and Arizona where they have their deserts. Deserts don't have leaves and grass so they won't be able to live there.

Mr. Plock: That's a neat inference. Caterpillars eat grass and leaves so caterpillars must live where there is grass and leaves.

Adam: Grass and leaves.

Mr. Plock: That's a great inference.

Mr. Plock finished the lesson by connecting the questions and inferences students generated in science to their questions and inferences constructed during reading. Making a plan to answer their questions was a next step for Mr. Plock to take in science, reading, and writing tasks. These interchanges revealed Mr. Plock's aims of overlapping reading comprehension strategies with active, inquiry learning to deepen students' content and process knowledge.

Talking with colleagues about students' abilities to overlap science and literacy strategies, Mr. Plock said,

I believe that using similar vocabulary has really helped my students as readers. The class has a better understanding of the comprehension strategies and students are more apt to use the vocabulary during discussion.

Ms. Nellans, another third-grade teacher participating in the project, concurred with Mr. Plock that students' reading improved during the year. Teachers surmised that the factors contributing to increases in achievement included students' use of writing and reading as tools to pursue their own questions, as well as frequent opportunities to talk about ideas, manipulate materials, record information, and test ideas collaboratively.

An additional phenomenon is that third graders' scores on the state-mandated writing test increased in both Mr. Plock's and Ms. Nellans's classrooms. While teachers attributed the increase to groups of students who clustered near the proficient achievement levels in academics, teachers agreed that changes in their overall instruction due to an emphasis on inquiry may also have contributed to the increases. Teachers also noted that increased quality and quantity of students' writing in science notebooks seemed to indicate increased understanding of science concepts and use of accurate word choice in writing. When results from future state science tests for fifth graders become available, they may provide evidence of increased student achievement in science as a result of science-literacy workshops.

Materials
The more teachers reflected on links between science and literacy, the more carefully they selected reading materials for and with students. Following are examples of quality books used when students raised researchable questions about life cycles, such as Lena's question, "Where is their natural habitat?"

- Hariton, A. 1996. *Butterfly story*. Boston: Dutton.
- Heiligman, D. 1997. *From caterpillar to butterfly*. New York: Harper.
- Woelflein, L. 1995. *Metamorphosis: Animals that change*. New York: Lodester.
- Zemlicka, S. 2002. *From egg to butterfly*. Minneapolis: Lerner.

Assessing Student Growth

Mr. Plock monitored students' growth through an inquiry guideline he used to assess student learning. To gain insight into students' thinking as inquiring scientists, he examined students' science notebook entries and oral responses captured on videotape or in his own anecdotal records. He began the year using a matrix entitled "Essential Features of Classroom Inquiry and Their Variations" (NRC 2000, p. 29) Later in the year, he used a set of questions we formulated with teachers based on that document to include both science and literacy growth. (In the list below, number two, for example, includes students' reading in relation to researchable questions, and number five incorporates attention to students' writing and speaking as they communicate how evidence does or does not support explanations.) The questions Mr. Plock used were as follows:

1. What types of questions is the student asking (testable? researchable? other?)?
2. How does the student select and collect evidence to test or research the question(s)?
3. How does the evidence support or not support the explanation(s)?
4. How does the student connect the explanation(s) to science learning?
5. In what ways does the student communicate how evidence supports or does not support the explanation(s)?
6. How has the student's thinking changed?

These questions guided Mr. Plock's assessment of students' thinking as revealed in their oral and written language and guided his teaching as well. He observed increased development of students' scientific thinking through their questions, use of reading and investigations to collect evidence that supported explanations, and speaking and writing to communicate how evidence does or does not support explanations.

Finally, educators involved in the project to overlap science and literacy in an inquiry-based workshop format agreed that they had made progress in relation to reasons for project involvement. First, teachers spent more time teaching science because it appeared throughout the school day and not merely during science blocks. Second, teachers recognized that they included more informational reading in classrooms than in previous years by working with school media specialists to integrate informational trade books. Part of this effort involved use of the Search It! website (*searchit. heinemann.com*) created by Saul and colleagues as the teachers sought books containing accurate science concepts as well as quality writing and illustrations. Third, teachers expressed satisfaction with their efforts to build on existing district curricula as they constructed science-literacy workshops.

Roles of Key Educators

Collaboration among people in four key roles opened spaces in the standard operating procedures of the school district for science-literacy workshops. This section describes the roles of educators involved—a university professor, school administrators, elementary teachers, and district curriculum and content specialists.

At the university level, Professor Wendy Saul, from the University of Missouri at St. Louis, was invited to Jefferson County School District to explore how an inquiry approach might enhance teaching and learning in science and literacy. Her publications (Saul 2002; Saul and Reardon 1996; Cole and Saul 1996; Saul and Jagusch 1992), publications of her colleagues (Pearce 1999; Bourne 1999), and their efforts in the NSF-funded Elementary Science Integration Projects provided jumping-off places for educators' reading, thinking, dialogue, applications, and adaptations in three classrooms in two Jefferson County schools. Throughout the school year, Saul and her colleagues dialogued, brainstormed, and problem solved with educators in the district as they implemented science-literacy workshops and made adaptations according to the needs of their students. During the second year of the project, the approach has extended to other schools in the district.

At the school-district level, several administrators assumed critical roles throughout the project. Saul insisted that an administrator attend the initial conference in Baltimore with teachers and content specialists. The curriculum coordinator from the English Language Arts Department attended the conference, gaining background by attending sessions, engaging in dialogue with authors and colleagues from around the country, and participating in planning sessions at the conference. His involvement was invaluable in carrying the project forward and sustaining it. The director of science and technology and the science curriculum coordinator at the time attended in-district meetings, supported technology needs required to document the project, and funded our national conference presentations that pushed us to examine and articulate the project. The district executive director of curriculum and staff development challenged those of us involved not only to integrate science and literacy but also to experiment with how time could be reconfigured in the elementary school day to create blocks for quality integration. She also used project videos we created for staff development of administrators and instructional coaches, thus stimulating interest among educators in other schools.

At the school level, two principals opened their doors to content specialists who worked regularly with teachers throughout development of the science-literacy workshops. They were enthusiastic, wanted to be informed, attended several project meetings, and acquired time, space, and materials to support the project. Principals also located funds for substitutes while teachers analyzed their videotaped instruction with us to guide decision making about next steps for the project. Without these administrators' commitment to the project, it could not have flourished.

At the district level, two science curriculum and content specialists worked with an English language arts curriculum and content specialist to stay abreast of current theory, practice, and research in literacy and science instruction and assessment; observe and record teachers' work in classrooms; and meet with teachers after school to analyze student writing and view and evaluate videotaped instruction. Specialists also worked with one building-level instructional coach who collaborated with Ms. Staggs, the sixth-grade teacher who participated in the project, to formulate a rubric for assessing students' science writing. During the second year, another English language arts specialist became part of the project.

At the classroom level, teachers were motivated to participate in the project because they knew their efforts and insights guided our work. When challenges or questions arose, teachers generated ideas with us, tried the ideas, and refined or changed their practices accordingly. Mr. Plock, for example, found overlapping science and literacy instruction to be time consuming. In this workshop approach, students stopped to articulate their thinking via writing and speaking so that investigations took longer than when students used worksheets alone, a finding that has surfaced elsewhere (Barker 2004). Additionally, students' reading to locate information on the internet, in books, or in magazines extended the time needed to complete investigations. Mr. Plock stepped outside the district-recommended model of time spent on each subject area by restructuring his schedule to meet students' needs. He periodically alternated a 60-minute science-literacy block on one day with a 60-minute math block the next, thus providing the time his students needed to fully understand and apply concepts and skills in a science-literacy workshop. Additionally, on days that the science-literacy workshop occurred, he used science trade books for reading and writing.

Concluding Thoughts

Our years spent constructing and investigating science-literacy workshops allowed us to understand why and how to overlap science and literacy within an inquiry context. It was an effort accomplished by collaboration among educators at the university, district, school, and classroom levels.

Images of energized teachers and students working in classrooms surfaced whenever we visited classrooms. We observed teachers' and students' heads clustered together in close-up observations, animated voices explaining why a phenomenon occurred, eyes riveted on a challenging text to answer a question, hands tickled by living things dancing across tiny palms, fingers rushing pencils to capture understandings, minds whirring with new learning and plans for next steps. Science-literacy workshops were and continue to be joyous, productive places.

References

Allington, R. L., and P. H. Johnston. 2002. *Reading to learn: Lessons from exemplary fourth-grade classrooms.* New York: Guilford Press.

Barker, H. B. 2004. *Teachers and the reform of elementary science: Stories of conversation and personal process.* Greenwich, CT: Information Age.

Bennett, A., B. L. Bridglall, A. M. Cauce, H. T. Everson, E. W. Gordon, C. D. Lee, R. Mendoza-Denton, J. S. Renzulli, and J. K. Stewart. 2004. *All students reaching the top: Strategies for closing academic achievement gaps.* North Central Regional Educational Laboratory. Naperville, IL: Learning Point Associates.

Bourne, B., ed. 1999. *Taking inquiry outdoors: Reading, writing, and science beyond the classroom walls.* York, ME: Stenhouse.

Calkins, L. M. 1994. *The art of teaching writing,* rev. ed. Portsmouth, NH: Heinemann.

Clay, M. 2002. *An observation survey of early literacy achievement.* Portsmouth, NH: Heinemann.

Cole, J., and W. Saul. 1996. *On the bus with Joanna Cole: A creative autobiography.* Portsmouth, NH: Heinemann.

Duke, N. K. 2000. 3.6 minutes per day: The scarcity of informational texts in first grade. *Reading Research Quarterly* 35: 202–224.

Duke, N. K., and V. S. Bennett-Armistead. 2003. *Reading and writing informational text in the primary grades: Research-based practices.* New York: Scholastic.

Fountas, I. C., and G. S. Pinnell. 1996. *Guided reading: Good first teaching for all children.* Portsmouth, NH: Heinemann.

Fountas, I. C., and G. S. Pinnell. 2001. *Guiding readers and writers grades 3–6: Teaching comprehension, genre, and content literacy.* Portsmouth, NH: Heinemann.

Harvey, S., and A. Goudvis. 2000. *Strategies that work: Teaching comprehension to enhance understanding.* York, ME: Stenhouse.

Jiménez, R. T. 2001. Strategic reading for language-related disabilities: The case of a bilingual Latina student. In *The best for our children: Critical perspectives on literacy for Latino students*, eds. M. de la Luz Reyes and J. J. Halcón. New York: Teachers College Press.

National Research Council (NRC). 2000. *Inquiry and the national science standards: A guide for teaching and learning*. Washington, DC: National Academy Press.

Pearce, C. R. 1999. *Nurturing inquiry*. Portsmouth, NH: Heinemann.

Pressley, M., R. L. Allington, R. Wharton-McDonald, C. C. Block, and L. M. Morrow. 2001. *Learning to read: Lessons from exemplary first-grade classrooms*. New York: Guilford Press.

Saul, E. W. 2002. Science workshop. In *Science workshop: Reading, writing, and thinking like a scientist*, ed. E. W. Saul. Portsmouth, NH: Heinemann.

Saul, E. W. 2004. Introduction. In *Crossing borders in literacy and science instruction: Perspectives on theory and practice*, ed. E. W. Saul. Newark, DE: International Reading Association.

Saul, W., and S. A. Jagusch, eds. 1992. *Vital connections: Children, science, and books*. Portsmouth, NH: Heinemann.

Saul, E. W., and J. Reardon, eds. 1996. *Beyond the science kit: Inquiry in action*. Portsmouth, NH: Heinemann.

CHAPTER 10

Developing Scientific Literacy Through the Use of Literacy Teaching Strategies

Textual Tools Study Group*
University of Michigan

C urricula that place students' science learning within real-world investigations (i.e., project-based science curricula) generally include the use of multiple tools for inquiry (Krajcik et al. 1998). Little is known, however, about how teachers and students use print-based tools in classroom science inquiry projects. Our group—the Textual Tools Study Group of the University of Michigan and Detroit Public Schools—is designing, studying, and enacting scientific textual tools (reading and writing materials) and teaching and assessment practices to support learning in middle school science classrooms. This work is embedded in the Center for Learning Technologies in Urban Schools (LeTUS). In previous studies, LeTUS materials and practices have been shown to enhance science learning among middle school students (Marx et al. 2004), but we know less about how teachers

*Members of the Textual Tools Study Group are

University of Michigan: Elizabeth Birr Moje, LeeAnn M. Sutherland, Mary Heitzman, Tanya Cleveland, Nonye Alozie, Joseph Krajcik

Detroit Public Schools: Kalonda Colson, Chevon Kay, Kerry Girardin, Yulonda Hale, Denise Wallace Hytower, Shomari Jabulani, Alycia Meriweather, Alissa Naymark, Deborah Peek-Brown, Theresa Rice and students use texts as tools in their project-based science work. However, we hypothesize that the integration and careful sequencing of certain types of texts within ongoing physical or "firsthand" (Palincsar and Magnusson 2001) inquiry activities can support students' learning of science concepts and discourse. These texts include a variety of forms, such as expository, narrative, and naturally occurring texts (e.g., newspapers). We are currently engaged in repeated tests of these textual tools and literacy instruction around these tools to specify the features of textual tools, curriculum, and instruction that support middle school students' science and scientific literacy learning. In this chapter, we focus on what teachers in the group learned about their students' science learning and scientific literacy development as they used the various literacy strategies and the text materials.

What Is Literacy and What Is Its Role in Project-Based Science?

All the members of our team—which is made up of classroom teachers, an instructional specialist, and university literacy and science education researchers—recognize that real-world scientists use print texts extensively in their own inquiries. Thus, we are committed to engaging students in reading and writing texts in ways that support their science investigations. Textual inquiry—what Palincsar and Magnusson (2001) conceptualize as one form of secondhand inquiry—should be closely integrated with physical, or firsthand, inquiry. Both forms of inquiry share important features (see Chapter 8 in this book), but are also different in important ways. Physical inquiry, for example, involves manipulating materials, theories, and ideas, whereas textual inquiry requires the decoding and negotiation of symbols, theories, and ideas. The fact that many of our students struggle either with basic reading and writing processes or with the technical and interpretive demands of science text in the inquiry process makes the integration of textual inquiry into the curriculum particularly challenging, however. In fact, many students require support in comprehension, composition, and meaning making or application of any content texts (Goldman 1997; Ivey 1999; Lee and Fradd 1999). Unfortunately, the constrained time periods for doing science during a typical school day make it challenging for teachers to *teach* students how to use print texts to engage in physical inquiry and build scientific literacy skills while also conducting the physical inquiry itself. Thus, one of our goals is to enable students to weave textual and physical inquiry together.

In addition, we are interested in providing opportunities for students in Detroit to read (and also compose) different kinds of texts because the ability to read and write a wide variety of science-related texts is key to developing a scientifically literate citizenry. Scientific literacy is referred to in the National Science Education Standards as "the knowledge and understanding of scientific concepts and processes required for personal decision making, participation in civic and cultural affairs, and economic productivity" (NRC 1996, p. 2). Science literacy is attained when students acquire knowledge of and fluency with the social practices, cultural assumptions, and tools of science in addition to learning the subject matter. These assumptions and tools can be taught explicitly through teachers' instruction of the ways of knowing, acting, reading, writing, and representing knowledge of scientists and in the texts they use (Lemke 1990; Moje et al. 2001; Moje et al. 2004). But what are those practices? How do scientists comprehend and produce science texts? What does it mean for anyone to comprehend text? How do text comprehension processes support scientific inquiry practices?

Comprehension of any text occurs at the intersection of the reader, a text, and a context. The elements that a *reader* brings to a text include word recognition knowledge, vocabulary knowledge, background knowledge, linguistic and textual knowledge, the ability to infer meanings, the ability to use strategies to make sense when comprehension is challenged, and motivation and interest to engage with a given text. The *context* that shapes a reader's meaning making can include the academic content area in which one is reading (e.g., science), one's ethnic background, the social situation in which one is reading, a broad political context, a family situation, the purpose for one's reading (e.g., to inform firsthand investigations), and even environmental factors such as temperature or noise around a person when she reads. Finally, the *text* itself contributes to the reading process because texts are written in a variety of ways. Texts can tell stories (i.e., narration) or explain information (i.e., exposition). Texts can pose problems to be solved, or can inform readers on ways to solve problems. Texts can be written in many different styles, relying heavily on technical language and particular ways of phrasing ideas, or they can be written to appeal to more general audiences (e.g., real-world texts, such as newspapers). The texts of science classrooms, in particular, often rely heavily on certain ways of stating information and on particular text structures (e.g., cause and effect relationships, problems and solutions). Science texts also employ a great deal of technical language, as well as everyday language that is used in unique, scientific ways (e.g., *property* or *solution* in chemistry texts).

Some independent reading strategies used by good readers include reading backward and forward to check comprehension; asking self-questions before, during, and after reading to set a purpose and guide and check comprehension; making predictions about the material to be read; and discerning word meanings from the context of the passage or looking up words in reference material when unable to discern meaning from context (Duke and Pearson 2002). Studies demonstrate that good readers perform many of these moves automatically or unconsciously, as *skills*, only employing them consciously as *strategies* when their comprehension is challenged or interfered with because of difficult text or their own lack of content knowledge (Wade, Trathen, and Shaw 1990).

We are committed to providing opportunities for students to learn reading strategies that will help them comprehend and use texts to engage in inquiry and, ultimately, learn science concepts and become scientifically literate. To that end, we have produced text materials, arranged in what we call "text sets," each made up of an expository text, a narrative case, and real-world text. We have prepared one text set to examine substances and properties, two text sets to support students' understanding of chemical reactions, and a final set to support their understanding of conservation of matter, all of which are key concepts and processes described in national standards and benchmarks and taught in an inquiry chemistry unit titled, "How can I make new stuff from old stuff?" Because we develop our own texts, they are always tied to the investigations, either being read prior to an investigation to inform inquiry (just as a scientist would conduct text research prior to engaging in an experiment) or read afterward to extend and cement concepts explored in the investigation.

Accompanying the text sets were six professional development sessions, in which members of the team came together to develop particular applications of general literacy teaching strategies for supporting students' comprehension and independent strategy use. The professional development activities included formal presentations of strategies by Elizabeth (Moje) and LeeAnn (Sutherland), but also involved the entire team working together to develop coherent applications of these strategies for the particular science curriculum under study. Because the work was part of an experimental study, treatment classroom teachers often worked on additional or unique versions of the strategies for application with the multiple text types.

Research Design

For the research aspect of our work, we rely on a mixed methods design, which integrates an experimental study of 11 seventh-grade classrooms at 10 different schools (student $N = 295$), with a qualitative study of 6 of the 11 classrooms (3 treatment classrooms and 3 control classrooms). The schools represent a range of achievement levels in literacy and science, with state proficiency reading test pass rates ranging from 11.8% to 78.9% (with a mean of 30.3%) and science pass rates on the same test ranging from 13% to 99.1% (with a mean of 42.4%). Student demographics at the 10 schools include mainly African American and Latino/a students, with some representation of Asian American and European American students. The teachers, who are all co-authors on this chapter, include Kalonda, Chevon, Kerry, Yulonda, Denise, Shomari, Alycia, and Alissa.

The data sources we are using to assess student learning and to examine our curriculum and teaching strategies include (a) pre- and posttest scores on assessments designed specifically to address content knowledge, (b) pre- and posttest scores on assessments designed specifically to address reading skills reflected in the curriculum, (c) classrooms observations in 6 of the 11 classrooms (chosen randomly), (d) student and teacher interviews in those 6 classrooms, (e) informal reading inventories for three focal students per six focal classrooms, (f) artifacts of student work, and (g) teaching artifacts. Data analyses are ongoing. In this chapter, we describe the strategies we designed as a group, and study group members describe modifications they made as they used strategies in their particular classrooms. To that end, we draw most heavily on field notes and teacher self-report. We do not report science gain scores or reading scores, although our overall curriculum work demonstrates that the students make high gains both on pre/post measures of the curriculum and on standardized state achievement tests as a result of participation in the curriculum (Geier et al., forthcoming; Marx et al. 2004).

Teaching Strategies for Building Strategic Reading of Complex Science Texts

As Alvermann and Moore (1991) asserted, content-area reading strategies can be conceptualized in two ways: They can be classroom teaching strategies designed to scaffold students' comprehension of target texts or they can be strategies that readers use independently whenever they encounter texts that challenge them in terms of the prior knowledge required, technical language, organization and text structure, or any number of other aspects of text that can make comprehension difficult. Ideally, however, a content literacy teaching strategy not only supports students' sense making of a target text, but also builds those independent reading strategies and even reading skills. The goal in using literacy teaching strategies in science or any content learning is not to have students perform the strategy "correctly," but to support students as they make sense of text and to prompt them to learn to use some of the independent reading strategies modeled through literacy teaching strategy. Drawing from the cognitive studies of good readers (e.g., Duke and Pearson 2002), reading comprehension and content literacy theorists have argued that content literacy teaching strategies should engage readers before, during, and after a reading activity in order to elicit knowledge, guide strategy use and build metacognitive strategies, and check or extend comprehension following a reading.

In the following sections, we present six different content literacy teaching strategies. These strategies—all of which have been studied scientifically in multiple investigations over the last 50 years—are (a) preview guides, which are similar to what Vacca and Vacca (2004) call anticipation guides; (b) vocabulary concept cards (Nist and Simpson 1997); (c) concept of definition maps (Schwartz, 1988); (d) list-group-label (Taba 1967); (e) story impressions (McGinley and Denner 1987); and (f) perspective-taking strategy, generated from Pichert and Anderson's (1977) research study.

Preview Guides

A preview guide is a series of statements, written by the teacher, that students respond to before, during, and after reading a specific piece of text. A preview guide may contain either (a) a series of statements with which students are asked to agree or disagree or (b) a series of questions to which students will respond in writing (see Figure 1). Statements should be designed so that they can be answered with information stated directly in the text (e.g., definition, cause and effect) or with information from various parts of the text, integrated as *inferences*. Statements should also require students to predict, summarize, synthesize, or challenge previously held misconceptions. Students' prior knowledge is activated as they respond to the items before reading. The statements help to establish a purpose for reading that shapes students' interest and encourages them to be actively engaged during reading. After reading, students revisit their initial responses and indicate whether and how their ideas have changed.

> **Denise's experience.** *The majority of my students struggle with reading, and many tend to find the content in most science texts very dry. I used the preview guide as a strategy to set up the purpose for reading, to get the students to focus on the objectives for reading, and to pique students' interest in the reading selection. I focused on what I wanted students to learn from the reading passage as a way to develop preview questions. I provided a copy of the preview guide to*

FIGURE 1 Preview Guide Example for a Passage on Solubility

Preview Guide Questions	Guess (before reading)	Answer (after reading)
1. Is solubility a property?		
2. What other words can you think of that might be related to solubility?		
3. What might make a substance dissolve?		
4. What kinds of substances might be soluble?		
5. When might one substance dissolve in another?		
6. Why is solubility important?		
7. List two key aspects of solubility.		

Adapted from Shomari Jabulani, Detroit Public Schools.

each student, and I read each question to them. I asked them to write their be-fore-reading ideas, to underline the answers in the text as we read the selection as a class, and then to answer the post-reading questions after we had finished. I think the strategy helps students focus on the "big ideas" in the reading passage. Their reading is more purposeful. I think it boosts students' confidence to be able to find and underline some of the answers in the text. With future preview guides, I would do a better job of making sure that after the preview guide pro-cess students understand the big ideas intended.

Alissa's experience. I posed four questions on the first preview guide I created, and we discussed our predictions before reading. Since the more vocal students were pretty sure of their answers, and most of the other students seemed pretty unsure, I decided it might be more motivating to challenge students to be the first to find the sentence that answered one of the preview guide questions as we read. I told them that when they thought they had found it, they should underline it and then raise their hand, and I would come and check out what they had underlined. Then they could share the sentence aloud to see if other students also thought it answered the question. If they found a good piece of evidence in the reading, then they got five points. This process helped motivate students who thought they already knew all the answers before they read the selection, and it helped provide stopping points where we put emphasis on the statements that helped to answer the preview guide questions. I think it helped some of the students, who were less sure of the answers, to figure out the answers to the questions and slightly shift their perspectives.

Shomari's experience. The use of the preview guide strategy was quite a success for me. However, after preparing an overhead transparency for solubility, I noticed that for my students to have ownership of the strategy, they needed even more active engagement setting up the task. So as part of the start-up strategy, I had students copy into their science notebooks each of the seven questions I had prepared on an overhead transparency. They were quiet, occupied, and writing from the start of the activity. After a set amount of time, I polled the class for their responses. This seemed to wake up many of the students who do not always cherish the notion of reading. The students read the selection in silence and immediately filled in post-reading responses. One surprise was that several students wanted to answer beyond yes or no, and several students asked for highlighters.

What did we learn about using preview guides? Several of us found that preview guides increased our students' interest in reading the informational text for which we designed the questions. When Alissa and Denise's students underlined (as they were instructed to), and when students in Shomari's class asked (on their own) for highlighters, active reading was clearly taking place. Underlining and highlighting are not necessary components of the strategy, but a teacher who looks at students' underlining and highlighting might gain important information about individual students' difficulties answering the post-reading questions. As they read, students in all of our classes developed their close reading skills, making connections between ideas and using text in a meaningful way. During a period of whole-group or small-group review of their responses, students could be asked to read aloud the part of the text that helped them answer a question (e.g., the text they had underlined). When asked to read round-robin style (proceeding around the room, one at a time), students often passively listen as their peers read or their minds wander rather than staying focused on the text. But when they have completed a preview guide and are asked to read aloud to prove a point (e.g., to justify a response), oral reading can become engaging for all students.

Denise's experience highlights an issue relevant to all strategy use: It is important that the teacher maintains learning as the focus. Even a research-based strategy that has been shown to be effective can be reduced to a work-sheet-completion activity if the teacher does not use the strategy as a learning tool. As students complete preview guides, they are experiencing an active reading strategy that, with practice, might become automatic for them. In the future, students will not write lists of questions for themselves before they read (just as none of us do unless challenged by a particularly difficult text), but they may develop a habit of self-questioning that is automatic and unconscious. In the process of becoming more active readers, they also better comprehend and retain information provided in the texts they read.

In the next section, we report on two strategies used to develop vocabulary. We focus on both scientific terms and everyday terms used in particular ways in science.

Vocabulary Concept Cards

Vocabulary concept cards (Nist and Simpson 1997) are easy to construct and can be used in many different ways, but the underlying premise is that the target term is taught conceptually, rather than as a memorized, canned definition. Thompson (2003) has demonstrated that, in addition to vocabulary breadth and depth, vocabulary *flexibility*—the ability to use the same word with different meanings in different contexts—distinguishes strong readers from average and poor readers. Vocabulary concept cards help to build vocabulary flexibility by requiring learners to examine word meanings from many different angles. To carry out the strategy, the target word is written on one side of an index card (or notebook page, depending on the classroom system). On the other side, the card is divided into at least four quadrants (additional divisions can be made, again depending on the particular goals one has for student learning) (see Figure 2). Initially, the teacher provides a scaffold for students by helping them record (a) what the word *is*, (b) what the word *is not*, (c) an example of the word (or a drawing or sentence using the word), and (d) the definition in the context of some reading material (or a dictionary definition—again, depending on learning goals). Critical to the use of the cards is the idea that with each new term, some quadrant is scaffolded in whole-class, small-group, or partnered instruction, at least until the word is learned independently.

Chevon's experience. My students have a great deal of difficulty reading and comprehending text. If they have a familiarity with some of the vocabulary, it encourages them to read further and attempt passages they would ordinarily ignore. One of the methods I use to introduce and further develop vocabulary knowledge is vocabulary concept cards. When we were studying properties of substances, students constructed cards for color, melting point, hardness, solubility, and density. Students were intense in their quest to have

FIGURE 2 Vocabulary Concept Card Template and Student Sample

	Side 1
What it is	Example/ Drawing/ Sentence
What it is not	Reader/ Textbook/ Dictionary Definition

Side 2
Target Word

Student Sample (Target word is *properties*.)

```
what it is          Examples
to distinguish if   MF Better is
Something is the    Soluble what color
Same or different   is it, Hardness and
                    Melting point or Dens?

what it is not      Defination, Properties
properties is not   are Characteristics of
the Shape or size   Subtances that scientists
                    use describe Subtance.
```

a "perfect" card to reflect their knowledge. They asked each other for opinions of what they had written. We punched holes in each card, and students used a ring to keep them together, adding new cards throughout the unit. Students used the cards to quiz each other as they prepared for a game or an assessment. Making vocabulary cards appears to help students understand words more than they do after simply looking up definitions.

Kalonda's experience. I have used vocabulary concept cards as an introduction to a new concept as well as a follow-up assignment after completing an investigation that presents a new concept. In both instances, the results have been beneficial. After sharing the information on their cards in a brief discussion in which their peers or I provide comments, students can make changes to reflect new knowledge or deeper understandings. The cards are a way for students to monitor their own learning. They look forward to learning new words. One of my students wrote, "I really enjoy using the vocabulary concept cards in science class. I like writing my own definition first because it allows me to reflect on what I have learned and then compare it to the reader definition." As a teacher, I must agree with this student that this is a great strategy. I also encourage students to use this strategy as they come across new vocabulary in other classes, in various readings, and even in conversations.

Alissa's experience. I used vocabulary concept cards for words like substances, mixtures, and properties. I chose this strategy because I thought it was an excellent way to help the students really think through each of the selected topics and then have a "souvenir" to help them remember the topic and think about the concepts on later dates. It was helpful to the students to think of examples of the words and to share their examples in class discussion. I plan to have students use their cards to create questions for a review game to play before they take the posttest.

Concept of Definition Maps

Concept of definition maps (CD maps) were developed and tested by Robert Schwartz (1988) to achieve a purpose similar to that of vocabulary concept cards. The CD map can be a tool for building prior knowledge before a reading; encouraging and guiding a discussion before, during, and after a reading; or for assessing students' understanding following a reading. As with the vocabulary concept cards, the ultimate goal is to encourage students to use the categories of the CD maps as they encounter and learn new words. That is, if learners begin to think of concepts as having (a) characteristics, (b) uses, (c) examples, and (d) verbal definitions, and start to learn words using those categories, then they have a heuristic for learning and remembering words independently (see Figure 3).

Alycia's experience. We had tried this strategy during professional development, and it really made me think, so I figured it would do the same for my students. I really liked this strategy from the beginning, because I thought it would give insight into students' true understanding of a word. We decided, as a group, that we would all use the word property, in the context of science, for our first concept of definition map. Because I had completed the map myself, and other teachers had taught the lesson before me, I was able to change some things that I thought might be problematic. For example, although characteristics might fit as a category for a different word, I felt that non-examples would be a better branch on the map related to properties because it is hard for students to conceptualize characteristics of a property. The term property, in science, represents, after all, a characteristic of some other thing. For an activity, I asked the students to record an activity that they had done or had seen me do that helped them know what a property was or was not.

Chevon's experience. Using CD maps is a way to focus students and help them obtain vocabulary knowledge. The students were able to complete the definition and example portions of the map quickly because of work we had previously done with vocabulary cards. However, we needed to review what uses and characteristics mean, and then we searched our texts and made a list of ideas for each category. I asked students to review previous material and to read new material to collect information. Although we had spent a great deal of time doing activities and reading about properties, what students wrote in the "examples" section reflected some of the prior knowledge that I thought had been revised. Some students listed items such as land, houses, cars, and jewelry. After a quick reminder of what the class had been studying, students replaced those answers with appropriate science terminology. They revised their maps as the lessons continued, and ultimately submitted them for assessment.

Kerry's experience. We spent a great deal of time constructing the meanings of property and chemical reaction through inquiry-based, hands-on activities. Then I used the CD map to make sure that students fully grasped the concepts we had been studying. The activity was as much an evaluation of their

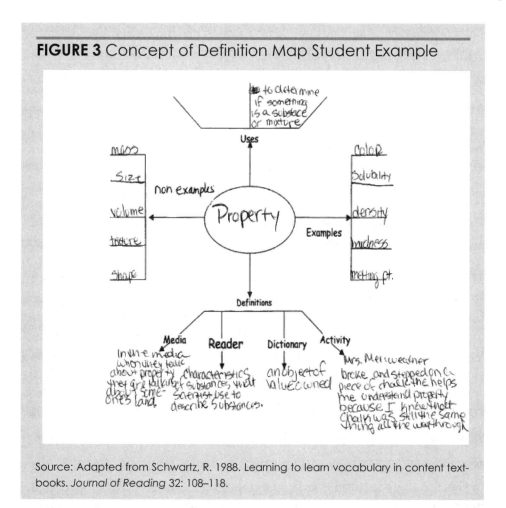

FIGURE 3 Concept of Definition Map Student Example

Source: Adapted from Schwartz, R. 1988. Learning to learn vocabulary in content textbooks. *Journal of Reading* 32: 108–118.

understanding as it was a review and affirmation of what they already knew about the concepts. Some students, however, felt overwhelmed by the amount of work or the amount of writing involved. Reassuring them and letting them work in groups helped ease their panic a bit. As a result, those who understood the concepts fairly well had a chance to learn more as they completed the task, to review what they already knew, and to excel by teaching others. Once students completed their maps, they were able to see just how much they had learned and how that information could be linked and logically organized.

Kalonda's experience. When looking for a way to give my students the opportunity to express their sense of new vocabulary concepts, I introduced CD maps. As a culminating assessment after we had studied properties, I guided students as they completed their maps. The results provided me with a *clear description of students' thinking. I was able to use the results to address any misconceptions and to ensure that the proper conceptual and relational knowledge were applied. Students were able to effectively use this vocabulary strategy, and I will continue to use it in my quest to build a solid bridge between science and literacy.*

What did we learn about using vocabulary strategies? We learned that it was not enough to provide students with blank concept of definition maps or blank vocabulary cards; they also needed us to model and to coach them as they used each strategy for the first few times. We recognized before using the strategies, or as soon as we began, that students needed to understand what each of the categories referred to before they could use the strategy effectively. Some of us used the labels as described in the original strategies we had practiced, and others among us changed the labels to ones we thought were more appropriate for an individual concept or for the learning goals we were aiming to achieve. Several of us noted that students took pride in and took ownership of the cards and maps they produced. We all agree that the vocabulary strategies we used helped our students build a deeper understanding of key vocabulary words than they typically develop by memorizing dictionary definitions. As Kalonda said, "A true understanding of key concepts in science is vital in helping students make meaning and apply scientific knowledge in everyday life."

List-Group-Label/Story Impressions

In this section, we present two strategies that we have linked together for the multiple purposes of building vocabulary knowledge, conceptual and word relation knowledge, and even knowledge of how text and language work in scientific texts and in other genres. These strategies also help to set a purpose for reading and motivate students to read and compare texts. The first strategy, list-group-label (LGL) (Taba 1967), asks students to group a list of words chosen by the teacher (or by groups of students, as they progress with the strategy) into categories that they think make sense, based on what they know about the words before reading (see Figure 4). Students are then asked to identify cover terms for the categories. This categorization activity encourages students to think about how words are related to one another, thus developing conceptual, rather than mere definitional, understandings of terms and phrases.

Our team combines the list-group-label strategy with an expository text application of McGinley and Denner's (1987) story impressions (SI), a pre-reading strategy in which students are asked to construct their own text passages from a list of words. We call our combination "text impressions" (TI). To use SI/TI, the teacher chooses key words of different parts of speech from a passage (these are the same words used for LGL, which we use as a precursor to SI/TI). After grouping and labeling the terms, and sharing their ideas about the terms with the class, students are asked to work in groups to construct their own texts from the list of terms. They must use the terms in order and exactly as they appear in the list. Another modification of the original strategy that we have developed is to assign different text types for the writing activity, such as a news report, an encyclopedia entry, or a popular science magazine. In other words, groups of students are encouraged to try writing different genres or types of text as a way of drawing the students' attention to how text differences may shape the ways that words get used in science-related texts and may even shape the presentation of the science concepts themselves (see student example in Figure 5).

We strongly suggest that teachers model this strategy with the whole class and use small-group writing several times before considering this activity an individual, independent activity. It is also important to keep in mind that the purpose of the activity is to set the stage for reading the target science text, so perfect writing is not the goal in this strategy. The key is to encourage students to think and talk about word meanings and relationships among words so that they will have a focus for their eventual reading. And it is especially important that the class or small groups discuss the differences between the texts they produced and the target text they read after the reading activity is concluded.

Alycia's experience. When we did this strategy in professional development, I thought it was so much fun, I had to restrain myself from jumping two lessons ahead and doing the lesson with the students the next day. When we got to it, I knew the kids would really enjoy the activity. I introduced the LGL strategy using a nonscience example, asking students how they could group the words cat, house, dog, *and* apartment. *Students decided that the words could be put into the categories "animals" and "places to live." I also encouraged students to think of other labels they could use for the groups. After that example, the students seemed to work through the assignment, but I certainly did get a few hands in the air from students who wanted help or clarification. I really tried to make them work it out by saying, "Ask your group, What do you think?" That seemed to work well, and I was fairly satisfied with their*

FIGURE 4 List-Group-Label Words

roof	chemical reaction
steeple	acid rain
green	pollutant
Statue of Liberty	automobile emissions
surface	coal-burning plants
copper	sulfuric acid
shiny new penny	copper sulfate

results, especially considering that it was their first attempt.

For the writing portion of the activity (TI), I created 3 × 5 cards each containing a genre in which the stories were to be written. The cards were labeled "National Enquirer," "encyclopedia entry," "TV news report," "internet site," "Hollywood entertainment TV show," "newspaper

FIGURE 5 Example of Student Text Impression Based on Words in Figure 4

Table 2
1/27/05
Science, 3
The word lists
Story.

Once upon a time there was a
Roof and a steeple. It was green,
~~compared~~ like the Statue of
Liberty. The surface was copper
like a shinny new penny. Then
a chemical Reaction occured because
of acid Rain, which is a pollutant.
There also was a automobile emission,
coal buerning plant which Released
sulfuric acid, and copper sulfate.
This also contributed to the
Reaction. In conclusion the
the pieces of the building never
turned back to ~~the~~ it's original
color.

story," and "a story about someone's life…or something from it." I also included one free choice, and the team who picked that card could write in any style they chose. I read all of the choices out loud first, so that all of the groups could hear the possibilities so that the group that drew free choice would have ideas about what they might choose to write. Each group then chose a card without seeing the genre. Once the students understood the task—to use the

words from the LGL strategy in order and to write in the manner of the genre on the card they drew—there was a buzz of productive noise and laughing for the 15 minutes they spent writing in groups.

Yulonda's experience. I gave my students a list of 11 words, some of which they were familiar with and some they were not: element, chemically, molecules, universe, magnified, millions, distilled, sodium fluoride, chloride, calcium, and representation. I told students that their job was to categorize (label) the words. Interestingly, one group labeled universe, magnified, millions, and distilled as "Air." My guess is that they were connecting what they learned in the previous Air Quality unit to the current unit. This made me think that in the future I will have students write a reason next to the label as to why they grouped the words the way they did, which will require them to put more thought into the process of grouping and labeling. This would probably mean that I would have to use fewer words until the students had more practice with this process.

When they had completed that portion of the activity, I told students that based on their groupings, they would next create a scenario using the words in the order they were presented. Of course the students asked, "What about the words we don't know? Can we use a dictionary?" I told them that they could not use a dictionary and that they needed to do the best they could. The students were both excited and flabbergasted as they attempted to categorize and write stories with words that they knew little or nothing about. The scenarios were just as interesting as the groupings and labels. While the students were excited by the writing task, many of them used the words out of context. Time constraints made it impossible to have the students read the actual text in which the words were used on the same day that they wrote their stories. However, I kept the words posted and held on to their stories so that we could do so in the next class period. I think it might be beneficial at the start of the day we are going to read the actual text to have the students read (not dramatize) their stories again. It might also be beneficial to have the students regroup or categorize the words once they have read the text.

Kerry's experience. Each week, I list vocabulary words that students are to use in a paragraph, which is to be turned in at the end of the week. So, my students have been practicing scientific stories all year long as homework. That said, the students' stories written for text impressions were interesting to say the least. Some stories were pretty good; however, many of the paragraphs students wrote were completely incoherent. This discouraged me, and I was *worried that I had wasted time on this exercise. The worst stories were those that tried to pack all the words into a small paragraph, most often used incorrectly. I warned students against doing this, yet they still packed the words in. They had a great time, yet a chug-through-it style of writing prevailed for some. I think I can learn from this experience, though. They needed a little more time for the activity; they needed encouragement to try to make sense rather than squeezing all the words in, and they needed fewer words than I provided. The results I observed were, I think, an issue of the quantity of words affecting the quality of their stories.*

When they shared their writing with the whole class, the students were excited and interested to hear what others had written. This is especially true because each group was assigned a different writing scenario. The options I gave them were a talk show (e.g., Oprah), Animal Planet, a Discovery Channel report, a fictional story, a factual report, and a gossip-column format. As they shared their stories aloud, students laughed and enjoyed the ones that made sense, but they had little-to-no reaction to the ones that were incoherent. They did not laugh at each other, but they didn't know what to do either. The groups that wrote the incoherent paragraphs either would not make eye contact (appearing embarrassed) or would blame each other. I try to maintain a positive and safe environment, so I did not spend too long on any one group's story so that students would not become uncomfortable. When it was time to read the actual text for which I used the strategy, I noted that the students' interest in the text seemed to increase. A few students put on their "Oh, no, boring reading!" faces, but some students really did seem to want to find the words and discover how they were supposed to be used.

***Denise's experience.** Before using the LGL strategy on the expository text that they were supposed to read, I decided to assess students' understanding of four vocabulary words and ways in which the words could be related to each other. I listed four science terms on the board and asked students to write a paragraph that included at least four sentences that would include the four vocabulary words. The students seemed to lack confidence in completing the assignment. They didn't ask questions, and I did not model the procedure prior to giving the assignment. Some students wrote sentences using the words outside of scientific context. A few students wrote sentences that had fairly accurate information. Many students didn't complete the assignment. The next time I use the LGL strategy, I will (a) model the strategy using examples, (b) make sure students have correct information in terms of context intended, and (c) start out with categorizing practice before implementing the full-blown strategy.*

What did we learn about using the list-group-label and text impressions strategies? Many of us found that a short list of words was useful for introducing the strategy, and then students could move to a longer list of words taken from the required reading assignment. But even after the initial practice, some of us found that the 10–12 words we thought we could start with may be too many. Another struggle we faced using these strategies was whether to let students write texts in which their use of the words was "wrong" scientifically, or to guide them so that the texts they wrote would turn out to be more scientifically accurate.

On the one hand, we all aim to help our students be successful, and we all try to establish a classroom atmosphere that is nonthreatening, as Kerry describes. On the other hand, we tell students that it is OK to be wrong, that people learn from wrong answers as much as or more than they do from right answers, and that wrong answers are a driving force in scientific discovery. In fact, these strategies are designed so that "wrong" uses of words are as important as "correct" uses of words. *Properties* means something quite different in science than it does in its everyday use (as Chevon describes in the CD map section). Getting it "wrong" in the story highlights those differences when students encounter the word in the expository text. If they have no idea what a word means, students are on the lookout for that word as they read. They read actively and deliberately to find out whether their use of the word was right or wrong in the context of this particular science text, and active engagement in reading is a primary aim of these strategies. In other words, it is important to remember that the strategy is not intended to produce a *good* written text, but to stimulate thinking about the words and the concepts to which words are linked before students read the target text. Practice using the words is not necessary because the object is simply to stimulate thinking. It may be wise, in fact, to start simply by having students write paragraphs, rather than by assigning different genres of text (e.g., newspaper versus encyclopedia versus science fiction novel), because the focus on genres may inadvertently draw attention to the writing, rather than to the reading process.

Finally, in using this, or any of these strategies, teachers need to consider both the learning *environment* that they wish to create and the learning *opportunities* they wish to provide within that environment. Strategies need to always be used with learning goals, students, and the particular text and context for learning in mind.

Perspective-Taking Strategy

This strategy was developed in response to our learning about a study of how the perspective from which a person reads shapes comprehension and retention (Pichert and Anderson 1977). In the study, participants were asked to read a brief story of two boys spending the day at home. The story provided great detail about the boys' house. Some study participants were asked to read from the perspective of a home buyer, others from the perspective of a burglar. All were asked to read and then recall as many details as they could. Findings indicated that readers' recall varied significantly depending on the perspective from which they read. Home buyers focused on structural aspects of the home (e.g., number of bedrooms) and those things that would stay with the house (e.g. hardwood floors), whereas burglars remembered the layout of the home (e.g., behind a hedge) and focused on items that could be carried out of the house (e.g., stereo equipment).

We were introduced to this study as a way of helping us think about how reading is shaped by students' background experiences, prior knowledge, and experiences. We engaged in the home buyer/burglar activity ourselves (see the particular version of the text we used in Figure 6). As we discussed our own experience, many of us agreed that perspective taking could be a useful literacy teaching strategy for reading different science classroom texts and conducting scientific inquiry, since awareness of one's perspective and bias is crucial for rigorous scientific inquiry. Half of the group agreed to use a perspective-taking strategy to help our students read an advertisement and a case about diamonds and cubic zirconia, and then to read a real-world article from the internet about manufactured diamonds. We hoped that a perspective-taking activity would set a purpose for reading and encourage students to think about why someone might care about substances outside of science class. These reading inquiry activities were directly linked to firsthand inquiry activities that asked students to test various substances to determine their properties (and, thus, whether they were the same or different substances).

Shomari's experience. *As we all agreed upon as a group, I asked each student to read from a particular role (i.e., perspective), such as the father of a teenage female who just received a pair of earrings, the teenager, a jeweler, a manufacturer of cubic zirconia, and a scientist. After a brief introduction to what they were to do, I had students draw a "role" from a bag and told them to keep their selection secret. After reading, the class responded to the questions we had also agreed to pose. The class responses were indicative of their*

FIGURE 6 Home Buyer/Burglar Text for Perspective-Taking Strategy

The house, a large stone structure with heavy casement windows, is buried deep in the woods. You can't even see it from the road, so tall and thick are the trees that surround it, and with nightfall fast approaching, you find the shadows around the house a bit eerie. Your shoes crunch loudly on the long and winding gravel driveway as you approach the home by foot. The grounds are well kept, you note, as you admire a thick, green carpet of grass and tall, well-manicured hedges that hug the walls of the home. The double front doors seem to be several inches thick, but the many large windows across the front promise a light-filled living space.

Craftsman-style lamps that appear to be original frame the door, but no other lighting system seems available to guide your path. Suddenly, lights flick on, startling you, until you realize that motion lamps are installed high in the eaves of the second story. Undeterred by the lights, you peer in the front windows and realize that you can see all the way to the back of the house on one side; it appears that French doors lead out the back of the house onto a porch or deck of some kind.

Circling the house, you find not only one set of French doors, but several sets lining one whole side of the house. The back deck is elevated, but sturdy stairs lead from the sloping, tree-covered hillside to the top of the deck. You scan the advertisement in your hand: 7 bedrooms, 5 full bathrooms, remodeled kitchen, original wood, air conditioning, security system, sauna, and media center. Yes, you think to yourself, this house will do quite nicely.

---

role's point of view. The activity was productive in pushing students to think, to analyze, and to recognize that point of view can color observations. The students seemed more receptive to learning the differences between a diamond and cubic zirconia after completing the perspective-taking activity.

Alissa's experience. I spoke to another teacher after she had already taught the lesson with this strategy, and she said that she had found it useful to first do the perspective home buyer/burglar activity, just as we had done in our professional development. I decided that this idea sounded like it would help my students understand the idea of perspective taking as well, so I did the home buyer/burglar activity and assigned the roles that Shomari describes above, and it worked out *well. I also found that it helped to have students underline the sentences or facts that stood out to them as they read based on their perspective. The students seemed to underline the appropriate sentences that linked with their assigned perspective. We did not have much time for the discussion at the end, but since this story is revisited throughout the unit, as students learn new properties and apply what they learn to the girl's earrings, I think it will help them remember the story and apply their new learning to the story.*

What did we learn about using the perspective-taking strategy? As with other strategies, perspective taking focused students' attention on their reading, encouraging them to read more closely as they read for a specific purpose. Alissa's students focused on the text that "linked with their as-signed perspective," and Shomari's students' responses "were indicative of their role point of view." This strategy serves not only that immediate goal, but also a larger goal, which is to have students recognize that perspective or point of view matter. This understanding can be revisited when students read other text—of any genre—in which the author shapes the text with a particular audience in mind. Knowing the author's goals (e.g., trying to convince the reader that his or her opinion is the "right" one) helps all readers to be more critical readers, a lifelong skill that applies to the reading of science texts in class and the reading of science as it is communicated via the mass media.

Conclusions

As a study group, we noted at least five outcomes of using these literacy strategies in the science classrooms. First, the strategies helped organize instruction and provide a structure for the reading-based activities that ac-companied students' investigations. Using these strategies helped us employ Palincsar and Magnusson's (2001) model of linking firsthand (physical) investigation with secondhand (textual) investigation in the classrooms. Kerry underscored the links among scientific physical inquiry and scientific textual inquiry (and assessment) with this comment:

I used the word map [concept of definition map] strategy on two occasions in my classroom. We mapped out the two most prominent concepts of the chemistry unit, property and chemical reaction. Beforehand, we spent a great deal of time constructing the meanings of these words through inquiry-based, hands-on activities. I used the mapping technique to make sure they fully grasped the concepts we had been studying.

Second, the strategies also helped teachers mediate—or interpret and model interpretation from text—for students. In the past, we have often read texts aloud and discussed them, but we have not really dug into the texts and component terms in the ways that the strategies allowed us to do. These strategies allowed teachers to target key words and concepts and have in-depth discussions about them. Although the strategies take time to enact in the classroom, the learning (and assessment) benefits seem to make the time investment worthwhile.

The third theme is related to text mediation. That is, the strategies allowed for modeling in various ways (some explicit, some implicit) independent reading strategies (e.g., predicting, questioning, setting purpose, rereading) and metacognition (recognizing when they did and did not understand the text). By having conversations about the texts with these strategies as a guide, teachers showed students how to think through text (not just what the interpretations should be, but how to engage in the process of interpretation).

Fourth, the strategies motivated students to read. All of the teachers in the group remarked on particular aspects of students' demeanors or their learning that resulted from the use of these literacy strategies in their science classrooms. Although it may take some time for students to understand the task itself when a strategy is first introduced, and some strategies require the teacher to do a fair amount of up-front work, the payoffs in motivation seem clear. Alycia summed up this motivation aspect when she wrote, "I love implementing strategies that I know the kids are enjoying, that make them think, and still accomplish an academic goal."

A final theme is particularly exciting to all of us in the Textual Tools Study Group. This theme of assessment became evident as the weeks wore on in the unit and we began collecting and analyzing artifacts of student work via the literacy teaching strategies. It seemed from our professional development sessions that the strategies produced artifacts that make visible student thinking and learning, allowing for formative or instructional assessment. For example, Alycia commented at one point, "I liked the map as an assessment tool, and especially with little prompting, it can give great insight into understanding of the topic." And one of Chevon's comments sums up what many of us on the team were thinking as we read student artifacts from the classrooms during our professional development sessions:

You can definitely see an evolution of understanding of concepts by using this literacy strategy [concept of definition maps]. As a culminating assessment of this term property I guided students as they completed their maps. The results provided me with a clear description of students' thinking. I was able to use this pertinent information to address any present misconceptions and ensure that the proper conceptual and relational knowledge was applied. I will continue to use this strategy in my quest to build a solid bridge between science and literacy.

In sum, literacy teaching strategies not only provided teachers with tools for guiding students' interactions with texts and with physical inquiry, but also motivated students to engage with the texts and provided a window into student thinking. All of us in the Textual Tools Study Group plan to continue to develop these strategies, together with the text sets we described previously (report forthcoming), thus continuing to examine the impact on teachers' practice and on students' general and scientific literacy development over time.

Acknowledgment

This material is based upon work supported by the National Science Foundation, under Grant No. ESI 0101780. Any opinions, findings, and conclusions or recommendations expressed in this material are those of the authors and do not necessarily reflect the views of the National Science Foundation.

References

Alvermann, D. E., and D. W. Moore. 1991. Secondary school reading. In *Handbook of reading research*, vol. 2, eds. R. Barr, M. L. Kamil, P. B. Mosenthal, and P. D. Pearson, 951–983. New York: Longman.

Duke, N. K., and P. D. Pearson. 2002. Effective reading practices for developing reading comprehension. In *What research has to say about reading instruction*, eds. A. E. Farstrup and S. J. Samuels, 205–242. Newark, DE: International Reading Association.

Geier, R., P. Blumenfeld, R. Marx, J. Krajcik, B. Fishman, and E. Soloway. Forthcoming. Standardized test outcomes for students engaged in inquiry-based science curriculum in the context of urban reform. *Journal of Research in Science Teaching.*

Goldman, S. R. 1997. Learning from text: Reflections on the past and suggestions for the future. *Discourse Processes* 23: 357–398.

Ivey, G. 1999. A multicase study in the middle school: Complexities among young adolescent readers. *Reading Research Quarterly* 34 (2): 172–193.

Krajcik, J., P. C. Blumenfeld, R. W. Marx, K. M. Bass, and J. Fredricks. 1998. Inquiry in project-based science classrooms: Initial attempts by middle school students. *The Journal of the Learning Sciences* 7: 313–350.

Lee, O., and S. H. Fradd. 1998. Science for all, including students from non-English language backgrounds. *Educational Researcher* 27 (3): 1–10.

Lemke, J. L. 1990. *Talking science: Language, learning, and values.* Norwood, NJ: Ablex.

Marx, R.W., P. C. Blumenfeld, J. S. Krajcik, B. Fishman, E. Soloway, R. Geier, and T. T. Revital. 2004. Inquiry-based science in the middle grades: Assessment of learning in urban systemic reform. *Journal of Research in Science Teaching* 41: 1063–1080.

McGinley, W., and P. Denner. 1987. Story impressions: A prereading/writing activity. *Journal of Reading* 31: 248–253.

Moje, E. B., T. Collazo, R. Carrillo, and R. W. Marx. 2001. "Maestro, what is 'quality'?": Language, literacy, and discourse in project-based science. *Journal of Research in Science Teaching* 38 (4): 469–496.

Moje, E. B., K. M. Ciechanowski, K. E. Kramer, L. M. Ellis, R. Carrillo, and T. Collazo. 2004. Working toward third space in content area literacy: An examination of everyday funds of knowledge and discourse. *Reading Research Quarterly* 39 (1): 38–71.

National Research Council (NRC). 1996. *National science education standards.* Washington, DC: National Academy Press.

Nist, S. L., and M. L. Simpson. 1997. *Developing vocabulary concepts for college thinking.* 2nd ed. Boston: Houghton Mifflin.

Palincsar, A. S., and S. J. Magnusson. 2001. The interplay of first-hand and text-based investigations to model and support the development of scientific knowledge and reasoning. In *Cognition and instruction: 25 years of progress,* eds. S. M. Carver and D. Klahr, 152–193. Mahwah, NJ: Lawrence Erlbaum.

Pichert, J. W., and R. C. Anderson. 1977. Taking different perspectives on a story. *Journal of Educational Psychology* 69: 309–315.

Schwartz, R. 1988. Learning to learn vocabulary in content textbooks. *Journal of Reading* 32: 108–118.

Taba, H. 1967. *Teacher's handbook for elementary social studies.* Reading, MA: Addison-Wesley.

Thompson, C. A. 2003. The oral vocabulary abilities of skilled and unskilled African American readers. Doctoral diss., University of Michigan.

Vacca, R. T., and J. Vacca. 2004. *Content area reading: Literacy and learning across the curriculum.* 8th ed. New York: Allyn and Bacon.

Wade, S. E., W. Trathen, and G. Schraw. 1990. An analysis of spontaneous study strategies. *Reading Research Quarterly* 25: 147–166.

Science, Literacy, and Culture

Una Jornada de Aprendizaje Valiosa Para Compartir (A Learning Journey Worth Sharing Out)

Jackie Rojas is a fifth-grade teacher at Patrick Henry School in the Anaheim City School District, Anaheim, California. Her students are 83% Hispanic, 10% Caucasian, 5% African American, and 2% other demographic backgrounds. Eighty percent are English language learners.

On October 8 Juan Rodriguez entered the school office promptly at 10:00 a.m. "Buenos día, Sr. Rodriguez. ¿En qué le podemos servir?" ("Good morning, Mr. Rodriguez. What can we do for you today?"), asked the office staff, while wondering why he would be coming in to school at this time. Juan Rodriguez has never attended school conferences or meetings. He only comes to pick up his younger daughter in second grade when she is dismissed before her brother Luis can walk home with her.

Mr. Rodriguez replied clearly and firmly that "Mi hijo, Luis, me pidió que viniera hoy día a las 10:00 para que él pudiera enseñarme ciencias en el salón de la Sra. Rojas." ("My son, Luis, asked me to be here today at 10:00 in Mrs. Rojas's classroom so he could teach me science.")

In Juan Rodriguez's hand was a personalized invitation from his son entitled "Family Science Shareout." The flyer, in English and Spanish, offered the basic information for the event: who, what, when, where, and why. Students had taken home the invitations to give to their family members.

Luis is the most active student in Jackie Rojas's fifth-grade class and has the most difficulty staying on task. Luis reads over two years below grade level and scored a 2 out of 5 overall on the California English Language Development Test. He recently qualified for special education in language arts for four hours per week. But, Luis is growing in confidence and persistence daily. A sample from Luis's science notebook appears in Figure 1. He wrote in response to a prompt to interpret his triple-beam balance—a difficult exercise for him. He includes a comment about the nature of science.

FIGURE 1 Luis's Notebook Sample

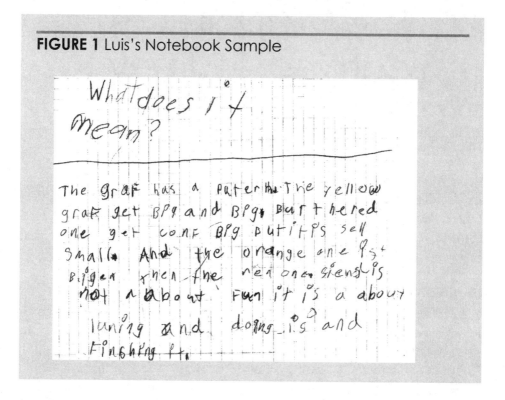

Background

At the start of each year I let my class know that we will learn together, teacher and students. I invite them to join me on this journey because I cannot get there on my own. I need them to teach me, too, so that I can learn from them. Then, I will be able to teach them more effectively so that they can think and understand at a higher level.

Jackie began the first trimester of school this year by teaching eight lessons from a unit on floating and sinking using a mode of instruction that incorporates student science notebooks.

I use science as my primary springboard for learning. It is the most concrete of all of the subjects. As a result, it allows for the most comprehensible input for all students, including English language learners. The use of student science notebooks levels the playing field for everyone to learn. Inquiry science provides the opportunity for all children to learn to think critically and make deep connections whatever their level of literacy and regardless of their socioeconomic, cultural, or linguistic background. I get more mileage out of integrating all of the language arts and mathematics standards that could apply into the science lessons. Because the investigations involve talking and thinking through minds-on discussions first, all children are empowered to be successful in analytical writing much sooner than would normally take place (usually not until high school for many minority children or English language learners).

Jackie developed the following writing prompt to serve a dual purpose: (1) as a post-unit assessment (for science) that showed growth in conceptual understanding of the factors that control the buoyancy of an object, and (2) as an evaluation of student writing ability in the persuasive domain from a multiparagraph composition to be scored according to a holistic rubric used by the fifth-grade teachers. The prompt was,

Write a multi-paragraph persuasive composition. What are the factors that cause an object to float (or sink)? Base your claims (arguments) on evidence from your student science notebook.

Figure 2 shows a student's first draft (paper and pencil) in response to the prompt. This student was in the resource specialist program (RSP). RSP students are identified as being capable of reaching proficiency at grade level, but for some reason (not solely the fact that they are learning English as a second language), they are at least two years below grade level in language arts and/or math. RSP students are only seen for an hour or two (depending on the goals) a day four days a week by a special education teacher. The student whose work is shown in Figure 2 "graduated" from RSP before the end of the school year.

I am not asking for complete sentences here. I need them to spend their time thinking, not writing. So, I allow them to use words, phrases, and abbreviations as their text. I also let them know the importance of dual encoding (verbal and visual) so that they are encouraged to both write and draw their predictions. The same is true later of their observations when recording their results.

FIGURE 2 Student Response to Writing Prompt Regarding Factors That Cause an Object to Float (or Sink)

April 28, 2003

Siz and Shape
I didn't think that siz really doesn't mather I think shape mathers becaues when we got the clay lump and tried to make it float we chaned the shape and it floated.

Ideas
Some ideas that we had were that something that will sink was too heavy and something that will float or sink—depends on wt put another person saed person can float in back, but not on front.

Cargo boats
I think when we did the cargo boats the shape had a lot to do to hole the cargo up like the cargo boat that coed supert more than 100. marbles.

Weight at the larg Cylinder
In the graph you can see that the aluminum cylinders weight more than all the others so I think that weight has a little to do with it to.

Prediction
In the measurent first, secent and three and average the clay all sink put the average was all seven-teen so I think the average and F/S and name were all the same because it was too hevey

I do not ever correct the science notebooks for conventions or content. I let students know that writing mechanics are important, but not in this context. They are to put down what they think without stressing over the spelling, punctuation, grammar, or handwriting. (I do use the notebooks as a source of material to identify and later teach standards or objectives in language arts or English language development.) Therefore, neither they nor I make "corrections," but rather we might make another entry (dated) to explain any changes in their thinking and reasons for those changes, citing evidence (mainly their own observations and data).

By working with a partner of differing ability, students in Jackie's class begin to respect each other and permit their partners to help with their weak areas without embarrassment. For example, Mario allows Heather to know that he really does not read well yet. He learns from her how to read with understanding to follow multistep written directions. Heather watches Mario patiently experiment with different ways to get the bobby pin on the spring scale to hold the slippery marble. She sees that he finds it fun, not frustrating, when he comes up with an original idea to make it work.

By emphasizing inquiry science at the beginning, my students quickly realize that "low"-achieving students are often the most successful and "high"-achieving students often feel the most frustrated. I think this is because the former group of students is used to being "wrong" the first time they try something and they are more comfortable with uncertainty. The latter group of students is used to knowing the "right" answer and expecting their ideas to work the first time.

After completing Lessons 1 through 8, Jackie prepared her students for the mid-unit embedded assessment. She asked each pair of students to prepare notes for an oral presentation on one of the eight lessons. Jackie modeled the process for them with Lesson 1, using evaluation criteria from the district's Listening and Speaking Language Arts Standards.

To meet standards for technology integration, the students transferred their notes from index cards used in these presentations into word processing software. These documents followed a format modeled on scientific papers: Number and Title of the lesson, Question investigated, Materials used, Procedure followed, Data gathered, Results obtained. The digital files are then used to create posters for the Family Science Shareout that Juan Rodriguez has come to see. The posters help students guide their parents through the same investigations they themselves had experienced. (See

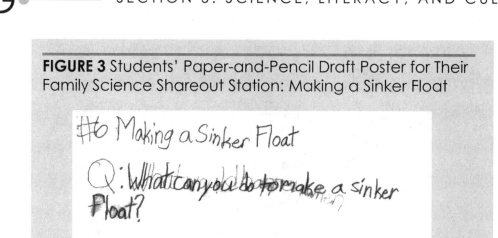

FIGURE 3 Students' Paper-and-Pencil Draft Poster for Their Family Science Shareout Station: Making a Sinker Float

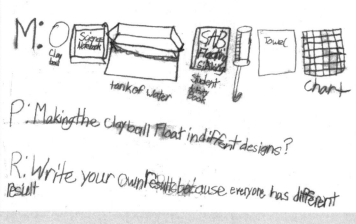

Figure 3 for two students' pencil-and-paper draft of a poster and Figure 4 for the same students' digital document.)

Family Science Shareout

Scheduling the Family Science Shareout in the daytime between 10:00 a.m. and 2:00 p.m. allows visitors from family, school, and the community to come and go as their schedules permit. Inviting stakeholders beyond parents allows for all of the students to interact with many more participants, including certificated and classified school staff, undergraduate future teachers, university teaching and research colleagues, and business or community partners.

The day before the event, Jackie's students set up eight stations in the classroom. Station 1 has the Know-Wonder-Learn (K-W-L) charts (with the Learn part covered) from the unit, but no hands-on materials. Each

---

FIGURE 4 Students' Digital Document for Their Family Science Shareout Station: Making a Sinker Float

Lesson 6:	Making a Sinker Float
Station:	11
Questions:	What can you do to make a sinker float?
	Do you think that you can make the clay ball float by changing only its shape?
	How many different ways can you find to reshape the clay so that it will float?
	Which ideas worked?
	Which ideas did not work?
	What designs were the most effective?
	Why do you think these designs worked best?
Materials:	N Mini-Notebooks
	2 Student Science Notebooks
	1 Student Activity Book
	4 Trays: Each with several clay balls
	2 Tanks of water
	N Paper Towels

---

of the other stations is set up with the student-created poster, two student notebooks bookmarked for that lesson, paper, pencil, lesson materials and equipment, and directions needed for the key activity.

On one side of the door is a sign-in table. On the other side is an information table for visitors to stop by as they leave. It displays brochures in English and Spanish from the Beckman@Science Program, Project Tomorrow, the American Association for the Advancement of Science, and the federal government's No Child Left Behind initiative. All of these materials provide suggestions for how parents can support their children's learning in science. Parents appreciate the bilingual resources to support their intentions to encourage science experiences at home.

Juan Rodriguez enters Jackie's classroom. The students are standing in three rows like a choir and begin to recite their Class Poem, a statement of aspirations that is very important to the class.

The Class Poem is the first step in creating a learning community in my classroom, which I expect them to extend beyond the schoolhouse door. Latino culture is truly family centered. The Class Poem states that each individual is a part of the human family. In order to have a successful Family Science Shareout, we extend our audience even further, to include not only their nuclear families, but also their extended families, and their school and community families. Latino culture loves collective performance and Hispanic parents love to watch their children perform. I warmly welcome visitors into my classroom by offering them this recitation of a Class Poem that parallels Latinos cordially and generously receiving guests into their homes. This seems to provide the students with the confidence to go ahead and take on their role as teachers for the day.

Students go to their assigned stations and start their families out at their own station. Juan Rodriguez and the other parents rotate through the stations, spending 10 minutes at each, with the students guiding them through a key activity from the lesson. Parents compare their own data recorded in "mini-notebooks" to the entries in the two student notebooks bookmarked for that lesson.

The families come to Jackie when they complete all eight stations. She keeps the flow going and talks to each family as they finish. The adults love it when every one of their children (students' siblings, cousins, etc.) or extended family members (grandparents, aunts/uncles, etc.) is acknowledged and attended to, even if only with a greeting and a cookie.

Interdependence is a way of life in the Hispanic home. The students and parents and other family members feel more comfortable learning together in the Family Science Shareout. Each group member is valued and plays a role in supporting the effort. Even toddlers are included as they, for example, are allowed to put marbles in a clay boat. An elderly grandmother can help to count the marbles (in Spanish) while a parent records the written results. Sharing with their families helps my students understand that, whether or not a student speaks English, he or she is intelligent; whether or not a student reads and writes English well, he or she can think; and whether or not parents went to school for many years, there are ways they can support us in our learning.

Jackie, an Anglo American, comfortably includes English-speaking as well as Spanish-speaking participants at the shareout. She accommodates the Anglo American parents by providing an exact timetable of events they can follow. The Hispanic parents appreciate that there is no real "start" or "stop" time, such that no one is considered "late." There is a continuous flow of visitors coming and going, although some stay all day. A child-care area occupies one corner of the room with blocks and books so a student can entertain toddlers who become fussy.

Within the four-hour time slot, Jackie conducts two group shareout sessions in the classroom for parent input. She has pizza delivered for the parents and invites them to begin sharing their impressions. Often, everyone in the group understands Spanish or the few English-only speakers will have a bilingual acquaintance, so she talks in Spanish only. Otherwise, Jackie simultaneously translates back and forth as the questions and comments are made. She uses a welcoming approach with a gentle but firm expectation that each parent has something valuable to say. She requests that they be honest and let her know what they liked and what needs to be improved. Jackie asks the parents to introduce themselves and give the name of their child. She then waits as long as needed for them to speak.

A mother looks as though she may want to speak so I gently prod her to share her ideas. Finally she opens up and says in Spanish: "I am Carmita's mother. Well, I did go to school for three years in Mexico and I learned some science like this. But, I have learned a lot more here today from my Carmita and your other students."

Luis's father, to my surprise, looks as though he might speak and jumps in! "Me llamo Juan Rodriguez. Soy el papá de Luis. Estoy de acuerdo. ¡He aprendido mucho!" ("I am Juan Rodriguez, Luis's father. I agree, I have learned a lot!")

Then, Carmita's mother turns to her husband and speaks for him: "And, my husband here did not have a chance to study at all. He never went to school even in Mexico. So, he is so happy that Carmita is learning so much that she can teach him what she is learning. Well, that is why we came to here, to this country, anyway."

Overwhelmingly, the most positive reaction is related to the opportunity to see their child's work and learn science from their own son or daughter. Most parents comment on the amount of language and math the students are mastering and the improvement in their English as a result of the focus on science.

Four years ago when I proposed a family science event I had no idea what it would look like. I did have two underlying criteria: I wanted it to be noncompetitive and I wanted it to center around involvement in actual student learning of the science curriculum. I conduct several Family Science Shareouts a year because I can accomplish a great deal. The parents see their child's language and math develop over time through their children's progress in the science notebook entries.

Assessment has become an integral part of the Family Science Shareout. Before the event, the students' attention to appropriate detail in making the poster and the enthusiasm they demonstrate in preparation for "the big day" reveals their engagement in the subject matter. During the event, because the students play the role of teacher with their families, Jackie can observe the level of questions they use in guiding their relatives through the investigations.

Most of the students in her classroom not only have to explain their thinking to their families, but also actually need to translate their thoughts from English to Spanish for the adults and younger siblings to understand. This ability to code switch is not as easy as it may seem to monolingual speakers of English who often assume that because a person speaks two languages, they can automatically interpret from one to the other.

The day following the Family Science Shareout, Jackie asks her students to reflect on their own learning from the event and on what they think their families learned. She requests that they also interview their family members to find out what they think went well and what could be done to improve for "next time." Figure 5 shows one student's reflections.

Lessons Learned

Since 1995, Anaheim City School District has focused on language arts. Now Jackie is spreading her love and passion for inquiry science and literacy integration. The effect of the Family Science Shareout is growing. Administrators discussed the benefits of this model of parent involvement with the faculty. Parents are "spreading the word" about the importance of science in their children's education and, to the delight of the students,

FIGURE 5 One Student's Reflection on the Family Science Shareout

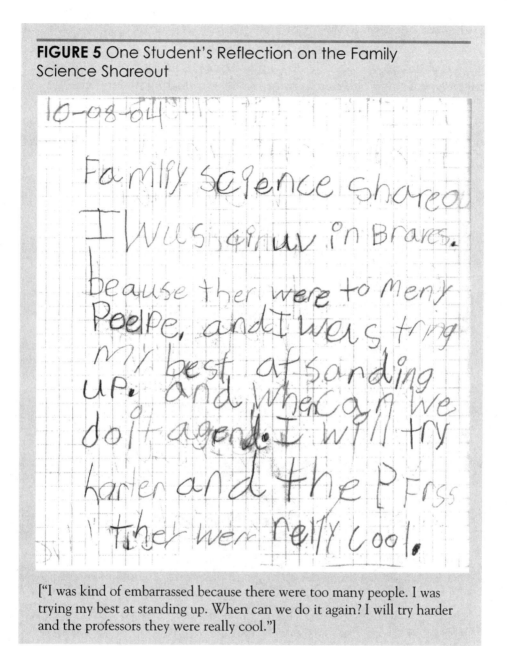

["I was kind of embarrassed because there were too many people. I was trying my best at standing up. When can we do it again? I will try harder and the professors they were really cool."]

they have begun to praise and encourage their children's pursuit of learning. The number of both primary and intermediate grade level teachers interested in teaching more science and implementing science notebooks has also grown. Now, all three special education teachers in Jackie's school have come on board as active participants in the Family Science Shareout.

Even more impressive, they now base much of their work with Jackie's students on science notebook entries and vocabulary from math and science.

By connecting science, math, and literacy, students in Jackie's classes have made from two to five years of progress in reading fluency in one year. Their writing has developed from a score of 1 or 2 to a score of 3 or 4 on the grade-level rubric, especially in content but also in mechanics. They have mastered math vocabulary and skills related to statistics, data analysis, and probability. (See student writing samples in Figure 6.)

Jackie reflected on teaching in an urban district with a high percentage of English language learner students:

Most of my students are living in two cultures. I want them to realize the richness that bicultural situation provides. Latino parents are interested, even if they are not involved in the way non-Latino parents might be. The more we can involve them, the more they will learn about how to support their children's learning. Whether or not Spanish-speaking parents approve of "bilingual education," the Spanish language is intricately woven into their lives. According to current California law, English language learners are taught through "structured English immersion." That means that I must teach overwhelmingly in English but may provide primary language support. Through using a bilingual homework calendar, I am honoring those limited-English-speaking students, even the newcomers, by assigning them the exact same homework as their fluent-English-speaking or English-only-speaking peers. I am thus enabling their non-English-speaking parents to assist with homework, especially when they understand the content as well as the language of the problems assigned.

There are different levels of support that children experience in the home. Traditionally, the quality of children's writing in language arts is directly related to the frequency, diversity, and richness of their experiences at home. This, combined with a high level of parental support and involvement with their schoolwork, ensures that children have something to write about! The Family Science Shareout, by enabling parents to become co-learners of instruction in school, serves as a model for how to make connections at home. This is why I distribute bilingual brochures that provide ideas for how to continue supporting children to learn science with their families and through community resources.

FIGURE 6 Student Science Notebook Samples

David, an RSP student at risk of retention, recorded his investigation plan (shown below) to compare the weight of a mystery cylinder to that of a cylinder of water (ten = 10 paper clips) in order to predict whether it will float or sink.

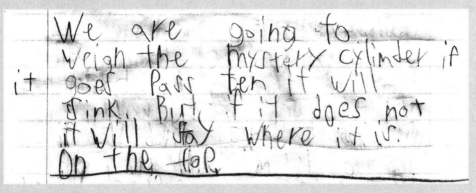

We are going to weigh the mystery cylinder if it goes Pass ten it will sink. But if it does not it will stay where it is. On the top.

Valencia's first draft (written directly on the computer) in response to the prompt on page 291 is shown below. Valencia, a limited English proficient student, was reclassified as fluent English proficient before the end of the school year.

April 28, 2003

What Floats and What Sinks

What I've found out is that some people think that some objects sink because the object weights a lot. That isn't true because gigantic ships weigh a lot and they still float. But like the Large aluminum cylinder weights the most and sinks doesn't mean that if a object is heavy it Will sink. Oh, no! It might also be like what the material it is made of. Like the large wood cylinder is made of wood and wood does float.

Like I said that the large wood cylinder floats because it is made of wood, and so is the small wood cylinder and it floats. Now, that is only one way of how an object can float or sink. There are more ways, like what the figure is. What we did in lessons 6 and 7 pages 30 to 39. We tried to make the clay lump [which sank] to a different shape. Some of those shapes floated but some did not.

Some people thought that bubbles had to do something with floating and sinking. They Thought other things that [maybe] have to do with floating and sinking like bubbles help things Float, balloons and sponges float, sink- too heavy [like what we were talking about], and, waves Make things sink by making water go in the floating object. That is what they thought that had to do with floating and sinking. Who knows it might be true or not.

At class, when we berly started floating and sinking some kids in my class thought that if an object weights a little it will float. That isn't true, and I can prove it because In the class graphthe alumanium beb was lowest in weight then came the small wood cylinder and then the 3thlowest object whitch weight about 3 paper clips and sank.

We'll, what all we've done on floating and sinking I think every one knows like what is The buoyant force and measuring and calibrating the spring scale, but most important knowing what makes objects float or sink.

About My Students' Parents

Whether or not they are "involved," they are interested. Most parents who were not brought up with student council, etc., do not "know the ropes" of PTA involvement. And there are many other factors to consider.

Even if they do not return a phone call or a note, they do care. Many parents do not live in a situation in which they can return a phone call or a note, especially in English. But there are many other factors to consider.

They appreciate being welcomed into the classroom to observe their child's learning while the teacher is teaching. Tasks often asked of parent volunteers are not necessarily what they might be comfortable with, but they love watching and listening to their children.

They learn much more about their child's schooling when allowed to experience the learning themselves in the classroom alongside their child and under their child's guidance. Their children often accompany them to the doctor, lawyer, or immigration offices and serve as their interpreters there both linguistically and culturally.

About My Students

Whether they speak English or whether they don't, they're all intelligent. This means that we do NOT have to "teach them English first" before teaching them science or in lieu of teaching them science. There are virtually no limitations to the types of students who can do inquiry-centered science.

Even if they can't read or write English well (yet), they can all think. This means that they do NOT have to learn to read first, before they can read to learn. Science actually motivates children to turn to books for more information and to find applications for their new knowledge and skills.

Although they may not come with the expected early childhood background, they do bring a wealth of knowledge and experience to the classroom. This means that teachers need to really truly get to know their students and learn how to use the strengths they have acquired from their linguistic and cultural home environment.

I conduct four Family Science Shareouts during the school year. Through repeating these events, we invite and welcome the parents and the rest of the community to join us on our learning journey at different points along the way.

It's January 25. Jackie happens to be at school late when Mr. Rodriguez comes to pick up Luis and his sister from the after-school program. Jackie asks Mr. Rodriguez,

Do you plan to attend the second Family Science Shareout this Friday?

Mr. Rodriguez smiles broadly and puts his arm around Luis:

Haré lo mejor posible para llegar. (I will do my best to make it.)

He squeezes his son's shoulders affectionately. Luis grins.

Resources

Clark, J. M., and A. Paivio. 1991. Dual coding theory and education. *Educational Psychology Review* 3 (3): 149–170.

Harlen, W. 2000. Interpreting evidence for formative assessment. In *Teaching, learning and assessing science 5–12.* 3rd ed. London: Paul Chapman.

Krashen, S. 1985. *The input hypothesis: Issues and implications.* Beverly Hills: Laredo.

National Science Foundation. 2000. *Inquiry: Thoughts, views, and strategies for the K–5 classroom.* Arlington, VA: National Science Foundation, Division of Elementary, Secondary, and Informal Education.

Ogle, D. 1986. K-W-L: A teaching model that develops active reading of expository text. *The Reading Teacher* 39 (6): 564–571.

Shepardson, D. P., and S. J. Britsch. 1997. Children's science journals: Tools for teaching, learning, and assessing. *Science and Children* (Feb.): 12–17.

Questions for Discussion

1. Student learning is enhanced in environments where students' cultures are understood and accepted. What are some ways in which Ms. Rojas uses her understanding of student and family culture to enhance science and literacy instruction?

2. Examine the chart of strategies to get started with Science Talks (Chapter 11, pages 313–314). Which strategies does Ms. Rojas use to prepare her students and their parents for success in learning science?

3. Teachers benefit from science talk in that they gain a new view of many students. What evidence is there that Ms. Rojas benefits in this way from the Family Science Shareout?

Using Diversity as a Strength in the Science Classroom:
The Benefits of Science Talk

Ann S. Rosebery and Josiane Hudicourt-Barnes
The Chèche Konnen Center at TERC

In the last 15 years, we have talked with teachers across the country about their concerns about teaching science to students from groups historically underrepresented in the sciences. Most often, these teachers have told us that they do not know how to best teach their students. This seems to be especially true for teachers who work with students from low-income families, students from families with little formal education, students of color, and students who do not speak English as a first language.

A recurring worry in these conversations is that teachers do not know how to connect the curriculum to what their students know and what they know how to do. Because of the distance between their own life experiences and those of their students, teachers are often unfamiliar with their students' out-of-school lives, including the ideas and perspectives they bring to learning, the ways they use language to communicate what they know and don't know, the ways they interact socially, and more. Sometimes we meet teachers who are so frustrated that they have begun to focus on those things they think their students can't do rather than on what they can do. An unintentional consequence of this focus can be lowered expectations for what their students can learn and achieve in science.

Since 1987, teachers and researchers at the Chèche Konnen Center at TERC, an education research and development organization in Cambridge, Massachusetts, have been identifying pedagogical practices that use diversity as a strength, rather than seeing it as an obstacle, in the science classroom. Chèche Konnen means "search for knowledge" in Haitian Creole. The first teachers who helped launch the center's work gave it this name. Although significant differences may exist between the life experience and language practices of some students and those valued by curricula, schools, and teachers, a growing body of research is demonstrating that these students, like all others, are capable of learning and achieving in science at high levels. Indeed, the varied ideas, life experiences, and language practices of these students represent sources of considerable intellectual strength when teachers know how to recognize and capitalize on them.

Using diversity as a strength in the classroom requires teachers to change their practices in some critical ways. It means learning how to listen to and look carefully for connections between students' ideas and scientific ideas and ways of knowing. In this chapter, we discuss three steps teachers can take to learn how to see and hear these connections. Teachers can do the following:

1. Deepen their understanding of how language use and life experience are related to teaching and academic learning
2. Expand their views of science and what scientists do, which carries deep implications for science teaching
3. Experiment with a pedagogical practice called "science talk" that allows students to mobilize their varied language practices and life experiences as intellectual strengths in learning scientific ways of knowing and helps make students' thinking visible to teachers

We address each step in the sections that follow.

How Do Children Learn? Relationships Among Language, Life Experience, and Learning

From birth, each of us is learning all the time. Among the first things we learn is how to talk and act in ways that are "correct" at home. At very young ages, children know how to communicate effectively with the adults and other children in their lives. They know how to learn new ideas and practices. And they know how to use what they know toward purposeful ends. In short, most children are competent at home and in their out-of-school lives (Labov 1972; Rogoff 2004). Successful teachers use a broad range of students' home-based knowledge and experiences as a foundation for building academic literacies (Hudicourt-Barnes 2003; Lee 1993; Moll and González 2004; Warren and Rosebery, forthcoming). Knowledge of students' language-use practices is particularly important because of the pivotal role that communication plays in learning and teaching (Hudicourt-Barnes 2003; Rosebery and Warren, forthcoming).

In the United States, the competencies that middle class, European American children learn at home pave the way for academic literacy (Heath 1983). The ways that they learn to talk and act are used in school as the foundation for learning written academic language and academic ways of thinking. For example, middle-class parents teach their children to talk and think about things according to attributes (e.g., color, shape, texture). This kind of thinking undergirds a predominant form of questioning in early school discourse (e.g., "What's the color of that truck?") and, in later years, modes of classification in academic sciences. Middle-class parents also teach their children to tell stories that assume the listener knows little or nothing about the topic (e.g., "Tell Daddy what happened today"). This kind of outside-perspective-taking lays a foundation for understanding and working with the decontextualized, "objective" stances typical of expository texts, especially textbooks.

Children from low-income families, children of color, and children who are learning English also acquire remarkable ways with words at home (Heath 1983; Ward 1971). Before they enter school, many can understand and use elaborate metaphors and imagery and produce captivating stories (Miller, Cho, and Bracey, forthcoming; Ward 1971). Some can do this by the time they are three years old (Miller, Cho, and Bracey, forthcoming). Many non-middle-class children also acquire robust and sophisticated argumentation skills at young ages. By intently watching interactions among adults and older children, they learn how to present concise points of view, marshal evidence, challenge the claims of others, and take multiple points of view (Hudicourt-Barnes 2003; Heath 1983). Unlike the language practices of middle-class children, the relationship of these language practices to academics, which is strong, for the most part goes unrecognized at school.

Children also learn different ways of knowing in their families and communities. Middle-class children are typically taught to concentrate on one thing, instead of several, at a time. In school, teachers look for this behavior as an indication that students are "paying attention" (Rogoff 2003). By contrast, children from non-middle-class families may learn how to pay attention to more than one thing at a time. They are able to manage several tasks simultaneously with ease (Rogoff 2003). This means that even very young children, for example, can listen to a story, play with a toy, and keep an eye on a younger sibling without skipping a beat. Middle-class teachers, however, who themselves have learned to focus on one thing at a time, find this ability startling and often misinterpret it as "not paying attention" when it happens in the classroom. In a similar vein, children from non-middle-class homes may also learn to learn through careful observation. Unlike their middle-class counterparts who learn to learn through verbal explanation, these children learn many things by paying careful attention to what is happening around them (e.g., how to play a game, how to construct an argument or tell a story, how to act in one situation versus another), not needing additional, explicit explanation.

In short, most teachers, owing to their own life histories, community traditions, and professional training, have been prepared to recognize and build on the ways with words and ways of knowing that middle-class children bring to school. But they have not been prepared to recognize and take up the knowledge and practices that non-middle-class children learn at home.

One implication is that teachers need tools to help them learn more about the children they teach. There are at least two things that teachers can do in this regard. First, they can gain firsthand knowledge by observing their students in settings where they are competent, such as on the playground, at home, or in other nonacademic settings (Ballenger 1999; Moll and González 2004). Paying attention to those times when students participate actively and take on roles of leadership or responsibility may be particularly informative. Making records (by taking notes or audio- or videotaping, with participants' permission) of what students say and do in in-school as well as out-of-school settings allows teachers to reflect on what their students know and how they express their ideas (BTRS 2004; Gallas 1995). Second, teachers can read about what others—fellow teachers as well as researchers—who are interested in exploring relationships among language, life experience, and learning have discovered through such inquiries. (A Recommended Resources list appears at the end of this chapter.)

An Expanded View of Science: Surprises From the World of Practicing Scientists

Simply put, science is the study of how the world works. Science standards and benchmarks define scientific literacy as including scientific knowledge as well as the practices that scientists use to construct that knowledge (AAAS 1993; NRC 1996). But what do scientists do when they are learning? And what, if anything, does this imply for learning science in school? To answer these questions, we look briefly at what scientists do when they do science.

The popular image of scientists has changed in recent years. The stereotype of a lone scientist (usually white and male) pouring chemicals from beaker to beaker has been altered to reflect a broad and rich range of activities and people. Thanks to studies of scientists at work, we know that in addition to using particular ways of observing, thinking, experimenting, and validating (i.e., the "scientific method"), scientists also routinely engage in practices that at first blush may not seem particularly scientific. For example, scientists argue with one another about ideas and evidence. They conduct these arguments within their labs, at conferences, through academic publications, and over e-mail, using spoken and written language as well as a variety of representations (e.g., diagrams, models, graphs, tables, and mathematical formulas) to bolster their claims (Latour and Woolgar 1986; Lynch 1985). Scientists also use their imaginations to pursue difficult questions, visualizing what they cannot actually see (e.g., the movement of chromosomes or the action of beta-blockers). They use models, metaphors, and analogies to conceptualize situations and to take on different points of view (Wolpert and Richards 1997). And as they grow intimately familiar with the phenomenon they are studying, scientists often develop an attachment to it, what the geneticist Barbara McClintock called "a feeling for the organism" (Keller 1983). These and other practices, which may at first seem anything but scientific, are in fact cornerstones of scientific thinking and work.

Take the case of Barbara McClintock, who won a Nobel Prize for her work on the genetics of corn. McClintock raised her corn plants herself, fertilized them by hand, and studied the genetics of their offspring microscopically, using techniques she developed specifically for that purpose. Eventually, she learned so much about the genetics of corn that it was hard for other scientists to understand her work; she had moved beyond what they knew. The importance of her work became clear, however, when her colleagues realized that she had learned how genes and chromosomes move from one location to another during fertilization. McClintock's findings showed that genetic organization and control are fluid and dynamic. This was in major conflict with the dominant thinking in biology at the time and thus helped revolutionize the fields of molecular biology and genetics.

According to her own description, McClintock's approach to science diverged in several ways from the standard scientific method:

I found that the more I worked with [the chromosomes], the bigger and bigger they got, and when I was really working with them I wasn't outside, I was down there. I was part of the system. I was right down there with them, and everything got big. I even was able to see the internal parts of the chromosomes—actually everything was there. It surprised me because I felt as if I was right down there and these were my friends…. As you look at these things, they become part of you. And you forget yourself. (Keller 1983, p. 165)

In McClintock's science, observation, imagination, perseverance, perspective-taking, and intimate knowledge of one's subject, among other things, fueled insight and progress.

Teachers often find McClintock's account, and others like it, exciting because it expands their notion of what counts as scientific and reconnects them to past learning experiences that they valued but have lost touch with (Warren and Rosebery 1995; Rosebery and Warren, forthcoming). As their view of science expands, they begin to see deep connections between scientists' ways of talking and knowing and those of their students (e.g., metaphorical thinking, imagining oneself inside a phenomenon, visualizing phenomena inside their contexts). To explore their view of science, teachers can read accounts of science-in-action written by scientists and by those who have observed scientists at work. Many of these are accessible to nonscientists and make enjoyable reading. (See Recommended Resources for suggested titles.)

Science Talk: Mobilizing Students' Language Practices and Life Experience

From our view, teaching is an ongoing inquiry into the nature of science and into students' ideas about the natural world (Rosebery and Warren 1998). To begin this inquiry, teachers must be able to hear their students' ideas. Unfortunately, authentic discussion happens infrequently in the science classroom. Jay Lemke, a former physicist interested in science education, recorded and analyzed conversations in junior high and high school science classrooms. He found that most consisted of impersonal, objective, expository language and lacked emotional content. Teachers and students did not use slang, figurative or metaphorical language, hyperbole, or exaggeration. They almost never engaged in arguments, told stories or jokes, or used other forms of humor (Lemke 1990). Ironically, these kinds of conversations are not representative of those that take place among scientists (Ochs, Gonzales, and Jacoby 1996). So they not only promulgate stereotypes of science as objective and impersonal, but perhaps more significantly, they marginalize students' home-based ways of talking and knowing.

At the Chèche Konnen Center, teachers interested in expanding the range of talk and thinking in their classrooms have experimented with a form of discussion called "science talk." Science talks are conversations in which students talk with one another openly and respectfully in an exploratory fashion about their ideas and questions about the natural world. Science talks are not about right or wrong answers. They are a time for students to think about how an idea fits into their understanding of the world, to identify and build connections between what they already know and what they are being asked to learn, to raise and explore questions, and to learn from one another.

Most teachers use science talks in conjunction with their existing science programs. They set aside a block of time once a week for students to discuss the ideas and questions that have emerged about the scientific phenomenon they are studying (e.g., plant growth and development, force and motion). Science talks are typically organized around questions the students have asked. Some teachers record their students' questions on chart paper and let students take turns choosing a question for science talk. Other teachers choose a question that they think will be productive.

Students' questions touch on a broad range of concerns, from where seeds come from to why pumpkins float to what it might mean to "waste" water in light of the water cycle to whether plants grow every day. Because science talks are a time for students to think out loud together, every student can have a voice in the curriculum. Even students who may be struggling with reading, writing, and mathematics have ideas and questions about the world that they can share. In fact, in our experience, these students often emerge as intellectual leaders during science talks.

Teachers, too, take on a different role during science talks. Their primary job is to listen to what their students are saying. Some teachers are most comfortable facilitating these discussions; others allow the students to manage them on their own (e.g., by calling on one other). Some teachers strategically "revoice" what they think students are saying, articulating connections they see among students' ideas or between a student's perspective and that of science. (In these cases, it is important for teachers to ask the original speaker if the revoicing adequately represents the student's meaning. If it does not, the student should have a chance to clarify or amend what the teacher has said.) Other teachers will ask students to elaborate or say more about their ideas when they think it is needed. The bottom line is that the teacher's goal is to listen to students' ideas and develop a reflective stance toward them.

Most teachers set aside 30 minutes once a week for a science talk. Often they find that as their students delve into a phenomenon over time and become increasingly knowledgeable about it, their science talks increase in length. Students want—and use profitably—more time to pursue their ideas and questions with one another. Some teachers are surprised to hear that the length of a science talk is not related to students' age. On many occasions we have seen students in first and second grade engage in serious discussion for 45 to 50 minutes.

Students engage with many aspects of scientific literacy during science talks. They grapple with important scientific ideas. They learn how to present and explain their ideas to others. As they participate, they learn how to present a point of view with clarity, make evidence-based arguments, answer challenging questions persuasively, revise their thinking in the face of counter evidence, and clarify their own thinking by talking to others.

Science talks also serve an important function for teachers. By listening carefully to students' ideas, teachers can figure out how to shape their curricula to best support students' learning. Because science talks make students' thinking public, they allow teachers to identify students' current views of the phenomenon under study. From a constructivist perspective, whether these ideas are right or wrong, they nonetheless constitute the intellectual "stuff" available for teaching and learning. Science talks allow teachers to gain insight into these ideas and, upon reflection, develop next pedagogical steps that will enable students to connect their ideas more deeply to scientific perspectives. Thus, science talks can be an essential tool for curriculum building and lesson planning (see box, "Seven Strategies for Getting Started With Science Talks," next page).

An Example: Do Plants Grow Every Day?

Imagine a class of third graders in a two-way bilingual program in which the students learn English and Spanish as well as regular academic subjects. The students are studying plant growth and development using the National Science Resources Center's "Plant Growth and Development" unit (NSRC 1991). They have collected and recorded data on plant growth for several weeks. On this day, their teacher has decided to try out a new kind

Seven Strategies for Getting Started With Science Talks

1. Engage your students in a common activity with a scientific phenomenon (e.g., rolling cars down ramps to investigate constant acceleration; raising plants to examine growth; floating pumpkins to explore buoyancy). This will give all students something to say. Engage your students in an open-ended discussion about the event. Ask them what they saw or what they think happened (e.g., "What happened when you tried to submerge the pumpkin?" "What was the pattern of the speed of the cars as they rolled down the ramp?"). The goal is to provide each student with the opportunity to articulate her thoughts and think with her classmates about the phenomenon.

2. As your students share their thoughts, *listen* to what they say. Your job is to understand their meaning and the perspectives they are bringing to bear, rather than to teach the right answer. Look for connections between your students' ideas and the big ideas of the phenomenon they are studying. Write down what they say; this will help you focus on their ideas and give you a record to return to for further reflection.

3. Encourage your students to talk to one another. When they are authentic, science talks often have the spontaneous, informal flavor of out-of-school conversation. Accept all contributions that are put forward with respect.

4. View yourself as facilitator of the conversation. Feel free to use those practices that will allow you to establish a reflective stance toward the discussion. Some practices that other teachers have found helpful are (a) repeating what a student has said, and then inviting other students to share their ideas. It is important to use the student's words in your restatement rather than your own; (b) "revoicing" what you think a student has said in your own words. Teachers often do this when they want to articulate connections they see among students' ideas or between a student's perspective and that of science, and when they want to invite other children to comment. After revoicing, it is important to follow up with the original speaker and ask if your words represent what she meant. This not only allows her to accept, reject, or amend your interpretation but gives her a chance to re-articulate her ideas if necessary; and (c) asking a student to elaborate or say more about her ideas. This is especially helpful if you are not sure you understand what the student is saying.

5. Think broadly about the scientific phenomenon—that is, be open to seeing it in a new light, to questioning your assumptions about what it is and how to explain it. Let your students introduce you to unexpected

(continued)

Seven Strategies *(continued)*

perspectives (e.g., the idea that growth might follow a punctuated rather than constant pattern or be three- rather than two-dimensional). Be open to learning more, for example, about how current scientific understanding developed, or how current understanding connects to varied traditions of knowing, reading, writing, and talking.

6. When a student says something you don't understand, do not assume she is wrong or confused. Assume she is making sense and that *you* do not yet understand her. Follow up and ask her to elaborate, explain further, or say more about her idea. Or ask if other students can help you understand. Think of the class as building meaning together. By taking notes, you can then revisit the student's words at a later time and explore their possible meaning with the class.

7. Reflect on your students' ideas. Revisit your notes and think about your students' ideas. (If you do not want to take notes, consider audio- or videotaping your students' science talks and listening to them later.) Look for ideas that surprise, puzzle, or confuse you. Consider meeting with other teachers to discuss your students' thinking, the relationship of their ideas to the discipline, and how you can use their ideas and perspectives to shape your teaching.

of discussion called science talk. The class is considering Desiree's question, "Do plants grow every day?"

Our example explores the depth of scientific thinking in which all children can engage when the range of what counts as scientific is allowed to expand. It focuses on the participation of two students, Elena and Serena. (All student names are pseudonyms.) Elena is from a working class family; her parents have little formal schooling. Her mother is from Mexico and the family speaks both Spanish and English at home. She is repeating third grade and her teacher is concerned about her progress. She rarely speaks during academic lessons and until now has been almost silent in science. Serena's parents are both professionals with advanced academic degrees. She speaks Spanish at home and is fluent in English. Her teachers see her as a strong student. She participates actively in school.

Serena begins the discussion by claiming that plants do grow every day but "our eyes can't see it." She explains that the measurement tools (i.e., "our rulers") they have been using to make their charts and graphs of daily plant growth may not be able to detect the small increments that the plants grow each day. Then Juana, another student who rarely participates, asks,

"How come we can't see them grow? And how come we can't see us grow?" In contrast to Serena, Juana focuses on the plant. She wants to see it grow, and see herself grow. Elena then says, "I don't think we could see them grow, but I think they could *feel* theirselves grow. Sometimes we can feel ourselves grow because my feet grow so fast cuz this little crinkly thing is always bothering my feet. That means it's starting to grow. It's starting to stretch out."

Prompted by Juana, Elena is thinking about the moment-to-moment process of growth. How would growth *feel* to a plant? As she describes the crinkles in her feet, she wriggles her nose, and she makes her voice high and throaty. It is as if she is trying to re-experience for herself, and at the same time dramatize for others, the crinkly feeling of growth by re-creating it in her imagination, and physically, in her intonation and body movements. Unlike Serena who was observing the plant from the outside, Elena is thinking and talking about growth from a perspective inside her own body, aligning herself with the plant. In her imagination, she is with the plant, not on the growth chart as Serena is.

Many teachers would be impressed by Serena's discussion of graphs and charts to find and justify an answer to Desiree's question. She seeks to represent the plant's growth through objective measurement, from a perspective outside the plant. Her response would rightly be heard as scientific, perhaps even as "the answer." And, in another situation, it might end the discussion. On this day, however, right answers are not what the teacher is after. Instead, she wants to hear the students' ideas; she particularly wants to hear from students like Elena and Juana, who typically do not participate in science. So after hearing what Serena has to say, she asks other children if they think plants grow every day. Elena's response catches her off guard. If she had not prepared herself to listen carefully for connections between the science and the children's ideas, she might have dismissed Elena's response. As it turns out, the contributions of both Elena and Serena play important roles in deepening the class's thinking.

Serena's approach highlights the value of recorded measurements and data. Learning to make, read, interpret, and use charts and graphs is key to scientific thinking; all children need to know how to do this and know the purposes it serves. But there is also much left to learn about growth that this perspective leaves untouched. Elena's approach invites her classmates and the teacher to wonder about growth as it takes place in real time. By imagining herself inside the plant and trying to feel what her own growth is like, Elena positions them all to wonder about exactly what is going on as something grows. She invites them to think with her about growth as three- rather than two-dimensional, as something that fills socks and shoes as well as gets taller. She also prompts them to think about *when* growth happens and what its pattern might be. Does it happen in constant little increments or is it more punctuated, less predictable? As the words of Barbara McClintock suggest, an important aspect of science is pushing beyond data and measurement to "imagine" the world at other levels in order to pursue fundamental questions. Elena's embodied, imagined way of thinking about plant growth has much in common with McClintock's, and proves to be an important perspective for her classmates, including Serena, to engage with.

Elena's contribution has additional consequences for her classmates. Her imaginative, sensory-driven approach makes it possible for them to question and examine knowledge they might otherwise neglect. Not only does their discussion and probing become more specific and grounded as the conversation continues, but more children—children who are typically quiet in science (like Elena and Juana)—participate. From here, the children go on to consider and imagine other aspects of a plant's life from a biological perspective, for example, visualizing how the Sun might get inside leaves.

As they participate in this discussion, the children also have opportunities to articulate and present their ideas to others, to think about the kind of evidence they need to build a convincing argument, and to disagree with someone else's idea on scientific grounds. All of these are important aspects of scientific literacy.

The children's teacher benefits from science talk as well. She is able to get a new view of many of her students. She hears from many quiet students, and to her surprise, discovers that despite their silence, they are thinking and learning. She also sees students like Elena and Juana assume roles of intellectual leadership, something she has not seen before in an academic context. Related to this, she sees students like Serena, whom she thinks of as academically strong, benefit from ideas and perspectives articulated by students whose academic skills have concerned her.

The science talk also reinvigorates this teacher's interest in plant growth. The children's ideas and perspectives stimulate her to think about it in new ways and to wonder what moment-to-moment growth in a plant might indeed look like. Finally, she is left with many exciting, potential directions in which to take the children's inquiry. For example, they could pursue growth as a three-dimensional idea. If they were to do this, how could they measure it in plants? in themselves? (For a more in-depth discussion of science talk, see Ballenger 2003.)

Conclusion

All students, no matter what their background, bring important and useful ways of knowing and talking to science. In most classrooms, the thinking of students like Serena is featured because it fits with prevailing views of science. Rarely are students like Elena given similar opportunities. As the example showed, however, students like Elena have as much to share and teach their classmates as do students like Serena. Science talks create a space that allows all students to participate in the ongoing intellectual work of the class, in ways that are scientifically meaningful. When this happens, everyone learns, including teachers.

Renote Jean-François, a teacher in the Boston Public Schools, has been using science talks as a regular part of her curriculum for several years. She teaches middle school students, all of whom are learning English at the same time they are learning to read and write. She uses science talks to enrich her literacy program:

> Having regular science talks in my bilingual literacy classroom is a great learning experience for both my students and me. My students learn and practice academic, social, and emotional skills. They use their abilities to think critically, to question and analyze the new ideas and concepts they encounter in science and in life more generally. Time and again, they demonstrate academic perseverance in their efforts to explore and understand their surroundings. Science talks allow my students to develop self-confidence, cooperative and listening skills, acceptance of others' ideas, and respect for diversity. I am no longer surprised when, each year, the most quiet and shy student in my room blossoms during science talks and begins to venture challenging ideas within the first few months of school. As for me, I find this experience humbling. It gives me the opportunity to learn from my students and to admire, again and again, their ability for deep, scientific thought.

Acknowledgments

We want to thank the teachers and children with whom we have collaborated over the years. We would also like to thank our colleagues Beth Warren, Mary DiSchino, and Mary Rizzuto for their helpful comments.

References

American Association for the Advancement of Science (AAAS). 1993. *Benchmarks for science literacy*. New York: Oxford University Press.

Ballenger, C. 1999. *Teaching other people's children: Literacy and learning in a bilingual classroom*. New York: Teachers College Press.

Ballenger, C. 2003. The puzzling child: Challenging assumptions about participation and meaning in talking science. *Language Arts* 81 (4): 303–311.

Brookline Teacher Researcher Seminar (BTRS). 2004. *Regarding children's words: Teacher research on language and literacy*. New York: Teachers College Press.

Gallas, K. 1995. *Talking their way into science. Hearing children's questions and theories, responding with curricula*. New York: Teachers College Press.

Heath, S. B. 1983. *Ways with words: Language, life, and work in communities and classrooms*. Cambridge: Cambridge University Press.

Hudicourt-Barnes, J. 2003. The use of argumentation in Haitian Creole science classrooms. *Harvard Educational Review* 73 (1): 73–93.

Keller, E. F. 1983. *A feeling for the organism: The life and work of Barbara McClintock*. New York: W. H. Freeman.

Labov, W. 1972. *Language in the inner city: Studies in the black English vernacular*. Philadelphia: University of Pennsylvania Press.

Latour, B., and S. Woolgar. 1986. *Laboratory life: The social construction of scientific facts*. 2nd ed. Princeton: Princeton University Press.

Lee, C. D. 1993. *Signifying as a scaffold for literary interpretation: The pedagogical implications of an African American discourse genre*. Urbana, IL: National Council of Teachers of English.

Lemke, J. L. 1990. *Talking science: Language, learning and values*. Norwood, NJ: Ablex.

Lynch, M. 1985. *Art and artifact in laboratory science: A study of shop work and shop talk in a research laboratory*. Boston: Routledge and Kegan Paul.

Michaels, S. 1981. "Sharing time": Children's narrative styles and differential access to literacy. *Language in Society* 10: 423–442.

Miller, P., G. Cho, and J. Bracey. Forthcoming. Working-class children's experience through the prism of personal storytelling. *Human Development*.

Moll, L., and N. González. 2004. Engaging life: A fund of knowledge approach to multicultural education. In *Handbook of research on multicultural education*, 2nd ed., eds. J. Banks and C. McGee Banks, 699–715. New York: Jossey-Bass.

National Research Council (NRC). 1996. *National science education standards*. Washington, DC: National Academy Press.

National Science Resources Center (NSRC). 1991. *Plant growth and development*. Washington, DC: Smithsonian Institution, National Academy of Sciences.

Ochs, E., P. Gonzales, and S. Jacoby. 1996. "When I come down I'm in the domain state": Grammar and graphic representation in the interpretive activity of physicists. In *Interaction and grammar*, eds. E. Ochs, E. A. Schegloff, and S. A. Thompson, 328–369. Cambridge, England: Cambridge University Press.

Rogoff, B. 2003. *The cultural nature of human development.* New York: Oxford University Press.

Rosebery, A., and B. Warren, eds. 1998. *Boats, balloons and classroom video: Science teaching as inquiry.* Portsmouth, NH: Heinemann.

Rosebery, A., and B. Warren, eds. Forthcoming. *Teaching science to English language learners.* Arlington, VA: National Science Foundation.

Ward, M. 1971. *Them children: A study in language learning.* New York: Holt, Rinehart and Winston.

Warren, B., and A. Rosebery. 1995. Equity in the future tense: Redefining relationships among teachers, students, and science in linguistic minority classrooms. In *New directions for equity in mathematics education,* eds. W. Secada, E. Fennema, and L. Adajian, 298–328. New York: Cambridge University Press.

Warren, B., and A. Rosebery. Forthcoming. Everyday experience: An analytic resource for learning science. In *Teaching science to English language learners,* eds. A. Rosebery and B. Warren. Arlington, VA: National Science Foundation.

Wolpert, L., and A. Richards. 1997. *Passionate minds: The inner world of scientists.* Oxford, England: Oxford University Press.

Recommended Resources

About the Relationships Among Language, Culture, and Learning

Ballenger, C. 1999. *Teaching other people's children: Literacy and learning in a bilingual classroom.* New York: Teachers College Press.

Gallas, K. 1995. *Talking their way into science. Hearing children's questions and theories, responding with curricula.* New York: Teachers College Press.

Heath, S. B. 1983. *Ways with words: Language, life, and work in communities and classrooms.* Cambridge: Cambridge University Press.

McIntyre, E., A. Rosebery, and N. González, eds. *Classroom diversity: Connecting curriculum to students' lives.* Portsmouth, NH: Heinemann.

Rosebery, A., and B. Warren, eds. Forthcoming. *Teaching science to English language learners.* Arlington, VA: National Science Foundation.

About Scientists at Work

Collins, H., and T. Pinch. 1993. *The golem: What everyone should know about science.* New York: Cambridge University Press.

Feynman, R. 1985. *What do you care what other people think?* New York: Bantam Books.

Keller, E. F. 1983. *A feeling for the organism: The life and work of Barbara McClintock.* New York: W. H. Freeman.

Wolpert, L., and A. Richards. 1997. *Passionate minds: The inner world of scientists.* Oxford, England: Oxford University Press.

CHAPTER 12

English Language Development and the Science-Literacy Connection

Mercedes Durón-Flores
Imperial Valley California Math Science Partnership
Elena Maciel
Heber Elementary School, Heber, California

P ublic schools in the United States are educating a student population more diverse than ever before. This student population represents large immigration patterns of predominately Spanish-speaking students (U.S. Department of Education 2002). With the national trend of standards, assessment, and accountability, school districts, schools, and classroom teachers face new challenges to provide these students with an opportunity to learn. Teachers face the challenge of developing English language fluency in students in the context of content, especially science content, without diminishing or "watering down" the content. We believe that classroom teachers who are well informed about "best practices" in English language development (ELD) can provide English language learners with the opportunity to learn and the ability to make meaning from their science classroom experiences.

The purpose of this chapter is to provide classroom teachers with a summary of ELD strategies used by one region in the United States. The integration of these strategies in science instruction has led to increased levels of vocabulary development by English language learners and their increased achievement in science (Amaral, Garrison, and Klentschy 2002). Many of the strategies, designed to help English language learners acquire standards-based science content, can be integrated across the curriculum. All of the strategies have been used by classroom teachers in the Vallé Imperial Project in Science in Imperial County, California, for more than a decade.

Imperial County is both one of the largest (about 4,600 square miles) and most sparsely populated (130,000) counties in California. Located in the extreme southeast corner of the state, the county lacks any large metropolitan area and residents must travel to San Diego (120+ miles) or Los Angeles (200+ miles) to reach the nearest urban area. Geographic isolation is especially acute in the San Pasqual Unified School District, located on the Quechan Indian Reservation, as residents from this district travel over 60 miles just to get to El Centro, the county seat (population 55,000).

Many Imperial County residents live in extreme poverty, with household incomes having declined in real dollars during the 1990s. The Internal Revenue Service reported a 2002 mean per capita income of $17,822, the lowest of all California counties. The county's unemployment rates increased from 17.1% in 1991 to 26% in 2004, while statewide unemployment rates remained under 5%. Imperial County ranks highest in poverty of all 58 counties in California.

Of the approximately 36,000 K–12 students in Imperial County, 81% are Hispanic, 5% African American, 11% Caucasian, 1% Asian, and 1% Native American. More than 60% of the students in the county are identified as limited English proficient, 81% qualify for free lunch, and 10% are migrant. Almost all schools qualify for the Title I program. Additionally, the schools face an annual influx of immigrant students, predominately from Mexico.

The Vallé Imperial Project in Science (VIPS) has served Imperial County school districts and teachers for almost a decade as the primary delivery service for a countywide, systemic program in science education and teacher professional development. The project was developed through a unique partnership between the 16 school districts of Imperial County, Imperial Valley College, San Diego State University-Imperial Valley Campus, the California Institute of Technology, the California Science Subject Matter Project, and, more recently, with the Imperial Valley California Math Science Partnership. The partnership and delivery system are based on a systemic model of reform identified by the National Science Resources Center (1994). The implementation of this model, especially for English language learners, is well documented in the literature (Amaral, Garrison, and Klentschy 2002; Jorgenson and Vanosdall 2002; Saul et al. 2002; Klentschy and Molina-De La Torre 2004).

VIPS has developed a professional development strand for classroom teachers that focuses on ELD strategies for teaching science content. The strategies were developed to be integrated into science, but can be used in any curriculum that addresses the special needs of English language learners. The focus of these strategies is to build coherence and contextual and relational understanding into the delivery of science content for English language learners.

The Nature of English Language Learners/Theoretical Model

Classroom teachers can be most effective in instructing English language learners when they have a deep understanding of their students' various levels of language acquisition and the appropriate strategies associated with each level. Mora (2000) provides a 4 × 4 model of the stages of language acquisition (Figure 1), categorizing students into four different levels. Each level has a different domain of emphasis. For example, in working with Level 1 students, teachers should focus on listening strategies. With Level 2 students, teachers should focus on speaking strategies. Level 3 students are developmentally ready to be exposed to reading strategies. Writing strategies are developmentally appropriate with Level 4 students.

A student's level of language fluency does not prohibit a teacher from exposing the student to language acquisition strategies in the other domains, but rather the focus of that level should be considered in conjunction with the other domains horizontally across that level to build fluency in order to move students to the next vertical level. As students move across the levels, teachers should plan to scaffold the various ELD strategies until the students reach a new level of fluency.

Gardner (1993) describes several strategies that teachers can use with English language learners. These strategies include *size* and *time*, whereby the teacher adapts the number of items the English language learner is expected to complete and the amount of time in which they are to be completed. Another strategy makes adaptations for both the *input* information from the teacher and the *output* information from the student. Teachers can use alternative vocabulary to help students make connections and to avoid diminishing or "watering down" the content. *Rephrasing* is a key teacher strategy in this regard. When the teacher is flexible in both *input* and *out-*

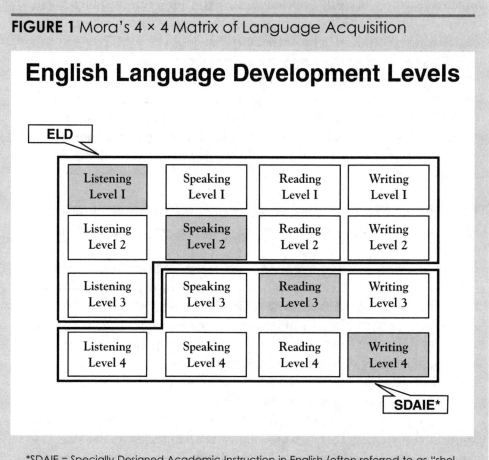

FIGURE 1 Mora's 4 × 4 Matrix of Language Acquisition

English Language Development Levels

ELD

Listening Level 1	Speaking Level 1	Reading Level 1	Writing Level 1
Listening Level 2	Speaking Level 2	Reading Level 2	Writing Level 2
Listening Level 3	Speaking Level 3	Reading Level 3	Writing Level 3
Listening Level 4	Speaking Level 4	Reading Level 4	Writing Level 4

SDAIE*

*SDAIE = Specially Designed Academic Instruction in English (often referred to as "sheltered instruction").

Source: Mora, J. K. 2000. *ED 526 course reader.* San Diego, CA: Montezuma Publishing.

put, the student has an opportunity to understand and respond. In some cases the adaptation may be in the form of primary-language support.

Many English language learners struggle with *participation* (Gardner 1993) in their classrooms. Allowing students to work with a peer or defining their specific role in a group lowers their anxiety levels and also increases the *level of support* they experience. Many Level 1 and Level 2 students are reluctant to participate orally in class discussions. Teachers can use *randomization* to provide all students with equal opportunity to participate. In this method, the teacher writes each student's name on a tongue depressor and places all of the tongue depressors in a can. The teacher then randomly selects a tongue depressor from the can and calls on the student whose name is on the tongue depressor instead of calling on students who have raised their hands.

Incorporating English Language Development Strategies Into Science Instruction

Educating English language learners can be overwhelming, but it is definitely manageable with the help of specific strategies. English language learners may be lacking specific linguistic skills, but at the same time they bring with them their own prior knowledge and experiences that can enhance classroom instruction. Strategies such as providing step-by-step instructions, posting terms/vocabulary where they are visible, rephrasing statements while checking for clarity, and actively involving students with peers or group work are just a few for classroom teachers to consider (Buck 2000).

Vocabulary Development

ELD applications integrated into science instruction provide excellent opportunities for students to make connections to science content and process skills. The primary application that provides a foundation for all areas is vocabulary building. As long as the vocabulary is coherent—that is, vocabulary that students have been exposed to and are able to make connections to—and introduced in context, students will conceptualize word meanings and therefore make concrete connections.

Teachers can help build vocabulary by discussing science materials with students prior to a lesson or unit in which the students will be using these materials. As each new word is discussed, a record is kept. This record may be in a student's individual science notebook, but we have found that a "working word wall" developed by the teacher while the vocabulary is being introduced works best.

Kit Inventory

Another strategy that VIPS has emphasized is the kit inventory. In this strategy students examine the items found in a science kit that will be used during a unit of study. They discuss the scientific name, use(s), and property description of these items. The kit inventory provides an excellent opportunity for students to build vocabulary in a coherent and contextual way. Acquiring the conceptual knowledge of what the items are, their use or function, where they came from, and how they are related to science is important for students to make meaning from their experiences.

The basic premise behind the kit inventory is to develop relational and contextual identification of vocabulary as it will be used within the unit of study. During this activity the teacher and students construct a working word wall with the name of the items, their synonyms, and illustrations and descriptions of the items.

Teachers can use different methods to inventory a science kit. One of the ways teachers in Imperial County have successfully used this strategy is to ask students to make predictions as to how an item will be used within the unit by removing one item at a time from the kit and asking the students to identify the item, discuss the item in terms of what it reminds them of, and then make a prediction as to the use of the item in the unit of study. The teacher may tap into the student's prior knowledge during the science kit inventory by asking questions such as, "Where have we seen this before?" and "What have you seen it used for?" The discussion that follows allows the teacher to assess student understanding of vocabulary that will be used in the unit of study (Figure 2).

FIGURE 2 Kit Inventory for a Unit on Rocks and Minerals

Item	Teacher	Students
goggles	What are these? What are they made of? Where have you seen them before? Why do people have them at the swimming pool? Why do you think they are in our science kit?	goggles plastic at the swimming pool to cover their eyes to cover our eyes
nail	What is this called? When do you normally see these? What do you do with a nail? Look at this nail, the ends are different. What can you tell me about it? Do you have any predictions about what we might be studying in this unit?	a nail when we are building pound it; put it in wood one end is flat, and one end is sharp. maybe building
paper clip	What is this item called? Why are paper clips in our kit? What do you think we are going to be studying?	paper clip to hold paper together building

Asking students to sort and classify the items in the science kit is another way in which the inventory can occur. Sorting and classifying provides opportunities for repetition of vocabulary and contextual understanding (Figure 3). (For a further explanation of the kit inventory activity, see Amaral, Garrison, and Durón-Flores 2006.)

Working Word Wall/Word Chart

A working word wall—also known as a word chart—is composed of vocabulary that is directly related to the items in a kit and the concepts in a unit being taught (Figure 4). An illustration is drawn next to the word for living organisms, or, if possible, the actual item is taped next to the word. As the teacher feels the need to introduce or review vocabulary, students write the words on chart paper or sentence strips and place the words in clear view of the class (Figure 5).

FIGURE 3 Sorting Activity for a Unit on Magnetism and Electricity

Conductors	Non-conductors
bolt	craft stick
wire	plastic bag
nail	plastic disk
paper clip	eraser
fastener	
screw	
penny	

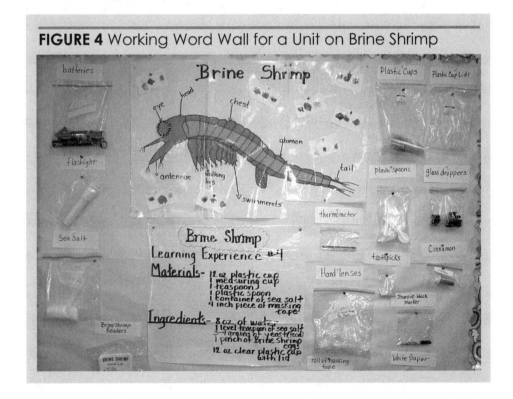

FIGURE 4 Working Word Wall for a Unit on Brine Shrimp

FIGURE 5 Word Chart for a Unit on Magnetism and Electricity

Properties						
metal	screw	nail	compass	paper clip	fastener	wire
flexible	wire	straw	fastener	paper clip	pipe cleaner	
nonmetal	straw	craft stick	pipe cleaner	plastic bag	tinker toy	

Developing working word walls in the classroom is extremely important for all students, but even more so for English language learners. A working word wall helps those students to develop an understanding of, and fluency in, key unit vocabulary. The teacher must model how to read the information from the charts as a class discussion. Students can refer to the working word wall when collaborating in a group and during class discussions. The working word wall also empowers English language learners when writing. Eventually, the word wall is converted into a resource area accessible to all students. Students need to be exposed to a variety of word charts to select from when they are required to document or interpret their data. As the school year progresses, classrooms should display a great library of different charts.

Sorting and Classifying
Once the students feel comfortable with the definition/description/property of the items introduced during the kit inventory, a sorting and classifying activity may take place. Students sort the same items that were introduced for the working word wall during the kit inventory. Students apply their prior knowledge of the properties of the items and discuss these properties in their groups and in a class discussion, explaining why the items have been sorted in a certain way. The teacher's goal is to reinforce the properties of these items. There is no right or wrong category as long as the students can explain their reasoning and provide a justification for placing items in a certain category. A grouping strategy may look like this

Group A	Human-made items
Group B	Natural items
Or	
Group A	Plastic
Group B	Metal

At this point, the words on the working word wall can be categorized into groups. Students can take the words from the working word wall and group them as follows:

Scientific Vocabulary—mainly process skills. These are words that are important to develop, and will include *hypothesis, prediction,* what *data* look like, what it means to give *evidence,* and what a *reflection* is.

Content Vocabulary—dealing with the unit at hand. These are words that directly connect to the science unit being studied—for example, *rocks, minerals, sedimentary, igneous,* and *metamorphic*.

Additional Vocabulary—words that connect (e.g., *and, into, through*) when discussing the groups, or descriptive words. Words that connect tend to be especially difficult for English language learners to use in a sentence.

Teachers follow up by asking students to give their reasons for grouping the words as they did. This strategy provides another contextual and relational experience for English language learners to acquire language and build fluency through repetition.

By this point, students usually feel very confident about writing down the names of the items in a kit or identifying them orally. The activities described above are all conducted before the first lesson in the unit of study. This foundation building for English language learners gives them the confidence they will need for the entire science unit.

Venn Diagrams

Once English language learners have been exposed to sorting and classifying activities, they can develop Venn diagrams using the actual kit items or the names of the items printed on index cards (Figure 6).

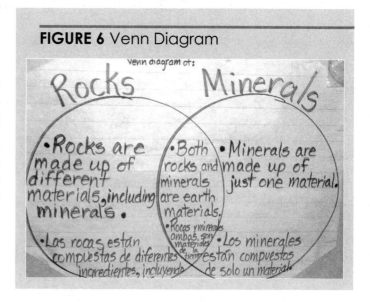

FIGURE 6 Venn Diagram

Hula hoops or large rings of yarn can be used to form the interlocking rings of the Venn diagram.

English language learners now have enough exposure to the kit items and sufficient language fluency to think of antonyms and synonyms for each term (Figure 7).

FIGURE 7 Synonyms and Antonyms

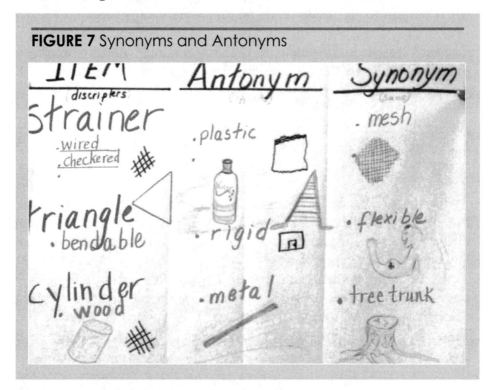

Sentence Stems
Sentence stems are an important tool for teachers to use to introduce students to writing about their science experiences and to make meaning about what they have learned. Examples of sentence stems used by the Vallé Imperial Project in Science include the following:
- Today I (or we) _____ .
- Today I learned _____ .
- I noticed _____ .
- I wondered _____ .
- Questions I have now are _____ .

Besides providing an excellent starting point for students, sentence stems offer a correct grammatical model and correct sentence structure.

Students can select vocabulary from the working word wall to help complete the sentence stems. (Student writing should be taking place in science notebooks as a way for students to make meaning from their science experiences and as a means to develop a permanent record of their progress. For an in-depth review of the essential elements for science notebooks, see Klentschy 2005.) Teachers can use a sentence stem in the following way: "Today, after this investigation, I would like you to write a reflection on the results of your investigation. Use the sentence stem 'Today I learned _____' to start your writing. Take four words from the working word wall or word chart and include them in your writing."

Labeling Diagrams and Illustrations

Labeling diagrams and illustrations also increases language acquisition and fluency. Student science notebook entries should contain drawings and illustrations. Teachers must encourage students to label every illustration using the scientific vocabulary introduced in earlier lessons. This reinforces the use of language in context and builds relational values. Students should be encouraged to use vocabulary for their labels from the working word wall or word charts in the classroom.

Cloze Strategies

Cloze paragraphs (Figure 8) are a strategy in which key vocabulary words are deleted from a passage. The passage is then presented to students, who insert the correct vocabulary as they read to complete the passage. For assessment purposes, teachers can develop cloze sentences or paragraphs with vocabulary from the working word wall or word charts.

FIGURE 8 Cloze Paragraph for a Unit on Rocks and Minerals

penny   gypsum   quartz   tools   mineral   nail

We found that some minerals could be scratched and some could

not. The _____ was the hardest mineral because the _____ and the

_____ could not scratch it. _____ was the softest _____ because

all of our _____ could scratch it.

Technology

Teachers can use technology to have students revisit their vocabulary, build fluency, and use language in context. Teachers in the Vallé Imperial Project in Science have taken vocabulary introduced during the science kit inventory and have created PowerPoint presentations that students use independently and in small groups. On each PowerPoint slide there is a photograph, a vocabulary word, and a description of each vocabulary word. The students sit at the computer for a few minutes a week and simply scroll though the vocabulary words to reinforce either the pronunciation or the meaning of the words.

Closing Thoughts

English language learners can achieve success across the curriculum with the integration of language acquisition strategies that accommodate their needs. The primary goal for teachers working with English language learners is to be aware of the student's language acquisition level, which will determine the specific strategies that should be implemented.

From our practice in Imperial County, California, we know that there are particular functional language forms that are common to reading, writing, and speaking that can be taught successfully through science. The language of science and English are complementary and the integration of ELD in science is a natural way for English language learners to fully participate in a high-quality program of instruction in science.

References

Amaral, O., L. Garrison, and M. Durón-Flores. 2006. Taking inventory. *Science and Children* 43 (4): 30–33.

Amaral, O., L. Garrison, and M. Klentschy. 2002. Helping English language learners increase achievement through inquiry-based science instruction. *Bilingual Research Journal* 26 (2): 213–239.

Buck, G. 2000. Teaching science to English-as-Second-Language-Learners. *Science and Children* 38 (3): 38–41.

Gardner, H. 1993. *Multiple intelligences: The theory in practice.* New York: Basic Books.

Jorgenson, O., and R. Vanosdall. 2002. The death of science? What are we risking in our rush toward standardized testing and the three r's? *Phi Delta Kappan* 83 (8): 601–605.

Klentschy, M. 2005. Science notebook essentials: A guide to effective notebook components. *Science and Children* 43 (3): 24–27.

Klentschy, M., and E. Molina-De La Torre. 2004. Students' science notebooks and the inquiry process. In *Crossing borders in literacy and science instruction: Perspectives on theory and practice*, ed. E. W. Saul, 340–354. Newark, DE: International Reading Association.

Mora, J. K 2000. *ED 516 course reader*. San Diego, CA: Montezuma Publishing. (Available at *http://coe.sdsu.edu/people/jmora/Pages/4X4Guidelines.htm*.)

National Science Resources Center. 1994. *Science for all children: A guide to improving elementary science education in your school district*. Washington, DC: National Science Resources Center, Smithsonian Institution.

Saul, W., J. Reardon, C. Pearce, D. Dieckman, and D. Neutze. 2002. *Science workshop: Reading, writing and thinking like a scientist*. 2nd ed. Portsmouth, NH: Heinemann.

U.S. Department of Education. 2002. *Educational statistics for United States student population: 2000*. Washington, DC: U.S. Department of Education.

Implementation and Policy Issues

Taking Literacy Integration out of the Closet

Fran Blaess taught second grade for eight years at Aquidneck Elementary School (preK–4) in Middletown, Rhode Island, and then served as the school's acting principal. The Middletown student population is 86% Caucasian, 8% African American, 3% Hispanic, and 3% Asian and Native American. Since this story was written, she has become principal of the Wilbur and McMahon Schools (K–8) in Little Compton, Rhode Island.

Fran is speaking:

When the emphasis in our district turned to reading, writing, and math skills at the sacrifice of our science program, to be honest, many teachers were relieved that they didn't "have to be bothered" with the science kits. I knew something had to happen. I knew that integrating science with literacy could enhance the teaching of inquiry-based science and develop essential reading and writing skills.

The story of how we became focused on literacy and science integration really begins with our science program. Science was going strong in our district. Being part of the East Bay Educational Collaborative (EBEC, a K–8 science education reform initiative in Rhode Island; see Chapter 5), we were in our fourth year of implementing a kit-based inquiry science program. The principal recognized my ability to facilitate and mentor my fellow teachers and encouraged me to become a kit trainer for EBEC. Being a trainer gave me additional opportunities to gain content knowledge and to improve and reflect on instructional practices.

When I also became lead teacher for the school in 2003, I realized that in that capacity I could really impact the teaching of science in my school.

As lead teacher I was able to serve on the Literacy Curriculum Committee at our school. Now I was able to advocate for the use of science notebooks when the committee discussed the need for introducing procedural writing into the elementary classrooms.

How did my school progress to effective notebook implementation across the grades? There were three important developments in our training and practice that happened almost simultaneously: (1) attendance at the Science and Literacy Integration Project (SLIP) conference at Rhode Island College, (2) use of the lesson study process, and (3) a new emphasis on the National Council of Teachers of English (NCTE)/International Reading Association (IRA) Standards for the English Language Arts.

Science and Literacy Integration Project

Two teams from our school attended the SLIP conference for two summers (in 2003 and 2004). The week-long training I had received as a kit specialist (including attending programs at the Elementary Science Integration Project at the University of Maryland at Baltimore County) and my eagerness to try new techniques led me to present a few workshops at SLIP, including one on the use of science notebooks in the primary grades. Reflecting on the experience at SLIP, one teacher wrote:

> The way I teach science has changed completely after going to the SLIP conference this summer. I think the biggest piece for me was listening to the presenters from El Centro, California. I loved how the literacy piece tied so closely to the inquiry model. We are asking kids to document their thinking instead of just filling in graphic organizers. The most powerful part for me was the El Centro model [see Chapters 5, 14, and 16] that included the Making Meaning conference, in which kids talk to each other and share their notebook entries while the teacher facilitates. When the kids gather for the meeting, they learn from each other. Now, instead of telling them to label their diagrams, I show them how a particular student labeled hers. Not only do I validate the student's work on display, but I show the kids a model. Most important, I give them time to revise their own entry.

Our supportive administration was a big factor in our school reform. By contract we have five hours of professional development each month. We also have a source of funds that, under state guidelines, must be used for literacy professional development. This allowed teachers who went to SLIP to share their discoveries at staff meetings and half-day professional development sessions led by the school literacy coach and me. Anyone who wanted to receive more training could attend additional in-school sessions and the administration arranged for substitutes to cover their classrooms!

The PTG (Parent Teacher Group) was also supportive. They agreed to purchase half-page composition notebooks for the third and fourth grade and provide the supplies for the kindergarten through second grades to create their own notebooks. Little by little we moved from the bound, duplicated, pre-made notebooks to science notebooks in which the students at all grade levels record their questions, observations, procedures, materials, and conclusions. Looking at the writing that even struggling student writers produced in their science notebooks became "bait" to entice reluctant teachers (see Figure 1 and Figure 2). When the teachers witnessed their most reluctant writers becoming productive writers in their science notebooks—that was invaluable.

FIGURE 1 Writing Sample From a Fourth-Grade Student

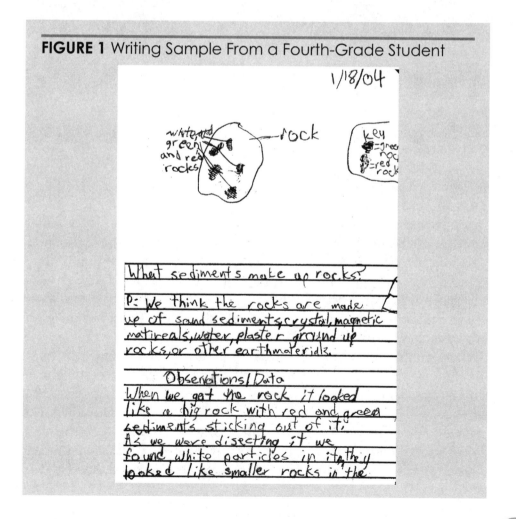

FIGURE 2 Writing Sample From a Kindergartner

Lesson Study

We involved the teachers who were not participants in the SLIP conference by combining SLIP information with lesson study, a new lesson assessment practice we were implementing. Lesson study is a form of long-term professional development in which teams of teachers collaboratively conduct research closely tied to lessons and then use what they learn about student thinking to become more effective instructors. (For more on lesson study, see Resources, Lewis 2002.)

For example, the first SLIP team had a representative from every grade level except for third grade. So third grade was the one in which the team chose to model using science notebooks and lesson study. The teams that attended SLIP designed a lesson that built on the use of science notebooks. The lesson was from a third-grade unit on water that focused on the number of water droplets that will fit on a penny. The lesson was taught by one of the teachers while her colleagues observed and collected data (student talk and notebook entries) in order to document how well the lesson's goals were achieved. That same lesson was then revised and refined by the group and retaught in another classroom. One version of the lesson plan with teacher notes reflects the fluid process and is pictured in Figure 3.

The lesson study process really only required us to do the lesson in two of the three third-grade classrooms, but we took it a step further and refined the lesson through the teaching of the same lesson in all third-grade classrooms. Our consistent focus on gradually involving all teachers was an important factor in transforming practice not only in third grade but throughout the school. As one of our fourth-grade teachers commented:

> *Science instruction has changed significantly over the past five years. The kits we use, although hands-on, do not always lend themselves to the best inquiry-based instruction. The lessons and materials are very scripted and teacher directed. I have learned to use real-life scenarios that my students can relate to and help them write focus questions from which they can guide their own inquiry. Three things were critical in changing my practice: (1) professional development through the SLIP Institute and the presenters from El Centro, California, (2) collaboration with colleagues, and (3) implementation and constant reflection, both self and collaborative. Rigorous guided practice and teamwork on a focused lesson study were instrumental in bringing these practices back to our school.*

Standards for the English Language Arts

Simultaneous with our district's switch from traditional science textbooks to inquiry science in 2001, we underwent a similar transformation in literacy instruction. In Rhode Island all schools are required by law to have a School Improvement Plan whose implementation is monitored annually by the School Improvement Team. The team was composed of a chairperson (me), the principal, and interested teachers and parents. When the School Improvement Team examined the state assessment scores in 2002, it became readily apparent that our students needed more direct instruction in the reading of informational text as well as procedural and report writing.

As we adopted the NCTE/IRA Standards for the English Language Arts, we weaned ourselves off of the basal reader. To encourage the use of trade books, our standards coach offered professional development at the district level and EBEC offered it at the regional level. We implemented a balanced literacy approach in which students at all grade levels read and wrote every day. We used the reader's and writer's work-

FIGURE 3 Lesson Plan for a Surface Tension Activity (With Teacher Notes)

Research Lesson Study
Activity 2 Surface Tension

Introduction: Real life activity to engage students and review the properties of water they are aware of from activity 1.

Explain today's starting activity by asking students to estimate

How many full drops of water do you think can fit on a penny?

Record guesses on chart paper
Guesses ┊ Counts
8
12
15

Partners will also predict using their notebooks. It is important to share information with your partner.

Prepare for the activity: Today's activity will have three parts.
In **part one** we will be observing the
Shape the water makes on the penny.

Materials: 2 pennies
2 droppers
2 paper towels
1 sponge
2 cups of water

Directions :
Use full drops of water. Drop water from about 1cm above the Penny. Be careful not to touch the penny with the dropper.
Reminder: Talk to your partner and write down in your notebook your observations.

(continued)

FIGURE 3 (*continued*)

A bell will signal when to stop and come back together for a scientist meeting. (ring bell) We will share findings and start the next part of the lesson.

bring notebook to meeting and a pencil

Scientist meeting: Discuss how close their guesses came to the final results. Record sample results on chart paper. *share findings*
students may want to add to their notebook

Question- ***What shape was the surface of the water on the penny before it spilled?***
Ask someone to draw a side view of the penny and water.

Introduce the property of **surface tension:**
   Surface tension causes water to stick together and try to form a ball.
 Introduce soapy water. Explain that some materials can change surface tension when added to water.

Question-*Find out if soap can change water's surface tension?*

Describe the soap activity: Partners will now work as a team.
  Start with a dry penny put 15 drops of plain water on a penny
  Next, place one drop of soapy water on the water dome and observe what happens. They may want to add 2 or 3 more drops of soapy water. Record your findings in your notebook.
Important: **Students should use only one dropper in the soapy** *have student demonstrate*
water. Droppers should remain in the cup. — *this*
   Pass out cups of soapy water(one partner gathers material)

Sound bell for scientist meeting
    Record on the chart a side view of the penny and the soapy water.

plain

soapy

(*continued*)

FIGURE 3 *(continued)*

Introduce salt water
Question-*Will salt change the water's surface tension?*

Students follow the same procedure to test what happens to the
surface tension with salt water. *15 drops of plain water*
Remind them to keep the droppers in their original cups. *then add*
salt water
drops
Record in notebooks your **findings** and **questions**

Salt did not change the surface tension. *– scientist meeting*
to share conclusions

CLEAN UP
  Pennies collected and cleaned in vinegar to remove any film.
  Materials returned to collection station.
  Cups and droppers rinsed.

molecule – to the word bank

rivet activity –
   m o l e c u l e

sample entry { *high*
               medium
               low }

then definition – on chart

include word in word bank
       then copy definition from chart

shop models from the National Council of Teachers of English to hold
students accountable for reading and writing at their level. By incorporating the various disciplines into these models of instruction, time
management problems were reduced.

Through reader's workshop, students learn to question as they read,
summarize important points, make inferences, and synthesize from the text.
Science lessons are enhanced as the teachers add to the students' background knowledge through literature.

A first-grade class working on a weather unit begins a reader's workshop:

Teacher:	I called you together because I thought it would be a good idea to read some nonfiction. You haven't read much of that lately. We have been talking a lot about the weather. Let's start by opening this book about weather to the very last page. Look it over. It's a storm timeline. Do you remember we made a timeline that described our year? And we put on it what happens during the year—for October we placed a pumpkin, for December a snowman. In this book, there is a storm timeline for Tuesday and Wednesday from morning to afternoon to evening. What do you think the pictures mean by the timeline?
Students:	They tell about when the storm comes. Yeah, it tells what the weather is like at those times of day.
Teacher:	Now we know it took two whole days for this storm. So we have a storm timeline. This book is about stormy weather and how it changed over two days. Now, take a picture walk through the book. This is not reading—just look at the pictures and notice some details. What's going on during the story? What's something you saw? What information did you pick up?
Students:	Trees falling down—strong winds—I saw a baby crying.
Teacher:	Why do you think it's crying?
Student:	Maybe it's scared of the weather. Thunder maybe scared the baby.
Student:	There is lots of rain and umbrellas.
Teacher:	What can happen when there is lots of rain?
Student:	Floods!
Teacher:	Why might it flood?
Students:	Drains get full. There is too much water.
Teacher:	I think we are ready to read. Today the strategy I want to practice is….
Student:	Skip and return?
Teacher:	That's a good one! Today I also want you to look for chunks and look for all the weather words you know.

In reader's workshop, students learn a variety of literacy strategies. They learn the art of questioning as they read to improve comprehension and reading level. I encourage them to record their questions on sticky notes, which are often shared and classified as a whole-class "wrap-up" activity at the end of a workshop. The students also learn to distinguish which answers they can find in books and which they are able to investigate themselves (researchable questions versus investigative questions). Students also learn to support their claims in science with evidence from their firsthand experience and from text. Vocabulary is expanded using games like the Four Blocks Literacy Model to introduce science vocabulary:

- Students are introduced to new terms that will appear in the text by practicing reading and spelling the terms using the "hangman" process.
- Students use the meaning of the words to predict information that will appear or events that will occur in the text.
- Students build on these skills by having conversations, which helps them learn how to listen to their peers.

Back to Teachers

As teachers became more comfortable with using trade books rather than the basal and discovered how important nonfiction can be in increasing test scores, the natural next step was to explore even more text genres. Since money and time are important concerns in education, learning to be creative and more efficient becomes even more important. With our principal saying, "Money previously used to purchase disposable reading workbooks will be allocated for trade books," we were set.

We established two "literacy closets" one for kindergarten–second grade and one for third–fourth grade, housing groups of leveled trade books for teachers to use in guided reading groups. The literacy closets were first stocked with narratives, and then in subsequent book orders we purchased books that supported the science kits, health books, and social studies texts. Most important, books were purchased that met all readers' abilities.

To support our move to trade books, the literacy coach shared research-based strategies for increasing reading comprehension. A staff resource library was established for the teachers. Even with this support, however, I can't say that all of the teachers have yet moved to integrating reading as well as writing. Some are slowly moving in that direction as they learn new methods to combine the teaching of science and literacy. I would say about 80% of the teachers at my school are using an integrated model of instruction because they have seen the results and have found it relatively simpler to teach that way. They view themselves as researchers and have a deep level of understanding that is reflected in their classroom practices and teacher-to-teacher conversations.

Our School Improvement Plan suggested a teacher book club. It took us a while to get the club going, but it is voluntary and books are purchased for those who attend. The goal is to "dig deeper" into student comprehension. We currently have a small group of teachers in the book club reading *7 Keys to Comprehension!* (see Resources, Hutchins and Zimmerman 2003) led by our literacy coach. Her involvement has been vital because her role for the past three years has been to model lessons for classroom teachers.

Second-grade students reflect on their learning:

I like being a scientist because I like learning a lot of things. Simple machines can help people go places and move things.

I'm a scientist because I ask a lot of questions. I decide on a focus question, watch what happens, and then make predictions.

I like when I do science because I can do and record experiments.

By looking at student work (performance-based assessments, notebook entries, literature responses) and listening to the students' discussions, the teachers had a new window into what the students were learning. The process of lesson study also helped in this regard as did Learning Walks, which follow the University of Pittsburgh's Institute for Learning protocol. With Learning Walks, a team of "walkers" (teachers and administrators) spend approximately 5–10 minutes in each classroom. They are given an area to collect data on, such as whether students display "accountable-talk" (in accountable-talk, students build on the comments of their peers in a respectful and inclusive manner; students use facts to support an argument; and students use appropriate methods of reasoning). Although the procedure is nonevaluative, walkers are required to take part in a debriefing session in which they first discuss what they observed in each classroom and then raise "I wonder" questions. The principal writes a feedback letter to the whole staff, in which he or she reflects the team's findings on the classrooms they visited. This has been a very effective tool for us.

Change Process

The entire change process at our school was one that evolved. The initial following of the kits' lessons in a step-by-step fashion was probably necessary for the teachers to develop familiarity with the content while becoming more confident about the teaching of science in general. By gradually integrating literacy and science, integration became a sustained effort rather than another swing of the instructional pendulum.

Now the teachers engage in scientific dialogue with their colleagues on a more regular basis. Just as we encourage our students to learn from one another, the teachers have learned that they too can benefit from this process. I often will find an e-mail from one of the teachers in my in-box asking for ideas to enhance the teaching of science and the use of science notebooks.

I don't think I can call myself *the* change agent. Even though I was the lead teacher at my school, I certainly can't take all of the credit for the advances our school made. We have 20 dynamic classroom teachers and another 25 dedicated specialists, resource persons, and support personnel.

I hope that in my new role as an elementary school principal my teachers will consider me as a "lead learner" and that together we'll explore ways to integrate literacy and inquiry-based science. Because of the tremendous results I have seen as a classroom teacher, this will certainly be a focus for professional development wherever I serve as principal. I plan to spend a great deal of time in classrooms, where I can continue to share two areas I'm really excited about—books and science.

Resources

Institute for Learning at the University of Pittsburgh (*www.instituteforlearning.org*)

Lewis, C. 2002. *Lesson study: A handbook for teacher led improvement of instruction.* Philadelphia: Research for Better Schools.

Miller, D. 2002. *Reading with meaning: Teaching comprehension in the primary grades.* New York: Stenhouse.

Saul, W. 2002. *Science workshop: Reading, writing, and thinking like a scientist.* Portsmouth, NH: Heinemann.

Science and Literacy Integration Project (*www.ric.edu/slip*)

Stigler, J. W., and J. Hiebert. 1999. *The teaching gap: Best ideas from the world's teachers for improving education in the classroom.* New York: The Free Press.

Vallé Imperial Project in Science, El Centro, CA (*www.vipscience.com*)

Zimmerman, S., and C. Hutchins. 2003. *7 keys to comprehension: How to help your kids read it and get it!* New York: Three Rivers Press.

Questions for Discussion

1. What strategies did Ms. Blaess use to create a shared vision for science and literacy in her school?

2. Effective leadership is essential to support a new vision for instruction. What evidence in this case story suggests that Ms. Blaess is an effective leader? What are some additional support strategies (for principals and other administrators) that might further promote connecting literacy and science?

Planting Seeds One at a Time

Though she had prior experience as a principal, Karen Harris is new to this role at Pot Spring Elementary School in Timonium, Maryland. Her five years as the principal at Baltimore's Perry Hall Elementary were formative for her approach to professional development. Karen's experience as an educator also includes work as an assistant principal and 12 years in kindergarten/first-grade classrooms as a teacher.

The Pot Spring Elementary student population is 59% Caucasian, 18% African American, and 23% other races. English for Speakers of Other Languages (ESOL) services are provided to 10.3% of the students, and 16.8% of the students qualify for free or reduced meals.

Karen is speaking:

Perry Hall was a challenging place to begin as a principal. It had a veteran staff that seemed resistant to change and staff development. However, by the end of my time there, we were all proud of what we had accomplished with our science program. After five years (1999–2004) at Perry Hall I was transferred. So here I am at Pot Spring Elementary, and once again, I am starting small to plant the idea of connecting literacy to learning about the environment.

Changing a School Culture

It's been six years since I began my idea-planting effort as a new principal at Perry Hall Elementary. The predominately middle-class suburban school had 570 students in grades preK–5. Our Maryland School Performance Assessment Program (MSPAP) scores had been relatively flat for the three preceding years. Our boys underperformed the girls on all subtests of MSPAP. Teachers used very traditional instructional methods, working mostly through textbooks with teacher-directed lessons that followed the Baltimore County Public School (BCPS) Essential Curriculum. There was very little engaging, authentic instruction.

I am not sure what staff development was done at Perry Hall prior to my administration. I do know that it was limited and didn't have any particular focus. Teachers relied on whatever was sent from central office (e.g., reading instruction updates, MSPAP information, math instruction updates, a writer's workshop). There was no strategic long-range plan in place.

I had to begin by changing the culture. I knew we needed a schoolwide focus to change the instructional program and to improve student achievement. Over the next several years the staff and I implemented three different but connected initiatives to improve staff development (the teaching), improve the quality of work we ask the students to do (the learning), and improve student achievement (the results).

I began by exploring what would become our first initiative—the Chesapeake Bay Schools project. This project helps schools develop an innovative environmental education program that uses the environment as an integrating context for learning to help improve academic achievement, school behaviors, and environmental stewardship. I considered this project for several reasons: it seemed like it would actively engage the teachers and the students; it offered incredible staff development for all teachers regardless of what grade or subject they taught; it could be integrated into the BCPS curriculum at all grade levels; a variety of other schools involved in the project around the state were creating a network for the teachers; there wasn't a cost to the school; and I liked the idea of focusing on science and thought that most students would as well.

Now, as to how I planted seeds. I took my most negative teacher to an informational meeting about the upcoming Chesapeake Bay Schools project. I knew that if I could win her over, I could get the rest of the staff on board!

The meeting outlined the program goals: to increase student awareness of the environment in order to create environmental stewards, to increase student achievement, and to improve teacher effectiveness. It was an inspirational meeting, and the teacher and I found ourselves more than willing to compete to become one of nine Bay Schools in Maryland.

Hallelujah! The teacher returned to the school enthusiastic and ready to sell the rest of the staff on the idea of applying to become a Bay School. A rigorous application process would follow (eventually, 100 schools applied from across the state and 9 were chosen), but the staff decided to go for it, and we were selected. The Bay Schools project provided our school with ongoing professional development for three years (2000–2003). The professional development was conducted during the summer on designated professional development days, through staff release days where I provided substitutes, during our regular staff meetings, and during teacher planning times. The entire staff began working together in teams as they learned how to use the environment to create engaging lessons for students. Each grade-level team worked collaboratively to develop integrated lessons that engaged the students in solving real-life problems related to our local environment and in support of their grade-level curriculum.

In addition, a staff member from the Chesapeake Bay Foundation education department came to our school one day a week to help teachers as they learned how to incorporate the environment into their daily lessons. The first summer, 17 staff members and I went to Smith Island for a week of training. An additional 14 staff members went to St. John's College for a week of writing curriculum with the other Bay Schools staffs. Each summer thereafter we trained new staff to get them on board and provided additional training for returning staff. We also built all of our school-year staff development around what we were doing with the Bay Schools project. I provided each grade-level team with a half-day release time each quarter to work on developing their Bay Schools curriculum. We also involved parents at the onset of the project through informational meetings and having them attend staff development.

Our Bay School action team was made up of at least one teacher from each grade level, one special-area teacher, one support staff teacher, the Bay Schools support teacher, and one administrator. We also involved community groups as we developed projects.

Positive Effects of the Bay Schools Project

One example of how the Bay Schools project changed our teaching and learning was a second-grade study of animals and their habitats. The unifying question of the unit was, "Is our schoolyard critter friendly?" Students discovered that our schoolyard was not attracting many native Maryland birds. So the students decided to create a bluebird trail to attract bluebirds. During science they studied bluebird habitats and in social studies they studied neighborhoods and communities. As part of language arts, students wrote letters to local newspapers about their projects. Students monitored the bird boxes, collected data, and wrote about their findings. The teachers were impressed with the quality of the students' work. The students were motivated and saw meaning to their learning—characteristics of high-quality work.

Students hang bird box to attract bluebirds to schoolyard.

When we were in our third year of threading science throughout our program, we were invited to participate in the science and literacy conference, Crossing Borders II: Connecting Science and Literacy in the Classroom, hosted by the Elementary Science Integration Project (ESIP) at the University of Maryland at Baltimore County (UMBC). Seven staff members and I went to that training (one from each grade). We attended workshops organized by reading, writing, inquiry, and curricular integration connections. Then we met in our school team to share observations, discuss implications for science and literacy teaching and learning at our school, and plan based on our own goals and vision. The team was responsible for training their grade-level partners when they returned from summer break.

That school year each grade-level team was given release time one-half day per month to work together to select books that would support their environmental projects. We also created a schoolwide database of the books that were selected. We held two staff development sessions to share the strategies that the team had learned at the workshop. The first one was held on our first day back to school, and the second one, at which teachers shared how they were integrating science and literacy, was held a couple of months later. Whenever possible the teachers used literature to enhance their science lessons. Teachers taught reading skills through content-related reading materials. They also used content books as motivation for lessons and as resources for the students when they researched their projects.

Throughout the 2003–2004 school year, ESIP corresponded with us and offered support that included giving us access to a database of trade books; helping us to make connections with other teachers involved in ESIP; and providing resources to use in developing lessons, follow-up workshops, and support for ongoing projects.

Using the Lesson Study Process

At about the same time, we looked at ways to help our teaching teams develop their capacity to plan, observe, analyze, and revise lessons based on student work using the lesson study process. Lesson study is a professional development process that focuses on improving teaching. It makes instructors responsible for the implementation of effective strategies for teaching and learning in classroom practice. Lesson study involves goal setting, designing "study lessons" as a collaborative team, and writing a very detailed lesson plan. The lesson is tried in the classroom and the design team observes the lesson. The lesson study group comes together to discuss the lesson and reflect on what they have learned from the observations. Often, the instructors choose to revise the lesson and repeat the process.

The staff read *The Teaching Gap: Best Ideas From the World's Teachers for Improving Education in the Classroom* (Stigler and Hiebert 1999), and we subsequently developed a structure that would support lesson study in our school. We started small. One grade level—fourth—tried the process. Our first round of lesson study observations that year involved having the teachers integrate the use of literacy into their science lessons. They selected a concept in math, reading, or science that had been difficult to teach, worked long hours to plan the lesson, and then took the plunge. The first teacher taught the lesson while lesson study team members observed. The entire team processed what had been observed and analyzed student work. Teachers revised the lesson based on student behaviors and level of work produced by the students. This process was repeated until all the teachers on the team had taught the same lesson. By the end of the process the teachers had developed a high-quality lesson that they all "owned" and they were discussing the qualities of effective teaching and learning!

At the end of the year, the fourth-grade team presented their experience with lesson study to the staff. The next year, all but one team decided to implement lesson study. Lesson study had taken our professional development to a higher level. One teacher commented, "My grade-level partners and I discuss our lesson during lunchtime, before school, on a break, or at playground duty. Each of us has a vested interest in the success of the lesson. What a way to experience personal professional growth!"

As lesson study fever spread, the teachers were encouraged to develop lessons that connected science and literacy with their Bay School projects. In this way we were helping the staff see the connectedness of their professional development.

We added one more facet to our professional development the year after lesson study took off. Over the summer I had the staff read *Working on the Work: An Action Plan for Teachers, Principals, and Superintendents (W.O.W.)* by Philip Schlechty (2002). So many of the design qualities outlined in the book were already being addressed through the Bay School project—authenticity, content and substance, choice, product focus, affirmation, organization of knowledge, affiliation, clear product standards, novelty and variety, and protection from initial failure. As a staff we decided that students didn't have enough "choice" in their instruction so that was the quality we would focus on for the first half of the year. We made a commitment as a staff to include choice at least once a week in instruction. Some teachers allowed students to choose their formative assessments; others provided choice in project topics. Teachers worked on weaving choice into their lesson study conversations as well as in planning their Bay School projects. The W.O.W framework fit easily into what we were already doing.

Over these years at Perry Hall I witnessed the school's climate and culture change, and along with these changes came improvements in academic performance, behavior, and student achievement. Students collaborated with their classmates, applied teacher feedback to their writing, and investigated real-life problems. Students were learning with a purpose and they knew what that purpose was.

Our boys made improvements by having opportunities to learn through hands-on, engaging work. We have seen steady improvement in the Comprehensive Test of Basic Skills (CTBS) scores. The number of second-grade students reading on or above grade level went up 9% and that of fourth graders went up 4.6%. In addition, our MSPAP scores improved so consistently that we received a cash award of $46,000 from the state.

Our commitment to a consistent focus year to year contributed greatly to our success. Following our work on connecting science and literacy using the Bay Schools Project we focused on examining the quality of student work and only added strategies that supported that focus.

Beginning Over

Six years later, sitting at my desk at Pot Spring, I reflect on the seeds I have begun to plant here, how they are growing, and the steps I will take to move my new school forward.

My first small step was to send a group of four teachers to an outdoor, environmental workshop last fall. The team has been encouraged to work with our science/math resource teacher to implement the ideas that they learned at the workshop. In addition, each staff member is involved in a professional book club at our school. One of the books, *Greening School Grounds: Creating Habitats for Learning* (Grant and Littlejohn 2001), is about using science to enhance instruction in all subjects. I am working with my science/math resource teacher to design further professional development. Next year we also plan to focus on connecting math, science, and literacy instruction by using a schedule with large blocks of instructional time at each grade level.

The staff has also been given the opportunity to participate in the lesson study process as a way for them to begin to analyze the teaching and learning process with their colleagues. The majority of the teaching teams opted to participate in this alternative form of observation and their reflections have been very positive. We will continue to expand the lesson study process next year.

During my tenure at Perry Hall Elementary School I learned many things about leadership, the change process, and how to create a positive school culture and to motivate people. It is crucial to involve all stakeholders in the decision-making process. Everyone needs support along the way. Not only do teachers need time to work together and learn from each other, but they also need time to work with and learn from "experts."

Any new initiative has to connect and enhance what we are already doing and move us toward our ultimate goal of increasing student achievement while improving instruction. Just as students need to see connections in their learning, so do adult learners.

By learning to have fun and celebrate any success, no matter how small, teachers become comfortable sharing their ideas with each other. This goes for students as well! A third grader, while writing in one of the student-created outdoor learning environments, turned to his teacher and said,

This is like recess with learning!

Another small seed planted. Yikes, Here I go again!

Resources

Chesapeake Bay Schools Project (*www.mdsg.umd.edu/Extension/msgsnn/msgsnn03_1/cbf.html*)

Elementary Science Integration Project, University of Maryland at Baltimore County (*www.esiponline.org*)

Grant, T., and G. Littlejohn. 2001. *Greening school grounds: Creating habitats for learning*, Toronto: Green Teacher.

Schlechty, P. C. 2002. *Working on the work: An action plan for teachers, principals, and superintendents*. San Francisco: Jossey-Bass.

Stigler, J. W., and J. Hiebert. 1999. *The teaching gap: Best ideas from the world's teachers for improving education in the classroom*. New York: The Free Press.

Questions for Discussion

1. A professional development program for principals is essential to support effective supervision and instructional leadership. What evidence in this case story suggests that Ms. Harris is engaged in planned professional development for instructional leadership in science? What are some learning experiences you might add to her plan?

2. Critical elements for effective and sustained teacher professional development are outlined in Chapter 16. Reflect on these critical elements as documented in both Ms. Blaess's story (Case Story H) and Ms. Harris's story. What are some things your school is doing well in supporting science and literacy connections through professional development? What are some areas for improvement? What is your evidence?

3. Lesson study is discussed in Chapter 14 and is an important element of both case stories in this section. What do you think makes lesson study such a powerful professional development experience in each of the case stories?

Professional Development and Strategic Leadership to Support Effective Integration of Science and Literacy[1]

Iris Weiss
Horizon Research, Inc.

This chapter begins with data on the current status of elementary science instruction in the United States in order to set the context for considering how professional development and other reform activities can support effective integration of science and literacy. It continues with a brief description of the "emerging consensus" on effective professional development; a case description of a major professional development initiative that reflects those design principles; and a discussion of possible implications for professional development around the integration of science and literacy. The chapter concludes with a discussion of some of the issues

---

[1]Chapter 13, "Professional Development and Strategic Leadership to Support Effective Integration of Science and Literacy," is copyright © 2005 Horizon Research, Inc., and is reprinted with permission from the Horizon Research, Inc., website (*www.horizon-research.com*).

involved in "strategic leadership" to help ensure that efforts to promote the integration of science and literacy have broad and lasting impacts.

The Status of Elementary Science Instruction

Elementary teachers are assigned to teach multiple subjects, but that does not mean that they are equally adept at all of them. For example, in the 2000 National Survey of Science and Mathematics Education, elementary teachers in self-contained classrooms were asked how well qualified they felt to teach each of a number of disciplines, and also how much time they spent on instruction in these disciplines. As can be seen in Figure 1, 77% of elementary teachers indicated they considered themselves "very well quali-fied" to teach reading/language arts. In contrast, percentages of elementary teachers reporting that they were very well qualified to teach the sciences ranged from a high of 28% for life science to a low of 14% for physical science. At the other end of the scale, only 1% of elementary teachers re-ported being "not well qualified" to teach reading/language arts, compared to 27% in physical science (Fulp 2002). We also know from self-report

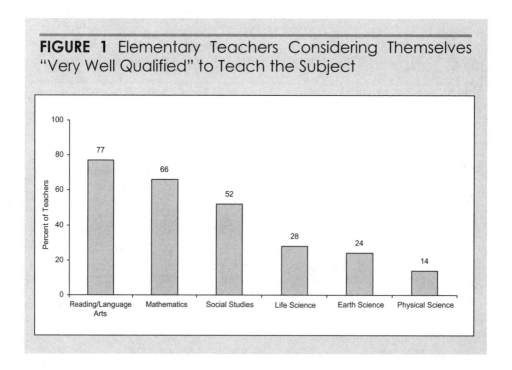

FIGURE 1 Elementary Teachers Considering Themselves "Very Well Qualified" to Teach the Subject

data that elementary teachers in self-contained classes spend considerably more time on reading/language arts instruction than on science instruction (Weiss et al. 2001). (See Figure 2.)

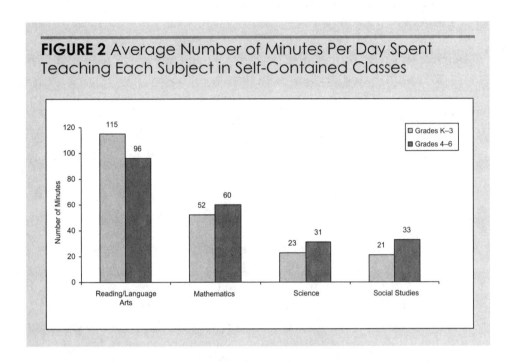

FIGURE 2 Average Number of Minutes Per Day Spent Teaching Each Subject in Self-Contained Classes

The *Looking Inside the Classroom* study (Weiss et al. 2003) was designed to complement and extend findings from the 2000 National Survey of Science and Mathematics Education, and included observations of a nationally representative sample of 364 mathematics and science lessons in grades K–12. Trained observers described each lesson in detail, rated various components of the lesson, judged the likely impact of the lesson on students along a number of dimensions, and provided an overall assessment of the quality of instruction. The results reported here are based on observations of 119 science lessons in grades K–8. Overall, 61% of elementary science lessons nationally are judged to be low in quality, 25% medium in quality, and only 15% high in quality.

Researchers saw some terrific lessons—classrooms where the students were fully and purposefully engaged in deepening their understanding of important science concepts. Some of these lessons were "traditional" in nature, including lectures and worksheets; others were "reform" in nature, involving students in more open inquiries. Observers saw other lessons, some traditional and some reform-oriented, that were far lower in quality, where science learning would have been difficult, if not impossible.

Based on the classroom observations, the relative strengths of K–8 science lessons are the following:

- Science content provided to students is generally significant, worthwhile, accurate, and developmentally appropriate.
- Instructional activities reflect attention to students' preparedness and prior experience, and to issues of access, equity, and diversity.
- Accurate participation of all students is encouraged.
- There is a climate of respect for students' ideas, questions, and contributions.

Prevalent weaknesses of K–8 science instruction are as follows:

- Whether or not they are engaged in hands-on activities, students are often not intellectually engaged with important science ideas.
- Science is often represented as "information," rather than as a dynamic body of knowledge enriched by hypothesis and investigation.
- Teachers' questioning tends to focus on factual information rather than probing for, or enhancing, students' conceptual understanding.
- There is a general lack of "sense making," both during and at the end of lessons.
- Intellectual rigor, including constructive criticism and challenging of ideas, is rare.

An in-depth analysis of descriptions of lessons judged very effective and decidedly ineffective identified a number of key factors that seemed to distinguish between the two. The bottom line is that the choice of instructional strategy doesn't appear to be as important as some have suggested. Rather, the key appears to be first providing students an opportunity to engage with important science concepts, and then ensuring that they in fact make sense of these concepts.

The "Emerging Consensus" on Effective Professional Development

Professional development is often the strategy of choice for efforts to improve teaching and learning. For example, in their evaluation of the National Science Foundation's (NSF) Statewide Systemic Initiatives, Zucker et al. (1998) noted that while there were many reform strategies included in the various projects, far more resources were devoted to professional development than to any other type of intervention. The centrality of professional development as a change strategy has led to considerable thought about improving the quality of professional development. According to Elmore (2002), even though there is not a great deal of empirical evidence on the impact of professional development, "much of the literature written by researchers and practitioners about professional development seems quite sensible and useful in thinking about how to design and operate professional development activities that have some likelihood of improving teaching and learning" (p. 6).

Included in this consensus are the ideas that professional development should be (1) based on a clearly defined mission that is grounded in student learning; (2) tailored to address the particular difficulties encountered by real students in real classrooms; (3) designed to develop and support collaborative practice within and across schools, including the involvement of administrators; and (4) sustained over time. Elmore (2002) suggests that these principles provide "an ample basis for designing activities that could be subjected to empirical testing" (p. 6).

The Case of the Local Systemic Change Initiative

The Local Systemic Change (LSC) Initiative supported by the National Science Foundation began in 1995 with eight projects targeting elementary science, and expanded over time to include 88 projects targeting various subsets of K–12 science and mathematics education. Formally titled Local Systemic Change through Teacher Enhancement, the LSC incorporates quite a few of these design principles for professional development, and has been the subject of extensive empirical work. This section describes the LSC initiative, including evidence of its quality and impact; explores the extent of support for Elmore's "sensible propositions"; and draws some implications for professional development to support effective integration of science and literacy.

The LSC Theory of Action

The LSC initiative differed from former NSF-supported teacher enhancement efforts in two important ways. First, it targeted all teachers in a jurisdiction for professional development; each targeted teacher is to participate in a minimum of 130 hours of professional development over the course of the project. Second, the LSC emphasized preparing teachers to implement project-designated science/mathematics instructional materials in their classes.

The LSC theory of action (see Figure 3) argued that providing teachers with opportunities to deepen their content and pedagogical knowledge in the context of high-quality instructional materials would result in better-prepared teachers. In addition to providing professional development for teachers, the LSC initiative promotes efforts to build a supportive environment for improving science instruction, including aligning district policy with the reform vision. The theory also predicted that teachers who participated in in-depth professional development, with ongoing support, would be more inclined to change their instruction in ways advocated by national standards, and would have more capacity to do so. Improved instruction would in turn lead to higher student achievement. (The dotted line lead-

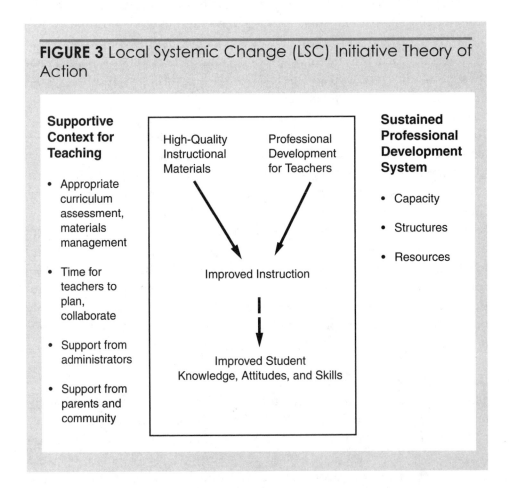

FIGURE 3 Local Systemic Change (LSC) Initiative Theory of Action

Supportive Context for Teaching

- Appropriate curriculum assessment, materials management

- Time for teachers to plan, collaborate

- Support from administrators

- Support from parents and community

High-Quality Instructional Materials

Professional Development for Teachers

Improved Instruction

Improved Student Knowledge, Attitudes, and Skills

Sustained Professional Development System

- Capacity

- Structures

- Resources

ing to student outcomes in Figure 3 reflects the fact that LSC projects were initially not required to assess their impact on students.)

Many factors influenced the design of individual LSC projects: the background and experience of key project staff; the history of prior reform activities in the district(s); district size and urbanicity; the involvement of a single district versus multiple districts; the types of partners involved in reform efforts; and so on. Whatever the individual design, however, LSCs were guided by a common set of principles to achieve their overarching goal of improving science/mathematics instruction.

Evaluation of the LSC

NSF contracted with Horizon Research, Inc., to coordinate a cross-site evaluation of the LSC. Project evaluators were asked to collect data using standardized questionnaires and protocols designed to answer core evaluation questions, and to complete ratings on the quality of LSC professional development programs. Data from the LSC core evaluation suggest that the initiative has had significant success in a number of areas. These data, summarized in Boyd et al. 2004, and reports from project staff (e.g., Pasley 2002) also provide insights into the difficulties that large-scale reform projects encounter in their efforts to provide professional development for substantial numbers of teachers and to develop a supportive context for scaling up and sustaining interventions.

Major Successes
High-Quality Professional Development

The LSC's primary goal was to provide teachers with high-quality professional development around the use of project-designated science and mathematics instructional materials. Core evaluation data suggest that projects had considerable success in this area. In particular, LSCs were strong in creating a culture conducive to teacher learning, in the quality of preparation of professional development providers, and in preparing teachers to use project-designated instructional materials and appropriate pedagogy in their classrooms. Further, ratings for overall program quality and the quality of individual sessions improved significantly over time, suggesting that LSCs became more adept at implementing high-quality professional development as they matured.

Impact on Teachers and Teaching

Data collected as part of the core evaluation suggest that LSC professional development had a positive impact on teaching and learning. Teachers' attitudes toward reform-oriented teaching in mathematics and science, and their perceptions of their content and pedagogical preparedness to teach these subjects, improved over time with increased participation in LSC professional development. Data from teacher questionnaires and evaluator ratings of classroom observations also suggest that teachers' participation in LSC professional development was linked to a number of positive outcomes in their instruction, including (1) overall improvement in the quality of science/mathematics lessons; (2) increased time spent on science instruction in the elementary grades; (3) enhanced quality of content presented to students; (4) more frequent use of investigative practices, questioning, and sense-making practices; and (5) a greater likelihood that the classroom culture promotes intellectual rigor and student engagement. Core evaluation data also suggest that the quality of classroom instruction improves over time as teachers' professional development hours accrue, although there seems to be a limited impact beyond 80 hours of professional development.

Widespread Use of Project-Designated Instructional Materials

Efforts to increase teachers' use of project-designated instructional materials in science/mathematics have been a cornerstone of the LSC program. The widespread use of these materials in the classroom by participating teachers points to success in achieving this objective. Core evaluation data suggest that the quality of instruction improved with teachers' use of the designated materials, and that teachers were more likely to use these materials as they accumulated LSC professional development hours. The LSC also played a major role in ensuring that project-designated instructional materials became a fixture in the educational landscape in participating districts by promoting the formal adoption of these materials. These efforts appear to have had a "systemic" effect on both participating and non-participating teachers in LSC districts, resulting in the increased use of these materials as LSC projects matured.

A Supportive Context for Reform

LSCs reported a steady increase in support for reform over time, suggesting that projects have had success in building stakeholder and policy support for the LSC vision and interventions. The adoption of project-designated instructional materials and aligned frameworks; the creation of science materials management centers; districts' allocation of funds to support teacher leaders in varying capacities; the development of partnerships with universities, nonprofit organizations, and others to support continuing professional development—all provide evidence of the success LSCs have had in building capacity and infrastructure to support and sustain reform.

Major Challenges
Preparing and Supporting Professional Development Providers

Evaluators noted some areas of weakness among providers that sometimes limited the impact of professional development. These weaknesses related to both content sessions (e.g., lack of rigor) and sessions on pedagogy (e.g., lack of explicit discussion of strategies). Even in projects that were highly attentive to the preparation and support of professional development providers, session quality sometimes suffered due to the limited skills of some providers.

Addressing Teachers' Content Needs

Among the dimensions of LSC professional development, deepening teachers' understanding of science/mathematics content proved the most challenging for LSCs. Professional development sessions designed to deepen content knowledge and support teachers' content needs during implementation sometimes failed to delve into the very content they were designed to address, due to other more pressing teacher concerns such as materials management or pedagogy. Teachers' limited understanding of the content may help explain the lack of attention to conceptual understanding observed by evaluators, and by project staff, in classroom visits.

Supporting Teachers

Supporting teachers during implementation also proved challenging for LSCs. While projects tended to excel at supporting teachers in terms of materials and supplies needed for the implementation of the modules/kits, LSCs devoted far less attention to providing ongoing individual and small group support, in part due to the lack of resources and staffing for these kinds of activities. Given teachers' lack of time and scheduling constraints, LSCs also encountered difficulty in recruiting teachers for participation in follow-up and support activities—for example, communities of learners designed to foster reflection around content, pedagogy, and materials.

Engaging Principals

In many ways, principals played key roles in determining the outcomes of LSCs—from encouraging teachers to participate in professional development, to supporting teachers' use of project-designated instructional materials and inquiry-based practices, to enabling the work of teacher leaders, to making time for teachers to participate in site-based professional development. LSCs struggled with balancing resources and level of effort devoted to teacher professional development as opposed to reaching out to key stakeholders. In fact, attention to principals was sometimes an afterthought or was neglected altogether.

Reaching Targeted Teachers

Despite efforts to provide a range of opportunities for participation, few LSC projects achieved the goal of reaching all eligible teachers with 130 hours of professional development. Teacher turnover, changes in state/district policies that reduced the number of professional development days available or shifted the focus to other subject areas, teacher reluctance to participate—all contributed to the problems LSCs encountered in reaching their targeted audience. In some districts, the large influx of new teachers, as well as mobility across schools and subject areas, hindered LSC efforts to meet the 130-hour goal. LSCs that underestimated teacher turnover—and many did—were forced to devise new strategies "on the fly" to meet the needs of new teachers, as well as those they had initially planned for.

Possible Implications for Professional Development to Support Integration of Science and Literacy

It makes sense to build on teachers' strengths in addressing their weaknesses, and the fact that teachers were willing to report their lack of preparedness to teach science lends some credibility to their reports of preparedness in reading and language arts. The emerging consensus on professional development, and the lessons learned in implementing a very large professional development initiative, can be used in designing professional development aimed at supporting effective integration of science and literacy.

Experience in the LSC suggests the need for a sustained level of effort around preparing and supporting professional development providers, especially in areas that pose particular difficulties for teachers (e.g., content, questioning, closure). Similarly, based on the LSC experience, it is clear that professional development efforts need to expect teacher turnover and build in a plan that includes new teachers and incentives for participation.

Beyond this, reform leaders need to look for more effective strategies to make the case for reform with both teachers and administrators to increase the likelihood of participation, and continue to make professional development relevant, accessible, practical, and of high quality to attract even those resistant to the reform vision.

Finally, the tendency for science content to be downplayed in LSC professional development, and in the classroom instruction of participating teachers, has implications for the design of professional development in support of the integration of science and literacy. While it seems possible on conceptual grounds to integrate disciplines while staying true to the key ideas of each, some previous efforts at integration have tended to give primacy to one of the disciplines, to the detriment of the other. For example, some mathematics-science integration efforts started with key ideas in mathematics, and brought in relevant science phenomena, but the science concepts were not developed in an organized fashion. Others started with key ideas in science, and brought in relevant mathematics, but neglected important mathematics ideas that weren't readily applicable to those science ideas. It is important in designing professional development to support integration of the two, not to lose the focus on quality *science* instruction in the service of literacy goals.

The Need for Strategic Leadership to Ensure Broad and Lasting Impact

Improving instruction is difficult work. It is unlikely people would embark on major reform efforts if they knew in advance that they would have an impact on only a small number of teachers and students, or that the reforms they worked so hard to create would quickly disappear. But in fact, that is what often happens. Certainly it is important to design high-quality professional development to develop teachers' knowledge and skills, and support them as they work to apply what they are learning to their classrooms. However, effective professional development is only a part of achieving the goal of high-quality, widespread, long-lasting integration of science and literacy.

Elmore (1996) makes the distinction between "scaling up" reform activities to reach a larger proportion of the current population of teachers, administrators, and students, and "going to scale" with the reforms, which entails changing the system so that the reform vision becomes part of its core mission. This section addresses "strategic leadership" in both scaling up and going to scale; it is based on research on large-scale reform, as well as on the "wisdom of practice" of people who have been engaged in planning, implementing, and sustaining improvements in education over the last several decades.

Articulating the Reform Vision

The first stage in planning a journey is deciding where you want to go. People who are working toward districtwide integration of science and literacy need to begin with the end in mind, identifying what effective integration would look like in classrooms. In articulating the vision, reform leaders need to consider the perspectives of all of the key stakeholders, creating opportunities for people with diverse views to provide input into the emerging vision. A vision that reflects the perspectives of a variety of stakeholders on what is important in both science and literacy, rather than one that adheres strictly to the views of a single group, is more likely to survive the tough times ahead, when pieces of the reform may not fall into place exactly as intended.

Garnering Support From Key Stakeholders

Although there is no formula for accomplishing it, securing the support of key players is critical as leaders engage in large-scale improvement. One way to think about key stakeholders is to consider whose support will be needed in order for the reform to succeed, and whose opposition could stifle it. Working with the appropriate combination of stakeholder groups will promote success; the actual mix of groups depends on local context.

Clearly, teachers are central stakeholders in efforts to integrate science and literacy. When teachers are well-informed, and recognize that their needs have been considered in the planning, they are more likely to work hard to make the planned changes a lasting reality. Principals also need to understand and buy in to the reform vision, so they will encourage teachers to implement the reforms, and ensure that school policies and practices are supportive of the vision.

It is particularly helpful to think about the incentives needed to encourage cooperation of the various stakeholders. For example, superintendents and principals are currently held accountable for student achievement in reading, with science achievement likely to be increasingly on the radar screen as it is incorporated into testing programs associated with the No Child Left Behind legislation. Administrators are more likely to provide release time for teachers to participate in professional development activities, and to provide support for teachers to take on leadership roles, if they anticipate that the initiative will lead to improved student performance. By highlighting how the improvement plan will help people achieve their own goals, reform leaders can increase the likelihood of support from a broad array of stakeholders.

Aligning Policy in Support of the Vision

States play a major role in regulating education, typically determining the content that should be addressed, teacher certification and renewal requirements, etc. Districts layer on additional policies, perhaps more detail about what content should be taught at particular grade levels, how much time should be spent on these subjects, what instructional materials will be used, what "counts" toward teacher certificate renewal, etc. Often there are assessments administered at both the state and district levels, with various stakes attached for students, teachers, and/or schools. To varying extents, and at various times, these policies influence the actions of key players throughout the system.

Rather than attempting to align every bit of existing policy with the science and literacy reform vision, reform leaders' efforts in the policy arena should be highly focused; it is likely that only a few policies really hold the attention of teachers, administrators, and other key stakeholders. An important first step in thinking about how to engage in policy work, then, is to identify the key policies, who makes them, and who pays attention to them.

Designing and Implementing Appropriate Interventions

People undertake reform because of one or more needs in the current system, and they choose a set of interventions they believe will address those needs and improve the performance of the system. For maximum effect, interventions need to be carefully chosen, well-implemented, and scaled up with their quality maintained. Note that it is neither necessary nor wise to start from scratch in developing interventions. Rather, reform leaders can choose from approaches to integrating science and literacy described in this volume and elsewhere that have proven effective in addressing their particular needs in similar contexts.

Of course, in order to be effective, the existing approaches have to be feasible in a given setting. If an intervention that appears promising on substantive grounds is likely to spark opposition, perhaps because it reminds key stakeholders of something that didn't work in the past, reform leaders would likely want to choose another approach.

Scaling Up Interventions With Quality

Success in integrating science and literacy for all requires choosing interventions that can feasibly be "scaled up" to reach all teachers and students. Choosing such interventions requires understanding that what works with the most willing and enthusiastic "volunteer" teachers will not necessarily work with every teacher. Similarly, if the interventions are so labor-intensive that the reform leaders won't have the necessary human or material resources to reach the targeted numbers, they need to either modify the approaches or choose others. The important consideration is that reform leaders select a set of science and literacy interventions that will be perceived as valuable *and* that they can do well on a large scale, so that they will *in fact* be valuable to the system as a whole.

References

Boyd, S. E., E. R. Banilower, J. D. Pasley, and I. R. Weiss. 2004. *Local systemic change initiative capstone report*. Chapel Hill, NC: Horizon Research.

Elmore, R. F. 1996. Getting to scale with good educational practice. *Harvard Educational Review* 66 (1): 1–26.

Elmore, R. F. 2002. *Bridging the gap between standards and achievement: The imperative for professional development in education*. Washington, DC: Albert Shanker Institute.

Fulp, S. L. 2002. *The 2000 national survey of science and mathematics education: Status of elementary school science teaching*. Chapel Hill, NC: Horizon Research.

Pasley, J. D., ed. 2002. *The role of instructional materials in professional development: Lessons learned from the LSC community*. Chapel Hill, NC: Horizon Research.

Weiss, I. R., E. R. Banilower, K. C. McMahon, and P. S. Smith. 2001. *Report of the 2000 national survey of science and mathematics education*. Chapel Hill, NC: Horizon Research.

Weiss, I. R., J. D. Pasley, P. S. Smith, E. R. Banilower, and D. J. Heck. 2003. *Looking inside the classroom: A study of K–12 mathematics and science education in the United States*. Chapel Hill, NC: Horizon Research.

Zucker, A. A., P. M. Shields, N. E. Adelman, T. B. Corcoran, and M. E. Goertz. 1998. *A report on the evaluation of the National Science Foundation's Statewide Systemic Initiatives (SSI) program*. Menlo Park, CA: SRI International.

CHAPTER 14

Science Education in a No Child Left Behind, Standards-Based World

Michael P. Klentschy
El Centro, California, School District

S chool districts throughout the United States are facing an ever-increasing series of challenges. These challenges are related to the growing national movement related to standards, assessment, and accountability. Classroom teachers are faced with the pressures of time, coverage, and assessment as they plan and deliver effective, standards-based instruction in science and other core subject areas. Many districts choose to have reading and mathematics make up the largest part of the instructional day. A large number of districts have little knowledge about research linking science and literacy, particularly as a means of improving instruction in both areas. While there are references to the science and literacy connection in the literature, there is little large-scale dissemination of the best practices at the district, school, or classroom level. As a result, a declining number of students are entering science, technology, engineering, and mathematics professions at a time when shortages in these fields exist. In fact, Saul and Jagusch (1992) reported that more people in the United States earn their livings by doing astrology than by doing astronomy.

To compound matters, there is a growing debate regarding what constitutes rigorous research evidence. The federal No Child Left Behind (NCLB) Act of 2001 calls on educational practitioners to use "scientifically based research" to guide their decisions about which interventions to implement (U.S. Department of Education 2003). This emphasis on scientifically based research practices in classrooms makes it increasingly difficult for school districts to identify the best practices and the types of evidence that are available to assist them in making instructional decisions. In many cases the best practices that will lead to increased student performance may or may not be practices that have derived evidence from "scientifically based research." School districts must make difficult decisions relative to what type of evidence is available and how it is used to inform instructional decision making.

There is a growing body of evidence related to science and literacy connections, some based on "scientific" research and some not. This evidence will be reviewed in depth in this chapter and has been divided into four categories: (1) student achievement in science, (2) science-literacy connections, (3) student opportunity to learn, and (4) fidelity of implementation.

Student Achievement in Science

Studies related to student achievement in science have been divided into two groups: the early studies and the recent studies.

The Early Studies

The early studies were conducted from the late 1960s though the early 1990s and were primarily focused on the impact of the implementation of science curriculum that was developed with the support of the National Science Foundation. In regard to best practices associated with improving student performance, particularly with historically underrepresented groups, there are four early studies that districts may want to consider: Breddermen 1983; Carpenter 1963; Shymansky, Hedges, and Woodworth 1990; and Wise 1996. These studies provided evidence that a strong relationship exists among high-quality instruction, teacher professional development, student achievement, and, eventually, closing the achievement gap.

The Recent Studies

More recent studies are available that examine standards-based, systemic approaches to the implementation of a science curriculum. These studies have also demonstrated a positive relationship between a systemic approach to the implementation of high-quality curriculum, teacher professional development, student opportunity to learn, and the subsequent impact on student science achievement and closing the achievement gap. These studies were conducted between 1995 and 2005 in Imperial County, California; Charleston, South Carolina; Green Bay, Wisconsin; East Bay Educational Collaborative, Rhode Island; Fresno, California; and Dade County, Florida. They are predicated on five critical elements of reform identified in *Science for All Children* (National Academy of Sciences 1997): (1) high-quality curriculum, (2) sustained professional development, (3) materials support, (4) administrative and community support, and (5) assessment and evaluation. It must be noted that these elements are interdependent. All five must be working together to provide the systemic approach that is necessary to attain the desired outcomes. For example in Imperial County, California, in the Vallé Imperial Project in Science (VIPS), there is a well-documented series of studies indicating the improvement of student achievement over time through the use of this systemic approach (Amaral, Garrison, and Klentschy 2002; Jorgenson and Vanosdall 2002; Saul et al. 2002; Klentschy and Molina-De La Torre 2004).

In the Imperial County study (for a detailed description of the study, see Amaral, Garrison, and Klentschy 2002), researchers investigated the impact of an inquiry-based program of instruction in science as the core of a systemic reform effort on student achievement in science and other subject areas. Fourth- and sixth-grade students were studied over a period of four years. The results of the study indicated that the longer the students were exposed to high quality in programs and participated in classrooms that were part of the systemic reform effort the more student achievement improved. In fact, fourth-grade students who had participated in the program for four years attained a mean percentile score 32 percentile points higher on the Stanford Achievement Test, Ninth Edition, Form T than those fourth-grade students who had no exposure to the program. In sixth grade the difference in the mean percentile scores on the same test was 37 percentile points higher for those students who had four years of participation when compared to those who had no exposure.

The researchers in Imperial County conducted an additional longitudinal study following the same students through middle school to investigate the impact of the program of science instruction over a longer period of time. This time the released items from the Third International Mathematics and Science Study (TIMSS) were used to measure the impact of the instructional program on student achievement. The sixth-grade students who were investigated in the earlier study were assessed as eighth graders. The results were significant and again indicated that the longer that the students were exposed to the program of instruction the better they performed on the TIMSS released multiple-choice items in science. The researchers then attempted to investigate the question, How much exposure actually made a difference? The differences between groups were significant related to time of exposure not only for the eighth graders but also for the seventh graders who were fifth graders in the original study. The investigators then asked the question, How much exposure is enough to produce a significant change in student achievement in science? The data indicated that two years of exposure for either the seventh graders or the eighth graders produced a significant difference.

Many times the impact of a science program or a systemic approach to teaching science to elementary children is not ascertained until high school graduation levels are examined. High school graduation levels can be examined in terms of percentage of students meeting university eligibility requirements. In that context the students in Imperial County have shown significant progress, as can be seen from the following account.

The University of California has entrance requirements based on grade-point averages of completed high school course work meeting specific criteria. Annually, these entrance requirements are benchmarked to allow 13% of graduating high school seniors to enroll in the University of California as freshmen. Historically, these entrance requirements have formed barriers and challenges for underrepresented students.

From 2000 to 2004, the five statewide graduating classes of underrepresented students met the University of California eligibility entrance rates at about 4%. In other words, 4% of all high school graduates who were part of underrepresented groups met the University of California freshmen eligibility requirements. In 2000, Imperial County was one of the systems where approximately 4% of the underrepresented high school graduates met those requirements. However, in Imperial County that percentage increased annually, reaching a high of more than 12% in 2004. The 2004 graduating class more than tripled the statewide entrance eligibility average. These graduating high school students were the sixth-grade students in the original study. In the past, success in algebra and laboratory science had been a barrier for these students.

Science-Literacy Connections

When examining science and literacy connections, it is important to consider how students learn science and the relationship between science process skills and literacy skills The Learning Research and Development Center at the University of Pittsburgh (2000) has developed a comprehensive set of grade-span content and process standards identifying what students should know and be able to do in the core subject areas. An examination of the standards for science and reading reveals that many of the standards are very similar (e.g., compare and contrast, predict, draw conclusions). There is a nice complement between these standards, providing classroom teachers with multiple entry points for the integration of literacy into the science program.

Glynn and Muth (1994) established a model of student cognitive processing. This model specifically addresses how students learn science content. A primary goal of instruction is for students to become metacognitive learners. In this context, the process of really learning science moves through three stages. In the first stage, the perception of the science phenomenon, students are actually doing science. In the second stage, the perceptions are transmitted to the students' working memory. In the third stage, connections are made from the working memory to the long-term memory. There are definite connections between science and literacy when students construct meaning from their classroom science experiences.

Guthrie et al. (1999) focus on the connections between science and literacy through the process of coherent instruction. Coherent instruction is teaching that connects the students' reading skills to writing, connects reading and writing to content, and connects content learning to student interest. Coherent instruction makes learning easier for students because it combines the strange (something new) with the familiar.

Many of the connections between literacy and science have been discussed for a number of years. More than 30 years ago, the National Commission on Reading in *Becoming a Nation of Readers* recommended that reading instruction and teaching about thinking strategies should occur in the content areas rather than in separate lessons about reading (Anderson et al. 1985). The importance of prior knowledge was also addressed, indicating that the more students know about a topic the better they comprehend and learn from text on that topic. In fact, according to the report, prior knowledge is the strongest predictor of a student's ability to make inferences about text.

Our understanding of the role of literacy in the acquisition of content has grown significantly since these recommendations were made. Bransford, Brown, and Cocking (2000) also note that prior knowledge is an important predictor for students to make inferences and that the more students know about something the more they will comprehend text on that topic.

Science and Reading Achievement

A series of recent studies has examined the impact on reading achievement, especially comprehension, of high-quality science programs with carefully engineered connections between science and literacy. These studies, drawn from Imperial County, California; Fresno, California; Dade County, Florida; Baltimore, Maryland; and Broward County, Florida, all indicate that there is a positive relationship between teacher professional development, student opportunity to learn in programs with integrated science and literacy, and impact on student achievement in reading and science and on closing the achievement gap.

In the Imperial County study (Amaral, Garrison, and Klentschy 2002), both English language learners and English-speaking students significantly improved reading achievement over time with exposure to a high-quality program of instruction in science. This improvement occurred with both fourth and sixth graders participating in the Imperial County study. In the Fresno, California, study (Valadez and Freve 2002), the results indicated that students who received four years of exposure to a systemic science program (from 1998 to 2001) scored significantly higher on the Stanford Achievement Test, Ninth Edition, Form T, Reading Subtest compared to students who did not receive the science instruction. Again, opportunity to learn in the systemic science program produced achievement results that closed the reading achievement gap between ethnic groups. In all cases a positive relationship was found between the number of years of participation in the systemic science program and the reading achievement score outcomes.

The Dade County, Florida, study (Dade County Public Schools 1996) found that a large number of students ($n = 2,420$) in grades 3 and 5 who received instruction in a systemic science program scored significantly higher (10 percentile points for each grade level) on the Stanford Achievement Test, Ninth Edition, Reading Subtest than students in the same grade levels ($n = 4,145$) who did not receive the systemic science instruction.

Guthrie et al. (1999) conducted a series of studies where students who received a high-quality program of science instruction in grades 3 and 5 made significant gains in science and reading achievement compared to matched groups that received traditional instruction. These series of studies yielded the same conclusions as the Imperial Valley and Dade County studies: that a high-quality program of instruction made up of a science activity followed by reading, writing, and classroom discussion focused on the activity led to higher achievement gains in both science and reading for the students participating in the treatment group.

Romance and Vitale (1992, 2001) conducted studies in 50 classrooms covering more than 1,200 students in Broward County, Florida. In these studies they implemented the Science IDEAS model, which is an integrated accelerated science curriculum strategy emphasizing science process skills, hands-on activities, and enhanced, content-area reading comprehension activities in science. The research results indicate that students (including at-risk populations) using the IDEAS model made significant gains in both reading comprehension and science on a nationally normed standardized test.

Science and Writing Achievement

The second important science and literacy connection takes place when students are exposed to writing in science. Such writing often takes the form of expository writing through the use of student science notebooks. Ruiz-Primo et al. (1999) indicate that the student science notebook is the best record of the lesson or unit implementation by the teacher. It is also the best record of student performance in terms of quality of communication and conceptual and procedural understanding. Furthermore, writing in science notebooks may enhance thinking because writing demands that students learn to organize their knowledge, link evidence to claims, and draw conclusions. There is a definite transfer effect to student achievement and an opportunity to develop student voice (Klentschy and Molina-De La Torre 2004). The notebooks are also assessment tools that can be part of a student performance portfolio related to a unit of science instruction (Ruiz-Primo, Li, and Shavelson 2004).

Writing in science notebooks as a way for students to make meaning in science has numerous applications, as shown in schools throughout the United States. Among these are projects in Imperial County, California; in Clark County, Nevada; in Tucson, Arizona; by the East Bay Educational Collaborative, Rhode Island; in Charleston County, South Carolina; and in school districts being studied by the California Institute of Technology and by the Center for Excellence at Tennessee State University. In each of these diverse locations, the preliminary data indicate a strong positive relationship between students engaged in keeping science notebooks and their achievement in both science and expository writing.

In these schools, classroom teachers have concluded that student science notebooks should contain certain components and criteria and that expectations for teachers and students should be developed for science notebooks in order to maximize their effectiveness. The components and criteria are as follows:

- Question/Problem/Purpose
- Prediction
- Planning
- Data/Observations (Claims and Evidence)
- What have you learned?
- Next Steps/ New Questions

These components are found throughout the notebook but not necessarily in each lesson. (For further discussion about student writing and the student writing process in science, see Klentschy 2005b; Klentschy and Molina-De La Torre 2004). The science notebooks also contain other aspects of student writing; many times students will write reflections, pose new questions, or express their feelings and attitudes about science.

When trying something new, such as writing in science, teachers often ask themselves, *Where [or how] do I start?* In this case, the easiest way for teachers to get started is to use a series of stems to encourage their students to write, such as the following:

- Today I (or we) _____ .
- Today I learned _____ .
- I noticed _____ .
- I wondered _____ .
- Questions I have now are _____ .

(For more information about getting started, go to *www.vipscience.com*).

Just as students go through a series of developmental stages in using science notebooks, teachers also go through their own stages of development in implementation. The data indicate that teachers may take several years to develop both the competency and the comfort level to integrate writing in science (Klentschy and Molina-De La Torre 2004).

Student outcomes in science achievement and writing proficiency are also important for school districts to consider when implementing high-quality science instruction that uses student science notebooks. In the Imperial County studies (Amaral, Garrison, and Klentschy 2002), the researchers explored the relationship between length of exposure to such instruction and the development of expository writing ability of sixth-grade students through the use of their science notebooks as demonstrated in an expository writing assessment. In the spring of 1999 there was an overall 64% pass rate on the district writing proficiency assessment for all sixth-grade students in the study. After disaggregating the data, the researchers found a direct relationship between the numbers of years of exposure to the science program and the student pass grade. The longer the students had been exposed to the program, the higher the pass grade. The differences between the students were significant. Only 23% of the students with no exposure to the science program demonstrated an ability to pass the writing proficiency assessment, compared to 89% of the students passing the writing proficiency with four years of exposure. The researchers concluded that there was a definite link between the use of student science notebooks and significant improvement in student ability to write expository text.

Student Opportunity to Learn

A third principle that districts need to consider in the implementation of high-quality programs of instruction in science with strong science and literacy connections is providing student opportunity to learn. This is particularly important for the integration of English language development (ELD) strategies and the application of academic content language development (ACLD) for English language learners within the context of their science instruction.

Recent trends in the United States indicate that there is a phenomenon of changing demographics underway. Reports to the U.S. Department of Education from 25 state education agencies indicated at least a 10% growth from 1999 to 2001 in the English language learner (ELL) population. Eleven state education agencies reported a growth of 25% or more. These increases in the ELL population were predominately Spanish-speaking students. Nationally there was a 72% increase in Spanish-speaking students during the 1990s (U.S. Department of Education 2002).

Word Walls

A best practice for teachers to consider is the development of academic content language and science conceptual knowledge at the same time that they provide instruction in word recognition. This will lead to relational and contextual understanding by students. Another best practice that teachers may consider is the use of working word walls and charts to give students opportunities for comprehensible input, the development of scientific vocabulary, and an introduction to the vocabulary of the materials that they will be using in science. Word walls and charts facilitate science notebook entries for English language learners during science instruction.

Kit Inventory

Another strategy for developing vocabulary is the kit inventory. Many schools and districts use a kit-based form of science instruction supported by reading and other text material. The kit inventory focuses on vocabulary development and oral language practice and provides English language learners with opportunities to scaffold their understanding. The big idea of the kit inventory is really an introduction of the unit to the students by the teacher and is a way of integrating ELD, science content, and language arts. The language emphasis of the kit inventory is on the building of descriptive vocabulary. The descriptive vocabulary is documented by the teacher with chart paper and ultimately aligned with artifacts to a working word wall. The implementation is actually very adaptable to student needs and again addresses relational and contextual understanding of the development of vocabulary.

Another aspect of a kit inventory is the development of the science process skills of prediction and classifying. In prediction the student or the teacher removes one item at a time from the kit and asks the other students to predict what they think the item is, what it is called, and what it might be used for. In classifying, the teacher distributes items from the kit and the students group the items by the same category or students may identify the properties of these items (see Chapter 12 of this book for more information regarding the kit inventory).

Concept Mapping

Concept mapping is a strategy in which students use declarative knowledge to demonstrate their understanding related to a science concept. In this process 10 or fewer science terms are placed on disks; linking verbs that indicate relational aspects between these items are placed on cards and are then manipulated by the students with arrows indicating relational value. Figure 1 provides an example of a student concept map.

An analysis of this concept map indicates that the student understands most of the important relationships in the water cycle. The concept map also indicates that the student has a misconception that oceans flow into rivers. Concept maps provide an opportunity for English language learners to manipulate vocabulary and demonstrate their relational understanding. Ruiz-Primo et al. (2001) report evidence that students who represent their learning on concept maps perform, on average, higher than students who study without using concept maps. Concept maps are also a means for teachers to identify any misconceptions that students may have in their understanding of the relationships of science concepts.

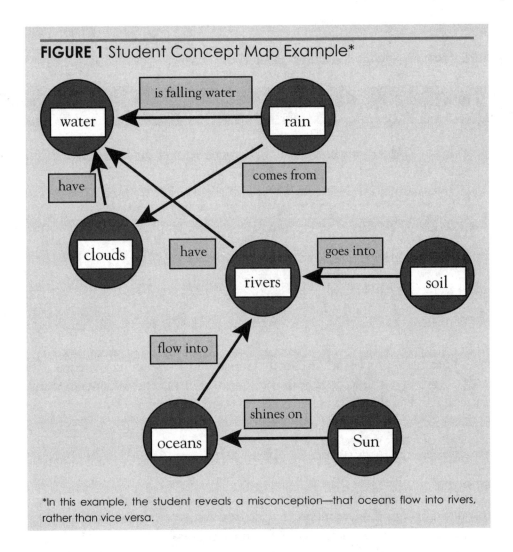

FIGURE 1 Student Concept Map Example*

*In this example, the student reveals a misconception—that oceans flow into rivers, rather than vice versa.

Word Clusters

Word clusters are also an important ELD strategy for students to use to build and demonstrate an understanding of vocabulary and relationships. Figure 2 provides an example of a word cluster using a simple object such as a Styrofoam cup to stimulate student use of language in context.

Cloze Paragraphs

In cloze paragraphs, a strategy to use language in context, key scientific vocabulary are deleted from a passage. The passage is then presented to students, who insert scientific vocabulary as they read to complete the pas-

FIGURE 2 Example of a Word Cluster With a Styrofoam Cup

What is it?	Material	Color	Size	Shape	Measure	Weight	Living thing?	Other
It is a <u>cup.</u>	It is made of <u>Styrofoam.</u>	It is <u>white.</u>	It is <u>small.</u>	It is the shape of a <u>cylinder.</u>	The <u>circumference</u> is 10 cm.	It is <u>light.</u>	It is a <u>nonliving</u> thing.	

Possible Questions for Use With English Language Learners:
- What can you tell me about the cup?
- Please complete this sentence: The cup is_____.
- What is the shape of the cup?

sage. Cloze paragraphs are useful in identifying students' knowledge and understanding of the science content and they encourage students to think critically and analytically about text and content.

Benefits of ELD Strategies

Through the use of ELD strategies there are many benefits to oral language development, reading, and writing. The benefits to oral language are opportunities for students to acquire precise terminology through academic content language development. It is also a way to introduce and repeat the vocabulary that the students will be using throughout the unit. Word walls and oral presentations are strategies the teachers use to stimulate the oral development of the class. The major benefit for English language learners is the association of vocabulary to items in the real world or placing vocabulary in context. The benefits to reading include the reading process skills identified earlier in this chapter, including repeating, sequencing, predicting, comparing and contrasting, inferring, analyzing, and summarizing. Expository writing is reinforced by providing students with opportunities to use and practice the language. Language is connected to students' immediate experiences, which also enhances writing conventions in the science and literacy connection.

Evidence of Effectiveness of ELD Strategies

Evidence for the effectiveness of these ELD strategies in student achievement can be found in the Imperial County, California, studies (Amaral, Garrison, and Klentschy 2002). Achievement data for both the fourth- and sixth-grade students who participated in the study indicated that the longer they were exposed to a high-quality science program, the greater their achievement. The achievement gap was closed between English language learners and English speakers after four years.

There are three other studies that are relevant to English language development in the science-literacy connection. Fradd and Lee (1999) indicated that a program of ELD instruction embedded into a high-quality program of instruction in science produced significant achievement gains for English language learners in science as well as in reading and writing achievement on state achievement tests in Florida. Morino and Hammond (2000) reported that a sheltered approach of ELD instruction with scaffolding embedded in a high-quality science program produced significant gains in science achievement and reading comprehension with English language learners in Northern California, where the instructional focus was on the relational and contextual development of language. Finally, Bravo and Garcia (2004) reported that in a large urban district of 58,000+ students, English language learners demonstrated significant gains in science and expository writing achievement when exposed to a high-quality program of science instruction with ELD, organizational skills, and contextual language development embedded into the science instruction.

Fidelity of Implementation

The fourth area that districts should consider is the fidelity of implementation of science and literacy connections within their classrooms. Educational Testing Service (2000) and Stigler and Heibert (1999) indicate that teachers bring a great deal of "craft knowledge"—the experiential knowledge they have gained from years of experience—to the workplace. That knowledge can be combined with best practices to strengthen the fidelity of implementation of science instruction in their classrooms.

Stigler and Heibert (1999) report that the lesson study approach addresses issues related to differences in levels of student accomplishment in classes of similar background and with teachers who have received similar training. It may be used as a process to assist teachers to move from novice to expert in their classroom instruction (Berliner 1994). In lesson study, a group of teachers from a similar school, similar grade level, or adjacent schools plan a joint lesson to establish best practices. In the context of building highly qualified teachers, lesson study is a way to chronicle best practices, becomes deeper with more practice on the part of the teachers, provides opportunities for pure collaboration and feedback, and promotes reflection and focuses on student work. This strategy is useful for teachers to receive feedback as they jointly design, implement, and evaluate student work using science and literacy connections. (For a detailed description on the planning, implementation, and evaluation of lesson study groups, see Amaral and Garrison 2004.)

Schools and districts may also wish to consider other emerging best practices for teacher capacity building and improving the fidelity of implementation of classroom instruction. The use of technology is one such tool. With LessonLab, an electronic platform that contains video, lesson plans, and student work, teachers can engage in professional development through the use of technology. LessonLab and lesson study then can be enhanced through an online web-based digital library available to teachers 24 hours a day, seven days a week, with a focus on key lessons emphasizing science and literacy connections with writing, reading, and ELD embedded into the digital lessons (Klentschy 2005a). LessonLab enhances lesson study through the promotion and development of reflective teaching practices. The lesson plan, teacher commentary, student work, and additional resources are available online, along with the actual lesson that was taught by that teacher. LessonLab and lesson study also allow schools and school districts to archive lesson study activities and to provide starting points for new lesson study groups.

Final Thoughts

Science and literacy connections are natural connections for teachers to make as they plan instruction. These natural connections extend and integrate expository writing through the use of student science notebooks, provide a contextual relationship between science activities and reading text, embed English language development strategies into the delivery of science content to assist English language learners, and allow for collaborative forms of teacher professional development through lesson study and technology-based models to increase the fidelity of implementation of standards-based science content.

A growing body of best practices is available for school districts, schools, and teachers to consider as they embark on this type of planning. Some of these best practices are drawn from so-called scientifically based research evidence. Other best practices come from common sense and are derived from teachers' developing craft knowledge. The key principle that should drive instructional planning is how this growing body of best practices will provide students with an increased opportunity to learn and increase their understanding of the science content.

References

Amaral, O., and L. Garrison. 2004. Lesson study: The Imperial Valley experience. *California Journal of Science Education* 4 (2): 45–79.

Amaral, O., L. Garrison, and M. Klentschy. 2002. Helping English learners increase achievement through inquiry-based science instruction. *Bilingual Research Journal* 26 (2): 213–239.

Anderson, R. C., E. H. Hiebert, J. A. Scott, and I. A. G. Wilkinson. 1985. *Becoming a nation of readers: The report of the National Commission on Reading.* Champaign, IL: Center for the Study of Reading.

Berliner, D. C. 1994. Expertise: The wonder of exemplary performances. In *Creating powerful thinking in teachers and students: Diverse perspectives*, eds. J. Mangieri and C. Block. Fort Worth, TX: Harcourt Brace College.

Bransford, J., A. Brown, and R. Cocking, eds. 2000. *How people learn: Brain, mind, experience, and school.* Washington, DC: National Academy Press.

Bravo, M., and E. Garcia. 2004. Learning to write like scientists: English language learners' science inquiry and writing understandings in responsive learning contexts. Paper presented at the Annual Meeting of the American Educational Research Association, San Diego, CA.

Bredderman, T. 1983. Effects of activity-based elementary science on student outcomes: A quantitative synthesis. *Review of Educational Research* 53 (4): 499–518.

Carpenter, R. 1963. A reading method and an activity method in elementary science instruction. *Science Education* 47 (4): 544–567.

Dade County Public Schools Research and Evaluation Department. 1996. *Report on achievement: Effects of hands-on science.* Dade County, FL: Dade County Public Schools.

Educational Testing Service. 2000. *How teaching matters: Bringing the classroom back into discussions of teacher quality.* A Policy Information Center Report. Princeton, NJ: Educational Testing Service.

Fradd, S. H., and O. Lee. 1999. Teachers' roles in promoting science inquiry with students from diverse backgrounds. *Educational Researcher* 28 (6): 14–20, 42.

Guthrie, J. T., E. Anderson, S. Alao, and J. Rinehart. 1999. Influences of concept-oriented reading instruction on strategy use and conceptual learning from text. *The Elementary School Journal* 99 (4): 343–366.

Guthrie, J. T., and S. Ozgungor. 2002. Instructional contexts for reading engagement. In *Comprehension instruction: Research-based best practices*, eds. C. C. Block and M. Pressley, 275–288. New York: Guilford Press.

Gynn, S., and K. Muth. 1994. Reading and writing to learn science: Achieving scientific literacy. *Journal of Research in Science Teaching* 31 (9): 1057–1073.

Jorgenson, O., and R. Vanosdall. 2002. The death of science? What are we risking in our rush toward standardized testing and the three r's. *Phi Delta Kappan* 83 (8): 601–605.

Klentschy, M. 2005a. Designing professional development opportunities for teachers that foster collaboration, capacity building, and reflective practice. *Science Educator* 14 (1): 1–8.

Klentschy, M. 2005b. Science notebook essentials: A guide to effective notebook components. *Science and Children* 43 (3): 24–27.

Klentschy, M., and E. Molina-De La Torre. 2004. Students' science notebooks and the inquiry process. In *Crossing borders in literacy and science instruction: Perspectives on theory and practice*, ed. E. W. Saul. Newark, DE: International Reading Association.

Learning Research and Development Center at the University of Pittsburgh and the National Center on Education and the Economy. 2000. *New standards: Performance standards and assessments for schools*. Pittsburgh, PA: Learning Research and Development Center.

Morino, B., and L. Hammond. 2000. Writing to learn: Science in the upper elementary bilingual classroom. Paper presented at the Conference on Acquisition of Advanced Literacy, University of California, Davis.

National Academy of Sciences. 1997. *Science for all children: A guide to improving elementary science education in your school district*. Washington, DC: National Science Resources Center, Smithsonian Institution.

Romance, N. R., and M. R. Vitale. 1992. A curriculum strategy that expands time for indepth elementary science instruction by using science-based reading strategies: Effects of a year-long study in grade 4. *Journal of Research in Science Teaching* 29: 545–554.

Romance, N. R., and M. R. Vitale. 2001. Implementing an in-depth expanded science model in elementary schools: Multi-year findings, research issues, and policy implications. *International Journal of Science Education* 23: 373–404.

Ruiz-Primo, A., M. Li, C. Ayala, and R. Shavelson. 1999. Student science journals and the evidence they provide: Classroom learning and opportunity to learn. Paper presented at the Annual Meeting of the National Association on Research and Science Teaching, Boston, MA.

Ruiz-Primo, A., M. Li, and R. Shavelson. 2004. Evaluating students' science notebooks as an assessment tool. *International Journal of Science Education* 26 (12): 1477–1506.

Saul, W., and S. Jagusch, eds. 1992. *Vital connections: Children, science and books*. Portsmouth, NH: Heinemann.

Saul, W., J. Reardon, C. Pearce, D. Dieckman, and D. Neutze. 2002. *Science workshop: Reading, writing and thinking like a scientist*. 2nd ed. Portsmouth, NH: Heinemann.

Shymansky, J. A., L. V. Hedges, and G. Woodworth. 1990. A reassessment of the effects of inquiry-based science curricula of the 60's on student performance. *Journal of Research on Science Teaching* 27 (2): 127–144.

Stigler, J. W., and J. Hiebert. 1999. *The teaching gap: Best ideas from the world's teachers for improving education in the classroom*. New York: The Free Press.

U.S. Department of Education. 2002. *Educational statistics for United States student population: 2000*. Washington, DC: U.S. Government Printing Office.

U.S. Department of Education. 2003. *Identifying and implementing educational practices supported by rigorous evidence: A user friendly guide.* Institute of Education Sciences, National Center for Education Evaluation and Regional Assistance. Washington, DC: U.S. Government Printing Office.

Valadez, J. D., and Y. Freve. 2002. A preliminary summary of the findings from a study of the effects of hands-on/inquiry-based instruction on SAT9 reading scores. Paper presented at the TERC Conference on Sustainability (*http://sustainability2002.terc.edu*).

Wise, K. C. 1996. Strategies for teaching science: What works? *The Clearing House* 32 (6): 337–338.

Science IDEAS:
Making the Case for Integrating Reading and Writing in Elementary Science as a Key Element in School Reform

Nancy R. Romance
Florida Atlantic University
Michael R. Vitale
East Carolina University

As the children at a local elementary school opened packages of seeds, they were surprised to see the great variety of seed sizes, shapes, and textures. They busily used hand lenses to closely examine the features of each seed. They entered their observations in their science logs, including the name and an illustration of each seed. One student posed the following question: "Do small seeds produce small plants and large seeds produce large plants?" This led to other questions and to the class groups' planning how they might collect evidence to test their questions.

As students carried out their investigations, they decided to gather research information about seeds—their characteristics and their patterns of growth. Students used informational text as well as other sources, such as the internet. Students had already learned how to take notes, paraphrase, and summarize what they were reading. Now, after setting up their investigations, they recorded and discussed their observations and data, relating the information to their initial claims. They focused on whether the evidence gathered supported their claims. As the lesson drew to a close, one student asked, "Which came first, the plant or the seed?"

This class example shows active science learning. There is strong evidence that "doing" science entails, logically, elements identified as inquiry-based experiences—as well as reading and writing—to build meaningful contexts that engender students' in-depth understanding of science concepts. While this may be considered an authentic approach to integrating science learning with literacy development, it is also, in fact, what scientists do. Communicating in science is inseparable from science itself and should be considered a basic in designing instruction. All too often, however, this connection is not realized in classrooms because reading and writing are viewed as separate, and often more powerful, components of the curriculum, relegating science instruction to far fewer minutes than are assigned to literacy development.

Problems Associated With Reading Comprehension and Science Learning in School Reform

It should not be a surprise to most educators that over the past 20 years of school reform student achievement in science and proficiency in reading comprehension have remained systemic problems. Results from the National Assessment of Educational Progress (NAEP) science assessments in the United States found that high school science achievement levels have decreased rather than improved (Campbell, Hombo, and Mazzeo 2000; NAEP 2000, 2003). Similarly, the Trends in International Mathematics and Science Study (TIMSS) (Schmidt et al. 2001) found U.S. science achievement weak in comparison to other advanced countries and U.S. science curriculum to be a mile wide and an inch deep. In literacy, both developmental reading (e.g., decoding, fluency) and content-area reading comprehension have remained significant educational problems (e.g., AFT 1997; Feldman 2000; National Reading Panel 2000) for low socioeconomic, disadvantaged students (see also Snow 2002) as well as for many high school students.

Lack of In-Depth Science in Elementary Schools

Because schooling is a continuous process of learning, one must consider K–8 science programs as a way to prepare students for success in high school science courses (and in reading comprehension). Yet, studies by Jones et al. (1999), Klentschy and Molina-De La Torre (2004), and Vitale, Romance, and Dolan (2002) have identified reductions in time allocated to elementary science instruction because of pressures from the reading community to increase instructional time allocated to basal reading and other state-mandated reading programs. At the same time, however, small gains in grades 3–6 reading achievement (NAEP 2003) have not been associated with a corresponding increase in academic achievement in science and literacy at the high school levels (e.g., AFT 1997; Feldman 2000; Roeber 1999). In addressing this decline, there are several perspectives that can be offered to make a logical case for relating elementary science learning to high school achievement.

The first perspective focuses on learning. Specifically, research suggests that student prior knowledge is a major determinant of successful learning in high school science courses (Bransford, Brown, and Cocking 1999; Hirsch 1996, 2003). When students do not have the prior knowledge (and understanding) required for such courses, then teachers are faced with the problem of reducing the scope and depth of their science courses in order to provide remedial instruction. Second, the resulting remedial instruction must, of necessity, focus on the minimum skills and prerequisite knowledge that students did not acquire in preceding grades. This leads to a continuing downward adjustment to what should be an articulated sequence of increasingly rich science courses across grades 9–12. Instead, the scope of learning opportunities for all students is limited because of the lowered ceiling on what can be effectively taught and learned. In effect, high schools are experiencing the negative consequences associated with the reduction or elimination of instructional time devoted to elementary science. Elementary students no longer have opportunities to interact with rich, motivating science instruction and science-related reading materials that are the foundation for success in science at the middle and high school levels.

What Does Science Integration With Literacy Development Look Like?

Recently there has been growing interest focused on understanding ways in which science learning and literacy development can be successfully integrated to promote in-depth learning experiences for all students. For this to happen, the school curriculum must provide time for children to do science as well as read and write science. Within this context, students can investigate to find answers to questions they have, address specific science concepts (and topics), and access multiple reading sources, including informational texts, internet materials, biographies, and, where appropriate, science texts. In doing science, students must be able to communicate their ideas, to develop cognitive skills and reasoning ability, and to gather evidence to support claims and draw conclusions. Instruction must include opportunities for students to engage in lively discussion and questioning as well as to learn how to represent their ideas through writing, journaling, and creative notebooks. Specifically, such classrooms are print-rich environments where inquiry-based experiences are complemented with numerous opportunities for students to engage in guided and independent informational reading (and writing) as a way to increase their reading comprehension ability and enhance their learning.

There are additional benefits for learners associated with the use of informational text in elementary school that further warrant its inclusion in instruction. For example, the use of informational text is inherently interesting to most students, and for some, it is preferred reading. Motivated children will choose to read many books on a specific topic, including books that may be considered more difficult. In doing so, these children satisfy their own curiosity and are motivated by their own interests. Classroom libraries rich with nonfiction books allow students to make their own reading selections and read across multiple sources. Furthermore, such active, in-depth engagement in learning and doing science builds intellectual capital (Hirsch 1996) in the form of knowledge of the world and rich vocabulary that serve as the basis for success in later science courses. Connecting hands-on learning experiences with multiple reading sources for science, combined with opportunities for writing in science, provides a cumulative context for in-depth science learning and development of reading comprehension (and writing) proficiency.

Effectiveness of Integrating Literacy Development in Science Learning at Upper-Elementary Levels

For those seeking a research-based rationale for increasing time devoted to science instruction at the elementary level, there is a growing body of evidence demonstrating the impact of integrating reading (and writing) in science learning on both science and reading comprehension achievement. Research by Romance and Vitale (1992, 2001), Guthrie et al. (2001, 2002,

2004), Magnusson and Palinscar (2004), and Klentschy and Molina-De La Torre (2004) provides cumulative evidence supporting the effectiveness of using an integrated approach in elementary classrooms.

Romance and Vitale (1992) began their investigation with three teachers who implemented the integrated Science IDEAS model in their fourth-grade classrooms. The Science IDEAS model, described below, is an integrated instructional model that links doing science with reading and writing informational text during a two-hour daily block of time. The results of the initial investigation implemented in grade 4 were very positive. In comparison to demographically similar controls, students participating in daily two-hour Science IDEAS instruction obtained significantly higher levels of achievement in both science and reading comprehension as measured by nationally normed standardized tests (adjusted mean difference in Metropolitan Achievement Test [MAT] science = .95 GE; adjusted mean difference in Iowa Test of Basic Skills [ITBS] reading comprehension = .32 GE). Additionally, compared to controls, Science IDEAS students were more motivated and displayed significantly more positive attitudes and self-confidence in learning science and reading.

Across the next five years, implementation of Science IDEAS was extended to 50 teachers and 1,200 students in grade 3–5 classrooms that had more ethnically diverse student populations and a wider range of academic levels (from above average to severely at-risk). The achievement results (Romance and Vitale 2001) in science and reading comprehension were similar to the original study as was the finding of consistent patterns of positive affective attitudes (attitude toward learning, self-confidence in learning).

Teachers implementing the model were also very positive. Romance and Vitale (2001) confirmed that teachers implementing Science IDEAS were professionally more satisfied than they had been when they taught science and reading as separate subjects. The teachers indicated that Science IDEAS more actively involved students in meaningful learning. Similar findings from a recent study, reported by Vitale and Romance (2005), indicated that grade 5 Science IDEAS students outperformed students in traditional basal reading programs as measured by the ITBS reading and science subsections.

The work of Guthrie et al. (2001, 2002, 2004) has also shown how the integration of literacy practices in science learning increases reading comprehension achievement for students at all achievement levels. In his model, CORI (Conceptually Oriented Reading Instruction), students engage in an extended unit of science study that includes multiple hands-on experiences related to the theme and an abundance of interesting texts to read and collaborative activities. Magnusson and Palincsar (2004) have also demonstrated how in-depth science instruction that includes opportunities for reading and writing as well as doing science improves student achievement in science and reading comprehension. The work of Klentschy and Molina-De La Torre (2004) emphasized active learning in science and the extensive use of science notebooks in elementary and middle school classrooms. Results indicated that each year students were in the program, achievement in science improved.

The combined research findings of Romance and Vitale, Guthrie et al., Magnusson and Palincsar, and Klentschy and Molina-De La Torre clearly indicate that in-depth science instruction produces increased student achievement and interest in science and reading. In each case, these researchers have shown how active learning and print-rich environments can serve as a meaningful context in which to promote reading comprehension strategies. In fact, such strategies are best learned in and readily transferable to the context of the conceptual knowledge being learned. Logically, if one considers reading comprehension as a form of understanding, then it is best developed where students possess the adequate prior conceptual knowledge to construct new and deeper understanding. This perspective is in stark contrast to current reform practices in which reading instruction (focused on narrative, basal reading materials) displaces science.

Science IDEAS Model as an Alternative to Traditional Reading/Language Arts Instruction.

Science IDEAS, an integrated instructional model, served as a viable replacement for more traditional reading and language arts/literacy programs being implemented in many classrooms. The Science IDEAS Model (see Figure 1) has six key instructional elements: hands-on, inquiry-based science activities/projects; reading informational text/trade books/internet science materials; writing/journaling about science; propositional concept mapping within a daily two-hour time block; application activities; and using or reviewing prior content knowledge.

In building curricular units or themes, core science concepts and relationships within the unit serve as the framework for identifying, organizing, and sequencing the different activities in which students engage. And because all learning tasks are related to the core concepts, each experience (especially hands-on activities) contributes to and sustains the desired

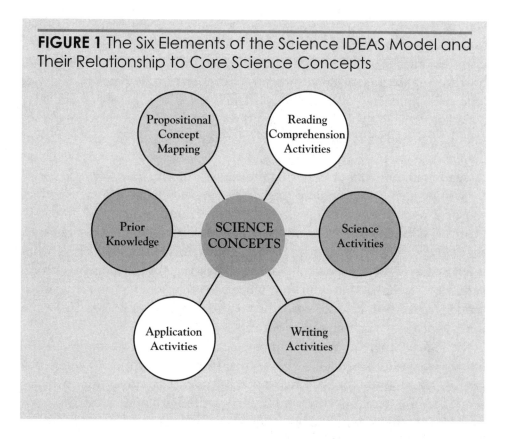

FIGURE 1 The Six Elements of the Science IDEAS Model and Their Relationship to Core Science Concepts

science learning outcomes. As a result, students are motivated to engage further in the multiple opportunities for reading informational books and for reading more purposefully. This additional reading enables teachers to guide the development of reading comprehension proficiency and associated language arts skills in an authentic fashion. Thus, as students enhance their own conceptual understanding, they are able to relate inquiry-based experiences to the underlying scientific principles that explain them.

Science IDEAS as a Knowledge-Based Instructional Model for Teaching and Learning

A concept map on evaporation represents an instructional model for teaching science with reading and writing. In effect, the illustration in Figure 2 shows how the propositional concept map (see Romance and Vitale 2001) on evaporation serves as a conceptual framework for organizing and sequencing a set of instructional activities to build meaningful student understanding. As you examine the concept map, you can see how teachers relate all instructional activities to support in-depth student understanding of the concept of evaporation. The ovals represent a sample instructional sequence illustrating how to amplify student understanding of evaporation. For example, as you follow the numbered ovals, you can see how prior knowledge and everyday experiences begin the lesson. This is followed by investigations, writing/journaling, and reading informational text. Finally, the teacher guides both student construction of a concept map and its use with expository writing. Upon close examination, it is evident that the concept map can serve as a blueprint for writing anywhere from four to six paragraphs including the details from the investigations. In planning science instruction in a manner similar to Figure 2, IDEAS teachers are able to follow a natural inquiry-oriented style that (a) continually emphasizes (and re-emphasizes) for students how what is learned over the sequence of different learning tasks (including hands-on activities) results in additional knowledge and understanding and (b) consistently guides students to see what they have learned as representative of the underlying (or overarching) core concepts.

In Figure 2, the concept map can be considered a sample planning guide. The lesson sequence could range from two to five days, depending on the amount of reading and writing integration built into the sequence. Remember, curriculum integration provides students with multiple learning experiences focused on the concept of evaporation. The example below, therefore, represents only one possible instructional scenario that would follow from the Science IDEAS instructional architecture. It illustrates how carefully planned curriculum integration can produce desired learning outcomes:

Activity 1—Prior Knowledge. The lesson begins with accessing relevant prior curricular knowledge, making certain that students understand phase change. This serves as a review.

Activity 2—Real-World Examples. The teacher engages students in a discussion of authentic examples involving evaporation (e.g., water droplets on a car in morning, a puddle of water on a concrete sidewalk, boiling water in a pot). Students are asked to explain their observations in terms of phase change. Ideas are recorded for later use. Concurrently, the teacher enriches the discussion by using the word *evaporation* to represent the process all the real-world scenarios have in common.

FIGURE 2 Curriculum Concept Map for Organizing and Sequencing Instructional Activities in Science, Reading Comprehension, and Writing

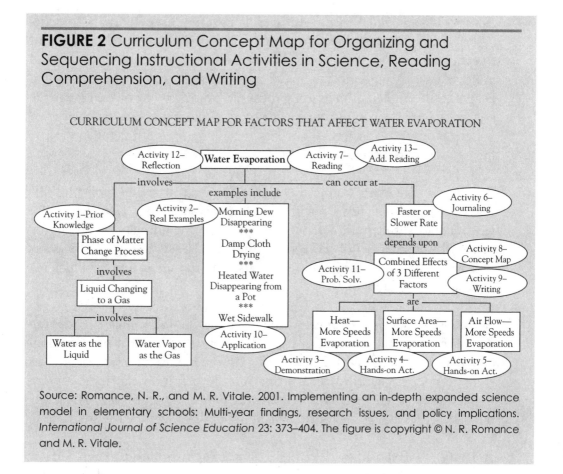

CURRICULUM CONCEPT MAP FOR FACTORS THAT AFFECT WATER EVAPORATION

Source: Romance, N. R., and M. R. Vitale. 2001. Implementing an in-depth expanded science model in elementary schools: Multi-year findings, research issues, and policy implications. *International Journal of Science Education* 23: 373–404. The figure is copyright © N. R. Romance and M. R. Vitale.

Activity 3—Hands-On Science Demonstration. Many different types of activities can be done. For example, one might use a wet paper towel and ask how one could speed up drying it. Demonstrations and open-ended investigations can occur at this juncture. Students record their observations and explanations in their science journals. The teacher then refers students back to evaporation examples (Activity 2).

Activity 4 and Activity 5—Student Hands-On Activities. Using two equally damp paper towels, one crumpled into a ball and one spread out, students explore other factors that speed evaporation. Students discuss findings and write their own conclusions in their science notebooks. The teacher refers students back to initial evaporation examples (Activity 2), to discuss the possible role of surface area and moving air on evaporation.

Activity 6—Journal Writing Activity. For Activities 3, 4, and 5, students describe in words and illustrate with graphics what happened with regard to evaporation. Next, students select one or all of the three activities and use evidence to support claims and relate experiences to the concept of evaporation. Students have numerous opportunities to practice language arts skills while writing about their observations, reflecting on their own understanding of the science concepts, recalling important detail, and writing expository passages.

Activity 7—Reading Comprehension. Whole-group guided reading follows. Students take turns reading passages about evaporation, while the teacher guides student discussion of the passage (including relating the passage to the previous set of classroom activities). The teacher guides students in learning how to paraphrase, relate concepts and ideas, and conclude using a summary paragraph.

Activity 8—Teacher-Guided Student Propositional Concept Mapping Activity. The teacher guides whole-class construction of a propositional concept map including the factors affecting evaporation. The teacher has students refer to key words and illustrations in their journals as well as from their reading as references for building the concept map. (Note: The original map serves as a guide for the teacher and is not seen by the students.)

Activity 9—Expository Writing From Propositional Concept Map. Teacher guides student use of the concept map constructed in Activity 8 as a blueprint for writing about evaporation. Each section of the concept map logically represents a set of related ideas, illustrating how a paragraph is constructed using a set of related ideas. The concept map helps students focus and organize their writing and provides an example of important and sufficient detail (claims, evidence, and observations) to support their understanding.

Activity 10—Out-of-School Application Activity. Students identify examples of evaporation (e.g., clothes in a dryer, food in a microwave, using a hair dryer), and learn how to interpret each in terms of the evidence (factors) they gathered from their previous investigations and their effect on evaporation. Students also learn how to use journals to record their data and explanations (claims, evidence, and arguments) for class discussion.

Activity 11—Problem-Solving Hands-On Activity. Students collaboratively solve additional problems related to factors that influence the speed of evaporation

Activity 12—Relating New Knowledge to Prior Knowledge Activity. The teacher displays the chart with key words from students' *original* ideas from the prior knowledge activity (Activity 1) and the concept map developed in Activity 8. The teacher guides reflective class discussion on how student knowledge has developed and become more organized.

Activity 13—Additional Reading Activities. The teacher selects additional reading materials for students to summarize in journals and share with the class.

Again, it is important to remember that the preceding is only a sample. Teachers could easily plan a wide variety of other sequences of activities in developing an instructional plan. In addition, virtually any activity could have been transformed into an assessment task rather than a learning task (Vitale and Romance 2005). While not discussed in this chapter, the Science IDEAS model encompasses both the six major elements illustrated above and six complementary forms of assessment (Vitale and Romance 1995, 2000, 2005, forthcoming).

Conceptual Foundations of the Science IDEAS Model

Underlying the Science IDEAS model are findings from cognitive science and applied learning theory (e.g., Bransford, Brown, and Cocking 1999). Science IDEAS can be described as a strong, knowledge-based instructional model because it requires (a) the explicit representation of the knowledge to be taught and learned in the form of core concept relationships and (b) subsequent explicit linkage of all instructional activities and assessment approaches chosen by teachers to the same core concept framework.

Ideas offered by Bransford, Brown, and Cocking (1999) and elaborated by Vitale and Romance (2006) offer an in-depth way of thinking about Science IDEAS as an instructional model that can be applied to any set of conceptually oriented concepts in science. First, the model emphasizes core concept relationships as the primary organizational focus of instruction. Second, the model emphasizes mastery of core concepts as a form of expertise that is the primary goal of instruction. Third, and often neglected in instruction, the model dynamically provides students with extensive and repeated practice on core concepts by using a variety of different core-concept-focused instructional activities (e.g., reading, hands-on activities, writing, propositional concept mapping) to engender in-depth conceptual understanding. That is, the varied learning activities are always related back to core concepts by students.

Rationale for Improving School Reform by Expanding Time for Science in Elementary Schools

In addressing the critical issues of quality science teaching and learning and how to increase time in elementary classrooms for that to occur, the preceding provides science educators with a strong rationale. Consider how expanding the time for in-depth science teaching can improve high-priority student achievement goals within a school reform and accountability framework through a dual focus: (a) the improvement of student general reading comprehension as measured by state- or nationally normed tests and (b) the development of the prior knowledge students need to be successful in high school science courses. Both of these are significant educational reform priorities that have not been adequately met.

In offering a rationale for curricular policy change, there are two other related factors that warrant consideration. First, as part of No Child Left Behind (NCLB), states are introducing state-mandated science testing in elementary (and other) grades. This NCLB component suggests that policymakers need to recognize elementary science understanding as an important reform priority (one that so far has been largely ignored). However, in states that plan to test science at the elementary level, schools are unlikely to have sufficient instructional time to address science content and reading comprehension separately. As such, schools need to become aware of the research supporting how their combined focus produces even stronger achievement gains across both curricular areas. Therefore, from a policy perspective, addressing reading comprehension within science instruction would become an attractive alternative to support high-stakes testing outcomes.

Second, simply adding some nonfiction reading materials to a basal reading program does not equate to in-depth science learning (as represented by the Science IDEAS model) or literacy development. In fact, research suggests that reading *any content-based science* materials is preferable to basal reading materials (e.g., Guthrie and Ozgundor 2002). However, science educators must understand that simply obtaining better results than basal reading programs in grades 3–5 is not sufficient. That is, obtaining better results than a basal reading program does not imply the development of the level of reading comprehension proficiency required for success in high

CHAPTER 15

school science. Nor does it imply that students possess the prior knowledge in science necessary for success in high school. Rather, only through in-depth science instruction do students develop the understanding that facilitates success in high school science courses, including being able to comprehend content-area texts.

Third, it is important to recognize that more reading time devoted to narrative, noninformational materials or adding more reading skills to the teaching of science at any level disregards the importance of prior conceptual knowledge as the basis for comprehension.

A final matter has to do with the tactic of gathering evaluative evidence to support pursuing the reform of elementary science programs (or more broadly, elementary school curriculum). In this regard, the most direct form of supporting data are cross-sectional student achievement trends (including reading comprehension) by grade level, from grades 2 or 3 (or earlier) through high school (at least grade 10). In addition to presenting data in aggregate form, the data should be disaggregated in terms of (a) different levels of initial achievement in grade 2 or 3, (b) student socioeconomic levels, and (c) race and/or possibly gender. The presentation of such achievement trends provides an empirical means to link existing curricular policy at the elementary level with the eventual problems in high school as a framework for justifying the rationale to increase the instructional time allocated to elementary science in grades 3–5. Finally, it may well be that present reflections on the persistent problems in educational reform may provide science educators with the opportunity to expand the role of science instruction at the elementary level on a long-term basis.

References

American Federation of Teachers (AFT). 1997. *Making standards matter 1997. An annual fifty state report on efforts to raise academic standards*. Washington, DC: AFT.

Bransford, J. D., A. L. Brown, and R. R. Cocking. 1999. *How people learn: Brain, mind, experience, and school*. Washington, DC: National Academy Press.

Campbell, J. R., C. M. Hombo, and J. Mazzeo. 2000. *NAEP 1999 trends in academic progress: Three decades of student performance*. Washington, DC: National Center for Education Statistics.

Feldman, S. 2000. Standards are working: But states and districts need to make some midcourse corrections. *American Educator* 24 (3): 5–7.

Guthrie, J. T., and S. Ozgundor. 2002. Instructional contexts for reading engagement. In *Comprehension instruction: Research-based best practices*, eds. C. C. Block and M. Pressley. New York: Guilford Press.

Guthrie, J. T., W. D. Schafer, C. Von Stecker, and T. Alban. 2001. Contributions of instructional practices to reading achievement in a statewide reading achievement program. *Journal of Educational Research* 93 (4): 211–225.

Guthrie, J. T., A. Wigfield, and K. C. Perencevich. 2004. *Motivating reading comprehension.* Mahwah, NJ: Lawrence Erlbaum.

Hirsch, E. D. 1996. *The schools we need. And why we don't have them.* New York: Doubleday.

Hirsch, E. D. 2003. Reading comprehension requires knowledge of words and the world. *American Educator* 27 (1): 10–23.

Jones, M. G., B. D. Jones, B. Hardin, L. Chapman, T. Yarbrough, and M. Davis. 1999. The impact of high-stakes testing on teachers and students in North Carolina. *Phi Delta Kappan* 81: 199–203.

Klentschy, M. P., and E. Molina-De La Torre. 2004. Students' science notebooks and the inquiry process. In *Crossing borders in literacy and science instruction: Perspectives on theory and practice*, ed. E. W. Saul, 340–354. Newark, DE: International Reading Association.

Magnusson, S. J., and A. S. Palincsar. 2004. Learning from text designed to model scientific thinking in inquiry-based instruction. In *Crossing borders in literacy and science instruction: Perspectives on theory and practice*, ed. E. W. Saul, 316–339. Newark, DE: International Reading Association.

National Assessment of Educational Progress (NAEP). *The Nation's Report Card: Science 2000.* (*http://nces.ed.gov/nationsreportcard/*)

National Assessment of Educational Progress (NAEP). *The Nation's Report Card: Reading 2003.* (*http://nces.ed.gov/nationsreportcard/*)

National Reading Panel. 2000. *Teaching children to read: An evidence-based assessment of scientific research literature on reading and its implications for reading instruction.* Jessup, MD: National Institute for Literacy.

Roeber, E. D. 1999. Standards initiatives and American educational reform. In *Handbook of educational policy*, ed. G. J. Cizek. San Diego: Academic Press.

Romance, N. R., and M. R. Vitale. 1992. A curriculum strategy that expands time for indepth elementary science instruction by using science-based reading strategies: Effects of a year-long study in grade 4. *Journal of Research in Science Teaching* 29: 545–554.

Romance, N. R., and M. R. Vitale. 2001. Implementing an in-depth expanded science model in elementary schools: Multi-year findings, research issues, and policy implications. *International Journal of Science Education* 23: 373–404.

Schmidt, W. H., C. C. McKnight, R. T. Houang, H. C. Wang, D. E. Wiley, L. S. Cogan, and R. C. Wolfe. 2001. *Why schools matter: A cross-national comparison of curriculum and learning.* San Francisco: Jossey-Bass.

Snow, C. E. 2002. *Reading for understanding: Toward a research and development program in reading comprehension.* Santa Monica, CA: RAND.

Vitale, M. R., and N. R. Romance. 1995. Technology-based assessment in science: Issues underlying teacher advocacy of testing policy. *Journal of Science Education and Technology* 5 (2): 35–44.

Vitale, M. R., and N. R. Romance. 2000. Portfolios in science assessment: A knowledge-based model for classroom practice. In *Assessing science understanding: A human constructivist view*, eds. J. J. Mintzes, J. H. Wandersee, and J .D. Novak, 168–197. San Diego: Academic Press.

Vitale, M. R., and N. R. Romance. 2005. *An experimental exploration of science- vs. traditionally-oriented reading/language arts instruction as mediators of the differential effectiveness of reading comprehension strategy training on student achievement in reading and science.* Technical Report 2.03, MURMSI Project. Boca Raton, FL: Florida Atlantic University.

Vitale, M. R., and N. R. Romance. 2006. Research in science education: An interdisciplinary perspective. In *Teaching science in the 21st century*, eds. J. Rhoton and P. Shane, 329–351. Arlington, VA: NSTA Press.

Vitale, M. R., and N. R. Romance. Forthcoming. A knowledge-based framework for classroom assessment of student science understanding. In *Assessment in Science: Practical experiences and education research*, eds. M. McMahon, P. Simmons, R. Sommers, D. DeBaets, and F. Crawley. Arlington, VA: NSTA Press.

Vitale, M. R., N. R. Romance, and M. Dolan. 2002. *A rationale for improving school reform by expanding time for science teaching: Implications and opportunities for changing curricular policy and practice in elementary schools.* Presented at the Annual Meeting of the National Association for Research in Science Teaching, New Orleans, LA.

CHAPTER 16

The Administrator's Role in Supporting Science and Literacy in Classrooms

Michael P. Klentschy and Patricia M. Maruca
El Centro, California, School District

Administrators play an important role in supporting science and literacy in classrooms. Support comes from a cohesive team of administrators at the district and school levels as school districts move toward institutionalization of best practices. The administrators at the district level take the lead in the design of new programs and provide ongoing support for schools in their implementation. Administrators at the school level, primarily principals, take the lead in providing ongoing support and feedback to classroom teachers to ensure a high level of implementation. This chapter will focus on one such team approach that has been in operation since 1996 through the Vallé Imperial Project in Science (VIPS) in Imperial County, California.

Imperial County is located in the southeastern corner of California along the U.S. border with Mexico, approximately 120 miles from San Diego. Most Imperial County residents have strong cultural and linguistic ties to Mexico and the county ranks among the highest in poverty of all counties in California. The population of the school system is predominately Hispanic (81%), with approximately 11% Caucasian, 5% African American, 1% Asian, and 1% Native American. More than 50% of students in the county are English language learners.

District-Level Support

At the district level, administrators play a critical role on a leadership team in the design of a systemic science instructional program. This systemic program addresses five critical, interrelated elements associated with successful programs by the National Academy of Sciences (1997): high-quality curriculum, sustained professional development, materials support, administrative and community support, and assessment and evaluation. The VIPS instructional model implemented in Imperial County is based on the National Academy of Sciences model.

High-Quality Curriculum

Administrators at both the district and school levels play an important role in the selection of curriculum that meets defined criteria. A high-quality curriculum is one that is developmentally appropriate and research-based. It is also one that leads the students to discover and understand the big ideas in science, as opposed to "factoids." A high-quality curriculum is balanced, with opportunities for students to be engaged in physical, Earth, and life science each year. Students study three to four major instructional units each year. The units focus on the notion that big ideas are attained through engagement in a series of activities that are integrated and developmentally sequenced so that students will develop an understanding of sub-concepts. When put together, the sub-concepts will lead to big ideas in science. The storyline depicted in Figure 1 is an example of such a unit.

A high-quality curriculum also provides opportunities for students to develop science process skills. These skills—exploration, investigation, inquiry, questioning, testing a hypothesis, collecting data, and analyzing data—are very similar to literacy skills. The Learning Research and Development Center at the University of Pittsburgh and the National Center on Education and the Economy through their New Standards Project have made a comparison of science process skills and literacy skills (2002). Figure 2 provides that comparison.

Sustained Professional Development

The second element in this design focuses on sustained professional development for teachers. In the Vallé Imperial Project in Science, there are 10 critical elements for school districts to consider when planning professional programs (Klentschy and Molina-De La Torre 2002):

FIGURE 1 "Mixtures and Solutions" Storyline Example

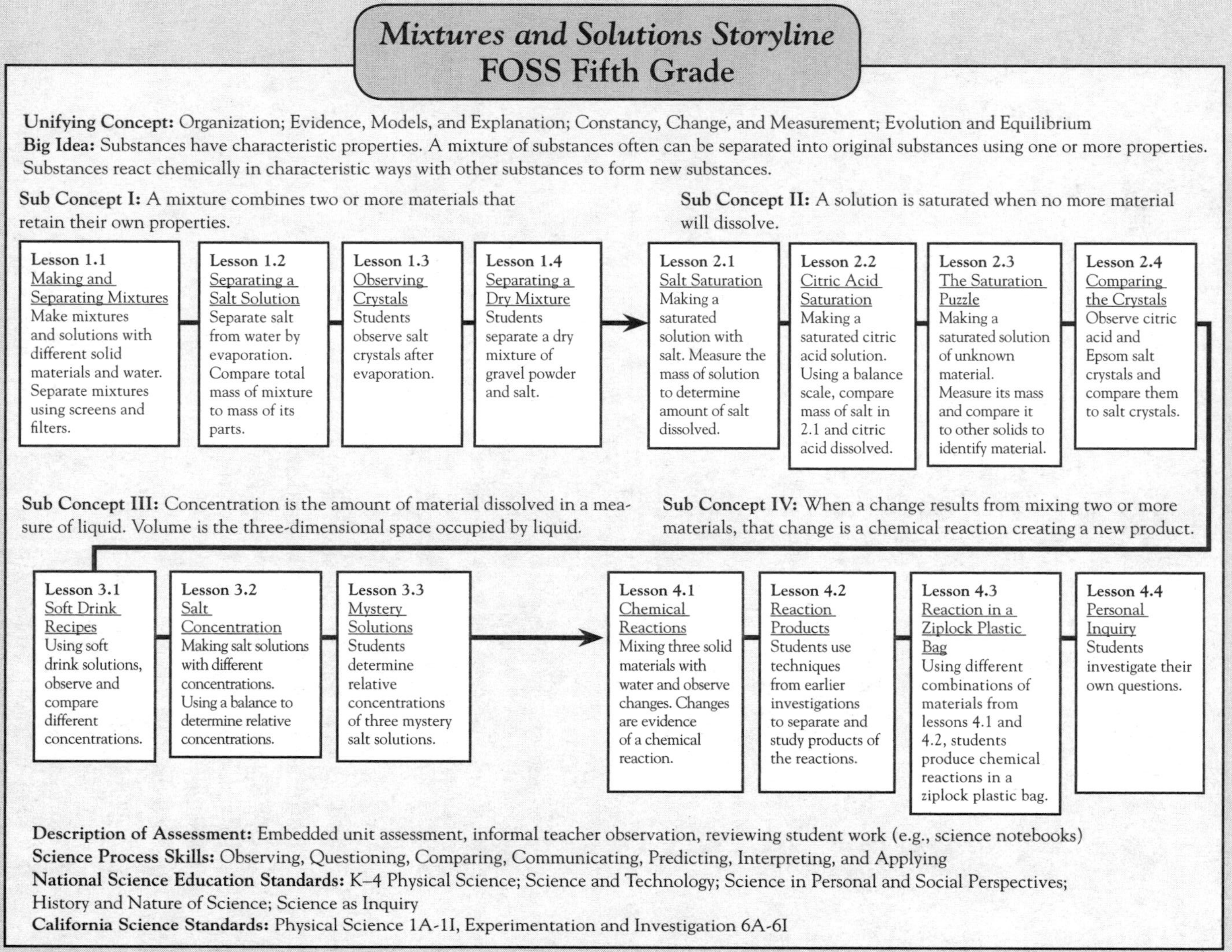

Mixtures and Solutions Storyline
FOSS Fifth Grade

Unifying Concept: Organization; Evidence, Models, and Explanation; Constancy, Change, and Measurement; Evolution and Equilibrium

Big Idea: Substances have characteristic properties. A mixture of substances often can be separated into original substances using one or more properties. Substances react chemically in characteristic ways with other substances to form new substances.

Sub Concept I: A mixture combines two or more materials that retain their own properties.

Lesson 1.1
Making and Separating Mixtures
Make mixtures and solutions with different solid materials and water. Separate mixtures using screens and filters.

Lesson 1.2
Separating a Salt Solution
Separate salt from water by evaporation. Compare total mass of mixture to mass of its parts.

Lesson 1.3
Observing Crystals
Students observe salt crystals after evaporation.

Lesson 1.4
Separating a Dry Mixture
Students separate a dry mixture of gravel powder and salt.

Sub Concept II: A solution is saturated when no more material will dissolve.

Lesson 2.1
Salt Saturation
Making a saturated solution with salt. Measure the mass of solution to determine amount of salt dissolved.

Lesson 2.2
Citric Acid Saturation
Making a saturated citric acid solution. Using a balance scale, compare mass of salt in 2.1 and citric acid dissolved.

Lesson 2.3
The Saturation Puzzle
Making a saturated solution of unknown material. Measure its mass and compare it to other solids to identify material.

Lesson 2.4
Comparing the Crystals
Observe citric acid and Epsom salt crystals and compare them to salt crystals.

Sub Concept III: Concentration is the amount of material dissolved in a measure of liquid. Volume is the three-dimensional space occupied by liquid.

Lesson 3.1
Soft Drink Recipes
Using soft drink solutions, observe and compare different concentrations.

Lesson 3.2
Salt Concentration
Making salt solutions with different concentrations. Using a balance to determine relative concentrations.

Lesson 3.3
Mystery Solutions
Students determine relative concentrations of three mystery salt solutions.

Sub Concept IV: When a change results from mixing two or more materials, that change is a chemical reaction creating a new product.

Lesson 4.1
Chemical Reactions
Mixing three solid materials with water and observe changes. Changes are evidence of a chemical reaction.

Lesson 4.2
Reaction Products
Students use techniques from earlier investigations to separate and study products of the reactions.

Lesson 4.3
Reaction in a Ziplock Plastic Bag
Using different combinations of materials from lessons 4.1 and 4.2, students produce chemical reactions in a ziplock plastic bag.

Lesson 4.4
Personal Inquiry
Students investigate their own questions.

Description of Assessment: Embedded unit assessment, informal teacher observation, reviewing student work (e.g., science notebooks)

Science Process Skills: Observing, Questioning, Comparing, Communicating, Predicting, Interpreting, and Applying

National Science Education Standards: K–4 Physical Science; Science and Technology; Science in Personal and Social Perspectives; History and Nature of Science; Science as Inquiry

California Science Standards: Physical Science 1A-1I, Experimentation and Investigation 6A-6I

Source: Adapted by Michael Klentschy from the FOSS (Full Option Science System) Science Curriculum, Lawrence Hall of Science, University of California, Berkeley.

FIGURE 2 A Comparison of Literacy Skills and Science Process Skills

Literacy Skills	Science Process Skills
note details	observe and retain small details
compare and contrast	compare and contrast
predict	_____ will happen because _____ If _____ then _____
sequence of events	process of logic and analysis
link cause and effect	what causes things to react in a particular way
distinguish fact from opinion	the use of evidence to support claims
link words with precise meanings through experiences	develop operational definitions of a concept
make inferences	make inferences based on observation and evidence
draw conclusions	draw conclusions by combining data from various sources

Source: Adapted from Learning Research and Development Center, University of Pittsburgh, and the National Center on Education and the Economy. 2000. *New standards: Performance and assessments for schools.* Pittsburgh: Learning Research and Development Center.

1. Link between preservice and actual classroom practice
2. Institutes to deepen content understanding
3. Opportunities to deepen pedagogical skills
4. In-classroom support and coaching
5. Leadership development
6. Materials support
7. Time for collaboration and networking
8. Applications of technology
9. Workshops focusing on student work as the centerpiece
10. Opportunities to refine and reflect on instructional delivery through lesson study

The program of sustained professional development follows a sequence that runs from preservice to inservice to advanced training. Inservice offerings include capacity building, institutes, debriefings, and lesson study groups. The program also includes in-classroom support, opportunities to develop teacher leadership, and opportunities to obtain advanced degrees through partnerships with universities. The notion of systemic reform and systemic development for teachers from a professional development perspective is exemplified in the Imperial Valley Science Project through a long-term partnership for teacher professional development. This partnership is composed of the 14 member districts of Imperial County, Imperial Valley College, San Diego State University-Imperial Campus, California Science Subject Matter Project, the Imperial Valley California Math Science Partnership, and an association with the California Institute of Technology.

The professional development design model used is one that was developed by Loucks-Horsley et al. (1998) and has been employed by administrators in districts and schools across the country. The first professional development program component in the model is university preservice, when preservice teachers are given coordinated experiences in science content, pedagogy, and student learning through their student teaching under the guidance of university supervisors. These experiences are aligned with the same basic principles that teachers will experience when actually teaching in Imperial County schools. This process has been jointly established through the collaboration and partnership of the Imperial County school districts and San Diego State University-Imperial Valley Campus.

The second level of training that teachers receive is through the district inservice that is implemented over a two-year period. Teachers, who are introduced to two science units a year, work in grade-level teams during the inservice training, which is led by teacher leaders, scientist volunteers, and staff members of the Imperial Valley California Math Science Partnership. In addition, inservice sessions are held at an advanced level. These summer institute sessions focus on advanced content training. Through the partnership, teachers participate in 40- to 80-hour science content courses specifically aligned to the California Science Content Standards. Teachers are also offered other institutes focusing on English language development (ELD) and literacy connections, as well as institutes on assessment and the analysis of student work.

The use of student science notebooks as a means of making meaning from classroom instruction is emphasized in all inservice activities. The

VIPS professional development model links science and literacy through the notebooks within an inquiry-based model of science instruction. Use of the notebooks is based on the belief that students should be provided with an opportunity to develop "voice" in their personal construction of meaning of science phenomena (Klentschy and Molina-De La Torre 2004). In addition, due to the high student population of English language learners, ELD strategies are integrated into science instruction in order to provide students with expanded opportunities to learn through the development of science academic content language. Reading comprehension strategies are also integrated into the professional development programs. Research-based comprehension strategies (Zimmerman and Hutchins 2003; Harvey and Goudvis 2000) are used in the context of making meaning from text.

A wide range of professional opportunities is also provided to teachers at the school level. For example, classroom support comes through a coaching model. Trained coaches and facilitators regularly visit schools to provide coaching and feedback to teachers.

Because the success of any professional development program is the legacy it leaves behind in terms of trained teacher leadership, an extensive leadership development component is also a part of the inservice program. Topics related to curriculum support, curriculum integration, institutes and seminars, monthly networking, facilitation and presentation skills, language institutes, assessment institutes, and inquiry are explored by current and future teacher leaders.

Administrators from district and school levels provide time, resources, and support for the design, implementation, and follow-up of a sustained program of professional development for classroom teachers.

Materials Support

The third critical element of successful programs is materials support. The Science and Mathematics Resources Center in El Centro, California, serves as the hub for the entire county. It is where the Imperial Valley California Math Science Partnership and the Vallé Imperial Project in Science are based. It functions as a countywide materials center and professional development center. As a materials center, it is where all of the science materials for the county are manufactured, ordered, inventoried, refurbished, and redelivered back out to the schools. A cost-sharing process is used whereby the cost for materials development, purchase, and refurbishment is shared by all participating districts. The center is staffed by a director, two media technicians, and an administrative clerk. The media technicians not only refurbish and remanufacture the instructional materials, but also serve as videographers who tape classroom lessons that are used for lesson study discussion and as exemplars of best practice. All materials and units are bar coded to make inventories current to facilitate delivery and pickup.

Administrative and Community Support

The fourth element is administrative and community support. This element contains several components:

- administrative training
- recruitment and training of professional science volunteers
- parent education
- family science nights
- presentations to school boards
- media relations

Each of these components is important to the overall design of a systemic program. The underlying principle of each is not only to build capacity for principals and other school administrators, but also to inform and garner support from parents, community leaders, local school boards and the local media. Also important is the recruitment and training of science professionals as volunteers who assist in professional development, model questioning and inquiry, and serve as community spokespersons for the science program.

Assessment and Evaluation

Assessment focuses on three components: performance tasks or products that students complete with each unit, standardized tests (both norm referenced and those based on state standards), and a student science notebook for each unit. These components result in a portfolio that is analyzed not only at the school and individual classroom levels but also from systemwide and countywide perspectives. An external evaluator provides feedback to the program's leaders to help them make modifications.

As a means for engendering significant growth in student achievement in science, reading, and writing (Amaral, Garrison, and Klentschy 2002; Jorgenson and Vanosdall 2002; Saul et al. 2002; Klentschy and Molina-De La Torre 2004), science notebooks are an important vehicle for extending student literacy and play an important part in the documented success of this program.

School-Level Support

At the school site, principals and other school administrators play an important instructional leadership role in the supervision and support of high-quality science instruction programs. Districts and systems must provide professional development opportunities for principals to learn more about science and literacy integration. To begin that process, districts must define the principals' instructional leadership role in science. Districts must also examine the barriers that principals and other school administrators must overcome to assume the role of instructional leader in science education. Historically, these barriers have been issues of time, their own backgrounds and experiences in science, their districts' expectations and instructional focuses, and the expectations of the local community. Often, school principals are faced with competing priorities, none of which will be successful.

The district must begin with an analysis of the type of support principals need. Support for the principal comes in two forms: (1) a coherent program of science instruction provided by the district and (2) a professional development program especially designed for principals. The professional development program for principals must consider the following elements in its design:

- The science content and skills that are expected to be taught in the district's classrooms
- The pedagogical practices to be used for implementation
- The underlying theories or research behind these practices
- Strategies to improve fidelity of implementation
- Lesson observation and feedback
- Student work as an indicator of success
- Principal networking
- Media and community relations

To this end, VIPS has developed a systemic program of professional development especially for principals and other school administrators. The program, Hand Lenses on Science, has been implemented with principals and other administrators in Imperial County and in Wake County, North Carolina (see the Appendix for the Hand Lenses on Science observation form).

Hand Lenses on Science consists of eight half-day segments. The focuses of the segments are as follows:

- State-required science content standards
- Science content associated with the state content standards

- Literacy connections through reading and writing in science, oral discourse, and ELD strategies
- Video study
- Teacher feedback
- Analysis of student work
- Fidelity of classroom implementation
- Administrative support
- Media and community relations

A typical professional development session contains most of the above components. All sessions begin with an explanation of science education in a standards-based world. Principals are referred to *Making Standards Work* (Reeves 2002) to provide focus for the session. Eight critical issues of planning effective standards-based instruction are addressed:

1. Power Standards (Which standards are essential?)
2. "Unwrap" the Standards (What is the science content?)
3. Determine the Big Ideas (How do numbers 1 and 2 lead to big ideas in science?)
4. Write the Essential Questions (What do I want students to know?)
5. Plan an Engaging Scenario or "Hook" (How are students best engaged?)
6. Decide the Learning Tasks (What activities can be planned to answer the questions?)
7. Find Connections (What literacy skills are involved?)
8. Write a Scoring Guide (How do students demonstrate proficiency?)

Principals then participate in a series of interrelated activities designed to strengthen their capacity to supervise the instructional program and to provide effective feedback to their classroom teachers to strengthen fidelity of implementation.

State-Required Science Content Standards
Principals and other school administrators must have a clear understanding of the science content standards that their students must know and be able to do. The opening activity of each Hand Lenses in Science session focuses on the science content standards by grouping them together to form big ideas in science. By understanding these big ideas, principals will come to understand how the individual content standards align to form larger ideas

and concepts. For example, in North Carolina one science content standard for fourth-grade students is that students should to be able to design an electric circuit as a complete pathway with an energy source, energy receiver, and energy conductor. An understanding of this standard is one of several that fourth-grade students must have in order to understand electricity and magnetism. The "big idea" is that electricity and magnetism are part of a single force.

Science Content Associated With the State Content Standards
Principals and other school administrators are exposed to an activity associated with the standard. The actual participation of the principals in an activity is designed to give them a firsthand experience of what a lesson taught in one of their fourth-grade classrooms would look like. A lesson, such as lighting a bulb through the creation of a complete circuit, is first placed in the context of where it would appear in the instructional unit (in terms of what came before and what comes after this lesson) through the use of a unit storyline (see Figure 2).

The activity then begins with an engaging scenario. For this fourth-grade activity on the standard of designing a complete electric circuit, the scenario is as follows:

> *You are out on a hike and stumble and fall to the ground. You roll into a hole and find yourself in a dark cave. The good news is that it is possible to find your way out. The bad news is you forgot to put your flashlight into your backpack. The good news is that you find some objects in your backpack that may help you—a small bulb, a battery, and a piece of wire.*

This scenario is designed to stimulate discussion, and ultimately the session leader asks each participant to write a focus question(s) in a notebook used for this activity. An example of a focus question could be "How can we use a battery, a lightbulb, and a piece of wire to produce light?" Individual focus questions are then discussed by the group.

The leader then asks the participants to make a prediction using a conditional statement about what they think will happen. Participants are provided with stems such as "If _____ then _____" or "I think _____ will happen because _____." Participants write their individual predictions in their notebooks and share them orally with the group.

Participants are then asked to find at least three ways the battery, wire, and bulb can be configured to light and not light the bulb. The participants are also asked to describe the role of the battery, the wire, and the bulb in this process. The leader encourages the participants to use accurately labeled diagrams as a means of recording their findings. (Before starting the activity, the participants are asked how they are going to organize their diagrams. This leads to a discussion of the importance of the use of graphic organizers to organize data. Most participants select a T-chart as a graphic organizer for this activity, with one column used for the diagrams of how the bulb lit and a second column for how the bulb did not light.)

After the participants conduct the activity and record their data in their notebooks, the leader brings the group together for a discussion about claims that individuals might have made about the ways the bulb lit and did not light and what evidence they had for both. The leader guides the discussion by using the stems "The bulb lit because _____ " and "The bulb did not light because _____." Participants then write a claim and provide the evidence for each of the diagrams in their notebooks. They orally share their sentences with the rest of the group. The leader then asks them to examine their diagrams of when the bulb lit. A discussion of where the wire touched the bulb and where the wire touched the battery takes place. The leader then introduces a new vocabulary term, *contact points*, places the term on the working word wall, and asks each participant to label the contact points on his or her diagram. Each participant writes a summary statement of the differences, which is then shared with the group.

At this point the leader asks each participant to examine the prediction that he or she wrote at the beginning of the activity. Participants are asked to affirm or revise their predictions based on what they now know. The participants then write a summary statement regarding what they learned today, using the stem "Today I learned _____ ." These statements are shared with the group.

Finally, participants write reflections on the activity in their notebooks and also write any new questions they have about circuits. Several of these reflections and new questions are then shared with the entire group.

Literacy Connections Through Reading and Writing in Science and ELD Strategies
The use of the science notebook and reading strategies by the principals and other administrators in this activity demonstrates the reading, writing, and ELD connections inherent in any science lesson. Participants have a permanent record in their science notebooks of what they achieved in the activity. The notebooks will contain the following elements:

- Focus question
- Prediction
- Graphic organizer containing labeled diagrams of when the bulb lit and when it did not light (data)
- Claims linked to evidence (data)
- Conclusions
- Reflection, including new questions

The principals and other administrators experience expository writing embedded in the science lesson and thus have a firsthand experience of a science-literacy connection. (For an in-depth discussion of the essential elements for science notebooks, see Klentschy 2005.)

The principals and other administrators then read text related to the science concept being investigated. Research-based comprehension strategies (Zimmerman and Hutchins 2003; Harvey and Goudvis 2000) are discussed in the context of making meaning from text by

- creating mental images,
- using background knowledge,
- making connections,
- asking questions,
- determining the most important information or themes,
- synthesizing information, and
- making inferences.

The hands-on learning experience, combined with reading, writing, and oral discourse, provides the principals and other administrators with a clear example of an effective strategy that teachers can use in their science classes. This science and literacy connection is further strengthened through ELD strategies such as introducing language in context and the use of labeled diagrams, graphic organizers, and sentence stems.

Classroom Observation and Supervision of Instruction

One of the major responsibilities of principals is to supervise the instructional programs in their schools. This is best accomplished when the principal has a clear understanding of what to observe and how to provide formative feedback to his or her teachers. Formative feedback should move teachers along three distinct pathways in the development of their teaching expertise. These three pathways are described by Berliner (1994) as knowledge of content, knowledge of pedagogy, and knowledge of student understanding. Berliner believes that as teachers move along the pathways they progress in stages from novice to competent to expert. Teacher expertise also involves having a great deal of knowledge in each of these three dimensions, organized in a way that reflects a deep understanding of content, pedagogy, and student understanding (Donovan, Bransford, and Pellegrino 1999).

Video Study

The next portion of a typical professional development session for principals focuses on video study of an actual classroom teacher teaching the exact activity the participants have just completed. Prior to viewing the video, principals are introduced to a classroom observation tool (see Appendix), whose purpose is to provide them with a focus for their classroom observations. Hand Lenses on Science uses an adaptation of a classroom observation tool developed by Horizon Research, Inc. (2004). The classroom observation tool was originally designed to be used with National Science Foundation–funded Local Systemic Initiatives in both mathematics and science. It has been modified by removing the numerical rating scale and focusing on specific observable elements of the lesson with a narrative constructed by the principal. The elements are grouped into four dimensions: lesson design, lesson implementation, science content, and classroom culture.

Prior to viewing the lesson, participants are organized into groups of four and are assigned one of the four dimensions to use as a lens to view the lesson. The participants are given a written pre-observation interview with the teacher who is conducting the lesson. The principals should be familiar with the content and the expected student outcomes as they have just experienced the same lesson. The video has been edited to focus on the lesson highlights and the interaction between teacher and students and between students working in groups. While watching the video, the principals take notes pertaining to the elements contained in the dimensional lens they have been assigned. These notes will be used later during the Providing Teacher Feedback portion of the session.

Analysis of Student Work

At the conclusion of the video, the participants are given a written post-observation interview with the teacher, highlighting what the teacher felt had worked and what had not worked in the lesson. Three samples of student work from the actual lesson are provided for analysis and discussion. The participants focus on the elements that the student work would need to contain in order to demonstrate an understanding of the standard. At this point the principals are introduced to a scoring guide to be used for the analysis of the student work. A sample scoring guide for this lesson is found in Figure 3.

Providing Teacher Feedback

Marzano, Pickering, and Pollock (2001) maintain that for feedback to be effective it must be (1) timely, (2) self-corrective, and (3) focused on a specific criterion. When designing a process for principals to provide effective formative feedback to teachers, all three of these elements must be considered. The participants in the Hand Lenses in Science sessions work within their groups to formulate two positive feedback statements and two corrective feedback statements to share with the teacher they just observed, based on the observation tool's dimension they used. After each group has formulated their statements, the statements are shared with the entire group. Other feedback strategies are practiced during this portion of the training, including role playing within the group and a whole-group "goldfish bowl" activity. Practicing the formulation and delivery of feedback statements by the principals is important in their development as instructional leaders.

Administrative Support

The final phase of each professional development session focuses on issues raised by the participants related to the curriculum, classroom supervision, and feedback. Homework is often assigned in the form of practice in actual classrooms. Additional topics, such as family science nights, community information and support, and media relations, are discussed. Each session concludes with the participants writing a personal reflection of the day and a personal goal they wish to accomplish before the next session. Often these reflections are shared with the entire group.

Concluding Thoughts

Administrators at both the district and school levels play an increasingly important role in supporting science and literacy connections in schools. District-level administrators must design a coherent and systemic program of instruction that embeds literacy connections into the science curriculum. This must be done in such a way that it supports students in their efforts to make meaning from their science classroom instruction. This design must also provide for a sustained professional development program with multiple entry points for teachers. Finally, a sustained professional development program for principals is necessary to enable them to build ca-

FIGURE 3 Scoring/Feedback Guide

Feedback Guide		
Teacher Comments	Student Self-Evaluation	Proficiency Criteria
		Focus Question • Student generated—relates to scenario • Investigable—relates to content goals
		Prediction relates to focus question
		Data • Graphic organizer listing 3 accurately labeled diagrams of when the bulb lit and when it did not light **Claims and Evidence** • Wrote claims and evidence to correctly identify when the bulb lit • Wrote claims and evidence to correctly identify when the bulb did not light
		Conclusion • Wrote accurate summary paragraph
		Reflection • Analyzed prediction correctly and wrote a new question

pacity in the supervision of instruction at the school and classroom levels, including effective strategies for providing formative feedback to teachers. If these conditions are addressed in districts and schools, administrators will strengthen their role in supporting science and literacy in classrooms.

Appendix

Hand Lenses on Science
Lesson Observation Tool

Unit:_____ Teacher:_____

Date:_____ Lesson:_____

LESSON DESIGN

Strengths:
Weaknesses:

	Notes
1. The design of the lesson incorporated tasks, roles, and interactions consistent with investigative science.	
2. The design of the lesson reflected careful planning and organization.	
3. The instructional strategies and activities used in this lesson reflected attention to students' experience, preparedness, and/or learning styles.	
4. The resources available in this lesson contributed to accomplishing the purposes of the instruction.	
5. The instructional strategies and activities reflected attention to issues of access, equity, and diversity for students (e.g., cooperative learning, language-appropriate strategies/materials).	
6. The design of the lesson encouraged a collaborative approach to learning.	
7. Adequate time and structure were provided for "sense making."	
8. Adequate time and structure were provided for wrap-up.	
9. Formal assessments of students were consistent with investigative science.	

(continued)

Appendix *(continued)*

LESSON IMPLEMENTATION

Strengths:
Weaknesses:

	Notes
1. The instruction was consistent with the underlying approach of the instructional materials designated for use by VIPS.	
2. The instructional strategies were consistent with investigative science.	
3. The teacher appeared confident in his/her ability to teach science.	
4. The teacher's classroom management style/strategies enhanced the quality of the lesson.	
5. The pace of the lesson was appropriate for the developmental levels/needs of the students and the purposes of the lesson.	
6. The teacher took into account prior knowledge of students.	
7. The teacher's questioning strategies were likely to enhance the development of student conceptual understanding/problem solving.	
8. The lesson was modified as needed based on teacher questioning or other student assessments.	

(continued)

Appendix *(continued)*

SCIENCE CONTENT

Strengths:
Weaknesses:

	Notes
1. The science content was significant and worthwhile.	
2. The science content was appropriate for the developmental levels of the students in this class.	
3. Students were intellectually engaged with important ideas relevant to the focus of the lesson.	
4. Teacher-provided content information was accurate.	
5. The teacher displayed an understanding of science concepts.	
6. Science was portrayed as a dynamic body of knowledge continually enriched by conjecture, investigation, analysis, and/or proof/justification.	
7. Elements of science abstraction were included when it was important to do so.	
8. Appropriate connections were made to other areas of science, to other disciplines, and/or to real-world contexts.	
9. The degree of "sense making" of science content within this lesson was appropriate for the developmental levels/needs of the students and the purposes of the lesson.	

(continued)

Appendix (*continued*)

CLASSROOM CULTURE

Strengths:
Weaknesses:

	Notes
1. Active participation of all was encouraged and valued.	
2. There was a climate of respect for students' ideas, questions, and contributions.	
3. Interactions reflected collegial working relationships among students (e.g., students worked together).	
4. Interactions reflected collaborative working relationships between teacher and students.	
5. The climate of the lesson encouraged students to generate ideas, questions, conjectures, and/or propositions.	
6. Intellectual rigor, constructive criticism, and the challenging of ideas were evident.	

References

Amaral, O., L. Garrison, and M. Klentschy. 2002. Helping English learners increase achievement through inquiry-based science instruction. *Bilingual Research Journal* 26 (2): 213–239.

Berliner, D. C. 1994. Expertise: The wonder of exemplary performances. In *Creating powerful thinking in teachers and students: Diverse perspectives*, eds. J. Mangieri and C. Block. Fort Worth, TX: Harcourt Brace.

Donovan, S., J. Bransford, and J. Pellegrino, eds. 1999. *How people learn: Bridging research and practice*. Washington, DC: National Academy Press.

Harvey, S., and A. Goudvis. 2000. *Strategies that work: Teaching comprehension to enhance understanding*. Portland, ME: Stenhouse.

Horizon Research. 2004. *Local systemic change 2004–2005 core evaluation data collection manual*. Chapel Hill, NC: Horizon Research.

Jorgenson, O., and R. Vanosdall. 2002. The death of science? What are we risking in our rush toward standardized testing and the three r's? *Phi Delta Kappan* 83 (8): 601–605.

Klentschy, M. 2005. Science notebook essentials: A guide to effective notebook components. *Science and Children* 43 (3): 24–27.

Klentschy, M., and E. Molina-De La Torre. 2002. A systemic approach to support teacher retention and renewal. In *Science teacher retention: Mentoring and renewal*, eds. J. Rhoton and P. Bowers. Arlington, VA: NSTA Press.

Klentschy, M., and E. Molina-De La Torre. 2004. Students' science notebooks and the inquiry process. In *Crossing borders in literacy and science instruction: Perspectives on theory and practice*, ed. E. W. Saul. Newark, DE: International Reading Association.

Learning Research and Development Center at the University of Pittsburgh and the National Center on Education and the Economy. 2000. *New standards: Performance standards and assessments for schools*. Pittsburgh: Learning Research and Development Center.

Loucks-Horsley, S., P. Hewson, N. Love, and K. Stiles. 1998. *Designing professional development for teachers of science and mathematics*. Thousand Oaks, CA: Corwin.

Marzano, R., D. Pickering, and J. Pollock. 2001. *Classroom instruction that works: Research-based strategies for increasing student achievement*. Alexandria, VA: Association for Supervision and Curriculum Development.

National Academy of Sciences. 1997. *Science for all children: A guide to improving elementary science education in your school district*. Washington, DC: National Science Resources Center, Smithsonian Institution.

National Association of Elementary School Principals (NAESP). 2002. *What principals need to know about teaching science*. Alexandria, VA: NAESP Press.

Reeves, D. 2002. *Making standards work*. Englewood, CO: Advanced Learning Press.

Saul, W., J. Reardon, C. Pearce, D. Dieckman, and D. Neutze. 2002. *Science workshop: Reading, writing and thinking like a scientist*. 2nd ed. Portsmouth, NH: Heinemann.

Zimmerman, S., and C. Hutchins. 2003. *7 keys to comprehension: How to help your kids read it and get it!* New York: Three Rivers Press.

Contributors

Nonye Alozie is a doctoral student in science education at the University of Michigan, where she is also a member of the Textual Tools Study Group.

Joan Armon is an assistant professor of education at Regis University.

Jacqueline Barber is associate director of the Lawrence Hall of Science, University of California, Berkeley.

Anne Barry is a teacher in the Chicago Public Schools and a member of the ISLE (Integrated Science Literacy Enactments) team at the University of Illinois at Chicago.

Marco A. Bravo is an assistant professor of elementary education at San Francisco State University.

Gina N. Cervetti is a postdoctoral scholar at the University of California, Berkeley.

Tanya Cleveland is a doctoral candidate in learning technologies, science education, and literacy at the University of Michigan, where she is also a member of the Textual Tools Study Group.

Kalonda Colson is a science teacher in the Detroit Public Schools and a member of the Textual Tools Study Group at the University of Michigan.

Begona Cowan is a teacher in the Chicago Public Schools and a member of the ISLE (Integrated Science Literacy Enactments) team at the University of Illinois at Chicago.

Ronald D. DeFronzo is a science specialist with the East Bay Educational Collaborative, Warren, Rhode Island.

Mercedes Durón-Flores is the resource teacher for the Vallé Imperial Project in Science, El Centro, California.

Hubert M. Dyasi is a professor of science education at the City College of the City University of New York.

Joan Gilbert is principal of Peter Howell Elementary School, Tucson, Arizona.

Sharon Gill is a teacher in the Chicago Public Schools and a member of the ISLE (Integrated Science Literacy Enactments) team at the University of Illinois at Chicago.

Kerry Giradin is a teacher in the Detroit Public Schools and a member of the Textual Tools Study Group at the University of Michigan.

Yulonda Hale is a teacher in the Detroit Public Schools and a member of the Textual Tools Study Group at the University of Michigan.

Brian Hand is a professor of science education at the University of Iowa.

Jennifer Hankes is a teacher in the Chicago Public Schools and a member of the ISLE (Integrated Science Literacy Enactments) team at the University of Illinois at Chicago.

Mary Heitzman is a doctoral student in science education at the University of Michigan, where she is also a member of the Textual Tools Study Group.

Josiane Hudicourt-Barnes is a researcher and teacher professional development specialist at the Chèche Konnen Center at TERC, in Cambridge, Massachusetts.

Denise Wallace Hytower is a teacher in the Detroit Public Schools and a member of the Textual Tools Study Group at the University of Michigan.

Uma Iyer is a research assistant and a member of the ISLE (Integrated Science Literacy Enactments) team at the University of Illinois at Chicago.

Shomari Jabulani is a teacher in the Detroit Public Schools and a member of the Textual Tools Study Group at the University of Michigan.

Chevon Kay is a teacher in the Detroit Public Schools and a member of the Textual Tools Study Group at the University of Michigan.

Michael P. Klentschy is superintendent of schools, El Centro School District, El Centro, California.

Marleen Kotelman is the science resource coordinator, K–5, for the Tucson, Arizona, Unified School District.

Joseph S. Krajcik is a professor of science education at the University of Michigan, where he is also a member of the Textual Tools Study Group.

Elena Maciel is a teacher at Heber Elementary School, Heber, California.

Patricia M. Maruca is principal of McKinley Elementary School, El Centro, California.

Katherine L. McNeill is a graduate student in science education at the University of Michigan.

Alycia Meriweather is a teacher in the Detroit Public Schools and a member of the Textual Tools Study Group at the University of Michigan.

Elizabeth Birr Moje is a professor of educational studies at the University of Michigan, where she is also a member of the Textual Tools Study Group.

Linda Morris is science coordinator for the Jefferson County Public Schools, Golden, Colorado.

Alissa Naymark is a teacher in the Detroit Public Schools and a member of the Textual Tools Study Group at the University of Michigan.

Ibett Ortiz is a teacher in the Chicago Public Schools and a member of the ISLE (Integrated Science Literacy Enactments) team at the University of Illinois at Chicago.

Christine C. Pappas is a professor of curriculum and instruction at the University of Illinois at Chicago, where she is also a member of the ISLE (Integrated Science Literacy Enactments) team.

P. David Pearson is dean and professor of language and literacy education in the Graduate School of Education at the University of California, Berkeley.

Deborah Peek-Brown is a teacher in the Detroit Public Schools and a member of the Textual Tools Study Group at the University of Michigan.

Eli Raymond-Tucker is a research assistant and a member of the ISLE (Integrated Science Literacy Enactments) team at the University of Illinois at Chicago.

Theresa Rice is a teacher in the Detroit Public Schools and a member of the Textual Tools Study Group at the University of Michigan.

Amy Rife is a teacher in the Chicago Public Schools and a member of the ISLE (Integrated Science Literacy Enactments) team at the University of Illinois at Chicago.

Nancy R. Romance is a professor of science education at Florida Atlantic University.

Ann S. Rosebery is co-director of the Chèche Konnen Center at TERC, in Cambridge, Massachusetts.

Toni Saccani is an instructional coach at Holladay Elementary School, Tucson, Arizona.

Neveen Shamah is a teacher in the Chicago Public Schools and a member of the ISLE (Integrated Science Literacy Enactments) team at the University of Illinois at Chicago.

LeeAnn M. Sutherland is a research scientist in literacy, language, and culture at the University of Michigan, where she is also a member of the Textual Tools Study Group.

Maria Varelas is a professor of science education at the University of Illinois at Chicago, where she is also a member of the ISLE (Integrated Science Literacy Enactments) team.

Michael R. Vitale is a professor in the College of Education at East Carolina University.

Iris Weiss is president of Horizon Research, Inc., Chapel Hill, North Carolina.

Jeffrey Winokur is senior research associate at the Center for Science Education, Education Development Center, Inc., Cambridge, Massachusetts.

Karen Worth is senior scientist at the Center for Science Education, Education Development Center, Inc., Cambridge, Massachusetts.

Eunah Yang is a research assistant and a member of the ISLE (Integrated Science Literacy Enactments) team at the University of Illinois at Chicago.

Index